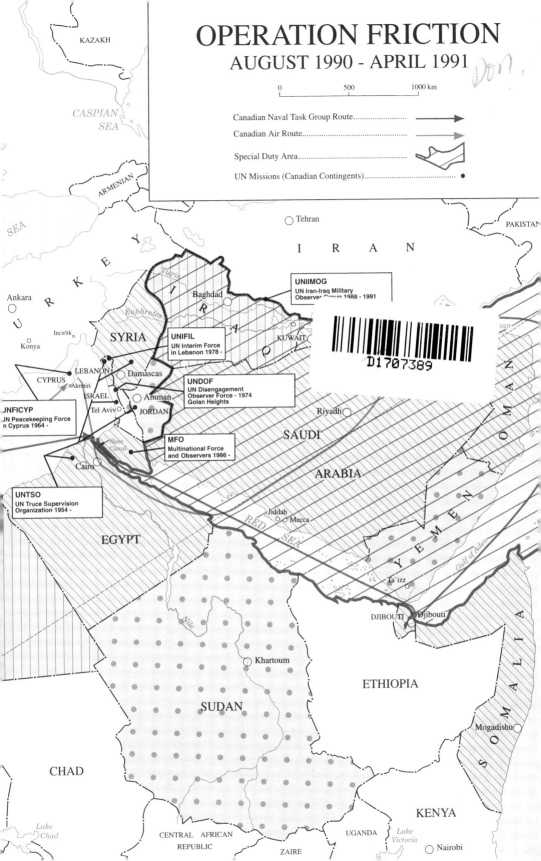

OPERATION FRICTION
AUGUST 1990 - APRIL 1991

Don,

| 0 | 500 | 1000 km |

Canadian Naval Task Group Route.........................
Canadian Air Route...
Special Duty Area...
UN Missions (Canadian Contingents)...•

UNIIMOG
UN Iran-Iraq Military
Observer Group 1988 - 1991

UNIFIL
UN Interim Force
in Lebanon 1978 -

UNDOF
UN Disengagement
Observer Force - 1974
Golan Heights

UNFICYP
UN Peacekeeping Force
in Cyprus 1964 -

MFO
Multinational Force
and Observers 1986 -

UNTSO
UN Truce Supervision
Organization 1954 -

D1707389

KAZAKH

CASPIAN
SEA

SEA

ARMENIAN

PAKISTAN

Tehran

I R A N

Tigris

Baghdad

Euphrates

TURKEY

Ankara

Incirlik
Konya

SYRIA

KUWAIT

LEBANON
CYPRUS
Akrotiri
ISRAEL
Tel Aviv

Damascus

Amman
JORDAN

Riyadh

SAUDI

ARABIA

O M A N

Cairo

Suez
Canal

RED SEA

Jiddah
Mecca

Y E M E N

Gulf of Aden

Ta'izz

EGYPT

DJIBOUTI Djibouti

S O M A L I A

Nile

Khartoum

ETHIOPIA

SUDAN

Mogadishu

CHAD

Lake
Chad

CENTRAL AFRICAN
REPUBLIC

ZAIRE

UGANDA Lake
Victoria

KENYA

Nairobi

THE CANADIAN FORCES IN THE PERSIAN GULF

OPERATION FRICTION
1990-1991

Friction

Everything in war is very simple, but the simplest thing is difficult. The difficulties accumulate and end by producing a kind of friction that is inconceivable unless one has experienced war ... Friction is the one concept that more or less corresponds to the factors that distinguish real war from war on paper ...

Moreover, every war is rich in unique episodes. Each is an uncharted sea, full of reefs. The commander may suspect the reefs' existence without ever having seen them; now he has to steer past them in the dark ...

Friction, as we choose to call it, is the force that makes the apparently easy so difficult ...

Carl von Clausewitz
On War

THE CANADIAN FORCES IN THE PERSIAN GULF

OPERATION FRICTION

1990–1991

Major **Jean Morin**

Lieutenant Commander
Richard H. Gimblett
Directorate of History of the Department of
National Defence

Dundurn Press
Toronto • Oxford

Editors: Michael Power and Kathleen Harris
Designer: Sebastian Vasile
Printer: Best Book Manufacturers

Canadian Cataloguing in Publication Data

Morin, Jean H.
    Operation Friction, 1990–1991

Issued also in French under the title: Opération Friction : Golfe Persique (1990–1991).
Co-published by the Department of National Defence.
Includes bibliographical references and index.
ISBN 1-55002-256-3 (bound)
ISBN 1-55002-257-1 (pbk)

1. Persian Gulf War, 1991 – Canada.   2. Canada. Canadian Armed Forces – History – Persian Gulf War, 1991.   I. Gimblett, Richard Howard, 1956– .   II. Canada. Department of National Defence. III. Title.

DS79.724. C3M67 1997   956.704'42371   C96-932103-1

1   2   3   4   5   NW   01   00   99   98   97

The publisher wishes to acknowledge the generous assistance of the **Canada Council**, the **Book Publishing Industry Development Program** of the **Department of Canadian Heritage**, and the **Ontario Arts Council**.

Care has been taken to trace the ownership of copyright material used in this book. The author and the publisher welcome any information enabling them to rectify any references or credit in subsequent editions.

Printed and bound in Canada.

Printed on recycled paper.

Dundurn Press	Dundurn Press	Dundurn Press
2181 Queen Street East	73 Lime Walk	250 Sonwil Drive
Suite 301	Headington, Oxford	Buffalo, NY
Toronto, Ontario, Canada	England	U.S.A. 14225
M4E 1E5	OX3 7AD	

TABLE OF CONTENTS

List of Illustrations

Preface

This official account of the participation by Canadian armed forces in the Gulf War, written by two officers who served in the Persian Gulf during the period of hostilities in 1991, is the fruit of four years of detailed research.

In January 1991, the Chief of Defence Staff authorized the Director of History to post Major Jean Morin as field historian to the staff of the Commander, Canadian Forces Middle East (Commodore Ken Summers). It was the first time since the Korean War that a historical officer had been posted to the staff of a Canadian commander overseas. Major Morin's duties were to maintain his own record of events as they unfolded and ensure the preservation of vital records while memories were still fresh. His terms of reference recalled the adage of a famous General who said that the naked truths of battle begin to get dressed five minutes after the battle is over. The historical record of Canadian military participation in DESERT SHIELD and DESERT STORM therefore, has its roots in prompt and rigorous examination of a very wide range of documentary, oral, and visual sources.

In the few crowded months during which the Gulf War ran its course, Major Morin was able to accumulate a vast quantity of data, although time naturally did not allow him to visit all the ships and squadrons which he wanted to see in person. He received full cooperation from Commodore Summers and his staff, for which we are extremely grateful. Morin's postgraduate degree in literature prepared him well for disciplined research methods and analysis, and he is an experienced soldier who has served in many peacekeeping missions. As a result, he was able to ask the appropriate questions at the appropriate times.

When the Gulf War came to its sudden end, the field historian's work began in earnest. Because Major Morin had been unable to witness naval and air operations, we obtained a historian from Maritime Command, Lieutenant Richard Gimblett, to deal with the naval side of events. An air force officer, Major Russ Cooper, Deputy Commanding Officer of the *Desert Cats,* also provided important support to the project with information about the Canadian contribution to the air war in the Gulf.

Lieutenant Gimblett (since promoted to Lieutenant Commander) has excellent qualifications. His 1981 postgraduate thesis on the origins of the Royal Canadian Navy had broken important new ground in Canadian military and political history, and he served as Combat Officer in HMCS *Protecteur* throughout the period of hostilities. His competence in historical research, combined with his practical experience before and during the Gulf War, made him the most suitable candidate in the Canadian Armed Forces for writing the naval side of this account.

The Canadian contribution, even if it was not a large one, merits the careful examination provided by these official historians. When a country embarks on hostilities, for whatever reason, a full and accurate history of events will provide valuable information for future decision makers. Among many other things, there are precedents to follow, mistakes to avoid, consequences to consider. If there is no objective analysis based on all the available sources, people forget, or depend on subjective memories, or frequently end up believing in a myth. There is ample evidence in our past to show how prevalent and how dangerous this can be. It is also necessary to place on record what the country and its armed forces did so that not only Canadian decision makers but the Canadian public — including the men and women who served their country in war — can have access to the information. Moreover, the writing of an official history can provide unrivalled leads into the sources for future academic studies. Finally, a full, accurate, and thoroughly documented account provides the means of informing the rest of the world about Canadian contributions to international undertakings.

For official history to be credible, it must be free from censorship. Canadian official historians always have enjoyed complete freedom to develop their own interpretation of events without interference from government. This is true of the present work. Of course, it will be understood that some documents remain classified; when Access to Information regulations make them available, another history of these events may become necessary. The contents of this book, however, represent the most accurate and complete interpretation of events possible at the present time, and they represent the honest views of the authors. I commend this study, without reservation, to the reader.

W.A.B. Douglas
Official Historian of
the Canadian Armed Forces,
(1973-1994)

Acknowledgements

This book was conceived through the original vision of Dr Alec Douglas, Director General History, whose instructions to the authors defined the scope of the project: to relate a "slice of life" of Canada's armed forces, the Gulf crisis serving as the cutting block. We have attempted to make good his vision in spite of the pressures to hasten the schedule. The retirement of Dr Douglas in 1994 was a great loss for the Historical Section. Dr Serge Bernier, his replacement, in his turn defended the authors from all sorts of ambushes, to permit the full latitude and time needed. These two men were the instigators and true defenders of this historical project.

General John de Chastelain gave his approval, early on, that a preliminary history of the Gulf conflict be included among the many projects of the Historical Section. He also assured the presence of an official historian in the theatre. Commodore Kenneth J. Summers agreed that Major Jean Morin would act as historian at his headquarters in Manamah from 16 December 1990, and made it possible for the official historian to visit Doha, Riyadh and the Canadian warships before his return. The Canadian Navy approved the appointment of Lieutenant-Commander Richard Gimblett to the Historical Section for three years (1991-1994) to work on the project.

Acknowledgement is due to all those who worked in preparing the unit war diaries, or who consented to provide interviews. Although too numerous to name individually, in particular Mr Bob Allen, Master Corporal Jocelyne Villeneuve and Major Bob Britten exceeded their mandate to produce in the NDHQ War Diary a document of great quality. Colonels William C. Leach, Tony Humphreys and Claude Auger, Lieutenant-Colonels Joe Kotlarz and Donald Matthews, Commander Rick Town, Lieutenant-Commanders Doug McLean and Ian Yeates, Majors Terry Honour, Roy Thomas, "Barney" Reid and Russ Cooper all aided our research greatly through their efforts.

We must also recognize our debts to the historians, archivists and administrative staff of the Historical Section, who assisted our work. The editing talents of Brereton Greenhous and the inquiring mind of Robert Caldwell intervened at critical moments to make this a better book than it might have been. Owen Cooke, Donna Porter, Réal Laurin, Andrea Schlecht, Laurette Blais, Jean-Pierre Gagnon, Mike Whitby, Warrant Officers Marielle Potts, Joanne Jensen and Howie Pierce, Jean Durocher, Gabriel Proulx, Hélène Desjardins, Private Jody Gervais all contributed, each in his or her own way, to this book. The work of Bill Constable, the cartographer-illustrator of the Historical Section, certainly will be recognized by the reader as probably his best.

Acknowledgements

The now-defunct journals *Sentinel* and *Der Kanadier* also were a precious resource. These two organs did much to conserve the corporate memory of the armed forces, and they regrettably have been cancelled because of Defence budget cuts (from which the Historical Section itself has not completely escaped). The Canadian Forces Photo Unit, the Director General of Public Affairs, and the Translation Service of the Secretary of State, in particular Josette Pelletier, Coordinator of Translation Projects, also contributed greatly. The assistance of Jacques Janson of the office of the Associate Deputy Minister (Policy and Communications) was invaluable in reviewing the French text. Michael Power and Kathleen Harris, as editors for Dundurn, contributed admirably to the final product, the latter in both languages.

Finally, we must acknowledge the independence we were allowed for this work, remarkable for uniformed officers. Still, the authors recognize that all errors and omissions are attributable only to ourselves. This book does not necessarily represent the views of the Government of Canada, the Minister of National Defence, or the Canadian Forces.

JM, RG
Ottawa
1996

CHAPTER 1

Determining the Commitment:
August 1990

Iraq Invades Kuwait

Long before the turning point of August, the events of June and July already had established 1990 as the summer of Canada's discontent. The dramatic last-minute failure, in late June, of the country's leaders to reach agreement on the Meech Lake Accord had renewed separatist sentiment in Québec and left the rest of the nation divided. Then, on 11 July, a dispute between developers and Mohawk band members in the community of Oka, over the proposed expansion of a golf course, erupted in violence. The armed standoff at Kanesatake quickly spread to nearby Kahnawake, where Mohawk "warriors" blockaded the Mercier Bridge to south Montréal. As an added aggravation, it appeared that the domestic economy was succumbing to the world-wide recession. What further ill remained to be added to the mounting score of problems?

It came from an unexpected quarter. During the night of 1-2 August 1990,[1] Iraqi forces deployed along their southern border were suddenly launched against the tiny emirate of Kuwait.[2] Resistance was minimal and by noon on the second, for all intents and purposes, the fight was over. At virtually no material cost, Saddam Hussein had come into possession of nearly one-quarter of the world's proven oil reserves.

Even though Saddam had been signalling his aspirations for some time, the world was taken aback by the sudden turn of events. Shortly after the indecisive conclusion of his eight-year conflict with Iran in 1988, he had renewed Iraq's longstanding claims against Kuwait. Still, the souring relations between Saddam Hussein and Kuwait's al-Sabah family raised no undue alarm amongst either the Kuwaitis themselves or the leaders of the Arab League attempting to broker a settlement to the dispute.

From the perspective of the West, in the decade after the declaration of the Carter Doctrine,[3] the oilfields of the Persian Gulf region remained absolutely vital to its interests. Having given more than tacit assistance to Iraq in its struggle against the Ayatollah-led revolutionary Iran, Western governments had hoped to encourage Saddam to adopt a more moderate political outlook. No one felt that he would be bold enough to threaten the oilfields and draw the Western world into an Arab dispute. For his part, Saddam must have felt that the West, specifically the United States, would not have the will to fight.

Nothing in the weeks before his invasion had disabused Saddam of this notion. Prior to the invasion, on 20 July the CIA had reported the Iraqi force massing on the border with Kuwait. In response, the National Security Council agreed that a limited show of force should suffice to stabilize the situation.[4] Consequently, during the last week of July, the United States Navy held joint manoeuvres in the Gulf with warships of the United Arab Emirates, the United States Air Force deployed several tanker aircraft to the Emirates for an aerial refuelling (AAR) exercise, and early on 1 August the USS *Independence* carrier battle group, steaming in the Indian Ocean near Diego Garcia, was ordered to make for the Arabian Sea. In the meantime, on the 25 July, the American Ambassador to Iraq, Ms April Glaspie, had an interview with the Iraqi dictator in which she was regrettably ambivalent about American concern.[5] On 30 July she went on vacation, happy with her assessment that Iraq's buildup along its southern border was little more than another act in the endless stage drama of Middle East posturing. The United States' intelligence agencies and diplomatic corps had misinterpreted the intentions of the Baghdad dictator, and the general assumption that the stabilization process would serve to hold Saddam Hussein in check proved to be wrong.

The U.S. was by no means alone in its misreading of events. As far as Canada was concerned, our Ambassador to Iraq had been recalled for normal rotation and his replacement, Christopher Poole, would arrive in Baghdad on 19 September and present his credentials on 4 November. In Kuwait, the Iraqi attack came only a few short hours after Canadian Ambassador Lawrence Dickenson's scheduled departure for holidays. Like Glaspie of the United States, he had left thinking that the existing situation would be resolved in a typical Arab compromise, without resort to force. At his stopover in Vienna he learned that Saddam had opted for a very different solution. Under these circumstances, first-hand information was, to say the least, hard to come by.

Managing the Response: The United Nations and the United States

In New York, shortly before midnight on 1 August, the members of the United Nations Security Council were informed of developments and summoned into emergency session. Their deliberations were unusually short and without acrimony. One member nation had been invaded and annexed by another. More importantly, the recent thaw in the Cold War meant that for the first time the Americans and Soviets did not find themselves automatically on opposing sides of so grave an issue. The unique situation demanded — and got — a united stand against the unambiguous criminality of Iraq's aggression. Before dawn, the Security Council, with only Yemen abstaining, unanimously passed Resolution 660, which

"Determined that Iraq's invasion of Kuwait constituted a breach of international peace and security, condemned the invasion, demanded an unconditional and immediate Iraqi withdrawal to the positions its forces occupied on 1 August and call[ed] on Iraq and Kuwait to begin negotiations to resolve their differences."[6]

Recognizing that at this point the best hope for a peaceful solution lay with regional players, the Security Council further affirmed its support for all efforts in this latter regard, "especially those of the League of Arab States." During the course of the day, King Hussein of Jordan, President Mubarak of Egypt, and King Fahd of Saudi Arabia all reassured President Bush that Arab leaders were intent on solving the problem among themselves. Their opinion was that after a period of cool-down and realistic negotiations on the part of the hard-headed Kuwaitis, Saddam Hussein would withdraw his troops, probably to a new frontier recognizing Iraqi control of the Rumeila border oilfields and the Gulf islands of Warbah and Bubiyan, which were the main points of contention between the two countries.

Otherwise, it was not immediately clear what could be done about the "Saddam problem." Estimates of the Iraqi forces varied but agreed upon two essentials: they were large and held awesome potential. The long war of attrition with Iran had exacted its toll, but it also had forced the expansion and reorganization of the Iraqi military and imparted to it an indefinable, but not negligible, degree of fighting experience. Building upon a foundation of Soviet equipment, with the financial assistance of the Gulf States and several Western powers, Iraq had acquired a range of sophisticated offensive weapon systems to become the dominant power in the region. The army counted a million men under arms, arranged in forty-three divisions, at least six of them being "elite" Republican Guard formations, and boasted 5,500 main battle tanks and 4,000 artillery pieces. The 700 combat aircraft of the air force included a variety of Russian bombers and *MiG* fighters as well as French *Mirages* capable of carrying *Exocet* anti-ship missiles. At first glance, the Iraqi navy did not amount to much. It was limited to a collection of fast missile-armed patrol boats, coastal *Silkworm* anti-ship missiles, and a variety of mines. However, if used in the proper combination, this collection of boats and arms could be used to deny much larger blue-water forces entrance to the shallow, northern Gulf waters, which were studded with oil fields.

There was also intense speculation concerning the state of the Iraqi chemical, biological, and nuclear weapons development programmes, and their capacity to be delivered by a locally modified version of the Soviet *Scud* missile. With such weapons, Saddam could threaten the capitals of his neighbours. He had boasted ominously of his new-found ability to strike at Israel "to cause fire to devour half of the Zionist entity ... "[7] In retrospect, noticeably absent from the descriptions of Iraqi military might was any qualitative perspective to the raw quantitative "force ratio analysis" provided by the intelligence community. However, one study of the ineptly fought Iran-Iraq War — the so-called first Gulf War —

published shortly before Saddam's invasion of Kuwait, included the apparently overlooked warning that "Force ratios are a remarkably uncertain measure of military strength, both in terms of battles and in terms of the strength and weakness of a nation."[8]

A regional settlement, it could be argued, would only delay the day of reckoning with Saddam. To counter the Iraqi expansion into Kuwait, there appeared to be only two real options — cut off the sources feeding the Iraqi machine, or amass the force necessary to evict and destroy it. Neither was a welcome prospect, and governments everywhere clung to the hope that Saddam would accept appeals to reason and withdraw without further incident. In the wake of the swift UN condemnation of the invasion, the world waited in vain for a constructive Iraqi reply. According to intelligence reports, the Iraqis instead chose to consolidate their initial gains by taking up positions near the Saudi border. Various countries, led by the United States and Great Britain, immediately froze all Kuwaiti and Iraqi assets. Canada would join the European Community in announcing partial restrictions on 4 August, with a total freeze established on the eighth, after a second UN Resolution, number 661.[9]

Almost as perplexing as the silence from Baghdad was that from Washington. Anticipating an unequivocal military response from the United States, Lloyd's of London announced the immediate introduction of a war premium payable by all ships operating in the Gulf area. The world's only remaining superpower, meanwhile, paused, perhaps in reaction to the swift and positive action of the Security Council. Although Iraq was still considered a client of the Soviet Union, the siding of the Eastern Bloc with the West indicated that however bad the situation, it was unlikely to deteriorate into a major East-West confrontation. Prudence demanded that General H. Norman Schwarzkopf, commander of the United States Central Command (CENTCOM), hastily review his contingency plans for a large-scale operation in the Persian Gulf. Established specifically for intervention in Southwest Asia (albeit as a counter to an expected Soviet thrust), CENTCOM existed only as a skeletal headquarters of 700, all ranks, to be reinforced with elements of other Commands when given a mission. The recently updated version of its primary operations plan, now known as OPLAN 90-1002, presciently shifted focus to the rising threat of Saddam's Iraq and identified Kuwait and Saudi Arabia as his next probable targets. It had been war-gamed in July as part of Exercise INTERNAL LOOK 90, in a scenario virtually identical to the actual unfolding of events on 1-2 August, and valuable lessons had been learned. The cold reality of the situation was all too apparent: the Americans could assemble forces quickly to demonstrate their concern, but it would take them time to deploy a significant fighting force.

In the evening of Thursday, 2 August, President Bush was in Colorado to address the renowned Aspen Institute on the topic of US defence strategy in what he heralded as "a new world order."[10] Prime Minister Margaret Thatcher of Great

Britain was also present, to receive the institute's Statesman Award. Meeting in private afterwards, the American and British leaders reviewed the events of the preceding twenty-four hours and concluded that Saudi Arabia was threatened by the still moving Iraqi forces and had to be defended immediately against a possible invasion. Moreover, an "Arab Solution" that entailed Kuwaiti territorial concessions would effectively reward the Iraqi aggressor. Nothing less than an "unconditional and immediate Iraqi withdrawal," as demanded by Resolution 660, could be accepted.

At the UN, meanwhile, it was also becoming obvious that Saddam had no intention of responding positively to Resolution 660. As soon as the members of the Security Council began discussions for a follow-on resolution, Canadian Ambassador Yves Fortier telephoned Prime Minister Brian Mulroney on 3 August to discuss Canada's position. Both men saw the absence so far of any precipitate American reaction as a unique opportunity for the world body to assume the role for which it had been created: to manage a global response to an international crisis. They recognized that Canada could be influential in this respect. Shortly after Mr Fortier's arrival as ambassador in the summer of 1988, Canada had assumed a temporary seat on the Security Council for the two-year period 1989-90 and was uniquely placed to exert its traditional middle power influence. While External Affairs was attempting to develop a national response from Ottawa, Ambassador Fortier already had demonstrated Canadian resolve by co-sponsoring Resolution 660. Indeed, as the crisis dragged on, Canada would vote in favour of each of the twelve resolutions on Kuwait, and it would co-sponsor eight of them, including Resolutions 660, 661, 665, and 678.

The Security Council was steering into territory seldom travelled. The familiar peacekeeping operations of the past were authorized under Chapter VI of the UN Charter. Measures to restore the peace — soon to be popularized as peacemaking — had been resorted to less frequently and came under the wider scope of Chapter VII.[11] Articles 41, 42, and 51 governed the employment of armed forces: Article 41 for non-warlike measures to support diplomatic and political decisions; Article 42 for supportive military operations by land, sea, and air to restore international peace and security; and Article 51 for unilateral self-defence or collective security action by the government of a member nation against a demonstrable threat.

As the Council moved to adopt sterner measures against Iraq, the Canadian ambassador worked hard behind the scenes to ensure continued solidarity. It was not to be a simple task. After their initial agreement, the Council members already were dividing into camps with differing views on further action. The United States and Britain felt that the Council had done its required business, and that further military action awaited only an invitation from either Kuwait or Saudi Arabia for assistance under the collective security provisions of Article 51. France and the

Soviet Union led the group which insisted that the possibility of economic sanctions provided by Article 41 should be explored first, in light of the fact that Article 42 offered the use of military force to give sanctions effect. Yemen, a member of the Arab League and by default its local representative, was reduced to reflecting the diverging opinions within that organization by abstaining from any too-abrasive measures.

Early Saturday morning, 4 August, senior American officials comprising the National Security Council convened at Camp David. They were aware that they could not afford to misinterpret Saddam's intentions a second time. However, the intelligence on which President Bush would have to act was ambivalent. The indisputable Iraqi buildup in Kuwait was open to two basic interpretations. It was either a defensive consolidation of gains or a preparation for further offensive action. Iraq now clearly posed a direct threat to Saudi Arabia. Various US intelligence agencies and the army staff had arrived at that conclusion, and — a significant consideration — Prime Minister Thatcher was expressing the same view. Military response was appropriate. Only the United States had the necessary resources to take on Saddam Hussein, and President Bush resolved to do so.

To create a buffer between Saddam's forces and the rich oilfields that lay to the south, US troops would have to be placed inside Saudi Arabia's northern border. The Saudis, however, were wary of any foreign, particularly non-Islamic, presence on their soil. Having taken the decision to intervene, President Bush immediately began to contact other heads of state to orchestrate a palatable combination of Arab and Western nations. Kings, presidents, and prime ministers around the world were asked if they would join the United States in the venture.

A Canadian Military Response?

Among the first calls exchanged that Saturday morning was one between the American president and the prime minister of Canada, in which Bush invited his northern neighbour, Brian Mulroney, to consider joining an American-led coalition of nations. Having discussed the developing sanction strategy of the UN with Ambassador Fortier, the prime minister affirmed the Canadian position to the president: the assembling forces should be mandated by the United Nations, and any Canadian contribution would be part of a UN-sponsored action. In this context, the two leaders explored the possibility that Canada might act to enforce an economic embargo by sending forces to the Gulf region.

A double imperative thus existed for a more direct Canadian involvement in a resolution to the crisis. The prime minister had made a personal, though tentative, commitment to a friendly power with interests similar to Canada's. At the same time, Ambassador Fortier was trying to orchestrate a UN response as a counter to unilateral US action. For either of these actions to be credible on the international political scene, Canada had to accompany its recommendations with a supportive military response. The time had come to investigate what realistic options the Canadian Forces could provide to the government.

Like the diplomatic community, the Canadian military establishment had been caught off-balance by the crisis. At the time of the Iraqi assault, both the Minister of National Defence and the Chief of Defence Staff (CDS) were away on separate out-of-country missions: Minister Bill McKnight was in Syria, relatively near the action but on unrelated business, and General John de Chastelain was involved in a two-week tour of the USSR and former Warsaw Pact countries. Apprised of the invasion while in Hungary, de Chastelain immediately reacted by saying that Canada would not become involved directly in the present crisis, but without a doubt it would have a peacekeeping role to play once the situation stabilized and a UN mandate was established.[12]

For the officers at National Defence Headquarters (NDHQ) in Ottawa, any idea of a military response seemed little more than professional speculation. While they watched with interest the unfolding of events in the Middle East, their attention already was focused on a crisis much closer to home. The vice-chief, Vice-Admiral Charles Thomas, who was the acting CDS, had been left to oversee, among other things, the worsening standoff between the Quebec Provincial Police and large groups of armed Mohawk protesters in the Montreal area. The situation had deteriorated steadily since erupting in violence on 11 July, when an officer of the Sureté du Québec was killed at Oka. Despite the arrival in force of the RCMP, the possibility remained that the Québec provincial government would call upon the Aid to the Civil Power function of the Canadian Forces at any moment.

It was in this setting that the prime minister concluded his conversation with President Bush. He quickly made calls to a number of key officials, including Secretary of State for External Affairs Joe Clark and Ambassador Fortier. Admiral Thomas was solicited for his recommendations concerning available forces. He soon decided on the ships of Maritime Command in Halifax, where one of the squadrons was preparing to deploy for a major NATO combined exercise. The ships were essentially ready to sail, and it was taken for granted that several of them could be diverted without undue strain on commitments.

The selection of Maritime Command to shoulder the Canadian response to a foreign crisis was unusual, if not exactly unprecedented. Undoubtedly, Admiral Thomas's background had been an influential factor in the choice of the navy. Still, there were few options. The army — Mobile Command — was anticipating a major commitment in Québec. The air force's combat aircraft in Europe were watching with caution the crumbling Soviet bloc, and the government was reluctant to tamper with that element of Canada's commitment to NATO. The navy, however, could forgo participation in an exercise in favour of an operational deployment.

Manoeuvrings on the World Stage

Events at the United Nations also dictated the form of the Canadian response. After a hectic weekend exchanging drafts of a new resolution which would be acceptable to all its members, the Security Council met Monday morning, 6 August, in formal debate. Once again an unprecedented near-unanimity was achieved, and Resolution 661 was adopted without a single dissenting voice. China and Yemen abstained. "Deeply concerned" that Iraq had not heeded the terms of Resolution 660, the Council called upon the rest of the world to exert pressure through the imposition of economic sanctions.[13] But almost immediately debate began on what this in fact meant. The American press and some politicians freely but inaccurately described the latest action as a blockade, while certain members of the Security Council recognized that the call for an enforced embargo could be construed as an unauthorized act of war. They wanted more time for a peaceful resolution before allowing armed enforcement, since the UN sanctions were effectively at the discretion of individual nations and only extended to economic action.

The most important voluntary measure in response to Resolution 661 came the next day, 7 August, when Turkey closed its pipelines to the shipment of Iraqi oil. Since Syria had shut the valves of its Iraqi lines some years earlier in support of Iran, Iraq was now faced with the closure of all land routes for the transport of its only significant export. With only ten miles of swampy marsh for a coast, Iraq's one remaining avenue was its newly acquired access to the Persian Gulf through Kuwaiti waters. Indeed, gaining an unrestricted Gulf waterway was one of Saddam's long-held ambitions. Occupation of the disputed Kuwaiti islands of Warbah and Bubiyan now gave unobstructed use of the Khawr 'Abd Allah for the shipment of goods from Basrah and Umm Qasr. Moreover, Iraq had gained possession of the fine port facilities of Kuwait City, and already Iraqi tankers were assembling there. The requirement under Resolution 661 to "monitor progress and compliance," therefore, pointed to the commitment of naval forces to undertake the patrols.

Naval forces were already in the Gulf. The Americans, British, French, and even Soviets all had instituted regular patrols to protect their shipping in the region during the Iran-Iraq War of 1980-88. In the present crisis, some eight USN warships were in the Persian Gulf at the time of the invasion, assigned to the commander of the USN Middle East Force (COMIDEASTFOR or CMEF), Rear-Admiral William M. Fogarty, and carrier battle groups were taking up station in the Arabian, Red, and Mediterranean Seas. HMS *York* and FS *Protet* were present in the Gulf too, but the remaining ships of the Royal Navy's ARMILLA and the French Navy's PROMÉTHÉE patrols were at other ports on the Indian Ocean littoral. On 5 August (after President Bush's calls to their leaders for concerted action), they were ordered back to their stations. Significantly, Soviet warships in the Gulf of Oman remained at anchor and did not interfere with the gathering of their traditional Allied adversaries.

The Americans remained anxious for a more visible demonstration against Saddam Hussein. While the UN was being urged to enforce an embargo, the *Independence* Battle Group arrived in the Gulf of Oman on 6 August to augment the Middle East Force. As the official US report observes, "during the first two weeks of the crisis, the focus was on defending Saudi Arabia from a possible Iraqi invasion and building a coalition in support of Kuwait."[14] Carrier air power ensured that even without ground troops present, some support could be given to Saudi Arabia if Iraq attacked across the border. Recognizing, however, that the striking power of carrier aviation had its limitations, Secretary of Defence Dick Cheney and General Schwarzkopf were in Jiddah on 6 August to meet King Fahd. They were intent on convincing him to allow US forces within his country. Supporting their case with satellite imagery, Cheney and Schwarzkopf showed that three divisions of Republican Guards were neatly aligned to threaten Saudi Arabia. There was no realistic defence which the Saudis themselves could mount against such forces. Nothing but a few hundred miles of desert separated Saddam from conquering their kingdom and effectively extending his control to over one-half of the world's proven oil reserves.

Despite his misgivings, the king could refrain no longer. All efforts of the Arab League to mediate a settlement had achieved nothing, and there really was no guarantee that Saddam would not try to match his intentions with his capabilities. King Fahd gave his assent to temporary American military assistance, contingent upon the eventual withdrawal of all US forces from Saudi Arabia once the task was completed. Intervention by other nations also was deemed acceptable in principle, but it would be negotiated on a nation-by-nation basis. On 7 August, King Fahd publicly issued a plea "for the participation of fraternal Arab forces and other friendly forces" to come to the defence of his kingdom.[15] Almost immediately President Bush declared that the United States was drawing a "line in the sand" against Iraq's aggression. Operation DESERT SHIELD was underway.

NDHQ Naval Staff Planning Commences

In Canada, Monday, 6 August was a civic holiday, and aside from a very few watchkeepers, National Defence Headquarters was deserted. When senior naval officers gathered for their first official meeting at 1000, it was a compact group: Captain (N)[16] M.B. MacLean, the Director of Maritime Force Development (DMFD), outlined the day's work to a single representative from each of the Directorates of Maritime Combat Systems (DMCS) and Naval Requirements (DNR). Together, they were to prepare a firm reply for Admiral Thomas in regard to the feasibility of a naval option, and the effect this would have on Canadian maritime resources. At the conclusion of the brief session, each departed to consult with his staff. They may not have realized it at the time — indeed, the loss of a holiday on an apparently futile paper exercise was resented by some of those involved — but they had embarked upon a process that would lead to the formation of a Canadian naval task group.

It was plain to everyone that according to equipment fit, the Canadian navy would be relegated to a very minor part on the fringes of the proceedings. For the past forty years the anticipated foe had been the Soviet submarine service, to be faced as part of a NATO task force in the open waters of the North Atlantic. The degree of "rust-out" of the navy and its consequent inability to meet this projected enemy had been the subject of debate for some years and indeed were the rationale for new ship procurement and upgrade programmes. More to the point in the present case, however, was the fact that the ships were armed and fitted for NATO Anti-Submarine Warfare (ASW). To meet the challenges of the Persian Gulf, the ships would have to be fitted to operate in Anti-Surface Warfare (ASUW) and Anti-Air Warfare (AAW) roles. Already the press was focusing on the potency of the Iraqi arsenal and the threat which it posed to a surface fleet. The government could not escape the fact that the combat-readiness of the navy would become a matter of some public discussion.

Admiral Thomas was acutely aware of this. He knew the ships intimately, having spent a large portion of his thirty-six-year career looking after them. Before entering the navy's command stream, he had spent his early service years as an engineering specialist. More recently, as Chief of Maritime Doctrine and Operations (CMDO) in the Ottawa headquarters, and then as the commander of Maritime Command in Halifax, he had steered the direction of the CPF,[17] TRUMP,[18] and ill-fated nuclear submarine programmes. When it came to the navy's acquisition programmes and new equipment, Vice-Admiral Thomas was perhaps the single most knowledgeable person, serving or civilian. Acting now as CDS, he already had indicated to the prime minister that some upgrades would be required to meet the present situation, and he proceeded to translate the political imperative into action. While the wishes of his political masters remained vague, Thomas was determined that the navy's ability to make a meaningful military contribution should not be limited by existing equipment. Naval staffs were directed to prepare their ships so that they could carry out a variety of duties and operate within range of Iraqi surface and air attack. A combined list of expected threats and anticipated missions was drawn up, from which a list of required equipment was developed.

The primary assumption from which the staffs worked was that the most serious threat in the Gulf was from the air. The Iraqi Air Force included amongst its weaponry the *Exocet* anti-ship missile, which the Argentineans had used with great effect against the Royal Navy in the Falklands War. Indeed, the Iraqis themselves had displayed no hesitation in using the *Exocet* against tanker shipping in the Gulf and also in the dramatic attack on the USS *Stark* on 17 May 1987. New-construction Canadian warships and those in refit would be equipped to counter the *Exocet*, but none were operational because modernization programmes had been delayed for years. The ships on the waterfront had only a minimal self-defence capability against the surface-to-surface and air-to-surface weapons in the Iraqi inventory. Saddam Hussein had used two other forms of warfare during his long war with Iran, against which Canadian ships had little effective counter: chemicals (poison gas) and mines. What little expertise had existed in the navy in the early years of the Cold War in either of these areas had been allowed to lapse and would take some effort to rebuild.

Anticipated missions dictated two other directions for equipment procurement. Firstly, although an embargo had yet to be declared, it was logical that a UN force should be ready to conduct boardings. A supertanker with a potentially hostile crew presented a very different prospect from the trawlers encountered during patrols for the fisheries. Therefore, an efficient means of transporting boarding parties and better personal weapons, communications, and body protection were required. Secondly, and perhaps most significantly, early on it was recognized that the presence of multinational forces meant that major enhancements to Command, Control, and Communications (C^3) also were required. Weapons can defend an individual ship, but if commanders cannot exchange information, it is difficult to coordinate the overall effort. Fortunately, recent developments in ASW had resulted in the navy acquiring sophisticated communications systems such as SATCOM (Satellite Communications) and SECVOX (Secure Voice radiotelephone) so that a measure of what is known as connectivity already existed with the USN and other NATO navies. Only a little effort was required to outfit the Canadian ships with what would prove to be the most all-inclusive variety of communications equipment in the Persian Gulf.

Having quickly established a preliminary tally of the potential threats and anticipated missions, the NDHQ staffs began to compile a master list of the necessary modifications and upgrades. Depending upon the ships to be tasked, they identified shortfalls of some twenty major systems. Although very few of the proposed systems were in use in the fleet, many had been selected for the CPF and TRUMP programmes. In fact, a great deal of equipment was available in Canada preparatory to fitting the ships.

By late afternoon of that holiday Monday, the investigating officers were able to confirm that far from being a mere paper exercise, the proposal to despatch a naval group to the Persian Gulf was practical. Enough equipment could be obtained in a relatively short time to outfit two ships. Working towards a mid-August departure, they arbitrarily assigned a period of one week (seven working days) to complete the upgrades. This was only a best guess that did not take into account the extraordinary demands which a coordinated simultaneous installation of the various systems would place on the Halifax shipyard. As for choice of ships, there proved to be very little selection. The large destroyers of the *Iroquois* (DDH 280 Tribal) Class topped the list. They were the most capable of the existing Canadian warships and required the fewest upgrades. Next in priority was a replenishment ship (AOR) to provide an independent logistics support facility.[19] Unmentioned, but in the back of everyone's mind, was the fact that between them the two ships could carry a total of five *Sea King* helicopters, a significant air element. Although the estimate couched the commitment in terms of "one Tribal Class Destroyer and one AOR," with ships laid up in refit there was actually only one of each available on either coast. Since the ships were to come from Halifax, being closer to the Gulf, it was already possible to put names to the hulls: Her Majesty's Canadian Ships *Athabaskan* (DDH 282) and *Protecteur* (AOR 509).

CANUKUS Naval Liaison

The afternoon and evening of 6 August was a busy time for the prime minister and pivotal in defining the Canadian commitment. The passing of Resolution 661 and the green light from King Fahd generated a flurry of activity in Washington, and President Bush invited Mr Mulroney to discuss the situation over a private dinner that evening. In preparation, the prime minister wanted Canadian intentions to be identified more precisely. After having been advised by Ambassador Fortier of the Security Council decision, Mulroney summoned him to his summer residence at Harrington Lake to discuss in person the implications of the UN resolution. Informed of Mulroney's meeting with Bush, the naval staffs turned their estimates into a formal position paper covering the dispatch of a destroyer and a supply ship. Armed with the navy's position paper and a brief on the situation in Kuwait, quickly compiled by a newly activated Gulf desk of the Current Intelligence Team, Prime Minister Mulroney departed for Washington.

During dinner, Mulroney and Bush expanded on their telephone conversation of 4 August. The prime minister, according to reports later published, reiterated that the price of Canada's support would be UN, rather than US, leadership. The president did not try to dictate the substance of the Canadian commitment, concerned foremost that there be one, and he was content that plans were being made to prepare Canadian ships for combat duty in the Gulf. Agreeing to pursue their separate but not incompatible approaches, the prime minister returned to Canada, determined to obtain Cabinet approval of participation in a UN-sponsored maritime embargo against Iraq.

Although the prime minister and the president were coming together in their approach to the crisis, the Canadian and American military establishments seemed to have very different ideas about Canada's place in any build-up of naval forces in the Gulf. Prior to the prime minister's impromptu dinner engagement, Rear-Admiral John R. Anderson, Chief of Maritime Doctrine and Operations (CMDO) and the senior naval officer in Ottawa, had advised the head of the Defence Liaison Staff in Washington of the plans under discussion. That officer then told his USN counterparts, informally, of the Canadian interest in a task unit, possibly a support ship and destroyer, as part of a multinational force, noting that Canada would prefer to exert command and control over its own forces. The American reaction was mixed: although interested in the idea of a Canadian supply ship in the Gulf, due to the perennial shortage of "tanker bottoms," the Americans were lukewarm to an escorting DDH 280. Without upgrades, it would be vulnerable to the Iraqi air threat. Moreover, anything the Americans said assumed that American operational control of all deployed forces was necessary to ensure the most effective employment of a carrier battle group in the Gulf. Admitting that this would not meet Canadian command and control requirements, the Americans suggested that Canada take over USN obligations in some other less threatening area, such as the Mediterranean, freeing American ships to deploy to the Gulf.[20] (The Germans, who were constitutionally limited in the scope of their military commitments, did exactly this in 1987-88.) But Canada had other plans for its navy. Any concerted action had to await further discussion.

The British response also reflected the Royal Navy's reluctance to operate within a multilateral context because it might limit independent action. At Rear-Admiral Anderson's request, the naval attaché on the Defence Liaison Staff in London spoke with the Assistant Chief of Naval Staff at the British Ministry of Defence. The naval attaché found that the British were aware as well of the limited air defence capabilities of the Canadian ships but were willing to acknowledge their superior command and control surveillance systems. The British agreed with the Americans on the potential usefulness of a tanker and said that they would gladly accept any Canadian support of "independent like-minded operations" in the Gulf to protect the flow of oil.

Canadian Political and Military Dimensions

During 7 August, a day of lively headquarters activity, naval planning quickly expanded to include other sections of the Matériel branch (Assistant Deputy Minister, Matériel, or ADM(Mat)) which would be responsible for procuring the equipment identified by DNR and DMCS. And although the emphasis was already directed very much towards a naval response, some staff contingency work began on land and air options so that the ministers could be appraised of all possible avenues for a Canadian reply. An air detachment or a specialized land unit might offer some advantages that had not been foreseen originally. At any rate, the military estimate was not to be definitively narrowed down to navy resources at this early stage.

That being said, the military decisions taken during the course of 5-9 August bear the unmistakable influence of one man. In addition to acting as Chief of Defence Staff, Admiral Thomas was at the apex of what can be called the Navy Triangle, the other two members of which were the commander of Maritime Command, Vice-Admiral Robert E. George, and the chief of the naval operations staffs in NDHQ, Rear-Admiral Anderson. With the aid of secure telephone and facsimile connections, these three senior officers discussed naval affairs on a near hourly basis, Thomas in Ottawa speaking to George in Halifax, and both of them consulting and directing Anderson, who would make the planning a fact through his NDHQ staff.

Admiral Anderson would regularly discuss the situation with the officer in charge of the day-to-day NDHQ management of operations, the Director-General of Military Plans and Operations (DGMPO), who at that time happened to be a naval officer, Commodore Bruce Johnston. DGMPO's role was to act as Chief of Staff of Operations to the Deputy Chief of Defence Staff (DCDS), Lieutenant-General David Huddleston (an air force officer), and as such Commodore Johnston had direct access to the executive officer at the highest level overlooking operations. Admiral Thomas, the Vice Chief of Defence Staff (VCDS) normally responsible for the administrative management of National Defence Headquarters and ostensibly at arm's length from operations, still could have a major influence on decision making, even without overextending his position as acting chief of the defence staff.

The circumstances of the moment thus allowed for an expedient circumvention of the existing NDHQ staff system, which was being sorely tested by the twin operational crises of the Gulf and Oka. After unification in the mid-1960s had done away with the individual service headquarters, NDHQ had been reorganized generally on the basis of function — operations, engineering and maintenance, policy, personnel, and finance. Each function was a unified sub-component in which senior positions were occupied in turn by officers of different elements and sometimes even by civilians. It was felt to be a joint headquarters, where staffs from different arms were called upon to integrate their plans and saw themselves as a unified force. What the present circumstances demonstrated, however, was that when pressure was applied to undertake operations in a short time, with limited resources and heavy political pressures, a closer decision-making network emerged. The single-service nature of each operation delineated more direct lines of communication among officers of the same element. With the response to the Persian Gulf situation becoming a maritime operation, naval officers became more prominent in its preparation. The attention of army officers was focused elsewhere (Oka), and for various reasons the air force was not directly involved in either operation. The naval connection happened to work in the precise way that it did because at this juncture naval officers occupied those NDHQ positions that could make it work. Had the VCDS or DGMPO not been from the navy, other channels would have had to be devised to streamline the naval planning. As things went, the Navy Triangle worked well. It is debatable if any other network of positions could have worked more efficiently to prepare the operation in the short time available. Still, the constraints implicit in its limited application were recognized, and it was not to be a lasting precedent.

Publicly, neither the prime minister nor his external affairs minister would acknowledge a direct role for Canada in the crisis other than that of diplomacy. They allowed that, as a member of NATO, Canada would react to an Iraqi threat against Turkey (which was not unlikely, given the pipeline closure) but would not be part of the US-led multinational military force in Saudi Arabia. Mr Clark, however, did admit that "private preparations" were being made of military plans,[21] and at a press conference on 8 August, Mr Mulroney hinted that Canada was "not entirely bereft of [military] equipment ... so we're capable of participating." But he did not elaborate on the possibilities.[22] Practically, however, the range of Canadian military options was not that broad. The need for Canada to be seen as supporting a potential UN embargo of Iraq, rather than siding with the US in defence of Saudi Arabia, argued strongly in favour of naval rather than air or ground forces.

There were also domestic concerns demanding urgent attention. The decision to send a naval force was influenced in part by the Canadian tradition that government cannot order forces to a theatre of war without an order-in-council approved by Cabinet, an order that must be debated in the House of Commons within ten days of its publication.[23] At the time of the invasion, the House was in summer recess and not scheduled to sit again until 24 September. But an early recall of parliament to deal with the Gulf deployment would provide the Opposition with an open forum to debate government action on the Oka crisis and the worsening economic situation. The type of force being sent, therefore, took on a political importance. If one assumed that the NATO commitment could be waived (and the tacit Soviet acceptance of the course of events was leading the North Atlantic Council to believe that this was possible), the most rapidly deployable Canadian forces were the squadrons of CF-18 *Hornet* fighters based at Baden-Söllingen, Germany. Naval forces, on the other hand, faced at least a week of preparation before a thirty-one-day passage to the theatre of operations. A month could pass before an order-in-council would be required. Circumstances could change greatly, allowing the government more time to refine the details of its commitment before making it the subject of parliamentary scrutiny. This indeed proved to be the case.

What did these considerations about a Canadian military response add up to in the form of pros and cons? A briefing to the Minister of National Defence and his staff on 8 August put the question in precisely these terms. Foremost on the pro side of the balance sheet was the fact that, by committing military forces, Canada would be declaring its utter disapproval of Iraqi aggression against Kuwait and its direct support to friendly countries potentially threatened by further Iraqi aggression, such as Saudi Arabia. Moreover, Canada would be indirectly supporting the implementation of UN sanctions against Iraq. Not to be overlooked was that this action could prevent further destabilization of world oil markets and sources of supply.

The list of cons was lengthier. The lack of an inclusive Security Council resolution meant that there was no framework in international law for Canadian military intervention; nor was there an existing regional collective security force with which to integrate for support and effectiveness. But there were greater issues than the lack of structure. A Radio Baghdad report of 6 August had announced that foreign "guests" — hostages — would be held at strategic sites to discourage retaliation against Iraq. By taking a hostile military posture against Iraq, Canada stood to compromise not only the 480 Canadian citizens registered in Iraq and Kuwait but also the fifteen Canadian servicemen then serving in Iraq as part of the United Nations Iran-Iraq Military Observer Group (UNIIMOG). Against all this was the reality that Canada's military effort would be so small that it would not make a significant difference to the military situation in the Gulf. There was also the danger that the Canadian government might be criticized if it were perceived as simply complying with the bidding of the United States. Finally, there was the recognition that this would be the first such action taken by Canada in forty years (Canada's involvement in Korea also had been based on a Security Council resolution). Rightly or wrongly, it would give rise to questions and criticism about a fundamental change in Canadian foreign policy.

The military concern over Canada's role as peacekeepers served to bolster the case for the naval option. Past peacekeeping operations had included naval forces only rarely and then in minor fashion. They had relied almost exclusively on soldiers in the field, air transport, and communications and logistical support. Unstated, but implicit in the argument, was the fact that since navies operate in international waters as a rule, they do not raise awkward problems such as territoriality or occupation. Most importantly, the navy never had been counted among the UN's blue berets. Its present participation in any Gulf action, therefore, need not detract from Canada's traditional peacekeeping efforts.

Canadian military and diplomatic actions were complementing each other closely. Defence Minister McKnight retained the two-ship naval option for presentation to Cabinet the next day. Ambassador Fortier was working to close the developing rift in UN solidarity. He argued in favour of strenthening the economic sanctions in Resolution 661 and for changes that would give a clear mandate to Canada's military intervention. A long period of negotiations was to ensue before a resolution satisfactory to all parties could be produced.

Cabinet Decides on the Naval Option

At 0900 Wednesday, 8 August, President Bush confirmed that US forces were in the process of being deployed to Saudi Arabia. The announcement was the first official statement to the public that a US military reaction had been ordered in response to the Iraqi invasion of Kuwait. Except in a context of a coalition of nations there was no direct mention of other national forces being involved, but the announcement confirmed press and public speculation that some concerted action was in the offing, adding to the pressure on the Canadian government to commit itself. That same day, Mr Clark finally announced action to implement the sweeping economic sanctions required by UNSC 661.[24] Saddam's response to the international pressure was to announce the annexation of Kuwait, a fullfledged member of the United Nations, as the nineteenth province of Iraq. The Security Council recognized that this would be a dangerous precedent if allowed to stand, and again it was called into emergency session. Ambassador Fortier added Canada's vote on 9 August to the unanimous adoption of Resolution 662, declaring "the Iraqi annexation null and void, calling on all states to refrain from any recognition of the annexation."[25]

The continuing escalation of the crisis was very much on the minds of all present when Cabinet was formally briefed on 9 August on the choice of options (sea, air, and land). General Huddleston, as operations spokesman for the Canadian Forces, made the presentation, giving particular but not exclusive attention to the naval option. There was one military impediment: the sorry state of anti-air defence in the Canadian navy. Correcting these deficiencies, even if it meant delaying departure by one to two weeks, was essential before embarking on the operation. If this was achieved, the commitment of two Canadian warships was a viable option.

After due consideration Cabinet agreed, but at some point in the deliberations it was accepted that the force should be enlarged to a task group of three ships. The ability to keep two ships at sea indefinitely must have raised some justifiable concerns; adding a third vessel gave that extra measure of insurance to maintain a continued presence. Mr Clark immediately left for a special closed session of NATO foreign ministers being held in Brussels to discuss collective action. Not expecting any dissension from within NATO, Cabinet agreed that a public announcement would be made by the prime minister the next day. Because the CDS would be returning from overseas at that time, Admiral Thomas would accompany Mr Mulroney to present the details of the deployment.

The sudden addition of another ship sent the naval staffs scrambling. The most obvious selections already had been made. Of the remaining available ships in Halifax, the thirty-five-year old destroyer *Terra Nova* (DDE 259) seemed to offer the best possibility. As a result, the task group would have three vessels from three different classes of ship, further complicating the developing modification plan.[26]

Late Thursday afternoon the Deputy Chief of Defence Staff issued a Warning Order formally alerting the Canadian Forces' senior commanders that a possible intervention in the Gulf, under the code-name Operation FRICTION, was imminent. Staff checks and deployment preparations, "including physical modifications," were to be initiated for the dispatch of a three-ship naval force, "the preferred option being to deploy one DDH 280, one IRE and one AOR ... Notice to Sail — Seven days."[27] Although the onus was therefore squarely upon MARCOM, the planning circle was widened to include Air Command (AIRCOM) and Mobile

Command (FMC). They were directed to lend whatever support was required. To facilitate that, General Huddleston took the extraordinary step of allowing DIRLAUTH (DIRect Liaison AUTHorized) among the commands as appropriate to complete staff checks. The National Defence Operations Centre (NDOC), normally only a skeleton crew during the silent hours, also was activated to round-the-clock operations in order to be able to respond immediately to their requests.

The next day, Friday, 10 August, the prime minister made a televised statement on the crisis. With Admiral Thomas at his side to provide technical details, he officially announced the Canadian decision: two destroyers, HMC Ships *Athabaskan* and *Terra Nova*, and the supply ship *Protecteur*, with their embarked *Sea King* helicopters, would deploy to the region "to deter further Iraqi aggression," arriving sometime after mid-September. The ships would sail as a naval Task Group representing Canada's resolve to uphold international principles.[28]

The media and Opposition critics immediately dismissed the move as "more symbolic than strategic." The prime minister admitted that the government would not decide on the ships' role or the requirement for active service until they arrived in the Gulf .[29] Joining the US-led multinational force was not practicable. Nor had the UN moved towards creating a workable structure. However, Canada was joining a growing coalition of nations pledging naval forces, with Australia, West Germany and Belgium also indicating their intentions that day, and the Netherlands shortly thereafter. But "the Coalition," as it was coming to be called, was without recent precedent, outside familiar structures such as NATO, and without a mandate. The Canadians were not alone in hoping that something would grow out of it.

Notes

1   Unless otherwise specified, all times are local, twenty-four-hour time.

2   This text assumes a basic knowledge of the Persian Gulf Crisis of 1990-91 and describes the unfolding of events only within the context of a Canadian perspective. For details on particular aspects, the reader is invited to refer to any of the published general histories of the conflict, the better of which to date include: Roland Dannreuther, "The Gulf Conflict: A Political and Strategic Analysis," *Adelphi Papers*, No. 264 (Winter 1991-1992); Lawrence Freedman and Efraim Karsh, *The Gulf Conflict 1990-1991: Diplomacy and War in the New World Order* (Princeton, N.J.: Princeton University Press, 1993); and Dilip Hiro, *Desert Shield to Desert Storm: The Second Gulf War* (New York: Routledge, 1992). An important reference source is Micah L. Sifry and Christopher Cerf (eds.) *The Gulf War Reader: History, Documents, Opinions* (Toronto: Random House, 1991). The official American account is tabled in United States Department of Defense, *Conduct of the Persian Gulf War: Final Report to Congress* [hereafter referred to as *CPGW*] (Washington, D.C.: April 1992). A useful popular account is Rick Atkinson, *Crusade: The Untold Story of the Persian Gulf War* (Boston: Houghton Mifflin Company, 1993). The only published Canadian account to date has been Jocelyn Coulon, *La dernière croisade: La guerre du Golfe et le rôle caché du Canada* (Montréal: Méridien, 1992).

3   The Carter Doctrine, declared by President Jimmy Carter in his State of the Union address, 23 January 1980 held that "An attempt by any outside force to gain control of the Persian Gulf region will be regarded as an assault on the vital interests of the United States of America, and such [an] assault will be repelled by any means necessary, including military force." The history of American interest in the security of the Gulf Region is discussed in Michael Palmer, *On Course to Desert Storm: The United States Navy and the Persian Gulf*, especially "Part Three: Assuring Access to Adequate Oil Supplies, 1950-1981" (Washington, D.C.: USNHC, 1992).

4   Norman Friedman, *Desert Victory: The War for Kuwait* (Annapolis, Md.: Naval Institute Press, 1991), p. 32.

5   "The Glaspie Transcript: Saddam Meets the U.S. Ambassador (July 25, 1990)," *The Gulf War Reader*, p. 122-33. [This transcript was released by the Iraqi authorities.]

6   Jane Boulden and David Cox, "Summary of United Nations Security Council Resolutions on the Persian Gulf," *The Guide to Canadian Policies on Arms Control, Disarmament, Defence and Conflict Resolution 1991* [hereafter *The Guide*] (Canadian Institute for International Peace and Security: Ottawa, 1991), p. 329.

7   Hiro, *Desert Shield to Desert Storm*, p. 73.

8   Anthony H. Cordesman and Abraham R. Wagner, *The Lessons of Modern War*, vol. 2, *The Iran-Iraq War* (Boulder, Col.: Westview, 1990), p. 591.

9   Canada, Department of External Affairs, "Canada Announces Further Measures Against Iraq," *News Release*, No. 166, 4 August 1990; and ibid., "Mr. Clark Announces Regulations on Sanctions Against Iraq," *News Release*, No. 170, 8 August 1990. External Affairs sources on 2 August stated "that the government lacks authority under any existing legislation to match the British and American actions;" that would require an order-in-council by Cabinet, which would have to await until 7 August (*Globe and Mail*, 3 August 1990).

10   *CPGW*, p. vi.

11   United Nations Department of Public Information, "An Overview," pt. 1 of *The Blue Helmets: A Review of United Nations Peace-keeping*, 2nd ed. (1990).

12   Coulon, pp. 43 and 47.

13 *The Guide*, p. 329.

14 *CPGW*, p. 62.

15 Quoted in *The Guide*, p. 214.

16 A captain in the navy is the equivalent of an army or air force colonel. See Appendix A for Canadian Forces rank equivalents.

17 The Canadian Patrol Frigate (CPF) programme would add twelve new ships to the navy, expanding the traditional ASW function to include an ASUW capability and good AAW self-defence.

18 The Tribal Update and Modernization Programme (TRUMP) was an expanded mid-life refit of the four DDH-280 *Iroquois* ("Tribal")-class destroyers, incorporating area air defence and command and control (C^2) improvements, in order to give the fleet the ability to conduct truly independent Task Group operations in any threatened environment.

19 DDH and AOR are respectively the standardized designations for "Destroyer, Helicopter-carrying" and "Auxiliary, Oiler Replenishment" (supply ship or tanker). The fact that the Canadian AORs had no self-defence protection at all was an identified deficiency due to be corrected in part in upcoming refits.

20 An RCN-USN precedent existed for just this sort of cooperation. During the Cuban Missile Crisis of 1962, the RCN established a patrol in the northeastern Atlantic, freeing USN ships for the close blockade of Cuba. See Peter Haydon, *The 1962 Cuban Missile Crisis: Canadian Involvement Reconsidered* (Toronto: The Canadian Institute of Strategic Studies, 1993).

21 *Edmonton Sun*, 8 August 1990.

22 *Ottawa Sun*, 9 August 1990.

23 The practice of obtaining an order-in-council for active service is not one of legality but of tradition, begun by Prime Minister Louis St. Laurent on 8 September 1950, when he gave notice that the regular forces of the Royal Canadian Navy, the Canadian Army and the Royal Canadian Air Force were being placed on active service for the purpose of participating in the UN Korean police action (P.C. 1950-4365, 9 September 1950).

24 Canada, Department of External Affairs, "Mr. Clark Announces Regulations on Sanctions Against Iraq," *News Release*, No. 170, 8 August 1990.

25 *The Guide*, p. 329.

26 Although no one in naval circles had spoken openly of a third vessel, by 8 August the secret naval staff estimates included the note that allowance for the commitment of an Improved *Restigouche*-class Escort (IRE) also had to be considered. The even older *St Laurent*-class DDHs which comprised the bulk of the Halifax-based fleet realistically could not be upgraded for the anticipated role.

27 DHist, War Diary (WD) NDHQ, CDS, "Warning Order - Op FRICTION," 9 August 1990.

28 Canada, Office of the Prime Minister, "Speaking Notes for Prime Minister Brian Mulroney Press Conference, National Press Theatre August 10, 1990."

29 *Globe and Mail*, 11 August 1990.

CHAPTER 2

Off to the Gulf:
August – September 1990

MARCOM Gets Involved

Meanwhile, as NDHQ-level planning progressed throughout the week of 2-9 August, the unsuspecting crews of the First Canadian Destroyer Squadron, HMC Ships *Athabaskan*, *Terra Nova*, and *Fraser*, and the supply ship *Protecteur*, were concluding their summer leave periods and getting ready for the traditional fall deployment to European waters. Returning late in the evening of the ninth, *Terra Nova* had spent two days at sea on a preparatory technical readiness inspection. The other ships were to go to sea the following week for an informal two-day combat readiness programme.

Those plans were quickly cast aside when Canada's navy suddenly became the focus of unusual national attention. The dispatch of a naval task group captured the imaginations of Canadians, and the media picked up the new national angle to the developing crisis with relish. While television and press reports underlined the age and lack of modern armament of the three vessels, they also allowed fair time to the navy. During the Ottawa announcement, Admiral Thomas, sitting beside the prime minister, vowed that the necessary upgrades would be completed. Immediately following Mulroney and Thomas, Admiral George held a similar press conference in Halifax. He proclaimed his confidence in the ability of his sailors and introduced the man who was to lead the expedition, the senior sea going Canadian officer, Commodore Kenneth J. Summers.

Then in his twenty-seventh year of service, Summers had been promoted to the rank of commodore the previous year and appointed commander of the Canadian Fleet, the seagoing extension of his shore-based responsibility as Chief of Staff for Operations at MARCOM. Earlier in his career, he had served under Admiral Thomas at NDHQ, first in the Directorate of Naval Requirements, and then as a Director himself in charge of Maritime Force Development. He was responsible for preparing the naval material for the 1987 Defence White Paper. Subsequently, he had spent the better part of the last three years in charge of formations of ships at sea, having commanded the Second Canadian Destroyer Squadron in Esquimalt. He was well-versed in the art of task group operations.

The idea of working in concert with other fleets was not an alien one to the Canadian navy. Indeed, the now forestalled European cruise in several ways continued to serve as a model for the new Gulf deployment. The original plan had been to have four ships participate in the annual NATO Exercise TEAMWORK, with the Canadian Fleet Commander in charge of certain anti-submarine warfare operations. To prepare for this exercise, the American officer in overall control was hosting a senior commanders' briefing and war game simulation at the Headquarters of the Supreme Allied Commander, Atlantic (SACLANT) in the second week of August. Up until then, none of the nations participating in the exercise had made a formal commitment to a Gulf deployment. However, aware of the possibility of Canadian action, Commodore Summers chose to remain in Halifax to follow the progress of political and military decision-making. In his stead, Captain Duncan E. ("Dusty") Miller, commander of the First Destroyer Squadron, departed as planned on Monday, 6 August, for Norfolk, Virginia, to attend the SACLANT briefings. Only indirectly aware of the pace of concurrent developments, he would not arrive back in Canada until the tenth, just in time to hear the official announcement of the deployment. Still, he had been privy to the USN's own preparations and to the professional speculation of his fellow senior NATO naval commanders. Indeed, at one point during the simulation someone reportedly commented that "we could probably shift this ... to the South after we got to the North Sea and we'd probably be where the action was really going to be."[1]

He was not far off the mark. Virtually all of the naval forces which would eventually gather in the Gulf region had been exposed to and were comfortable with the tactical doctrine and procedures of the Western allies. As well, the recent regular TEAMWORK operations of aircraft carrier battle groups in the confined waters of the Vestfjord, in northern Norway, had served to erode the long-standing naval dogma that carriers were an open-ocean force that could not operate effectively in constricted waters.

Although the deployment of the task group was not announced until 10 August, the shift from TEAMWORK to FRICTION was already well underway in Maritime Command Headquarters. During the NDHQ estimate preparation on the sixth, the first formal contacts were established between the Ottawa staff and that of Commodore Summers. In the absence of any more definite direction from Ottawa, the small circle of those in the know kept its activities under the strictest security until Thursday afternoon, when the outline of the naval option became widely known. Later that evening, in the wake of a Cabinet meeting and in anticipation of a warning order from NDHQ, Summers chaired the first of Maritime Command's many sessions tracking the daily progress of the preparatory work on the ships. Close coordination was required to put into effect a complex programme that included installing equipment, fuelling, loading ammunition, storing, issuing clothes, and training. Work would continue around the clock.

Among those present at the meeting of 9 August were the captains of the ships *Protecteur* and *Athabaskan* (*Terra Nova* was still at sea on her technical inspection), who learned at this point of their change of destination. For the three commanding officers the undertaking was doubly challenging. After only a month in command of their respective ships, they were confronted with a daunting task. On 10 July Captain Doug McClean had assumed command of *Protecteur*, the unarmed supply ship which would undergo the most extensive upgrade. The next day Commander John Pickford took over *Athabaskan*, which as flagship for the operation would have to accommodate the additional staffs. Finally, on the twelfth, Commander Stuart Andrews accepted charge of *Terra Nova*, a compact ship which could not be outfitted to the same extent as the larger destroyer. For the two destroyer captains, these were their first sea commands. Lastly, their squadron commander, Captain Miller, who did not return from Norfolk until 12 August, was also new to his position.

Summers faced the prospect that each of the four officers next in seniority to himself had assumed their commands only within the past month. These five officers were not unknown to each other, but it would take time, working in close association, to form operational cohesiveness. This was another consideration in the endeavour to prepare the ships and their crews for a demanding and possibly very long operation.

Institutional Reorganization

Friday, 10 August, was a momentous day for Canada's military. Several hours after the announcement of the Gulf deployment, Lieutenant-General Kent Foster, Commander of Mobile Command, came to Ottawa from his St-Hubert, Québec headquarters to present his plan for the restoration of order at the Mohawk reserves near Montréal. Code-named Operation SALON, it proposed a phased intervention by the 5th Canadian Mechanized Brigade Group (5 CMBG) from CFB Valcartier. General de Chastelain, recently returned from his interrupted trip to the Warsaw Pact countries, had resumed his Ottawa position as Chief of Defence Staff at a unique juncture. His approval of SALON, coming so close upon that of Operation FRICTION, suddenly thrust the Canadian Forces into action on two highly visible and potentially volatile fronts.

The two operations made for a study in contrasts. From the start, SALON was conceived and directed from the Command level. It envisaged the employment of existing army resources and required only NDHQ approval of what was essentially an internal security operation in aid of a provincial government. In contrast, the international dimension of FRICTION necessitated federal government involvement from its inception. Operational authority was only delegated to Maritime Command when it was decided that the naval option was the least risky. Even then, NDHQ remained intimately involved because the extensive modifications to the ships required continued coordination by the various directorates which were responsible for procurement of the new equipment.

By the second week of August 1990, Operations FRICTION and SALON were generating a frenzy of activity just short of a full mobilization of NDHQ. For what was effectively an administrative establishment, this precipitated a much-needed overhaul of its crisis response organizational structure. Informal arrangements, such as the Navy Triangle, could not be expected to cope. A brief attempt was made to implement a Battle Staff — an assembly of senior officials at Headquarters — as a way to stage the NDHQ response to the two crises. However, the familiar Matrix, the name by which the existing peacetime departmental structure was known, quickly proved too cumbersome for rapid decision-making. With requests from the two commands arriving day and night, the power to respond had to be channelled through a smaller circle of people assisted by duty staffs. An organizational plan to do this existed in NDHQ but had never been implemented except as an internal paper exercise. The Joint Operational Staff, or the J-Staff, took existing positions with an operations function from the Matrix and put them in a direct line to the Operations Centre, effectively streamlining the crisis response process.[2] Anticipating this development, NDOC had adopted an increased posture on 9 August. Now those officers on duty had a full operational staff at their call, allowing unexpected events to receive due attention. To formulate a longer-range perspective, the senior members of the J-Staff would gather at regular intervals as a Crisis Action Team (CAT). At one of their first sessions, immediately following the prime minister's public announcement on the tenth, Commodore Johnston decreed that the process was to be formalized. The J-Staff system was affected, and all staff functions related to Operations FRICTION and SALON would be coordinated by J3 Operations — the new title for his division.

When responsibility for an operation is delegated from Ottawa, the normal relationship with NDHQ is significantly altered. The designated Command is allowed to exercise a fair degree of autonomy, while the national staffs turn their energies to supporting the implementation of the operation. The fact that SALON was essentially within the purview of Mobile Command, and FRICTION within that of Maritime Command, assumed that these two operations could be run on a traditional basis of non-interference. This assumption, however, proved short-lived. The transfer of responsibility from the national headquarters for the respective operations began smoothly enough, but soon the coordination of the sometimes conflicting army and navy demands for matériel required some external management in allocating the finite resources of the defence department. Mobile Command was able to keep greater control of SALON, which had few demands that could not be satisfied by Command's own resources, but FRICTION almost immediately came to make heavy demands on certain army resources. Furthermore, each operation resulted in extraordinary air transport requirements. Above all, coming at the recognized beginning of an economic recession, the unplanned expenditures signalled a serious budgetary impact. Together, the two operations were to tax the military resources of the Forces in general, and of Maritime Command in particular, to the limit.

The strategic necessity to administer the allocation of these resources nudged open the door to an ever-increasing NDHQ involvement in what had been intended as arms-length operations. Early on 10 August, even before the official announcement of FRICTION and the approval of the SALON plan, in his first external edict as J3 Operations, Commodore Johnston ordered the Commands to route all requests for the commitment and tasking of resources through NDHQ's Operations Centre for prioritization. That too quickly became unmanageable. The overburdened operators passed the matériel requests to the Logistics and Movements Coordination Centres at headquarters. Renamed J4 Logistics and J4 Movements, these sections subsequently were accorded greatly expanded control over the requisition and transfer of matériel. In the short term, the result was an arbitration mechanism established to prioritize demands and allocate accordingly. Moreover, rather than waiting to respond to the normal supply system "demand-pull" process, which was not conducive to the hasty ship preparations, NDHQ was able to "supply-push" materiel required in Halifax, often in a matter of hours. What had begun as an internal crisis management tool was slowly transforming NDHQ into an operational headquarters.

Air Transport Group (ATG) felt the effect of the new arrangement almost immediately. With its small fleet of twenty-eight CC-130 *Hercules* and five CC-137 *Boeing 707* aircraft, ATG even now was working at full capacity to meet the routine worldwide air transport needs of the Canadian Forces. Normally, the Commands passed their respective demands to the Transport Group's Trenton, Ontario headquarters for action. The need to coordinate resources for FRICTION changed this by routing the requests through Ottawa and requiring ATG to respond to the requirements of the national Logistics and Movements Coordination Centres. The scope of the ship preparations meant that innumerable pieces of equipment had to be ferried across Canada and from abroad. Already immersed in locating and prioritizing this equipment, the Ottawa J4 group took the next obvious step: it promulgated the shipping instructions and took over the tasking of aircraft. The NDHQ sections were not used to coordinating air movements, and ATG never really accepted its loss of autonomy. The cross-nation air transport venture nevertheless got underway. In the evening of 10 August, the first two *Hercules* aircraft were tasked to transport equipment from Esquimalt. A continuous airlift operation had begun. At any particular hour of the day or night for the next eight months, Canadian transport aircraft could be found airborne in support of the forces deployed to the Gulf.

Quite apart from these logistical concerns, NDHQ was also responsible for promulgating certain ground rules governing the scope of the deployment. The Operations Order prepared on the tenth established national guidelines for Maritime Command to follow but did not specify the exact purpose of the deployment. The statement of the task group's mission left much room for interpretation. It simply required the commander to establish a military presence in the Persian Gulf in support of Canadian policy. That policy remained undefined. Nevertheless, it was clear that the Canadian squadron was intended to monitor, not to enforce, the implementation of sanctions from a vantage point in the Gulf of Oman. Its rules of engagement were essentially defensive. Admiral George was directed not to assign the Canadian ships to a foreign commander. However, once they were in-theatre, Commodore Summers was to coordinate his actions with those of foreign task group commanders. How to pay for everything was the next question. In an attempt to keep a cap on costs, Halifax was warned that expenditures should be absorbed within present allotments and additional funding requirements identified by cyclical forecasts if required.

If the mission was unclear, at least the navy had its sailing orders. The schedule for Task Group (TG) 302.3, as the three-ship force was designated, began to take shape. The plan foresaw a seven-day work period — the minimum time expected to effect the preparations — with at-sea trials of the new installations on 18-19 August, and then a day for fixing any "bugs" and final storing. The departure, tentatively set for 21 August, would be followed by a direct passage, with a fuelling stop in Gibraltar on the twenty-ninth and transit of the Suez Canal on 5 September. If all went well, TG 302.3 could arrive in the Gulf of Oman by mid-September.

Preparation of the Task Group I: The Ships
Official receipt of the Warning Order from NDHQ on Thursday, 9 August, allowed the thrust of the ship modifications to change from planning to implementation. By 0900 Friday, the Halifax Headquarters and Dockyard had become a beehive of activity. Anti-submarine mortars were removed from both destroyers and replaced with *Phalanx* Close-in Weapon Systems (CIWS, the rapid-firing anti-missile defence system, an acronym creatively pronounced "Sea-Whiz"). *Harpoon* surface-to-surface missiles were fitted on *Terra Nova* in place of ASROC (an anti-submarine weapon). And new chaff systems intended to confuse the attack radars of anti-ship missiles were added to all three ships.[3] Of all the upgrades, *Protecteur*'s was especially dramatic as the previously unarmed supply ship was brought up to a minimum self-defence level, with new radars, electronic warfare equipment, SATCOM, and two CIWS mountings.

Virtually all of the new installations were completed without the benefit of detailed design studies, or even the preparation of full sets of drawings. Workers simply responded to engineering sketches and verbal instructions, and exact placings were often determined as the tradesmen were welding the units in place.

There was no realistic alternative to this ad hoc procedure, but it did point to a significant risk — the danger of electromagnetic interference or compatibility problems (EMI/EMC) among different equipment. Whenever systems requiring a great deal of energy transmit at high power in close proximity, there is a danger that the energy radiated from one will interfere with or blank out another. More difficult to anticipate is the EMI from the electromagnetic fields produced around the miles of power cables strung throughout a ship. Intercomputer signals are particularly vulnerable. The ability to predict any adverse effect is an imprecise science at best and normally demands many hours of isolated testing and grooming before installation. In the short time allowed, the navy was forced to make the installations and hope for the best, but the situation did underline the absolutely critical requirement for two days of pre-deployment trials.[4]

Dividing the work among three ships and standardizing the equipment between them in some ways simplified the problem. But even these advantages had hidden drawbacks. The same workers sometimes would be required in three different places at the same time. Moreover, since each of the ships were from three entirely different classes, the installation of a particular system usually posed three distinct challenges. Several of the above points are illustrated by the installation of the *Phalanx*. In *Athabaskan* and *Terra Nova* space was made available for the new mounting by the removal of the obsolete anti-submarine Mortar Mk 10 from the quarterdeck area near the stern. In *Athabaskan*, however, the towering *Phalanx* had to be installed in such a way that it could have a clear arc of fire and not interfere with the safe launch and recovery of helicopters from the flight deck just a few feet forward. In *Terra Nova* the replacement of several tons of equipment from near the waterline by a much higher but still massive mounting precipitated a rather tricky change to the ship's centre of gravity. For her part, *Protecteur* did not require the removal of any other systems (she had so few to start with), but she was fitted with two of the *Phalanx* units, one forward above the bridge and one aft atop the hangar. Each required some simple but imaginative mountings that were able to transfer the heavy loads (seven tons) not planned in the original ship design to the vertical support frames on either side of the underlying aluminum superstructures. The power supply and firing circuit wiring was unique to each ship.

Top-heaviness was of little relative concern in the massive *Protecteur*, but stability changes remained a major worry in both *Athabaskan* and *Terra Nova*. The DDH-280s as a class were always tender ships (the TRUMP refit was required in part to address this problem). So in *Athabaskan* weight was rigidly controlled to such an extent that even dishes and cutlery were strictly rationed. The pre-deployment sea trials confirmed that *Terra Nova* was trimmed by the bows. Among the possible remedies were the addition of fifty tons solid ballast in the mortar well — not considered a good option — or limiting the fuel load in the forward tanks, with a consequent undesirable reduction in the operational capability and endurance of the ship. The navy chose the latter option.

Not as obvious as the new weapons mountings were the extensive command and control (C^2) and communications upgrades undertaken in varying degrees in each of the three ships. The flagship *Athabaskan* received the majority, to ensure high-level compatibility with the major allies, as well as a secure National Rear Link to the headquarters in Halifax and Ottawa. *Protecteur*'s fit was expanded to a similar capacity so that she could operate as an Alternate Command Ship. *Terra Nova* received a scaled-down package to retain interoperability within the task group. The fits were constantly modified to ensure the optimum flexibility. For example, shortly before the task group sailed, the attaché in London forwarded a Royal Navy recommendation that the ships be fitted with the British secure telephone system known as *Brahms*. Both the Australians and Dutch had done so. The recommendation was accepted immediately. By adopting *Brahms* — in addition to possessing the American *STU-III* system — the Canadian task group widened its allied communications network and gained unique access to both the American and British senior commands.

A good, all-Canadian example of the sort of original thinking which inspired the preparations went largely unnoticed. Fitted underwater to the bow of each ship was a new Mine Avoidance Sonar (MAS), a proven requirement for Persian Gulf operations. For decades, designers had tried but failed to find a device reliable enough to enable large, vulnerable surface ships to detect this simplest of weapons. Finally, in the late 1980s, modern technology and commercial demand had combined for quite a different purpose to produce a device which neatly fitted the present requirement — the simple fish-finding sonar, with a sufficiently high-frequency signal and processor to discern small objects. Among the best available anywhere in the world was the C-Tech *Spectra-Scan 3000*. It was the cheapest on the market and was produced in nearby Cornwall, Ontario. Three of the sets were bought literally off the shelf and quickly installed to complement the ships' existing anti-submarine sonars.

As detailed and far-reaching as the original refit plan was, in reality it had been a quick staff estimate. It was natural that some refinements would be made and implemented as the actual work progressed. The most significant, in terms of expense and operational concept, was the decision to fit *Terra Nova* with *Harpoon*, an anti-surface-ship missile with a maximum range of over sixty miles, roughly double that of the Iraqi's *Exocet*. *Harpoon* was added to the task group's inventory, not for its commonly advertised offensive capability, but more as a defensive measure, necessitated in part by the last-minute inclusion of *Terra Nova*. The small IRE-class destroyer, more so than the DDH-280, was a specialised close-in anti-submarine ship, without even the advantage of an embarked helicopter. Enlarging the task group gave an insurance of sorts in numbers, but there was no commensurate gain in defensive ability against missile-armed surface ships. As the Halifax staffs planned the passage of the task group to the Middle East and its subsequent employment in-theatre, the poor anti-surface posture of the force became startlingly apparent. *Harpoon* was the obvious answer to the problem. The weapon had been acquired for the CPF programme, was available in the national supply system, and as a stand-alone system (not unlike the *Phalanx*), it could be integrated easily into the combat suite. The removal of *Terra Nova*'s anti-submarine ASROC launcher provided the perfect physical location for the canisters. As soon as the modifications were completed, the commanding officer of *Terra Nova* was able to boast that " ... an incredible whirlwind metamorphosis ... [had] transformed TERRA NOVA into a class of her own, the DDG 259 class, Canada's first surface-to-surface missile [armed] destroyer."[5]

Other changes arose from the fact that the early NDHQ modification concept had not benefited from an interservice exchange of ideas, despite the fact that NDHQ had envisioned air and even army ingredients. This was quickly put to rights when planning was broadened after 9 August. At that point, army input resulted in variations to the planned modifications of at least two major weapon systems, the *Javelin* missile and the 40mm Boffin (Bofors) guns. Each system highlights some interesting aspects of the preparations.

When the naval staffs conducted their initial assessment on 6 August, they recognized that certain of the ships' defensive shortcomings could be addressed in part by a portable, very-low-level anti-aircraft missile system, which also could be effective against small vessels. Investigation revealed that *Stinger* was not available from the United States, but an alternative — *Blowpipe* — was already in Canadian Forces use with the air defence batteries at CFB Chatham, New Brunswick and in Europe. However, air defence staff officers in Halifax, Ottawa, and St-Hubert all preferred a third system, *Javelin*, over both *Blowpipe* and *Stinger*, for a variety of reasons: as essentially a second-generation direct development of *Blowpipe*, the *Javelin* aiming unit offered significant improvements over its predecessor, especially for firing from a moving ship; conversion to *Javelin* could be made more quickly than to *Stinger*, given the troops' familiarity with *Blowpipe*; and, perhaps most importantly, acquisition of *Javelin* from its British manufacturer was well underway, with partial funds approved under the *Blowpipe* Life Extension Programme. The fact that the new aiming unit could fire the existing stocks of *Blowpipe* missiles, and thus minimize capital expenditure, made the prospect particularly attractive.

At CFB Chatham, 119 Air Defence Battery made preparations for three nine-man detachments — one per ship — to join the task group, while the staffing proceeded apace. By the time the matter was put before Admiral Thomas and General Huddleston on 16 August, it had become almost a foregone conclusion. They ordered the acceleration of the acquisition process for the upgrade to *Javelin* aiming units and a *Hercules* aircraft to stand by in Lahr to transport the equipment to Canada.

At the same time, the three designated air defence detachments were conducting a live *Blowpipe* missile firing practice at CFB Gagetown. It proved to be a most useful exercise, not only giving the troops a much-needed refresher, but also demonstrating quite graphically that the aging *Blowpipe* ammunition was of questionable reliability: of the twenty-seven missiles shot, nine misfired. The staggering failure rate served to remove any lingering consideration of making do with *Blowpipe*, and General Huddleston directed that the pending order be revised to include stocks of *Javelin* missiles to complement the new aiming units. The old *Blowpipe* stock would be used up in training. The next day, 17 August, Mr McKnight invoked his Ministerial discretionary purchasing limit of $10 million — extended by Cabinet to facilitate the FRICTION acquisition process — to authorize the *Javelin* purchase. That afternoon the chief of supply signed the contract with *Short* Brothers — the British-based subsidiary of Quebec's Bombardier — at a final price of £5,026,543. The equipment and its British army instructors arrived in Shearwater by *Hercules* on 19 August, in plenty of time to deploy with the ships.

Any discussion of army matériel fitted on the ships begs for reference to the 40mm Boffin (Bofors) mounts.[6] These 40mm weapons had had a long association with Canada's armed forces, having been acquired during the Second World War, and the RCN continued to use them until the last of the wartime frigates and HMCS *Bonaventure* were paid off in the late 1960s. Then they were transferred to the artillery for the air defence of Canadian bases in Germany where they were still in use in 1990. Despite their age, they were functioning well, and the navy was planning to take back some of the guns to mount on the soon-to-be acquired minesweepers, not for their original air defence function, but in order to dispose of surfaced mines. Someone now observed that the small-calibre 40mm also offered unique capabilities during boarding operations. It was more easily controlled at close range than the ships' more powerful main armament. The preparations plan was accordingly altered to incorporate two per ship.

By Monday, 13 August, all six of the required guns had arrived in Halifax, in various states of disrepair. Even with the assistance of qualified army weapons technicians from Chatham and Gagetown, five days later only four of the guns were serviceable. For the others, the problem was the availability of parts, Halifax's local supply having been exhausted. Additional parts were available through the national supply system, but their procurement was on a lower priority than other items, such as the *Phalanx* and *Harpoon*. With time becoming critical, the weapons technicians decided to check the 40mm mount at the Maritime Command museum for anything useable. It turned out that that mount was not the same as the Boffin version, but one of the original Bofors. No useful parts were obtained. Still, the incident gave rise to the apocryphal story that the task group was being outfitted with museum pieces.

In time, the required parts arrived and the refurbishing was completed. The guns may have been somewhat dated, but they had a useful purpose.

As the installations of all the various weapons and communications systems progressed during the week of 11-18 August, Commodore Summers began to appreciate that the planned departure for the twenty-first was in jeopardy, through no fault of anyone involved. To meet the deadline, the Ship Repair Unit had mounted a sustained operation, splitting its 1300-strong workforce into two twelve-hour shifts. All the required matériel was arriving from scattered points according to a coordinated schedule. Even the elements were unusually cooperative. The late summer normally was foggy and drizzly through the morning with thunderstorms in the evening, but this year the Halifax skies remained clear. Only one hour of topside work was lost to rain in the whole of the period.

The simple fact remained that the sheer enormity and complexity of the task had been underestimated. The status of the task group preparations was the constant topic at daily briefing and planning sessions in Halifax and Ottawa. At midweek, on 15 August, General de Chastelain summoned a special conference to discuss the situation, and Commodore Summers flew to Ottawa to bring his perspective to the discussion. Joined by Admiral Thomas, the naval officers were able to argue convincingly that if the new defensive weapons were to be fully operational on sailing, there could be no compromise on their installation; if necessary the work period had to be extended and sailing delayed. All parties were forced to concede that they had been somewhat optimistic in allotting only seven days to the preparation phase and that sailing would have to be delayed beyond the twenty-first.

Further delays were encountered during the rest of the week, but *Athabaskan* and *Terra Nova* finally were able to proceed to sea in the forenoon of Monday, 20 August, for two days of equipment trials and weapon firing in the local Halifax exercise areas. *Protecteur* remained alongside, pending completion of the installation of her *Phalanx* systems, and was scheduled to join the others the next day after taking on ammunition. The results of the first day's trials were somewhat mixed. *Athabaskan* reported that some technical targets were met, such as achieving a good Citadel positive pressure, something essential to the gas-tight integrity of the ship in case of chemical attack, but several new problems arose, particularly with the new communications equipment, causing some of the trials to be postponed. Commander Andrews ominously reported serious problems with the operation of *Terra Nova*'s mine avoidance sonar and the air search radar. So much work remained to be completed on *Protecteur* that not much was expected of her trials other than the psychologically important achievement of getting the ship to sea.

The next day was much better, especially for *Athabaskan*. She still was encountering some minor problems, but Commander Pickford could hardly contain his enthusiasm in his mid-afternoon progress report. He wrote that his vessel was "proud to boast the first ever successful firings of both the Shield [chaff] and CIWS systems in a Canadian warship."[7] *Protecteur* was also underway. Although many of her trials had to be deferred pending final hookup, tests of the critical systems were more than satisfactory. Dockyard workers sailed with the ship and worked through the night to ready her two *Phalanx* mounts for a trial firing the morning of 22 August, on completion of which Captain McClean echoed *Athabaskan's* confidence with a report that "CIWS in stereo is sweet music."[8] Except for the troubles with *Terra Nova's* mine avoidance sonar, none of the ships had encountered any evidence of the feared electromagnetic interference (EMI) affecting their various systems. With two days for the dockyard to rectify the identified defects, Admiral George informed the Chief of Defence Staff that "Preparations for OP FRICTION [are] proceeding extremely well and … accordingly, unless otherwise directed TG 302.3 will slip and proceed … Friday 24 August."[9]

Preparation of the Task Group II: The Helicopters

A similar but separate effort was underway at CFB Shearwater to prepare the *Sea King* helicopters which were to embark on the ships. Their upgrading process was smaller in scale but no less sweeping in its purpose, although it started somewhat after that of the ships. *Athabaskan* would sail with a standard DDH 280 detachment of two helicopters, but *Protecteur* would embark an augmented AOR detachment of three, with an expanded maintenance section to better support an extended period away from the home base. The Commanding Officer of HS 423 *Eagle* Squadron, the operational *Sea King* unit in Shearwater, was Lieutenant-Colonel Larry McWha. He would be Captain Miller's senior adviser on air operations.

For some years, naval exercises had simulated surface search techniques, but little existed in the way of formal doctrine. Also, many of the self-protection deficiencies of the *Sea King* were well known, but the necessary new equipment acquisitions had been deferred to the New Shipborne Aircraft (NSA) *Sea King* replacement programme.[10] The statement of requirements for the NSA project now provided a planning basis. A group of officers from 423 Squadron and Halifax's Maritime Air Group Headquarters (MAGHQ) identified eleven major systems to be fitted to the aircraft:[11] five for the new surface surveillance role, including a Forward-Looking InfraRed surveillance device (FLIR), stabilized binoculars, and improved navigation (GPS) and secure communications (*Havequick*) outfits; and six for self-protection, ranging from chaff and infrared countermeasures dispensers to radar and laser warning receivers. The bulky sonars were to be removed to provide the needed space and reduce the weight. Some of the helicopter upgrades were taken from other Forces aircraft, but many had to be purchased outright. The scope of the modifications was so extensive that the aircraft were given the unofficial designation CH124C; officially, they retained their CH124A status.

If the refitting of the *Sea Kings* was simplified by the fact that the design and installation process was applied to only one aircraft type, it was complicated by the stringent requirements of flight safety. Essentially, nothing being installed on the ships would make them sink (except for their sheer weight — witness the stability problems in *Athabaskan* and *Terra Nova*), but electromagnetic interference with certain delicate aircraft controls could cause a helicopter to fall out of the sky. Maritime Air Group did not possess the resources to undertake extensive aircraft modifications, and Shearwater's aeronautical engineering organization was geared to the maintenance of the locally stationed helicopters. As a result, there was no on-site engineering and production equivalent of the Dockyard's Naval Engineering and Ship Repair Units. However, on 13 August, an Installation Control Team was established. It comprised teams of aeronautical engineers from NDHQ's Director-General of Aerospace Engineering and Maintenance (DGAEM) section, the Aerospace Maintenance Development Unit (AMDU) from CFB Trenton, and the Aerospace Engineering Test Establishment (AETE) at CFB Cold Lake.

The aim of the control team was to avoid any circumvention of the existing tried and proven installation and test procedures. Instead, they determined that the normal procedures could be compressed by integrating the two activities. Essential to this was the early decision to prepare a total of six aircraft. The sixth would be the first completed, the idea being that the new systems would be fitted and tested in this "prototype" to resolve any installation problems. It would then remain in Canada for later detailed testing.

Although Shearwater's effort initially lagged behind that of Dockyard by a full two days, it very quickly reached the same level of intensity. Even while the lists of new equipment were being put together, the air maintenance section at Shearwater was busy removing obvious surplus equipment such as the dipping sonars. With the arrival of the installation control team, the changeover got into full swing. To assist tracking the progress of the installations, all three headquarters (NDHQ, MARCOMHQ and MAGHQ) adopted a format in which each major item was listed and then updated daily according to a colour code: green ("Low risk, no known impediment"); yellow ("Medium risk"); or red ("High risk"). At the naval coordination meeting on the crucial afternoon of 15 August (when the delay in departure was being considered), the commander of Maritime Air Group admitted that most of his items were still coded red. He estimated that one aircraft would be ready for the departure on the twenty-first, and the ground crews would finish the rest on the way. Test flights of some of the individual systems began the afternoon of 16 August, and the prototype aircraft was completed on the twentieth. Of the originally intended installations, only the AWR-47 MAWS (Missile Approach Warning System) proved technically unmanageable. Further prototype investigation was never completed. The early concern over EMI/EMC was justified when the ALQ-144 infrared jammer "was found to create aircraft heading errors of up to 130 degrees!"[12] Its operational employment was restricted for some time before the Defence Research Establishment in Victoria proposed a workable solution in September.

Maritime Air Group was able to boast on 21 August — the original sailing date — that the installations were complete; it was said that eighteen months of peacetime work had been accomplished in eight days. The delayed departure was still to the air group's advantage, for the final maintenance checks and acceptance test flights were not completed and the aircraft signed over to HS 423 until the twenty-third.

Preparation of the Task Group III: Training and Personnel

Of even greater concern to the task group's commanders was that, despite the perceived threat of further Iraqi aggression, the group's real mission, the monitoring of an embargo, involved what is known in military circles as a Rules of Engagement, or ROE, scenario. Military officers, of whatever service, are always most comfortable in a well-defined, black and white situation with no restrictions on engaging an identified enemy; the present situation fell very much in that unwelcome grey area of "no peace, no war," which was short of open hostilities. No Captain would want his ship to be the next *Stark* or *Vincennes*.[13]

The task group would require stringent command and control arrangements and quick-reaction self-defence measures. With only seven days before the planned departure, Commodore Summers' staff busied themselves preparing the operational principles or Battle Doctrine which would guide the group's response to any of the several situations that might be encountered. At the same time, Captain Miller and the combat teams of the three ships ran a hastily prepared gamut of tactical training exercises at Halifax's Fleet School and the Maritime Warfare Centre.

The political and tactical situations were developing apace, sharpening the focus of the training. Even though the United Nations had not yet declared an embargo, the Americans were taking steps towards the institution of one. On 16 August, President Bush authorized the United States Navy to use the minimum force necessary to check Iraqi shipping. The first merchant ships intercepted on the seventeenth were allowed to proceed because they were empty of cargo, but on the eighteenth the USS *Reid* caught the world's attention when she fired the first shots of the blockade across the bow of the fully laden Iraqi tanker *Khanaquin*, which was subsequently diverted to Yemen. While that drama was unfolding, Iraq's National Assembly declared two measures of defiance: it ordered the detention of the nationals of those governments which had decided to participate in the embargo and were planning to attack Iraq, and it directed all embassies in Kuwait to close and move their offices to Baghdad by noon local time, 24 August. In response, the Security Council immediately and unanimously countered with Resolution 664, demanding "the release of nationals of third countries from Iraq and Kuwait and that Iraq take no further action to jeopardize their safety."[14]

The preparation for the deployment was not without its human dimensions. The new equipment and the seemingly never-ending augmentation tasks (such as the Air Defence detachments) all required additional sailors, airmen, and even soldiers to bring the ships up to their wartime operational complements. The executive officers of the three ships and HS 423 were in regular contact with the personnel staffs of the Maritime and Air Command headquarters and NDHQ, in the scramble to fill the open billets with men and women (*Protecteur* had had a mixed crew since 1988) with the requisite talents. *Protecteur* was a prime example of the changes in personnel: in addition to having unfilled billets, the ship's new combat systems required the kind of tradespeople already aboard the destroyers; as well, her skeleton medical staff was expanded to include a full surgical team of doctors, technicians, and nurses. In all, her ship's company increased from 247 to 375, virtually overnight. The harsh facts of life were that many service members received last-minute postings, while the media, television in particular, were bombarding their families with graphic reminders of the perils ahead. These pressures led the navy and the air force to adopt what for them were novel approaches to preparing families for a lengthy deployment. At CFB Halifax, the fledgling Military Family Support Centre came into its own, scheduling a series of information sessions and organizing support groups for dependants.

The Departure of Task Group 302.3

Finally the day of departure arrived. In Halifax, Friday, 24 August 1990 dawned bright and sunny. As the sailors, soldiers, and airmen reported aboard their respective ships and at CFB Shearwater, the pace of Dockyard activity slowly slackened. Last-minute preparations were interrupted briefly while Mr McKnight, accompanied by General de Chastelain, went first with Admiral George to address the three ships' companies, and then with Lieutenant-General F.R. Sutherland (commander of Air Command) to Shearwater to see off the aircrews of the 423 Squadron detachments.

The official departure went exactly as planned, with *Protecteur* slipping her lines to pass in front of the reviewing stand at 1400, followed in quick succession by *Terra Nova*, *Athabaskan*, and the embarking *Sea King* helicopters in a finger-five formation flypast. The citizens of Halifax and Dartmouth lined the shores for an emotional send-off, and small craft followed well past the harbour mouth. Superstitious sailors were pleased that the ships were escorted past Chebucto Head by a pod of dolphins, rarely seen in the area. Not to be left short of any good-luck omen, at least one of the aircrews reported two eagles flying with them.

Task Group 302.3 sailed from Halifax harbour two weeks to the day from Prime Minister Mulroney's announcement of their deployment. This fourteen-day period has been compared, often negatively, with those required for similar expeditions. After all, Canadian warships sailed for Korea in 1950 a mere five days after receiving the order. A comparable Australian task group of two frigates and a replenishment ship sailed for the Gulf on 13 August, their departure having been announced by Prime Minister Hawke also on the tenth. The dissimilarities in preparation times can be explained by the fact that the two latter cases involved the dispatch of ships which were essentially ready for the stated mission. In August 1990 the Canadian ships were totally unprepared for operations in the Persian Gulf region. In the final analysis, round-the-clock efforts at Halifax Dockyard and Shearwater airbase, at an unprojected cost to the Canadian Forces of $54 million, corrected serious operational deficiencies. With the Canadian Task Group having undergone a fundamental shift in role and equipment, the miracle was that the departure originally scheduled for 21 August took place only three days later. Ship preparations for Operation FRICTION initiated massive materiel transfers and capital acquisition programmes in a remarkably short period of time. A subsequent Treasury Board review proclaimed it "an example of successful materiel management."[15]

The First Canadians in the Gulf

The focus of the Canadian response to the invasion of Kuwait was to dispatch a naval task group to join an anticipated blockade of Iraq. Interestingly, while the ships were undergoing their fast-tracked preparations, other members of the Canadian Forces were active or arriving in the region.

For the previous eighteen months, fifteen Canadian Forces officers had been serving as part of the 350-member United Nations Iran-Iraq Military Observer Group (UNIIMOG), created in July 1988 to supervise the disengagement of Iranian and Iraqi forces. It had been an uneasy truce. Saddam's troops still occupied large sections of Iran which they had gained only in the dying months of years of bloody stalemate (significantly, it was this late military triumph of sorts upon which the myth of Iraqi military prowess was built). As the West took an increasingly belligerent stance towards Iraq, the safety of the troops wearing the blue beret was watched closely. Surprisingly, Saddam took no action, overt or otherwise, against the military observer force, perhaps in the interest of retaining what little goodwill there was for Iraq, especially amongst third-world nations in the UN. One sobering incident involved a Canadian soldier whose family was visiting him in Baghdad when the invasion occurred. Their return to Canada was initially delayed as Saddam began to detain his foreign "guests," but they were repatriated in good time without incident. Saddam's unexpected settlement with Iran on 14 August, and Iraq's subsequent withdrawal from Iranian territory, made the continuance of UNIIMOG superfluous. In September, UN Secretary-General Javier Pérez de Cuellar agreed to reduce the force by 40 percent, dropping the Canadian representation to nine officers. Later, anticipating that hostilities would make the mission untenable, the last Canadian observers were withdrawn in January 1991.

Other Canadians began arriving in the region because they were serving in exchange positions with American, British, and French units. As their squadrons, regiments, and ships deployed, these Canadian officers and men quickly proved the value of the exchange programme in promoting wartime interoperability of forces. Chris Sutherland, a cadet from the Royal Military College, was one of the first Canadian exchange officers to arrive in the Gulf. He was aboard the missile cruiser USS *Antietam* in the Indian Ocean when it was ordered to join the *Independence* carrier battle group in the Arabian Sea. Sutherland eventually made his way to Diego Garcia and returned to Canada. Another officer, Captain G. Kenneth Campbell, was much closer to the centre of activity, serving as a communications officer in Central Command Headquarters. By a succession of circumstances, his team played an important role in configuring and connecting the tactical communications network for the theatre of operations. Over the next eight months, some forty Canadians were to find themselves in positions as diverse as British armoured squadrons and signals regiments, Royal Navy and French Navy ships, RAF fighter squadrons, and USAF transport and AWACS (Airborne Warning and Control System) squadrons.[16]

Two small contingents from opposite ends of the military spectrum deployed in mid-August to vital positions on the fringe of the action. Air force pilots and weapons controllers stationed with the NATO AWACS group in Geilenkirchen, Germany served in rotation from a forward operating base at Konya, Turkey, bolstering Turkey's defences while surveying activity in northern Iraq. As well, teams of military police were dispatched to augment the security staffs at the Canadian embassies in Amman and Riyadh against any terrorist threat.

Since the above measures were elements of missions already in place, they required little additional national coordination. There was, however, one unusual initiative undertaken expressly as part of the Canadian contribution to the Coalition effort. In the event of war, it was anticipated that both sides would sustain large numbers of casualties. A surgical team from the Forces hospital in Halifax was assembled to run *Protecteur*'s reasonably well-equipped casualty handling facility. Its capacity was limited because the task group could not provide extended care for casualties, but on 18 August NDHQ learned that the USN had dispatched the hospital ships *Mercy* and *Comfort* to the Gulf under the terms of the Red Cross and Geneva Conventions. American medical reserves had been called up, but with all of the demands ashore the ships remained understaffed and were looking for foreign augmentation. Reacting quickly, the office of the Surgeon-General secured an agreement whereby in return for Canadian personnel being made available for employment in American facilities, Canada would gain access to the vast US treatment and evacuation organization. A nine-member team was assembled primarily from the National Defence Medical Centre in Ottawa and the Forces' hospitals in Halifax and Borden. On 14 September the United States Navy issued instructions for them to join *Mercy* within the week. The team departed Canada late on 18 September, arriving in Bahrain the next day, and were flown immediately by helicopter to join *Mercy*, on-station in the Persian Gulf. In early January 1991 they were relieved by a similarly constituted group, which was embarked until after the cessation of hostilities.[17]

Other contingency options continued to be explored, and the planning actually expanded in scope after attention had settled on the naval task group. The various proposals were known collectively as SANDY SAFARI. They addressed possibilities as diverse as the evacuation of Canadian nationals from the Gulf region, the deployment of fighter aircraft to Turkey in support of NATO air defence operations, the reinforcement or replacement of the FRICTION task group, the deployment of ground combat forces, and the provision of logistical and airlift support to the multinational forces.

The Odyssey of Task Group 302.3

For the task group's 932 men and women of all ranks what was jokingly known as the "Persian Excursion" was in every sense a voyage into the unknown. The destination was unfamiliar waters, never before entered by Canadian warships.[18] The departure ceremony came in the midst of a rash of war fever, overshadowed by the possibility of adverse Iraqi reaction to two developments: the general refusal of Western countries to close their embassies in Kuwait (Saddam's deadline was 1200 local time, 24 August), and the pending decision of the Security Council to authorize the use of force in conjunction with Resolution 661. Television, radio, and print journalists reflected the growing American impatience with Saddam by filing their reports under jingoistic headlines such as "War feared imminent ... Shots expected by week's end"; "Le Canada ne fermera pas son ambassade au Koweït"; and "Showdown looms as warships sail."[19]

If Commodore Summers was certain of one thing upon sailing, it was that his biggest challenge would be to develop a sense of combat urgency. Forty years of peace, despite all the training, would make this difficult. The goal of the transatlantic crossing was to familiarize the crews with their new equipment and roles in preparation for intensive training in the Mediterranean. While Captain Miller was leading the ships' Combat Teams through their paces in the simulators, Commander Jean-Yves Forcier, captain-designate of HMCS *Algonquin*, the first TRUMP DDH-280, and the task group operations staff designed a phased work-up package. They began with basic procedural drills in damage control, defence against chemical attack, and weapons firings to familiarize the crews with the new systems. Surface surveillance and contact reporting drills would be practised with another Canadian destroyer,

Fraser, and CP-140 *Aurora* maritime patrol aircraft. They were scheduled to escort the group on their Atlantic passage.

Beyond this Canadian-made package, it was recognized that coordination with allies was essential to the en route training. The traditional CANUKUS (Canada-United Kingdom-United States) allies were the obvious starting point. Without any firsthand knowledge of the Persian Gulf area, the Canadian navy relied heavily upon the lengthy experience of the Royal and American navies. The preferred plan was to sail with the USS *John F. Kennedy* carrier battle group, departing Norfolk, Virginia on 21 August. But that plan had to be waived when the Canadian task group's sailing was delayed to the twenty-fourth. Other opportunities were to be found along the length of the Mediterranean. Foremost among them were the British facilities at Gibraltar standing guard over the western entrance to the sea. From there the Royal Navy coordinated several major exercise areas, including standardized work-up training for its own ARMILLA patrol-bound ships. When queried, the British Flag Officer in Gibraltar was quite receptive to the proposal of a Canadian visit.

As a third line of approach, after the public announcement on 10 August, unofficial contacts with the Americans and British were expanded to include the French. Even without the formal channels of a Defence Liaison Staff, the Canadian Forces Attaché in Paris was only at a slight disadvantage when he spoke to his French military contact soliciting opportunities for coordination with their naval forces. The Canadians were particularly interested in Iraq's use of the French-made *Exocet* anti-ship missiles (which now included missiles captured from Kuwait). The attaché found the French willing to assist. They agreed to provide the desired technical details and also to fly simulated missile profiles against the transiting task group if it could make a detour towards the French side of the Mediterranean Sea. This was an opportunity not to be missed, and the offer was quickly written into the passage plan to follow immediately after the work-up at Gibraltar.

NATO provided a fourth avenue of allied cooperation. Contacts were established with the Italian navy for communications support for the Mediterranean passage, and they were later expanded to include a stop at the major naval base at Augusta, Sicily. The water and magnetic conditions at this port most closely approximated those to be found in the Gulf. They were seen as the perfect location for a proper degaussing[20] on the local range and for training on the new mine avoidance sonar, for which there had been no time earlier in the programme.

With these broad objectives in mind, Task Group 302.3 sailed from Halifax, and the training began to unfold as planned. The unseasonably clear weather and calm sea conditions enjoyed throughout the preparations continued for the first several days, presenting no significant restrictions to training or flying. Steady, measurable progress was made. The crews undertook increasingly complex exercises, progressing from individual familiarity with weapons and equipment to structured team events. Battle problems steadily advanced to include weapons firings and chemical warfare conditions.

Troubles were developing in a different quarter. Despite their extensive overhaul, the ships and aircraft continued to age mechanically. There was no denying this fact, which was brought home in a dramatic series of breakdowns with Halifax barely out of sight astern. *Protecteur* was the first to report an operational deficiency, late on 24 August. Because it affected only secondary machinery and not her main propulsion plant, there was no immediate disruption to the programme, but repairs could only be made with the ship stopped dead in the water for two hours. Then, on the twenty-fifth, two new problems arose in quick succession. At 1830 one of the helicopters declared an in-flight emergency because of a problem in her main gearbox transmission. After some very tense moments, the aircraft eventually returned safely to *Athabaskan*, but that was not the end of the matter. If the malfunctions were to be confirmed, it would have a major effect on the available air resources — the aircraft would be grounded until the gearbox could be replaced, a major repair rarely conducted away from home base and never before on a ship underway. Within an hour of that incident, *Terra Nova* reported that one of her two turbo-alternators was unserviceable and required complete replacement as soon as possible. With only one electrical generator in operation, the ship would be restricted to 50 percent of her full power, and if that one also were to fail, it would be powerless. *Terra Nova*'s worries increased the next morning, when the breech of her starboard Bofors gun cracked during a firing practice. It too had to be replaced. The critical spares carried by the ships included neither of these bulky items, which would have to await repair at some stop along the route.

The built-in capacity of warships to allow for battle damage enabled the task group to continue its transatlantic passage. Despite the concern provoked by these mechanical failures, the equipment casualties were taken in stride. The two hours which elapsed while *Protecteur* was successfully effecting repairs were used to conduct an intership boarding exercise. A simple flush of the transmission fluid of *Sea King* 412 was sufficient to solve the gearbox problem, and the helicopter was pronounced serviceable. *Terra Nova* continued to proceed on reduced power, but Commodore Summers decided to hasten the whole group's progress, increasing speed above the economical cruise level in order to allow her to proceed into Gibraltar a day in advance of the other ships for repairs.

Early arrival in the Gibraltar approaches also permitted the scheduling of a twenty-four-hour Freeplay tactical exercise to consolidate the many procedures learned thus far. The term was a bit of a misnomer. The exercise actually had a planned structure (albeit unknown to the ships' crews) to test reaction to a developing scenario. Building upon the picture compilation and weapons control practised to date, the unfolding scenario incorporated strict adherence to Rules of Engagement. It stressed the importance of avoiding any chance of "friendly fire," the unintentional engagement of friendly forces. On completion, the other ships passed between the Pillars of Hercules and sailed into Gibraltar the evening of 2 September. Commodore Summers signalled back to Ottawa that Phase One of the transit had ended on a positive note: "although there have been highs and lows in coming together, the combat teams have earned my complete confidence."[21]

The crews welcomed the time alongside in Gibraltar, but the pace of activity hardly slackened. A succession of *Hercules* flights from Shearwater and Lahr arrived to replenish ammunition stocks used up on the crossing as well as to deliver stores not available earlier. The replacement turbine for *Terra Nova* had been whisked to the waiting engineers and the defect was soon put right. Besides completing the maintenance on the ships and helicopters, the two days were put to good use finalizing details with Royal Navy and Air Force staffs for the upcoming official training period.

The earlier Freeplay period, however useful, had been only an introduction to the advanced scenario to be conducted after the port visit. This next session would be the last chance for group training before arrival in-theatre, and as such would constitute a Readiness Check for Commodore Summers. The ships sailed from Gibraltar the morning of 5 September under the battle conditions of a simulated sabotage attack. The *Fraser*, Royal Navy fast patrol boats, and British and Canadian aircraft, once again simulating Iraqi units, tested the task group's mettle in a scenario that escalated from harassment to outright attack. The exercise culminated in a boarding of *Fraser*, with live weapons firings and an advanced air defence exercise, in which the CF-18 *Hornets* and RAF *Buccaneers* played the aggressors and flew missile profiles against the ships. To make up for lost time, *Terra Nova* bore the brunt of the training, but every member of the task group was challenged over the course of the two-day exercise. There were problems along the way. For example, the initial anti-aircraft gunnery exercise was less than inspiring, and at one point *Athabaskan* mistakenly conducted a simulated engagement against a friendly reconnaissance aircraft. However, by the end of the Freeplay Readiness Check, the crews had established confidence in their new weapons systems and their own abilities to meet a variety of situations.

As *Fraser* parted company late on 6 September to return to Canada, *Athabaskan*, *Protecteur*, and *Terra Nova* conducted a critical aspect of their training. Taking a slight detour to the northeast, the task group had a rendezvous with French navy forces for *Exocet* training on the eighth. For over seven hours, a French Navy *Atlantique* aircraft equipped with an *Exocet* missile seeker head flew pass after pass over each of the three ships, providing invaluable familiarization and an opportunity to conduct one of the most intensive electronic warfare exercises in Canadian naval history. The combat teams experimented with chaff and manoeuvring combinations to decoy the missile.[22]

Meanwhile, political considerations in Canada had brought the issue of Active Service to the fore. The Privy Council's new legal interpretation of the order-in-council, delivered on 7 September, held that the requirement for Parliament to debate the order-in-council within ten days meant that to avoid an early recall of the House, the order could not be signed before 15 September, the tenth full day before the actual sitting of Parliament. At roughly the same time, General Huddleston was agreeing to a definition of the associated Special Duty Area, which said that the sea area for the Canadian task group commenced roughly at the entrance to the Suez Canal.[23] By inference, the task group could not even begin transit of the canal until after the order-in-council had been signed. Not willing to put their political masters in a predicament for the sake of one day, the military opted for a slight pause in the progress of the ships.

Two other seemingly insignificant but immutable facts now took on new importance: the time difference between Ottawa and the Middle East was seven hours, and southbound traffic through the one-way Suez canal began just after midnight daily. These facts meant that the order had to be signed in Ottawa (local time) the day before the task group entered the canal. Two days before their scheduled stop in Sicily, Commodore Johnston in the National Defence Operations Centre signalled the order for a check on their progress. They would commence the Suez Canal transit at 0100 local time, 16 September. This allowed for a longer stay in Augusta, where some minor maintenance and resupply as well as the degaussing and sonar training took place. The task group commander decided that the readiness and morale of the ships' crews would benefit from spending the extra time alongside. Quick arrangements were made with the Italian authorities for in-harbour berths and the minor retasking of a scheduled sustainment flight from Canada.

It was with mixed emotions that Task Group 302.3 passed through the Strait of Messina and arrived at Augusta on 10 September. Few sailors are ever disappointed at the prospect of a visit to a foreign port, but with their training complete, they were anxious to get on with their mission. Frustration at the last-minute delay, however temporary, was palpable, and there was more than just a messdeck audience at hand to take in the customary griping. Following the Freeplay exercise, Canadian media correspondents had been embarked from Gibraltar for the Mediterranean passage. Arriving aboard in the post-Readiness Check euphoria, they had established an early empathy with the crews, reinforced by the successful exercise off France. It was perhaps inevitable that they now would hear a few unguarded comments. "Unscheduled" became "unnecessary," and soon the journalists had their first scoop. A succession of simple mistakes — including admittedly poor Defence Department liaison with the Privy Council Office and the media drawing conclusions of law from background discussions — quickly compounded into a comedy of errors. Reports filed from Sicily announced that "Iraq must wait for Canada's fleet," and that the ships were being "stranded" awaiting the Cabinet order. The general tenor was one of objection to the government, not the navy. The accompanying journalists felt that the service was being short-changed again.

The navy now had a damage control problem of a different sort on its hands. Commodore Johnston hastily called a special press conference in Ottawa on 11 September in an attempt to redress the effect of reports based on inaccurate information. He spoke of legal necessities and coincidental timings, but the media interpreted the whole thing as an attempt to divert criticism away from the government and onto the department, although they did acknowledge that the explanation was valid and that the delay was not meant to be a complicated government plot to foil Parliament.[24]

Intermediate Resupply and Forward Support

The problem of forward support for the task group required special attention. Modern naval task groups often operate for extended periods at sea — a supply ship like *Protecteur* carries enough fuel, ammunition, and frozen food to sustain itself and two destroyers for over three months[25] — but the need for fresh food and occasional maintenance poses special recurring problems. These problems, of course, were hardly new. Squadrons of ships frequently deploy for extended periods, requiring shore-based national support, and it was customary to establish a small Canadian Forces logistical cell at the nearest allied naval base to liaise with the port authorities. This network being in place, the problems were rarely beyond the capabilities of a competent junior staff totalling no more than a dozen personnel of all ranks.

The Gulf deployment, however, was unique in several ways. The Deputy Chief of Staff for Logistics in Maritime Command Headquarters, Captain Gregory Jarvis, was among the first to appreciate the fact that Canada did not have bilateral defence agreements with any of the nations in the region, and that there was no American or allied naval facility in the theatre from which to draw support. As well, the supply line back to Canada was some 13,000 kilometres long. A much expanded organization was required to coordinate the logistics and the technical and administrative support requirements. Jarvis successfully lobbied for a logistical officer (instead of the traditional engineering officer) to lead the Forward Support Unit, and he offered one of his own senior officers, Commander David Banks, to command the in-theatre detachment.

Though long-range forward support was still at the conceptual stage, the ships en route had to be resupplied. Planning continued concurrent with the necessities of immediate support. Gibraltar, as the first landfall after the transatlantic voyage, offered an obvious starting point, and the Halifax staffs made a special effort to conduct a comprehensive resupply there, fully expecting that it would be the last such opportunity before arrival in-theatre two weeks later. The subsequent stopover in Augusta, coming so soon after Gibraltar, was not essential from a logistical viewpoint, but the staffs took advantage of the opportunity to forward more supplies and arrange a top-up of *Protecteur*'s fuel tanks.

Beyond the Mediterranean, the options were not so immediately obvious. The one sure resupply point was the facility maintained by the French Navy in the tiny Republic of Djibouti, on the Horn of Africa, which was the headquarters of the French Navy's Indian Ocean Command (ALINDIEN). Indeed, the French Navy's primary operational response to the crisis was concentrated in Djibouti. It monitored the traffic passing through the strategic Straits of Bab-el-Mandeb (joining the Red Sea to the Gulf of Aden) and activity in the nearby Yemeni port of Aden, where several Iraqi merchant vessels were waiting out the embargo. The French military had communicated to the attaché in Paris their offer to coordinate Canadian use of the facilities, but no firm plans had been made because of the uncertainty surrounding the departure of the task group.

As a forward operating base, Djibouti was too far removed from the theatre in which the Canadians planned to operate. Aside from the French in Djibouti, however, none of Canada's traditional Western allies maintained a permanent port facility in the area. The USN had a rather complicated basing arrangement with Bahrain, but Bahrain was dismissed because it was too close to potential Iraqi attack and too distant from the planned operating area in the Gulf of Oman. With little firsthand experience of the area to guide the selection of an appropriate port, planners came to rely upon British familiarity with the region. The Royal Navy intended to support its task group from the port of Dubai.

Dubai, one of the United Arab Emirates, is located on the southeastern coast of the Persian Gulf. One of the assumptions of early Canadian planning was that the task group would operate in the Gulf of Oman and not inside the Strait of Hormuz, in order to avoid Iranian *Silkworm* missile sites overlooking the narrow waterway.[26] This explains why planners considered Muscat, Oman and even Karachi, Pakistan as possible forward bases. When the Canadians learned that the British intended to undertake regular transits of the strait, to and from Dubai, their planning took two different directions. The primary search for a port on the Gulf of Oman continued, but an increasing amount of attention was directed to Dubai.

In the course of the investigation, the logistical planners in Halifax and Ottawa contacted nearly all of the major Coalition partners. Supplementing the aforementioned linkages with the Americans, British, and French, logistical arrangements were worked out with the USN to extend existing fuel and supply agreements to cover the present situation; with the British to allow use of the Royal Navy's Fleet Auxiliary vessel *Diligence* as a repair facility; and with the Australians, who suggested that the Canadian and Australian navies coordinate their efforts to ensure adequate sources for fuel and support. Indeed, the Canadians wanted more than just to ensure their own forward support. The task group itself, supported by *Protecteur*, offered certain logistical benefits which could be put to good diplomatic advantage. The USN had already expressed interest several times in the desirability of another tanker bottom, and the Department of External Affairs requested the Canadian ambassadors to the United Nations and the United States to approach allied delegations to determine what logistical support the Canadian task group could provide to forces deployed in the Gulf region.

The only suitable ports on the Gulf of Oman were the relatively primitive facilities at Fujayrah and Muscat. The third port under consideration, Karachi, was far afield. None of these alternatives was very appealing, and Captain Jarvis refused to make a firm decision without a firsthand survey of the options. With Ottawa and Halifax completely absorbed by minute details of the 24 August departure of the task group, nothing concrete on supply ports materialized before then. The Monday following the departure ceremony, 27 August, Admiral George hosted a conference dedicated to the subject of the sustainment of the task group. The participants included representatives from MARCOM and NDHQ, in particular the J4 Logistical member of the Crisis Action Team, Colonel William C. Leach, an army logistician with considerable peacekeeping experience in the Third World. On conclusion, Captain Jarvis drafted terms of reference for Commander Banks, the designated commander of the support unit. Colonel Leach returned to Ottawa and reduced the number of options concerning operating bases to three: Dubai was first and Muscat in Oman and Manamah in Bahrain were second and third. Leach was made the leader of a reconnaissance (Recce) team that included Banks, two of his designated staff, and a communications specialist from NDHQ. They were scheduled to depart Ottawa on 4 September.

In any event, the Recce party did not leave until 6 September. The delay was not their choice but was taken in order to coordinate their assignment with another development. Their CC-144 *Challenger* finally departed CFB Uplands late that evening. After a quick stop in Shearwater, it flew to Gibraltar to pick up another passenger.

Multinational Naval Cooperation and the Bahrain Conference

Commodore Summers was not with the ships for their arrival in Augusta. Upon completion of the Readiness Check late on 6 September, he had turned command over to Captain Miller for the task group's passage of the Mediterranean. The commodore had returned to Gibraltar to meet the Canadian Forces *Challenger* flight transporting the several logistical officers for their reconnaissance of Gulf region ports. Joining the Recce was in itself a useful exercise, but Summers had a larger purpose — to participate in a conference in Bahrain with senior representatives of the many navies joining the embargo against Iraq. The extended port visit of the task group to Augusta afforded him an opportunity to rejoin the ships late on 11 September before sailing the next morning for Suez. He brought momentous news.

The majority of nations, including Canada, which had dispatched forces to the Persian Gulf region had done so to display resolve in the face of Saddam Hussein's aggression. Most of them had longstanding defence arrangements and were familiar with Western tactical doctrine, which was easily adaptable to the existing situation. But alliances such as NATO had definite geographical limits that did not extend to the Persian Gulf. King Fahd's invitation to assist in the defence of his kingdom, therefore, was made under the collective security provisions of the United Nations Charter, and accordingly both precipitated and legitimized the Coalition buildup of land and air forces in Saudi Arabia.

The situation in international waters contiguous to the Arabian Peninsula was not so clear. The original unanimity which had met Iraq's aggression came near to falling apart when the Big Five debated the means that would give substance to the existing sanctions resolution without abdicating control to the Americans. On the one hand, the US and Britain, anxious to bring pressure on Iraq, held that Article 51 of the UN Charter allowed them to interpret Resolution 661 as granting them independent authority to intercept shipping. On the other hand, France and the Soviet Union, worried that the US and UK were being too impatient, argued that Article 51 was legally inadmissible at this juncture and "felt that more time should be allowed to explore the prospects of a political solution." They "wanted to reactivate the Military Staff Committee (MSC) ... to coordinate the naval forces in the Gulf."[27] At the same time, special care had to be taken to make sure that China continued to abstain from the debate.

Canada's position lay between the two extremes. Ambassador Fortier held that Resolution 661 needed amplification to justify the use of force and that any chance of effective coordinated action should not be lost by subordination to the MSC. He suggested instead that other sections of the UN Charter, specifically Article 42, allowed sufficient scope for coordinated actions by a group of like-minded states.

Despite the seeming impasse, on 16 August President Bush announced that the United States Navy had formally established an Interception Force, and he encouraged other nations to join in the interdiction — he was careful to avoid the word blockade — of Iraqi traffic. Recognizing the political dilemma facing their allies, Pentagon briefers elaborated that naval forces would remain under their respective national commands and that coordination would be provided by COMIDEASTFOR, Rear-Admiral Fogarty, from his flagship USS *LaSalle*. To discuss the details of its proposed Multinational Force Enforcing Sanctions (MNFES), the USN planned a conference for senior representatives to take place tentatively on 25-26 August. There were few takers. Most governments followed a line of thinking similar to Canada's and waited for the adoption of a Security Council resolution endorsing the proposed action. In the meantime, they also waited to see if the situation would change substantially.

The Canadian options were somewhat limited, but by opting for the dispatch of naval over land or air forces, the government had aligned itself on the side of UN-sponsored interception operations. Canadian officers were sensitive to the ongoing political-diplomatic debates and established a close working relationship with their counterparts in External Affairs to avoid any display of contradiction in government policy. They also knew that successful operations would require the cooperative efforts of the gathering naval forces. There was a risk in coordinating operations, but a mechanism had to be organized and agreed upon well before the arrival of the task group in-theatre.

Canada was not alone in this predicament. As the task group prepared to sail from Halifax, the lack of a coordinating structure for what was becoming a formidable array of naval forces was very conspicuous. The Netherlands and Britain had agreed to work together. France, however, wished to operate its forces independently and was resisting all American efforts at coordination of naval activities, despite French involvement in training and its willingness to share facilities. Instead, Paris was attempting to resurrect the Western European Union (WEU), a postwar defence arrangement which generally had been supplanted by NATO but was not encumbered by the latter's territorial constraints.[28] In practice, it proved difficult for these countries, whose foreign policies nearly covered the entire spectrum of opinion on Iraq's invasion of Kuwait, to come up with a workable solution. The Belgians were sensitive to domestic politics, and German involvement was limited by their own constitution. Both countries chose to restrict their ships to the Mediterranean, where they were able to relieve American forces on their way to the Gulf. On 21 August, the foreign and defence ministers of France, Britain, the Netherlands, Germany, Belgium, Italy, Denmark, and Spain issued a communiqué in which they agreed to coordinate their efforts but did not specify any details. No such alternative existed for the Canadians, except the possibility of joining Britain and Australia, her Commonwealth partners. This prospect was overtaken by events.

The American proposal languished while the Security Council went into a second and then a third week of debate. Finally, on 25 August, the day after the task group sailed from Halifax, the UN issued Resolution 665:

> [Calling] on states cooperating with Kuwait, by deploying maritime forces to the area to monitor the sanctions, to use measures commensurate with the circumstances to halt all inward and outward maritime shipping in order to inspect and verify their cargoes.[29]

Resolution 665 took the middle road desired by the Canadians. It provided justification for the use of force in conducting interceptions but did not impose a military command structure. The resolution merely "requested" participating states "to coordinate their actions … using as appropriate mechanisms of the Military Staff Committee …" As one author has noted, for the first time in its history "the United Nations had authorized the use of force (implied in the phrase 'such measures commensurate to the specific circumstances as may be necessary') by its members without a UN flag or command structure to implement it."[30] With the Security Council itself remaining in charge of operations, Canadian diplomats were assured of representation at the policy-making table.

Above all, Resolution 665 clarified the status of the deployed Canadian forces. Task Group 302.3, at first the result of a political decision, now clearly had a military function to fulfil. After weeks of deliberation, the Defence Department finally was able to issue a policy statement, qualified though it was, explaining the purpose of the Canadian naval units deployed to the Middle East. They were to have a role in implementing UN economic sanctions by means of surveillance, monitoring, and, if necessary, the interception of shipping in order to verify cargoes and destinations. Canadian naval units would be authorized to take all necessary measures to enforce the sanctions. They were to be part of a huge multinational naval deployment. Its mere presence, rather than any specific military threat, would deter any further Iraqi aggression in the region.

Nonplussed, the Americans reiterated their invitation for combined naval action, announcing a Naval Conference to be hosted by the Emir of Bahrain, Emir Isa Ibn Sulman al-Khalifah, on 9-10 September. The conference would discuss coordination of a Multinational Interception Force (MIF). The response this time was far more positive, for two reasons: there was an applicable UN resolution to govern any action, and there were assurances from the USN that deliberations would be kept at the working or technical level and not extend to an all-encompassing political discussion. Commodore Summers planned to attend on Canada's behalf.

The date for the naval coordination meeting obviously would overlap the Canadian logistical survey. Since the final selection of a forward site hinged upon the results of the Bahrain discussions, the Crisis Action Team decided to combine the two objectives. Thus it came about that the *Challenger* from Ottawa arrived in Gibraltar to embark Summers. After a quick stopover to refuel and pick up another passenger in Cairo — the attaché, Colonel J.L. Orr, who knew the region and its customs — the combined conference delegation and recce party arrived in Bahrain in the early evening of Saturday, 8 September.

The naval interception effort faced special problems. In theory, a naval blockade against the essentially land-locked Iraq was a relatively simple undertaking. In practice, though, the American coordinator, Admiral Fogarty, found that he was required to conduct operations with limited resources and perhaps for many months in three widespread areas ringing the Arabian peninsula. The inability of Jordan to seal its land border with Iraq demanded the inspection of vessels in the Red Sea bound for the port of Aqaba. Concerning Iraq itself, the Americans believed that a blockade of the distant Strait of Hormuz, while necessary, would not be completely effective because it would lack the impact of a visible presence on Saddam's doorstep. Consequently, they drew their interception line across the natural choke point of the central Persian Gulf, northeast of Qatar. This meant, however, that they also had to direct attention to the possibility of a preemptive Iraqi *Mirage-Exocet* attack. The central Gulf warships acted as a trip-wire for outbound traffic, and suspected violators were to be shadowed through the lines of naval forces collecting in the southern half of the Persian Gulf. Boarding would take place in the Gulf of Oman, and impounding would be carried out in the nearest ports. It was a complicated but unavoidable process.

The rest of the first day of the conference was given over to national delegations. One by one, senior naval officers outlined their government's policy on enforcing the sanctions and spoke about the unique capabilities and requirements of their forces and their preferred operating area. The Americans, of course, had all the bases covered. Their interception forces were already in position across the central Persian Gulf and the Gulf of Aqaba, and additional forces gathering in the Arabian Sea were available to assist them. The Australians and the WEU decided upon the Gulf of Oman. Britain and France, although members of the WEU, were willing to continue their present patrols in the southern Gulf. France would maintain watch on the Strait of Bab-el-Mandeb and work with the Greeks and the Spaniards in the Gulf of Aqaba.

When it came to his turn, Commodore Summers was noncommittal, indicating that Canada had no preference for one operational area over another but was prepared to operate where it could best contribute to the interception effort. Indeed, he had come to the conference with no specific instructions to lobby for a particular area, and much of his circumspection derived from his reading of the conference dynamics thus far. The Gulf of Oman, which had been the anticipated Canadian operating area, was obviously well-covered and increasingly recognized as a fringe area. There was good work to be done in the southern Gulf, but a rift was growing between the British and the WEU over the thrust of operations there, and Canada would be well-advised to distance itself from that if possible.[31] Finally, the Americans were stretched thin in the central Gulf, where the threat was more immediate. When the session adjourned at the end of the day, American officers approached Summers to ask the obvious question: Would Canada consider operating in the central Gulf and help fill the void on the front-line? The same question was on his own mind, and before making any commitments he wanted to weigh his options overnight.

The possibility of operating within the Persian Gulf had been discussed as early as 15 August. The decision that day to delay sailing, in order to assure the fitting of upgraded systems equal to any eventuality, now gained added significance. Summers' own Battle Doctrine listed the Persian Gulf as one of the planning situations, and Dubai became the primary choice for an operating base. However, Summers could not accept a central Gulf patrol without sharing such a dramatic decision with his superiors in Canada. Taking advantage of his portable secure telephone, he immediately placed calls in quick succession to Admiral George in Halifax and General Huddleston in Ottawa to explain his initial inclination to pursue the proposal. They advised him that there was no political constraint on him to agree to work in any of the areas and that he should go where his forces would be most valuable, with all due regard to their safety.

The second day's deliberations were dedicated to discussions on the technical aspects of multinational cooperation: communications, intelligence, deconfliction,[32] interception procedures, and logistics. During the course of the day, Summers became convinced that the Canadian task group should partner the Americans in the central Gulf. His force would have access to the vast USN supply train, for which procedures were already in place, and the facilities at the naval base in Bahrain. The Canadians were outfitted with systems compatible with the Americans over their full range, including satellite and secure voice nets, whereas concentrations in the other areas would be limited to the usual UHF and VHF circuits. Finally, the USN *Ticonderoga*-class Aegis air defence cruisers, stationed to the north of the central sectors, and the Royal Navy's ARMILLA Patrol to the south, augmented by USAF AWACS surveillance and Marine Corps F/A-18 *Hornet* fighters flying protective cover in Combat Air Patrols (CAPs), diminished the likelihood of an Iraqi attack getting through without advance warning. However, the factors that finally convinced Summers that his task group was ready to meet the challenge were the successful Readiness Check off Gilbraltar and the valuable anti-*Exocet* training with the French. The only possible reason for hesitation was the readiness of the ships to meet the mining threat, but to date there was no evidence of Iraqi mines. If they became a threat, the decision could be reassessed.

Following the conclusion of the conference on 10 September, Commodore Summers remained in Manamah another day for further discussion with Admiral Fogarty and to prepare a summary of the events of the past two days. Once relayed to NDHQ through Admiral George, his summary was quickly transformed into a briefing to the Privy Council. The thrust of Summers' proposition was that patrolling an independent sector across the middle of the Persian Gulf was within the Canadian task group's capability and would represent a meaningful contribution to the UN effort.

Sicily to Suez

While in Bahrain, Commodore Summers kept in constant contact with his superiors in Halifax and Ottawa, but his task group subordinates, biding their time in Sicily, were unaware of developments. Upon his return aboard *Athabaskan*, late on 11 September, he advised Captain Miller that the question of the Canadian task group's destination had been resolved — they had assumed responsibility for the important "Area Charlie" patrol sectors in the central Persian Gulf.[33] Now it was necessary to formalize the appreciation for confirmation by the government the next day. Quick action was required because Cabinet was reviewing the entire Canadian response to the crisis in the Gulf. In his briefing to NATO foreign ministers, following the 9 September Bush-Gorbachev talks in Helsinki, American Secretary of State Baker had called for "more Allied responsibility sharing" in the defence of the Gulf and more economic assistance to compensate for the economic dislocation resulting from the sanctions. The hardest hit were Turkey, Egypt, Jordan, and Eastern Europe.[34] Prime Minister Mulroney was planning to hold a press conference in two days, on 14 September, to announce the signing of the order-in-council. That would be the perfect opportunity to present any new decisions, including the one on the operating area, to the Canadian public.

The ships were set to sail the next morning, Wednesday, 12 September, on the final Mediterranean leg to the Suez Canal. Nonetheless, the task group staff undertook an all-night marathon session to compile the official appreciation. Captain Miller later described the midnight to dawn undertaking as "eight weeks' staff work in eight hours."[35] All the various factors affecting the choice of operating area were examined dispassionately, without undue prejudice for or against any particular location. Item by item, they undertook a realistic threat assessment, compared their findings with the capabilities of the Canadian and Coalition ships, and evaluated communications interoperability and available logistical support. As the ships were sailing from Augusta, the staff appreciation was transmited by secure facsimile to Maritime Command Headquarters: the task group commander concluded confidently that if Canada was to play a high profile, meaningful, and professionally challenging role in the Gulf, it should operate in patrol area Charlie in the central Gulf.

As they sailed from Sicily, the three ships' companies (other than the members of the task group staff) wcrc unaware of the imminent change in their circumstances. There was much to be accomplished in the remaining relative quiet of the Mediterranean, and Summers wanted nothing to take his sailors' minds from their task. Included among the variety of exercises were two which he watched with special interest, a staff-level Rules of Engagement exercise to prove the effectiveness of communications links with the government through the NDHQ Operations Centre, and a simulated minefield transit by the three ships. The operators in *Athabaskan*'s Operations Room also successfully established a computer datalink communication net (Link-11 for short) with one of the Turkey-based NATO AWACS aircraft, similar to those operated by the United States and Royal Saudi Air Forces in the Gulf. On conclusion of these various events, the task group commander was satisfied that the training was complete. The group was ready for operational patrol.

The passage from Sicily to Suez had its frustrating moments. Once again, equipment was the problem. Two new deficiencies became apparent. Neither was immediately critical, but each would have a major influence on future operations of the task group. In the course of a storm south of Crete, *Protecteur's* mine avoidance sonar was torn away, compromising the tanker's capability to transit mined waters and therefore limiting her area of operations. The full import of the second problem, which developed in *Terra Nova's Phalanx*, was not immediately recognized. Her combat systems technicians felt that it was a minor case of unserviceability, but replacement of the defective parts with spares carried in *Protecteur* failed to resolve the problem. Arrangements were then made for a factory support representative to meet the ship in Djibouti.

The ships anchored in Port Said at the northern approaches to the Suez Canal in the early afternoon of 15 September, joining the southbound convoy due to depart at midnight. In a strange twist of normal military practice, for the better part of a day the Canadian public knew more about the final destination and concept of operations of Task Group 302.3 than did the embarked sailors, soldiers, and airmen. Even the journalists were in the dark! As Governor-General Hnatyshyn was signing the order-in-council placing them on Active Service, Commodore Summers went to each of the ships and explained to the crews the significance of their new central Persian Gulf patrol sector.

The rest of Canada had been presented with the news the previous day, in the context of a widely expanded Canadian commitment. A press conference had been convened that Friday, 14 September, when the prime minister, flanked by Secretary of State Joe Clark and Minister of National Defence Bill McKnight, gave the expected word that the order-in-council soon would be presented to the governor-general and then tabled "when the House resumes, on September 24." Mr Mulroney stated the government view that in the face of Iraq's unrepentant naked aggression, the crisis had become "Saddam Hussein against the world." To give the national response a more global perspective, Cabinet had met that morning for a thorough review of the situation and decided to adopt several of the measures requested earlier by Secretary Baker to assist the Coalition effort. These measures included: doubling the $2.5 million already contributed to international relief agencies to assist displaced people; leasing transport aircraft to help convey Third-World refugees to their home countries; airlifting ground forces of other countries to Saudi Arabia; increasing development assistance funds for Sri Lanka, the Philippines, and Bangladesh (countries with sizable Muslim populations) by up to $10 million; and contributing $30 million to the three countries which were suffering the most severe economic setbacks from the sanctions, Turkey, Jordan, and Egypt. But the highlight of the conference was the following announcement:

The government has also further accepted the advice of our military staff to have Canadian ships operate within the Persian Gulf. They will be under Canadian command and control and will have responsibility for a sector across the middle of the Gulf north of the Strait of Hormuz and south of Bahrain. Our ships will be operating in the same general area as the ships of the United States, the United Kingdom and other allied navies. This decision, taken after consultations with other countries contributing navies, is based on military considerations. Canadian ships have recently been equipped with their own upgraded air defence capability. They will benefit as well from the combined air defence capabilities of allies in the region.

After only a slight pause, the prime minister continued:

As a further initiative, the government of Canada today decided to deploy a squadron of CF-18 fighter aircraft from Lahr, West Germany to the Gulf to operate under Canadian control and provide air cover for our own ships and the ships of friendly nations. With supporting elements this will engage up to 450 additional Canadian military personnel in the region.[36]

Each of the three arms of Canada's forces now had a major operation as the focus of its activities, a rarity in peacetime: the army, under Operation SALON, was still preoccupied with the standoff at Oka; all the navy's energies were devoted to Operation FRICTION, the deployment of the task group to the Persian Gulf; and now the air force, already heavily tasked by air transport demands, would undertake Operation SCIMITAR, the deployment of a fighter squadron to the Middle East.

FRICTION and SCIMITAR were separate operations, despite the common regional focus — the Gulf — and the overview of national headquarters. Commodore Johnston had warned Maritime Command earlier that it had no monopoly on planning for Operation FRICTION. The naval option was only Canada's initial military response to the crisis in the Persian Gulf and did not preclude the commitment of land or air forces. Attention was now beginning to shift away from the naval task group, even before the ships could arrive in-theatre. For the time being, however, it remained a navy story, and the real drama was about to begin.

Notes

1   Captain (N) Duncan E. Miller, interview by Jean Morin and Richard Gimblett, tape recording, Ottawa, Ontario, 30 March 1992.

2   See the schematic summary in Appendix B: Canadian Forces Crisis Management - Operation FRICTION 1990-1991. *NDHQ Defence Plan 900 - Emergency Measures* had been in preparation for ten years but been given only inadequate testing during limited exercises.

3   Refer to Appendix C, listing new fits by ship, with description of equipment.

4   Not all of the modifications were high-tech. The additional combat systems required the ships' internal communications to be either modified or expanded to ensure proper weapons control and coordination. Recognizing that this posed an insurmountable problem, the Halifax Headquarters authorized the ships to purchase readily available commercial Radio Shack-type intercoms.

5   DHist, *Ship's Historical Report - 1990 HMCS TERRA NOVA - 1274*, DTA: 1326-1, 11 March 1991.

6   The Bofors 40mm gun was originally produced with a hand- and foot-driven mounting. When adapted to the twin Oerlikon power mounting it was given the appellation "Boffin."

7   WD *Athabaskan*, "Trials SITREP 004," 21 August 1990.

8   WD *Protecteur*, "(Final) Trials SITREP 004," 21 August 1990.

9   WD CTG, MARCOMHQ, "CATG Departure Op FRICTION," 21 August 1990.

10 As the *Sea King* replacement programme, NSA was the naval air complement to the CPF and TRUMP programmes and represented a quantum advance in the capabilities of shipborne helicopters for the Canadian navy. Besides improvements in ASW, the airframe of the selected EH-101 aircraft allowed for significant surface surveillance (ASUW) and transport capabilities, as well as a measure of self-defence.

11 Refer to Appendix D, which lists new fits with description of equipment.

12 Capt M.M. Korwin-Szymanowski, "AETE Support of Operations in the Persian Gulf," *Flight Comment* no. 1 (1992), p. 24.

13 USS *Stark* was struck by an Iraqi Mirage-fired *Exocet* on 17 May 1987, with the loss of 37 of her crew; on 3 July 1988, USS *Vincennes* shot down an Iranian *Airbus*, killing all 290 passengers. Both incidents occurred in the Persian Gulf. See Cordesman and Wagner, *Lessons of Modern War*, pp. 549-58 and 573-84.

14 *The Guide*, p. 329.

15 Treasury Board of Canada Secretariat [Stephen Tsang coordinator], "OPERATION FRICTION: Refitting Three War Ships for the Persian Gulf - A Success Story in Matériel Management," (September 1991), p. i.

16 For a sample of the published accounts, see: Captain Marsha Dorge, "The Eye of the STORM," *Sentinel* 27, no.4 (1991), pp. 8-13; Captain Marc Rouleau, "Fighting under a different flag," *Sentinel* 27, no. 5 (1991), pp. 6-9; Captain Marsha Dorge, "Fighting for the Stars and Stripes," *Sentinel* 27, no. 5 (1991), pp. 10-11; and Captain Steve McCluskey, "View From the Turret", *Legion* 67, no. 7 (February 1993), pp. 6-10.

17 Captain Jane McDonald, "MERCY in the Gulf," *Sentinel* 27, no. 2 (1991), pp. 11-14.

18 Hiro, *Desert Shield to Desert Storm*, p. 128. A succession of Muslim countries not unsympathetic to Saddam's venture bordered its course, making an attempt to disrupt the passage of Western naval forces a not so remote possibility. Algeria, Libya, Jordan, Sudan, and Yemen all had either opposed or expressed reservations to a resolution denouncing Iraq's aggression and calling for

the dispatch of troops to Saudi Arabia, when it was placed before a summit of the Arab League in Cairo on 10 August. For the task group's route to the Gulf, see map 1.

19 *Winnipeg Free Press*, 23 August 1990; *La Presse* (Montréal), 23 August 1990; and *Halifax Daily News*, 24 August 1990. The *Toronto Globe and Mail*, 24 August 1990, filed a more temperate account by Hugh Winsor entitled "Three ships sailing eastward with little sense of direction."

20 Degaussing is the process by which a ship's magnetic signature is neutralized to reduce its susceptibility to mines triggered by the magnetic influence of the great mass of metal in a ship acting as a natural bar magnet. To counter this effect, every warship is ringed by a series of wire coils through which a compensating low-power electrical current is passed, essentially turning it into a floating electromagnet. The settings vary by latitude, among other factors; hence the importance of the Augusta testing.

21 WD CTG, "ASSESSREP," 2 September 1990. The ASSESSREP, or assessment-report, was a daily message from the task group commander to his superiors in Halifax, Ottawa, and later Manamah, to report the day's events, and provide an assessment of the situation.

22 The decoying of a missile through the use of chaff (shredded aluminum, presenting a false radar echo) or electromagnetic jamming, causing it to miss its target, is known as soft-kill, as opposed to the hard-kill destruction by a weapon such as *Phalanx*.

23 The proposed definition was: Sea Area, all navigable waters between 32 and 75 degrees East Longitude and 12 and 32 degrees North Latitude; and Land area, the Arabian Peninsula, including the countries of Saudi Arabia, Kuwait, Iraq, Yemen Arab Republic, Peoples Democratic Republic of Yemen, Oman, United Arab Emirates, and Qatar.

24 DHist, "Canada-Iraq" Press Roundup file, "Press Conference, Commodore Johnston, Director General Military Plans and Operations, 11 September 1990" [transcript].

25 The standard loading of a Canadian AOR is ninety days stores for herself and three destroyers. In this instance, *Protecteur* was so heavily laden that her draft on sailing from Halifax was reportedly the deepest in her history. She carried sufficient stores for up to five months, with the exception of fresh fruit, vegetables, and dairy products.

26 The Strait of Hormuz, one of the busiest waterways in the world, also forms the international boundary between Iran to the north and Oman to the south. Under the International Law of the Sea convention, transiting vessels, including warships, have the "right of innocent passage" but may not conduct operations in the waterway. Still, the strait had witnessed many attacks on tankers during the final phases of the First Gulf War, by both the Iranians (*Silkworm* missile) and Iraqis (*Mirage-Exocet*), and was considered a perilous passage. For legal and practical discussions, see respectively Said Mahmoudi, "Passage of warships through the Strait of Hormuz," *Marine Policy*, 15, no. 5 (September 1991), pp. 338-48, and Palmer, *On Course to Desert Storm*, Chapter 12: "The United States and the Tanker War," pp. 121ff.

27 Dannreuther, *The Gulf Conflict*, p. 29.

28 The Western European Union as such was not formed until 1954. It was an economic offshoot of the Western Union (formed under the earlier Treaty of Brussels of 1948), a way to allow West German rearmament through an exclusively European mechanism. The military defence provisions of the earlier treaty were never repealed when overtaken by the creation of NATO in 1949, which itself did not incorporate the economic ties desired by the Europeans. More than just a subset of the larger European Community, the WEU provided a mechanism allowing its member states (Belgium, France [then occupying the rotating position of chair], West Germany, Italy, Luxembourg, the Netherlands, and the United Kingdom) to project the semblance of united foreign and defence policies beyond the territorial restrictions of NATO. Based upon its apparent success in the Gulf crisis (five of the seven nations dispatched naval forces - the only exceptions being Luxembourg, which has no navy, and Germany, which has overriding constitutional limitations on

its military forces), it has been proclaimed as the model for future European military cooperation and even a replacement for NATO after American withdrawal from the European continent.

29 *The Guide* p. 329.

30 Hiro, *Desert Shield to Desert Storm*, p. 152.

31 The Anglo-French rift within the WEU is referred to in Thomas-Durell Young, "Preparing the Western Alliance for the Next Out-of-Area Campaign", *Naval War College Review*, 45, no. 3, seq. 339 (Summer 1992), pp. 34-36.

32 Military parlance for measures to avoid interference between friendly forces.

33 The patrol stations established for the multinational forces were given alphanumeric designations according to the area of operations: Alpha for the southern approaches to the Strait of Hormuz in the Gulf of Oman; Bravo for those just inside the southern Persian Gulf; Charlie for the central Persian Gulf; and Delta for the northern Red Sea approaches to the Gulf of Aqaba.

34 "NATO ponders bigger gulf role," *Ottawa Citizen*, 11 September 1990.

35 Miller, "Interview," 30 March 1992.

36 Canada, Office of the Prime Minister, "Speaking Notes for Prime Minister Brian Mulroney Press Conference, National Press Theatre, September 14, 1990."

CHAPTER 3

The Multinational Interception Force: September – November 1990

The Odyssey Continued

"The [working] day started just after midnight," recorded the task group public affairs officer, on Sunday, 16 September, when *Athabaskan*, *Terra Nova*, and *Protecteur* slipped their moorings to join the procession of ships southbound through the Suez Canal.[1] As the banks slipped silently past on either side, lush green to the west, battle-scarred desert to the east, the men and women in the three ships put the uncertainty and controversy of the previous five weeks behind them, to face the challenges still ahead. Gathered on the shore at the southern exit was a contingent from the Canadian embassy in Cairo, waving a big banner proclaiming that all of Canada was watching and wishing the sailors godspeed.

After clearing the canal, the Canadians noticed an immediate increase in the tempo of activity. Tracking the greater volume of ship and air traffic put the Operations Room operators through their paces. It was reassuring that they were not alone. Coalition naval forces abounded when the Canadian ships passed through the patrol areas of the USS *Saratoga* and *John F. Kennedy* carrier battle groups off the approaches to the Gulf of Aqaba. Monitoring the VHF radio circuits, the officers and sailors on the bridge and in the operations rooms gained valuable insights into USN interdiction methods.

The Canadian task group had been joined at Port Said by HMS *Gloucester*, a guided-missile destroyer en route to reinforce the British ARMILLA Patrol. The joint passage for the 1600-kilometre length of the Red Sea had been arranged to afford both the Canadians and the British the added safety of each other's company and to provide fuel support to the Royal Navy destroyer. A number of joint exercises were planned, including a demonstration for the Canadians of the boarding techniques employed by the Royal Marines embarked in *Gloucester*. With *Protecteur* acting as a suspicious merchant ship, *Gloucester*'s *Lynx* helicopter hovered low over the tanker's fo'c'sle and dropped a rope out the side door, down which rappelled five marines in a matter of seconds. While these secured the immediate area, the helicopter quickly picked up a second group and deposited them in the same manner. The boarding was completed. The Canadians were impressed by the vigorous and professional display and appreciated the method's many merits. Canadian doctrine called for a boatload of sailors to motor from their ship and use rope ladders to scramble up the side of the suspect merchantman. The newly acquired RIBs (Rigid Inflatable Boats) took some of the adventure out of the trip across, but actually getting onto the target ship remained a daunting prospect. It was no easy task to climb up the wet side of a ship in heaving seas. Moreover, an interdicted crew might not cooperate. While a helicopter solved these particular problems, it did not greatly extend the range over which boardings could be conducted, because whichever method was employed, a warship was still required nearby to keep the proceedings under her watchful guns should something go wrong. Nor were Canadian sailors British marines. These caveats aside, however, the capacity of the bigger Canadian helicopters, and the fact that *Athabaskan* and *Protecteur* each carried more than one, suggested further possibilities. An investigation was begun into the possibility of adapting Canadian boarding procedures as a means to employ the *Sea Kings*.

Shortly after the boarding demonstration, during a mid-afternoon crew training flight, one of *Athabaskan*'s *Sea Kings* suddenly experienced a failure in one of its two engines. Procedures existed to handle such an emergency in the cool and often windy environment of temperate waters, but in the extremely hot and humid conditions of the Red Sea the single remaining engine could not generate enough power to allow the big helicopter to hover and land in a controlled manner. Even after dumping most of its fuel to reduce weight, the crew of SK404 were unable to maintain a stable hover at the thirty knots relative wind *Athabaskan* could produce with her engines full ahead. After two unsuccessful attempts, the war diary entry noted:

> Eventually [the relative wind] came up to 35 knots which was enough for an attempt at a recovery, keeping ditching beside the ship an option ... The initial skid mark where the wheels touched down showed the tail wheel 6 inches ahead of the back lip [of the flight deck]. We also found out later that the engines on the ship were 0.6 degrees below a full shutdown emergency of their own.[2]

This incident dramatically underlined the ill effects that severe conditions in excess of 40 degrees Celsius and near 100 percent humidity could have on ships and aircraft, let alone their human occupants. Other examples soon followed. After conducting a flight in full chemical warfare protective gear, the pilot war diarist wryly recalled that "when I was in Moose Jaw, [when] the temperature was above 30 [degrees] or some ridiculously low temperature like that they cancelled flying ops."[3] The ships' upper decks became intolerably hot for prolonged periods, and ready-use ammunition lockers reached temperatures at which the reliability of the stowed rounds became suspect. Nor was there much relief inside. The air conditioners operated on the chilled water principle, but the sea water on which they relied for their initial intake was now too warm for optimum efficiency. The machinery was quickly overworked, and the captain of *Protecteur* found that with all of the new combat systems he had to order certain equipment shut down in order to reduce the amount of heat generated. The only acceptable long-term solution was to install an additional air conditioning plant. Fortunately, the temperatures experienced in the lower reaches of the Red Sea were to be the most severe during the deployment. The moderating climes of the winter months were nearing. Still, the potentially adverse effects of heat on men and equipment could not be dismissed, especially with the prospect of a lengthy deployment extending into the next summer.

In the evening of 19 September the sweltering journey down the Red Sea neared its end, and the ships prepared for the transit of the narrow Strait of Bab-el-Mandeb, which separates the Arabian Peninsula from the Horn of Africa. The strait was controlled on one side by the Republic of Djibouti, from which French naval forces were operating. Earlier that day the task group had passed the aircraft carrier *Clemenceau* and her escorting cruiser *Colbert* and been overflown by *Atlantique* and *Alouette* aircraft, but now none of these were at hand. On the other side, the strait was overlooked by the *Silkworm* missile sites of the Yemeni forces. Although Yemen, recently united after centuries of civil strife, had shown no outward sign of hostility towards the Coalition, the government was under immense strain as it tried to steer a middle course in the Arab League, and its armed forces were known to be reliant on Iraqi military advisers. Given the unknown intentions of the Yemenis, Commodore Summers kept the ships at the ready, and the sailors of the Canadian task group, with *Gloucester* in company, stood to their weapons and sensors in tense anticipation. In the event, the transit was conducted without incident. The following morning, after a quick top-up replenishment, *Gloucester* parted company to continue east for the Persian Gulf while the Canadians entered the safety of Djibouti harbour.

Djibouti was a resupply point, and the stop gave the task force an opportunity to discuss ongoing operations with their French counterparts. The French Navy maintained a large facility in the ex-colony to support their extensive operations in the lower Red Sea and Gulf of Aden. Beyond the dockyard gates, however, the Canadians had their first real exposure to the Arab world — and a poor portion at that — and it was a severe culture shock. An en route logistical detachment had arrived some days earlier, and its commander had warned Summers in advance of the ships' arrival that the Muslim weekend started Thursday afternoon and continued through Friday, the sabbath. Unfortunately, this coincided with the scheduled arrival on 20 September (a Thursday) and departure the next day, making the support from commercial suppliers minimal. Moreover, what was available locally was of questionable quality. *Protecteur* decided not to embark fuel from the oil depot after inspection indicated possible contamination. The task group's few material requirements had to be satisfied by the single *Hercules* shipment. Even rest and relaxation ashore was limited. On a one-night stop, only a fraction of the crews could get ashore, and those that did encountered abject poverty and simmering violence. Two days after the ships left, one of the hotel bars frequented by the sailors was destroyed by a terrorist bomb which killed several French légionnaires. In all, the Canadians were happy to leave the port in their wake and relieved that it had not been named the forward logistical site.

The stop was not wasted, however. *Terra Nova* had embarked a civilian factory support representative to repair her *Phalanx*, and before departure Friday morning *Athabaskan* came alongside *Protecteur* to accomplish the major task of "craning-off" the helicopter which had experienced engine failure a few days earlier. Within a short time, the air maintenance detachment aboard the supply ship had restored the helicopter to the serviceable list, but SK404 continued to demonstrate, through a disquieting series of mechanical malfunctions, an aversion for hot and humid operating conditions. The aircrews irreverently christened her the "Persian Pig."[4]

After departing from Djibouti the ships proceeded out the Gulf of Aden eastward into the Arabian Sea. Their destination now only days away, the crews made the final preparations before commencing operations. The true gravity of the situation hit home when Summers ordered all beards shaved off — to ensure a better gas mask fit — before entering the Strait of Hormuz. In irrepressible fashion, the sailors turned the moment to advantage, auctioning off the opportunity to shave the beards of senior officers, the proceeds going to various charities.

On 24 September, the Canadian task group rounded the toe of the Arabian peninsula and turned northwest into the Gulf of Oman. Soon they were passing through the patrol area known as the Alpha sectors, which the USS *Independence* battle group shared with the Australian and WEU task groups, the latter then composed of French, British, Dutch, and Italian forces. Command of the *Indy* group had been assumed by the commander of the US Navy's Carrier Group One, based in Norfolk, Virginia. Summers finally met this officer who had invited him to the TEAMWORK pre-exercise brief, in early August. At that time, Summers had had to waive the invitation and give it to Miller.

When Summers returned to his own flagship, the Canadian task group once again adopted a higher alert state for the nighttime transit of a narrow sea. "Silkworm Alley," as the Strait of Hormuz was known in deference to the Iranian coastal batteries on its northern shores, was another unknown quantity, but the task group's weapons were not called to action. Shortly after midnight on 26 September the Canadian warships entered the Persian Gulf. After making a quick pass through the central Gulf sectors, to test the waters in which they would spend the foreseeable future, Her Majesty's Canadian Ships *Athabaskan*, *Terra Nova*, and *Protecteur* arrived at Bahrain just after sunrise the next day, five weeks since their departure from Halifax.

The Establishment of CANMARLOGDET

When the ships arrived in Manamah harbour, they were greeted by Commander David Banks and his staff of the Canadian Maritime Logistics Detachment (CANMARLOGDET), as the Forward Support Unit had come to be known. After taking the decision to move his task group into the Persian Gulf, Summers had directed the Recce group to examine the logistical implications of Bahrain as a support base for a central Gulf operating area. Manamah certainly had much to recommend it. Relatively Western in outlook, the port had supported the United States Navy's Middle East Force in the Gulf for nearly four decades and was currently the focus of Admiral Fogarty's Interception Force activity. His flagship, USS *LaSalle*, was berthed there. So too was USS *Blue Ridge*, the vast command ship of Vice-Admiral H.H. Mauz, commander of the naval component of General Schwarzkopf's Central Command (NAVCENT). For the Canadian naval group, staff liaison was a simple matter of walking down the jetty. The modern, bustling international airport was easily accessible from the dockyard and offered an excellent airhead for sustainment flights from Canada. The airfield was also within range of the *Sea Kings* flying from the ships in the Charlie sectors.

Colonel Leach had arrived at the conference in Bahrain with a draft Status of Forces Agreement (SOFA) modelled after the existing USN arrangement with Bahrain but designed to be adaptable to whichever site was chosen. It now proved its worth. On 12 September, he met with officials at the Bahrain Amiri Naval Base to discuss issues of mutual concern for the planned military cooperation, specifically in preparation for the arrival of a thirty-two-person Forward Support Unit, and they signed a memorandum of understanding to be ratified by their respective governments. In the meantime, Banks was meeting with local agents and officials to lay the groundwork for his forthcoming establishment. The work of the Canadian Recce party supported Commodore Summers' evaluation: each of the ports they had set out to survey had its advantages and drawbacks, but given the proposed central Gulf operating area, Bahrain was the best location, with Dubai as an alternate. On 21 September, Admiral George issued an order activating the Canadian Maritime Logistics Detachment. Working initially out of the local Holiday Inn, Banks and an advance staff of eleven officers and men prepared to greet the ships upon their arrival a few days later.

In carrying out its mandate to provide logistical, engineering, and personnel services to TG 302.3, CANMARLOGDET obviously was intended to be fully responsive to the needs of the embarked task group commander. However, to ensure the detachment some independence of action while maintaining a direct reporting link to Halifax, Banks was designated a commander in his own right, as CTG 302.4 (an administrative appointment, since he commanded no forces). The scope of activities conducted by his detachment ranged from coordinating local services for the ships at the various ports which they would visit during their stay in the Gulf, to assisting in the travel arrangements of sailors repatriated to Canada and their replacements. The most obvious task was to satisfy the ships' requirements for matériel. Wherever possible, and particularly for such necessities as fresh foodstuffs and fuel, supplies were procured locally. The three ports frequented by the Canadian ships — Manamah in Bahrain, and Abu Dhabi and Dubai in the United Arab Emirates — boasted modern, European-style facilities. All had sizeable expatriate communities and were able to cater to a surprising degree to Canadian needs, although certain North American items were either prohibitively expensive or unavailable. Local markets provided spares unique to Canadian equipment or replenished ammunition stocks. Once the ships arrived in-theatre, the Maritime Command headquarters' sea logistical section undertook weekly sustainment flights. The first regular *Hercules* flight arrived at Manamah International Airport in the early afternoon of 4 October, with a load of two passengers, 81 bags of mail, approximately 20,000 pounds of ammunition, and 400 pounds of IOR OPDEF related stores, which were special items of an immediate operational requirement to repair essential equipment. As the scope of the Canadian contribution in the Gulf region widened, longer range *Boeing 707s* with greater cargo capacity joined the airlift, and the frequency of the flights increased apace to a four-day interval.

Even with the steady stream of *Boeing 707* and *Hercules* flights, not all of the task group's supply needs had to be transported by air. In mid-October, Commander Banks reported that where it was possible to make long-range forecasts of projected needs, it was more cost effective to reprovision meats, dry goods, and selected canteen items from Halifax rather than in-theatre. Within two weeks, the sea logistical staff back in Halifax organized the despatch of five commercial bulk sea containers (two of frozen goods and three general cargo and canteen stores) to depart Halifax at the end of October, and arrive in Bahrain a month later (it was redirected en route to be met by *Protecteur* in Dubai). Single shipments followed in late November (canteen goods, to arrive in time for Christmas) and early December (frozen foods, including "Beaver Tails" donated by an Ottawa firm). With no end in sight to the Gulf commitment, an expanded shipment of six containers was dispatched in early February. In all, a total of 245.3 tons of matériel in thirteen containers were shipped commercially to the task group. This amount plus the 1,741 tons of vehicles and containerized matériel shipped for the field hospital in January 1991, came to just under 2,000 tons of chartered sea lift to the Gulf forces.

Still, the experience tended to confirm the view of Maritime Command — later echoed by Air Command — that small forces can be largely self-sufficient, and are served best by the flexibility inherent in a judicious combination of local purchase and air transport sustainment. Over the duration of Canadian Forces' operations in the Gulf against Iraq, Air Transport Group delivered some 5,600 tons of matériel. The price was the virtual dedication of the ATG fleet to FRICTION and its associated operations, with little excess capacity for other activities. A comparison to the immense American effort, which was heavily dependent upon sea lift and saw some 2.8 million tons of matériel delivered by ship, highlights the difference in support concepts (as well, of course, of scale) between the two nations.[5]

Bahrain was not without its disadvantages as a forward operating base. These could not be appreciated at the time of the conference and Recce, but difficulties became apparent even as the members of the logistical detachment were settling in. To begin with, although close to the area of operations, the mid-Gulf location was within reach of the Iraqi extended range Al-Hussein *Scud* missiles, making it a less than ideal port for "rest and relaxation" from frontline activities. From a different perspective, the Canadians often found the local culture perplexing. Insh'allah — as God wills it — became a familiar refrain heard in response to any problems not immediately solvable. Even with the logistical detachment in place to facilitate shore arrangements, necessities such as diplomatic clearance for the ships were difficult to obtain and usually only at the last moment.

The biggest problem was also the hardest to resolve. When the ships first arrived, the destroyers were allowed to berth alongside wharfs, but *Protecteur* had to remain at an outer anchorage, some eight miles from the others. Upon setting up, CANMARLOGDET had confirmed one of the task group staff's worst fears: the advertised existence of deep-draught berths was misleading. The maximum depth in the inner harbour was thirty feet, only slightly more than the twenty-five-odd feet drawn by the destroyers. Fully loaded, *Protecteur* drew thirty-three feet, and her crew was forced to take measures to reduce it to within the allowable limits, an exercise which needed to be repeated each time the supply ship entered the harbour. Since most of her disposable tonnage was in fuel, timing arrivals in Bahrain carried the operational implication of reducing her available fuel state. The harbour authorities were driven in part by a concern for the explosive potential of the tanker's cargo should the port come under Iraqi attack, but more relevant was the fact that all of the deep-draught berths were taken up by, or reserved for, American vessels. A temporary resolution was reached when, as Captain Miller later recalled, "I personally called on the Harbour Master and presented him a Squadron crest [a backdrop outline of the Gulf, superimposed by a sea snake]. This obviously helped as he took up the phone to send tugs out to *Protecteur* to bring her alongside."[6] But this was to be a recurring problem, making resupply an awkward undertaking. It also underlined an irrefutable fact of life — the United States dominated every aspect of naval and military activity, and any other force paled in comparison. The result was low priority for services.

Preparing for Operations
The situation in the central Gulf had not changed substantially since the Bahrain Conference earlier in September. In several ways the ranks of the embargo forces had been bolstered: during September the British, French, and Italians all

reinforced their task groups; a joint Danish-Norwegian task group (composed of a Danish frigate and Norwegian Coast Guard cutter) was due to arrive early in October; and on 15 September Argentina announced the despatch of two frigates. But the bulk of these forces were earmarked for the Gulf of Oman or the northern Red Sea stations. Except for the occasional foray by a British or Italian destroyer from their southern Gulf stations, Admiral Fogarty's Middle East Force maintained a lonely vigil in the central Gulf sectors. His ships had withstood several Iraqi challenges, the most recent being the attempted breakout on 20 September of a group of merchant ships led by the MV *Hittin*; they were duly intercepted and subsequently boarded in the Gulf of Oman, but the Americans had been on-station nearly continuously since early August and were in need of a respite.

The tentative commitment Commodore Summers had made at the Bahrain Conference to patrol in the central Gulf sectors was awaiting government approval. Only when Task Group 302.3 began its Red Sea passage could he advise Admiral Fogarty of its arrival in Bahrain. After a weekend of staff consultations, he promised that his ships would be ready to proceed 1 October to sectors C1 and C4 (or, as Summers styled them, "Canada 1 and Canada 4").[7]

In adjusting to the looser command and control arrangements put in place for the embargo, US Navy officers were well aware that within the Gulf Coalition otherwise dependable allies were following their own national agendas. The Americans had adopted a wait and see approach to promises of assistance and were pleased with the arrival of the three Canadian ships in Manamah. Even before the ships were settled in their berths, the Canadian staff officers met their counterparts. Their immediate concern was to coordinate the details of joining the embargo effort in the central Gulf. The concept of operations proposed by Summers envisioned two of the three ships on-station at any one time while the third would be in port for maintenance and to allow the crews some rest. This was based on a fairly ambitious cycle of ten days on patrol and four days off. The earlier decision to upgrade the command and control capability of the tanker proved fortuitous because it enabled the task group commander and his staff to shift from *Athabaskan* to *Protecteur* whenever the flagship took her turn off-station. Arrangements also were made to embark an officer in *LaSalle* to maintain liaison with Admiral Fogarty's staff in their management of the multinational effort.

In the short term, other than getting the latest operational and intelligence briefings, and finalizing details such as the inter-ship computer data-Link setup and codes, there was very little staff coordination required in preparation for the commencement of interception operations. The ships' communications suites were found to be remarkably complete, and the few inconsistencies that remained were quickly rectified over the course of the weekend to ensure full connectivity with the USN. The basic tracking and reporting techniques used for the embargo differed little from the familiar NATO procedures. For a merchant ship to be intercepted in the Gulf in 1990, it had to be called or hailed on the international VHF radio frequency monitored by all vessels and queried as to its cargo and intentions. Then this information had to be passed to the local area coordinator for correlation before a decision on whether a boarding for closer inspection was necessary. In such cases, it was agreed that warships from two or more nations should cooperate, in order to stress the multinational character of the embargo. Routine inspections might be undertaken in the central Gulf, but boardings of Iraqi ships would occur in the Gulf of Oman, outside the range of Iraqi military interference. As soon as the Canadians were satisfied with these arrangements, the crews of *Athabaskan* and *Terra Nova* were ready to begin their first patrols on 1 October. *Protecteur* would remain in Manamah, finally alongside, to store up. She then would sail on the fifth to take her turn on patrol, relieving *Terra Nova*.

Events were unfolding elsewhere, however, which would affect the character of the Canadian involvement in the Gulf, and ultimately the task group itself. During September, both the United Nations and the United States had spearheaded efforts to increase the diplomatic and military pressure on Saddam to withdraw. With no apparent Iraqi reaction to Resolution 665, which gave substance to the maritime embargo, the Security Council passed in quick succession a series of follow-on measures. Resolutions 666 (13 September) and 669 (24 September) were essentially administrative refinements to the earlier resolution, respectively "[Requesting] the Secretary-General to seek information about the sources and availability of food in Kuwait and Iraq ... [and to] use his good offices to facilitate delivery and distribution of foodstuffs," and "[Entrusting] the Committee established to monitor sanctions with the task of examining requests from [third country] states for assistance because of hardships experienced due to the sanctions."[8] The passage on 25 September of Resolution 670, which extended the embargo to include aircraft leaving or entering Kuwait or Iraq, made the blockade of Iraq virtually complete.

Earlier, on 14 September, the Iraqi occupying forces had drawn renewed attention on a different front when they had stepped up their harassment of the international community in Kuwait City, including the sacking of the French embassy and the temporary detention of a Canadian diplomat. In response, on the sixteenth the Security Council passed by unanimous vote Resolution 667, "Strongly [condemning] Iraqi acts against diplomatic premises and personnel in Kuwait and the abduction of foreign nationals from diplomatic premises and [demanding] the immediate release of all foreign nationals."[9] The incidents were viewed ominously by the few countries still represented in Kuwait and under increasing pressure to close their embassies. By 10 October, besides Canada, the only Western embassies still open were those of the United States, Britain, and France.

In less than two months, Operation DESERT SHIELD had quickly grown to staggering proportions. On the ground in Saudi Arabia were the XVIII (US) Airborne Corps and I Marine Expeditionary Force. Overhead, USAF fighters flew protective Combat Air Patrols (CAPs) and were poised for strike missions. At sea were two carrier battle groups in the Red Sea (*John F. Kennedy* and *Saratoga*) and one carrier battle group (*Independence*) and an embarked Marine Expeditionary Brigade (4 MEB) in the Gulf of Oman. Also, the Marines flew their own fighter patrols over the Middle East Force in the central Gulf. The Final Report to Congress stated that "By early October, CINCCENT was satisfied the 'window of vulnerability' [against an Iraqi assault] had narrowed and that he could conduct a successful defense of Saudi Arabia."[10] With only minor refinements yet to come, the Coalition against Saddam took its final shape: in addition to the Americans, Arab League members Egypt, Syria, and the GCC states dispatched units to augment the Saudi forces, and several Western allies, including Canada, announced new or further commitments.

On 14 September, as we have seen, Prime Minister Mulroney held his press conference, and at the same time London gave notice of a greatly expanded commitment of British forces to the Gulf. The existing air and naval deployments would each be reinforced and an armoured brigade would be dispatched. The next day, in response to the Iraqi violation of diplomatic immunity, the French government unveiled Opération DAGUET, under which an air-portable brigade was sent to Saudi Arabia and eventually a squadron of *Mirage* fighters to Qatar. In short order Italy also joined, adding her own squadron of *Tornado* ground attack fighters and more warships to the ranks.

In Canada, Minister of National Defence Bill McKnight tabled the Active Service cabinet order before Parliament when it reconvened on 24 September, igniting a much anticipated acrimonious debate. The disquiet across the country was reflected in the House. The government's majority easily passed the enabling motion, but the opposition refused to give the traditional all-party support for an order-in-council that put Canadian troops on a war footing.

Unexpectedly, on 27 September NDHQ advised Commodore Summers, as well as the senior officers of the various Commands, of the necessity to consolidate the Canadian naval and air deployments into a joint operation. The next day Summers was designated commander of the proposed joint Canadian headquarters and ordered back to Ottawa to discuss his terms of reference (see Chapter 5). For the interim period of Summers' absence, Captain Miller was appointed acting commander of Task Group 302.3, and he and the junior staff officers continued the by now almost routine preparations for the embargo patrols.

For Summers the order to return to Ottawa was ironical. He might become theatre commander, and his interim plans to transform the Canadian supply ship into an American-style command ship might come to pass, but he was destined never to have an at sea command of ships in an operational theatre, the greatest ambition of any naval officer. Having brought the Canadian task group so far in terms both of distance from home and readiness for action, it was "with more than a little regret"[11] that he took his leave just as the ships were to join the action.

MIF Operations in the Central Gulf

Athabaskan and *Terra Nova* sailed as ordered for their first patrol on Monday, 1 October 1990. At 1220 local time, as his flagship entered area Charlie-1, Captain Miller, in his new capacity as acting commander, announced to his superiors in Halifax and Ottawa that the Canadian navy finally had joined the multinational interception effort, reporting that the "Barber Pole [returns] to action."[12]

The first patrol was to be a breaking-in period for the ships' companies. They needed the time to become familiar with their new surroundings and to get acquainted with the conduct of the interception operations. The crews looked forward to a change in pace from the very busy preparations and subsequent work-ups on the transit from Canada. They expected little else on the first patrol other than to challenge the merchant vessels that steamed through their patrol sectors. Within half an hour, *Athabaskan* conducted her first hailing, and by the end of that first afternoon the two destroyers had undertaken six interceptions without incident. At 1625, an hour before sunset, *Athabaskan* launched *Sea King* SK417, "Big Bird," in accordance with standing instructions that a helicopter be airborne and on the lookout for mines an hour before and after each dusk and dawn. The quiet was broken shortly after 1700, when the on-watch staff officer received a radio call from his counterpart aboard the USS *O'Brien*. MV *Tippu Sultan*, one of two relief vessels chartered by the government of India to remove their nationals from Iraq, was en route from Dubai to Khor az-Zubayr in Iraq for her second refugee evacuation. For some reason she had not been inspected in the southern Gulf to confirm that her cargo holds were empty, and one planned boarding by another warship had been aborted due to deteriorating weather and sea conditions. HMS *Jupiter* was in pursuit, but the British frigate, well to the south, could not catch the Indian ship until after dark. *Tippu Sultan* had passed between Charlie-1 and Charlie-4 patrol areas that morning, before the Canadian ships had arrived on-station, and was now some thirty miles to the north. Although certain that the ship was not in violation of the UN sanctions, the local MIF coordinator was concerned that she be inspected as a reminder to the Iraqis that the Coalition blockade was working. Could the Canadians attempt a boarding?

Captain Miller answered without delay and ordered *Athabaskan*, the closest of his ships, to proceed "with all despatch" to make good the interception. As the destroyer began her race to the north, the on-task helicopter was sent ahead. Just as the sun was setting, at 1730, the crew of "Big Bird" spotted the *Tippu Sultan* and advised her she would be boarded by a Canadian inspection team. The master was most cooperative, reducing speed, and rigging lighting and a ladder over the side to facilitate the procedure. Still, it was another hour and a half before *Athabaskan* could close *Tippu Sultan*. By that time, it was quite dark and a strong wind was blowing from the northwest, kicking up a six-foot sea and causing a slight delay in the destroyer getting her boarding party away. Not yet trained in the new helicopter-borne technique, the eight Canadian sailors had to manage with the existing boat procedure, despite the adverse conditions. Finally they boarded the Indian vessel, just as both *O'Brien* and *Jupiter* arrived to take up stations nearby to provide mutual support (watching for any signs of Iraqi retaliation or trouble aboard the vessel). Once on the relief ship, the boarding party swiftly determined that the vessel was empty, as declared. Within twenty minutes the boarding was complete, the team returned to *Athabaskan*, and *Tippu Sultan* was released to continue her passage.[13] Less than twelve hours on patrol, and under trying circumstances, Commander Pickford's crew had conducted a textbook MIF boarding, involving coordinated ship-helicopter procedures and multinational cooperation. The Canadians came away with a new appreciation of the value of their recent training.

On 3 October, *Athabaskan* undertook her second boarding. This time it was the other Indian relief ship, MV *Akbar*, which was also en route from Dubai to Iraq. This boarding was another multinational effort but in a different fashion. The vessel was initially located during the night by ITS *Orsa* in patrol area Bravo-1, and a boarding by HMS *Battleaxe* was planned for first light. The watch officer in *O'Brien* requested the Canadians to conduct a joint boarding with the British and keep an eye on the proceedings. Miller again tasked his flagship. Between them, the two ships quickly agreed that the boarding party would comprise an officer and three sailors from each. The heat-sensitive infra-red detector (the FLIR or Forward-Looking Infra-Red) mounted on the Canadian *Sea King* helicopter was put to good use that night when *Athabaskan* passed control of Big Bird to *Battleaxe* to locate the Indian ship. Once the ship's identity was confirmed, the helicopter returned to transfer the Canadian contingent to the British ship. By then it was daylight. With *Battleaxe* on the port beam of *Akbar*, and *Athabaskan* on the starboard quarter for mutual support, the combined Canadian-British team took to their boat and clambered aboard the Indian vessel. Once again, the master was most helpful. No discrepancies were noted. The vessel was confirmed empty and cleared to proceed.

Athabaskan chalked up her third boarding during the night of 9-10 October, the last night of her first ten-day patrol. Accompanied by USS *O'Brien*, *Athabaskan*'s search for *Akbar*, which was returning from Iraq, began late on the afternoon of the ninth. After sunset, *O'Brien* passed control of her *LAMPS III* helicopter to *Athabaskan*. Without a FLIR, however, it had difficulty investigating the many radar contacts and confirming which was the vessel of interest. (On a viewing scope, most radars can only produce an ill-defined image, best described as a blip; the infra-red FLIR has better definition, although over shorter ranges, using variances in temperature to produce an image not unlike a film negative.) If there had been any lingering doubts about the effectiveness of the FLIR mounted on helicopters, this experience dispelled them. *Protecteur*'s helicopter, SK404, the Persian Pig, was airborne at that time, conducting a test flight (the night before she had experienced yet another single engine failure in-flight emergency and had been repaired during the day). As soon as she was assessed satisfactory, she joined the search. With the aid of the FLIR, she located the ship and was able to distinguish not only her form but also her decks which were covered with people. Thereupon, the MIF Coordinator instructed *Athabaskan* and *O'Brien* to conduct a joint boarding. Refuelling aboard the Canadian destroyer, the Persian Pig took her party to the American ship and returned to *Protecteur*. The joint team was aboard *Akbar* by 2300, but this inspection, unlike the earlier searches of empty vessels, was complicated by the masses of people aboard and took about an hour. Just after midnight on the tenth, the relief ship was cleared to proceed.

Those first patrols set the tone for the participation of the Canadians in MIF operations. There was no low-key breaking-in period. *Terra Nova* had no opportunity to participate in any boardings before being relieved on 5 October by *Protecteur*, but she did conduct her share of hailings. Together, the three ships intercepted and challenged over one hundred vessels in the first seven days of operations. Task Group 302.3, newcomers to MIF operations in the Gulf, had moved quickly and relatively easily to achieve veteran status.

But there was a downside to peaking too early. In his daily report for 2 October, Captain Miller observed that "Patrol ops have settled down after an intensive first 12 hours." By the fourth he was reporting that it was a "Quiet day. Have had more interesting FISHPATs"[14] (single-ship fisheries patrols on the Grand Banks, well-known for their boring routine). For the crews working outside of the Bridge and Operations Room, who were the majority on board ship, it was even harder to maintain great enthusiasm for the mission. Coupled with the uncertainties posed by the potential for an Iraqi attack, plus the absence of an end date to their deployment and rumours of *Protecteur*'s imminent change of role to command ship, Commodore Summers' quick departure for Canada fuelled speculation concerning the future expansion of the commitment in the Gulf. There runs a common adage that "Sailors are not happy unless they are complaining," and it was inevitable that grumbling would start, although it started much earlier than anticipated. The shift in attitude did not escape the attention of the embarked media representatives. On 5 October, in stark contrast to a rather positive report three days earlier of *Athabaskan*'s busy first day on patrol, Paul Koring, the correspondent from the *Globe and Mail* aboard the flagship, filed a story citing various gripes amongst that ship's crew which indicated that "Morale, buoyed by adrenalin and intensive training on the long voyage to the gulf, already is sagging in the reality of boring patrols in a small patch of sea."[15] That article overstated the mixed feelings aboard, but the flagship's executive officer acknowledged that prominent amongst his sailors' several complaints was that "'It doesn't matter how long the tunnel is, but they want to know where the end is.'" He hoped to be able to tell them by the end of the month.

Barring that, the best way to improve morale is to increase activity. A semblance of the early hectic pace had to be maintained, and the ships began a friendly unofficial competition for the highest interception tally. Once they got into this new business, they took it to heart. On balance, that first week was judged a success, both within the Canadian group and outside. As recounted later by Commodore Summers:

> ... the heavy work was in the central Gulf and the USN, even with its considerable size, was stretched too thin. Canada responded to the need and we were the first non-USN ships to operate on the front line. I believe we showed the way and know that we embarrassed some nations: the others gradually followed our lead and moved north.[16]

With the now continuous presence of Canadian and also British warships in the area, Admiral Fogarty proposed the addition of three patrol sectors (C5, C6, and C7) to the existing four in the Charlie area, extending coverage to the northwest. Miller felt sufficiently emboldened not only to reiterate the commitment made by Summers to maintain two ships on-station, but also to offer to fill the new Charlie-5 sector when the two destroyers were at sea together. For her patrols, *Protecteur* was to be permanently assigned the southerly Charlie-1 sector with the at-sea destroyer then falling back to Charlie-2. These were precautionary measures for the protection of the tanker.

On 8 October, NAVCENT advised the multinational forces throughout the Gulf to adopt a higher alert status while combined British, Australian, and American teams conducted forcible boardings of two Iraqi merchant ships in the Gulf of Oman. Despite the diversion of one of the vessels, *Tadmur*, to an Omani port, no reaction developed. The day passed without further incident, but the threat of a retaliatory air strike was taken seriously because there were indications that the Iraqis were moving *Mirage* fighters to southern airfields, from which they were beginning over-water training. Heightening the tension was the lack of knowledge of Iran's overall military goals. The multinational interception forces throughout the Gulf were the regular subjects of Iranian air force and navy surveillance patrols, especially in areas where the MIF sectors came close to Iran's twelve-mile territorial limit. In his memoirs, the British theatre commander, General Sir Peter de la Billière, described the potential danger to the central Gulf forces if an Iraqi air strike had been allowed to pass undetected through the valleys of the Zagros Mountains, which run parallel to the Iranian coastline, and breakout from an unexpected quarter to attack the warships on patrol:

> In theory a jet could come straight off the coast at ultra-low level, without warning, and because the ship would not be able to engage it in Iranian airspace, she would in effect have about a fifteen-kilometre or thirty-second warning before she could

counter-attack an intruder armed with lethal *Exocet* missiles, which were used with such devastating effect against HMS *Sheffield* and other ships during the Falklands campaign.[17]

It was clearly difficult to establish hostility in the air. Commercial air traffic, except for that originating in Iraq-Kuwait, had scarcely slackened, and some airlanes were actually busier with the steady stream of Coalition transport flights. At the same time, Coalition fighters were constantly in the air, maintaining protective patrols over the fleets or engaged in tactical training exercises. In mid-October, Captain Miller, reporting to the minister on the operational conditions in the Gulf, described the air situation as "congested … on [average] 20-35 a/c are being tracked in [the Central Persian Gulf] airlanes … 17 commercial air are in transit at any time and at dawn some 8-10 Iraqi aircraft and as many USN/USMC/Cdn fighters airborne in CAP [stations]."[18] The potential for a blue-on-blue, or worse an innocent civilian engagement, was high. When suspicious situations developed — and they did, quite frequently — the warships went through a quick reaction procedure known as Resolve, whereby all available radar and electronic sensor information (such as IFF and ESM) was rapidly collated to determine an aircraft's true identity, while other operators using military and civilian air distress frequencies alerted the suspicious aircraft to the developing situation and warned it to steer clear or risk engagement.

The Bridge and Operations Room watchmen were constantly balancing these various factors. On 16 October, their fears seemed about to come to pass as *Athabaskan* conducted a Resolve to verify an Assumed Hostile Link-11 track apparently originating in Iran. It was quickly determined to have been a bad or false track, but for some time things were "very exciting." That same day, the problem of the unreliability of *Terra Nova*'s *Phalanx* surfaced again. Very soon this awkward situation was aggravated by an increasing number of technical problems with the ship's forward (3inch70 calibre) main gun mounting. Incidentally, a Canadian Press story alleging the use of "museum-piece" weapons in the fleet (the 40mm Boffin, see Chapter 2) was receiving wide distribution in Canada, raising anew the question of the air defence preparedness of the ships.[19]

The reporter had the right issue but the wrong weapon. The *Phalanx* was the real problem. Public knowledge of it would have been all the more embarrassing because it was this same reporter who had championed the *Phalanx* as the centrepiece of the task group's self-defence.[20] Captain Miller considered that the present level of tension posed an acceptable risk for *Terra Nova* to remain in Charlie-2 without a functioning Close-In Weapon System, but he allowed that should tension increase the decision would be reviewed carefully. He was given almost immediate pause to reconsider. Late on 18 October a Saudi patrol boat reported that she had come under attack, leading the Americans once again to put the Gulf forces on alert. It turned out that the Saudis had been overflown by homebound CAP, but the Canadian destroyer was ordered to the southern edge of Charlie-1 as a precautionary measure until the confusion was resolved.

The Coalition at Sea: MIF or MNF?

In situations of heightened alert, the multinational forces appreciated the air defence umbrella provided by the American cruisers in conjunction with the Marine Corps F/A-18 air patrols. In mid-October, two new elements were in the process of being integrated into the network — British Type 42C guided-missile destroyers (such as *Gloucester*) and Canada's own CF-18 fighters. Altogether, they reduced the airborne anti-ship threat to a level that allowed the remaining warships of the US, Royal, and Canadian navies to concentrate on the business of interception operations.

But the omnipresent might of the United States Navy was at once reassuring and disquieting. The USN was also engaged in non-MIF activities. When the Canadian destroyers arrived on-station for their first patrol, the battleship *Wisconsin*, with her three triple 16-inch gun turrets and rows of *Tomahawk* cruise missile canisters, was making a slow transit of the northern reaches of their sectors. Then, while *Athabaskan*'s second boarding was in progress (with *Battleaxe*, on 3 October), the American carrier *Independence* and escorts steamed by within eyesight to the west, making their way northwestward on the carrier battle group's first foray into the Gulf, her flight deck alive with activity as she exercised launching air strikes ashore.

These and various other incidents serve as a point of departure in our examination of the structure of the Coalition against Saddam Hussein, and how the various nations, especially those dispatching naval forces, saw themselves in the Coalition. During August, September, and October 1990 the naval Coalition developed in very different fashion from that formed on land. The participants were different and their aims varied. Both these factors were reflected in the operations conducted on the waters of the Persian Gulf.

The Coalition of popular perception was that of the Multinational Force (MNF) established in Saudi Arabia in response to King Fahd's invitation to defend his kingdom from further Iraqi advances. Because his request came under Article 51 of the United Nations Charter which allowed members to respond to a defensive request from another, it was made without the specific blessing of the Security Council. The nations which responded came from various quarters. Besides the Western forces represented by the Americans, British, and French, there were also sizeable contingents from the Muslim world. Saudi Arabia, Egypt, Syria, and the Gulf Cooperation Council member states formed the Arab Joint Task Force, or JTF. It was important to the Saudis that the overall command and control of the Coalition be seen to be exercised between General Schwarzkopf and their own General Khalid, and the two came to an arrangement on their combined command. Still, the overwhelming majority of the forces were American, and they deployed under the terms of OPLAN 90-1002, which was essentially a quick reworking of a rapid deployment to counter a

Soviet thrust to the Persian Gulf. Although initially a defensive action, it was inevitable that the American deployment would develop an offensive stance, an option to which the air force component in Central Command quickly turned its energy.

At sea, aside from the increased presence of the Middle East Force in the central Gulf, further US Navy and Marine Corps reinforcements proceeded in tandem with the Army and Air Force buildup ashore. The Royal Saudi Navy maintained the front-line patrol in the northern Gulf to monitor Iraqi movements. Otherwise, there was little attempt at operational integration with the regional navies, and the coastal forces of the other Gulf states were more noticeable by their absence from the multinational effort.

Countries other than the United States which dispatched naval forces were similarly determined to display resolve against Saddam Hussein's aggression, but they were reluctant to adopt too aggressive a stance at this early stage. However, NAVCENT was charged with building the naval Coalition, and Admiral Mauz was aware of the hesitation of other naval forces to engage in operations other than embargo enforcement. Once the immediate security of Saudi Arabia was assured, he could turn his attention to other options. Ironically, it was the USN that began the interception effort, albeit as an alternative to the inaction in the drawn-out negotiations preceding the adoption by the Security Council of Resolution 665. Even then, the overriding principle of the USN was to monitor shipping without compromising the security of its own vessels. Admiral Fogarty, still acting as COMIDEASTFOR, was assigned the additional task of "Commander, United States Maritime Interception Force" (COMUSMIF, CTG 150.2).[21] Besides his own Middle East Force (Task Group 150.1), warships from the Independence and *Kennedy* battle groups (TGs 150.4 and 150.5, respectively) were put at his disposal to carry out the additional mission (see Figure 1).

The inherent mobility of naval forces and fluctuating force levels due to reinforcements and replacements make the comparison of national deployments to the Gulf problematic. The beginning of October, however, was a period of relative stability in the multinational Coalition. Coincidentally, this is when the Canadian task group commenced operations. By then, the American naval deployments for DESERT SHIELD were complete. Some sixty vessels had arrived in the region, constituting the reinforced Middle East Force, three carrier battle groups, an amphibious task force, and logistical support forces. The remainder of the naval Coalition also had taken shape, with only minor refinements yet to come. These other (non-USN) naval forces have often been overlooked or dismissed as lesser participants because, when taken individually and then compared with the American naval deployment to the region, they looked insignificant. Even the British and French task groups were small. Taken collectively, however, the other forces totalled nearly fifty ships, approximating the American effort (compare Figures 2 and 1).

They were all deployed to a common purpose — the enforcement of United Nations sanctions. When analyzing the naval Coalition at this stage, given the other

COMMAND TITLE	DESIG	SHIP(S)	SIDE NUMBER	AREA[1]
COMUSNAVCENT VADM H.H. MAUZ	TF 150	BLUE RIDGE	LCC 19	CAG
COMIDEASTFOR RADM W. FOGARTY	TG 150.1	LASALLE WISCONSIN *ENGLAND *ANTIETAM *O'BRIEN *TAYLOR *R.G. BRADLEY *BARBEY	AGF 3 BB 64 CG 22 CG 54 DD 975 FFG 50 FFG 49 FF 1088	CAG
COMUSNAVLOG-SUPFOR	TG 150.3	COMFORT MERCY +3 SUPPORT	T-AH 20 T-AH 19	AG/GOO
COMCVBG NAS (COMCARGRU 1)	TG 150.4	INDEPENDENCE *JOUETT *GOLDSBOROUGH *REASONER *BREWTON +7 AUXILIARY	CV 62 CG 29 DDG 20 FF 1063 FF 1086	NAS
COMCVBG NRS (COMCARGRU 2)	TG 150.5	J.F. KENNEDY MISSISSIPPI MOOSBRUGGER *SAN JACINTO *T.C. GATES *MONTGOMERY *THOMAS C. HART *S.B. ROBERTS +3 AUXILIARY	CV 67 CGN 40 DD980 CG 56 CG 51 FF 1082 FF 1092 FFG 58	NRS
COMUSAMPHIB TF	TG 150.6	NASSAU +17	LHA 4	GOO
COMUSCLF	TG 150.8	SARATOGA PHILIPPINE SEA BIDDLE SAMPSON	CV 60 CG 58 CG 34 DDG 10	NRS

1   During the course of the crisis, the Coalition adopted use of the name 'Arabian' Gulf, at the request of their Saudi partners, who refused to acknowledge 'Persian' (i.e., Iranian) dominance of the Gulf. It also made for a more pronounceable series of acronyms to identify the various Gulf sector areas: NAG for the North Arabian Gulf, CAG for the Central, and SAG for the Southern. Except where required in acronyms, such as in this and the following table, or for the occasional quote, the text holds to the 'Persian' usage more familiar to readers.

      Acronyms used to identify the other operating areas were: GOO for the Gulf of Oman, NAS for North Arabian Sea, NRS for Northern Red Sea, and BEM for the Strait of Bab-el-Mandeb.

Figure 1. USN Deployments to the Gulf Region, 1 October 1990 (with ships available for COMUSMIF [CTG 150.2])

COUNTRY	DESIG	SHIP(S)	SIDE NUMBER	AREA
CANADA CAPT(N) MILLER	TG 302.3	ATHABASKAN (CTG) TERRA NOVA PROTECTEUR	DDH 282 DDE 259 AOR 509	CAG
UNITED KINGDOM	TG 321.1	YORK BATTLEAXE JUPITER LONDON (CTG) GLOUCESTER BRAZEN (8 Oct.) CARDIFF (25 Oct.) RFA FORT GRANGE RFA OLNA RFA DILIGENCE +3 MCM +4 LST	D 98 F 89 F 60 F 95 D 96 F 91 D 108 A 385 A 123 A 132	CAG /SAG /GOO
BELGIUM	TG 418.2	ZINNIA +2 MCM	A 961	BEM
DENMARK / NORWAY	TG 420.5	OLFERT FISCHER (DA) (CTG) ANDENNES (NoCG)	F 355 W 322	SAG /GOO
NETHERLANDS	TG 429.9	WITTE DE WITH (CTG) PIETER FLORISZ	F 813 F 826	SAG /GOO
ITALY	TG 620.1	LIBECCIO (CTG) ZEFFIRO ORSA STROMBOLI	F 572 F 577 F 567 AOR 5327	SAG /GOO
FRANCE	TF 623	MARNE (ALINDIEN) DUPLEIX MONTCALM COMMANDANT BORY DOUDART DE LAGREE PROTET COMMANDANT DUCUING DURANCE +3 (CLÉMENCEAU GROUP)	A 630 D 641 D 642 F 726 F 728 F 748 F 795 A 629	SAG /GOO / NRS /BEM
AUSTRALIA	TG 627.4	DARWIN (CTG) ADELAIDE SUCCESS	F 04 F 01 A 304	GOO
SPAIN	TGO 665.1	SANTA MARIA DESCUBIERTA CAZADORA	F 81 F 31 F 35	NRS /GOO
GREECE		LIMNOS	F 451	NRS

Figure 2. MIF Deployments to the Gulf Region, 1 October 1990

members' emphasis on MIF embargo operations rather than the broader MNF objective of power projection, it is more accurate to include only those US Navy units available to Admiral Fogarty for the interception operations. Discounting minesweepers and auxiliaries (Canada's *Protecteur* was the only auxiliary engaged in the daily task of interceptions), the "others" had fully thirty warships dedicated to the MIF tasks. Of the twenty American cruisers, destroyers, and frigates in the region, fifteen (only one-quarter of all USN forces) were available to the United States' Maritime Interception Force (USMIF). Within this narrower definition, out of the total vessels dedicated to sanction enforcement, the Americans accounted for only one-third (15 out of 45), and even then the cruisers and destroyers were charged primarily with providing defence against air attack, effectively reducing their availability for the other tasking. As a whole, the USN deployed forces so large and varied that it could afford the luxury of taking on the secondary priority of sanction enforcement. The other navies, as individual services, had insufficient forces available (on average each ranging from two to six vessels deployed) to cover such a variety of contingencies. With each country's deployment geared to reflect a specific political aim, their navies were left little choice but to concentrate wholly on the embargo enforcement. The Multinational Interception Force was quite literally their raison d'être in the Gulf.

The relative balance of forces at sea between the USN and their allies meant that the Americans did not enjoy the same dominant position on the seas as they did on land, despite their lead in the naval effort. Working collectively under the MIF banner allowed the lesser navies a larger voice in operational discussions when these pertained to interception operations. At the first meeting of representatives of the Coalition naval forces in Bahrain, on 9-10 September, the Western naval officers gathered around the table had little difficulty establishing a framework for multinational interception operations. But the fact that the enterprise fell outside the bounds of any of the traditional alliances (such as NATO) meant that there was no binding structure to the Coalition. The primacy of national command and control was agreed upon, but some sort of working arrangement was required to avoid both duplication of effort and any mutual interference. Since the formal C^2 principle — by which Command and Control is delegated to a recognized central authority — was out of the question, an informal C^2 was adopted: Coordination and Cooperation became the maxim.

This tended to underscore further the differences between the Coalitions ranged on land and at sea. In its fundamental nature, the multinational naval Coalition was at once a greater problem but a lesser concern for the Americans: more problematic in insistence on the embargo option, but within those bounds, much more Western and easier to coordinate. These dynamics complicated relations between the United States and the other navies. The commander of the United States Navy's Middle East Force was tasked with a variety of responsibilities, including coordinating the multinational interception effort. Therefore, it was inevitable that the lines between MIF and MNF would be blurred. As the crisis dragged on without apparent end, the members of the naval Coalition came under increasing pressure to adopt a more forceful stance. In the tense conditions of the central Persian Gulf, the demands of self-defence tended to blur even more the line between MIF and MNF priorities.

Another complication was that the fundamental nature of MIF operations was new to the Canadian navy. These boardings were very different from those undertaken in the course of fisheries patrols on the Grand Banks. Moreover, unlike the army and air force, veterans of peacekeeping operations throughout the world, the navy had no long tradition of UN operations. Naval operations off Korea, from 1950 to 1953, had been a tenuous exception and were a distant memory. All attempts to compare the multinational participation in the Gulf Interception Force to Canada's role in the Korean war came up short. Even a comparison to NATO was useless.

"Glory is fleeting ... "

Building upon the experience of the first week, the Canadian task group quickly adapted to the routine of central Gulf interception operations. *Protecteur* began her first patrol on 5 October, relieving *Terra Nova*. With the return of *Terra Nova* to relieve *Athabaskan* early on the tenth, and the consequent departure of his flagship for Manamah, Captain Miller and his staff transferred to *Protecteur*, using the tanker as an alternate command ship. The next day, Commodore Summers embarked in *Protecteur* to brief Miller and the ships' captains on the results of the NDHQ meetings. The immediate consequence was that the commodore returned ashore to make his headquarters preparations and on 12 October Miller formally assumed the command of Task Group 302.3.

Protecteur soon found herself in a more traditional role. While aboard the tanker on the eleventh, Summers witnessed the underway replenishment (UNREP, or RAS [Replenishment At Sea]) of USS *O'Brien*. It was *Protecteur*'s first replenishment of a non-Canadian warship in the Gulf. Because of the increased risk of air attack against unarmed tankers, central Gulf warships had to vacate their stations and refuel in Manamah, or the *Independence* battle group oiler, *Cimarron*, would journey occasionally from the Arabian Sea to make the rounds. However, the local American commander was keen to continue exploiting this new-found resource. When the air defence cruiser *England* was replenished on 12 October, her captain signalled *Protecteur*: " ... [I]t's good to have a friend with fuel close by. See you again soon." In his report to Halifax for that day, the task group public affairs officer boasted, "PROTECTEUR is quickly establishing its reputation as the floating gas station of the Persian Gulf."[22] Captain Miller was quite willing to assist the multinational effort in this fashion, with the sole proviso that the receiving ship make its way to Charlie-1 where *Protecteur* was on patrol. The deal was done. *Protecteur*'s captain, a westerner from Calgary, Alberta, gave his supply ship the nickname "Chuckwagon." During the course of her first two patrols in October,

Captain McClean's "Chuckwagon" came to be a popular sight. At the end of those two weeks, *Protecteur* had carried out eighteen at-sea replenishments, fully one half with other MIF navies. The trend would continue during the coming months.[23]

Three days into her second patrol, on 13 October, *Terra Nova* finally conducted her first boarding. It was a virtual repetition of *Athabaskan*'s effort ten days earlier. *Terra Nova* and the frigate USS *Barbey* conducted a joint inspection of MV *Akbar*, which was returning to Dubai with yet another load of refugees. From his temporary vantage in *Protecteur*, Miller passed his congratulations to Commander Andrews, welcoming him to the "Persian Gulf Veteran's Club" with the observation: "Glory is fleeting but obscurity is nothing."[24]

As if to capitalize on the successful combination, the next day the MIF Coordinator requested *Terra Nova* to join forces with *Barbey*, for a boarding of *Tippu Sultan*. This time Miller declined because the Indian vessel was passing some distance outside the assigned Canadian patrol area. After some discussion, the Americans accepted the suggestion that HMS *London* was closer and should be tasked. But within the week, the Canadians were making a fifth visit to an Indian relief ship. Early on 18 October, *Athabaskan*, for the first time patrolling farther to the north in sector Charlie-5, intercepted the *Akbar*, which was returning from Iraq on her final mission, bound directly for India without stopping in the Gulf. Back aboard his flagship, Miller informed the MIF Coordinator of his intention to board the vessel. Due to a noticeable increase in Iranian air and sea activity, USS *O'Brien* positioned herself between *Athabaskan* and an inquisitive Iranian frigate. The boarding was conducted without incident. The inspection was valuable as much for continuing the embargo as for the insights into conditions in Iraq gained from interviews with those on board.

For the first three weeks of October, Captain Miller was able to meet the commitment to occupy continuously two of the Charlie sectors. He knew that he was pushing his ships but was confident that the extensive engineering preparations undertaken in August would keep them going until a relief task group appeared. Then, on 25 October, the plan began to unravel. *Protecteur* had conducted an early-morning replenishment of an American frigate and was scheduled to service the Canadian destroyers as part of their turnover of patrol duties when she experienced a major engineering casualty — a high-pressure steam leak. The ship's technicians were able to isolate the problem and rig a temporary repair, but a permanent fix required extended repairs alongside. *Protecteur*'s next rest and maintenance period was not anticipated until 30 October — 4 November. On completion of the refuelling, as *Athabaskan* detached for her own maintenance period in Dubai, the task group commander and his staff transferred as planned to the tanker, which then departed from the operating area for Manamah. Hoping that an accelerated diplomatic clearance could be arranged to get *Protecteur* alongside on 27 October, Miller planned to continue to direct operations from his alternate command ship and employ the tanker's helicopters flying from Manamah International Airport to help maintain coverage of the Canadian sectors. Still, *Protecteur*'s MIF replenishment programme was off until further notice. *Terra Nova* would be the only Canadian representative afloat in the Charlie sectors, and she had problems of her own. Despite extensive attention during a recent maintenance period, her *Phalanx* was still unserviceable, and until it was repaired, she would be restricted to patrolling sector Charlie-1.

The outlook did not improve appreciably over the next few days. Attempts to get *Protecteur* alongside in Manamah met the same resistance experienced by the tanker on its first visit to the port a month earlier. By the time the bureaucratic red tape had been processed to obtain the required diplomatic clearance, the harbour master informed Captain McClean that there were no berths available. But proper repairs by skilled craftsmen were essential before the ship could sail again safely. The catastrophic potential of an engineering breakdown was underlined on 30 October when, in sight of *Protecteur* at her anchorage, the American amphibious assault helicopter carrier USS *Iwo Jima* ran aground while exiting Manamah harbour. A subsequent explosion in her boiler room left six sailors dead and twenty-two injured. The engineering officers attached to the Canadian logistical detachment quickly made arrangements for Manamah dockyard workers to be ferried aboard *Protecteur* to begin the repairs while she was at anchor.

Nor was *Terra Nova*'s air defence capability faring any better. Not only did her *Phalanx* continue to confound the efforts of yet another factory support representative, who cannibalized one of *Protecteur*'s weapons for parts, but the destroyer's SPS-503 air search radar (itself the subject of earlier problems) had to be taken off-line for a period on 26 October. The associated air conditioning plant shut itself down, and the sea water inlets were clogged with marine life, which included shrimp, squid, and poisonous sea snakes. There were several tense hours on the twenty-eighth when the Americans raised the threat warning for the interception and inspection of the large Iraqi crude carrier MV *Amuriyah* in the North Arabian Sea. This was "the most violent boarding to date," accomplished by a joint force of Australians, Royal Marines, and US Marines taking control of the ship after the master refused to heed the warning shots fired across his bow.[25]

Just when it seemed that could things get no worse, tactical communications between the task group staff embarked in *Protecteur* and the patrolling ship and helicopters became intermittent due to anomalous propagation, abnormal transmitting conditions brought on by high temperature and humidity variations. The task group commander had no immediate voice communications with *Terra Nova* in nearby sector Charlie-1, but he could converse with *LaSalle* and *Wisconsin* in distant Abu Dhabi. In the midst of this situation, General de Chastelain and the Deputy Minister, Mr Robert Fowler, visited *Terra Nova* in Charlie-1 and *Protecteur* at anchor, as part of a tour of the deployed Canadian Forces. While reportedly impressed by the spirit and morale of the task group, they must have been worried about the physical state of the ships.

The prospects for a resolution to the Kuwait crisis provided no cause for optimism. On 19 October, after holding out for over two months, the Canadian Embassy in Kuwait finally closed its doors, with the remaining staff evacuated to Canada after a temporary delay in Baghdad. Saddam Hussein still refused to release his "guests," except in token numbers to distinguished foreign supplicants, leading the Security Council on 29 October to adopt Resolution 674:

> Part A of the resolution demands that Iraq stop taking third-state nationals hostage and stop mistreating Kuwaiti nationals. The resolution reminds Iraq of its obligations under international law in this regard and demands that Iraq facilitate the immediate departure of third-state nationals and provide the nationals and Kuwaiti nationals access to food, water and basic services. Part B of the resolution reposes the Security Council's trust in the Secretary-General to use his good offices to pursue a peaceful solution to the crisis.[26]

Speaking to the resolution, Canada's Ambassador Fortier considered it a signal "that should Iraq continue blatantly to ignore the will of the international community ... further measures under the Charter will be required and we will not shy away from considering such measures."[27] Secretary of State Baker was less circumspect, warning: "We will not rule out a possible use of force if Iraq continues to occupy Kuwait."[28] His admonition "was taken seriously in Baghdad, which put its forces on 'extreme alert'."[29]

In his daily summary for 31 October, Captain Miller finally was able to report that *Terra Nova*'s *Phalanx* system was working again and *Protecteur*'s engineering problem was resolved. But by then *Athabaskan* was returning to station, and it was decided that *Protecteur* would remain at anchor off Manamah for her scheduled rest and maintenance, while Miller and his staff returned to the flagship. The two destroyers resumed patrolling their Charlie-2 and Charlie-5 sectors. *Protecteur* took advantage of the opportunity to refuel and take on some stores that had arrived on the recent sustainment flights, but the inability to get her alongside in Manamah only injected another element of frustration. The stores had to be barged out, which was time-consuming and expensive. As an alternative, when in port the destroyers took on as much of the higher priority stores as possible, but a quantity inevitably remained behind, to be added to within days by yet another sustainment flight. Captain McClean proposed moving the airhead to Dubai, despite that emirate's distant location from the operating area. It was a black time for the task group, and the staff officers began to re-examine the Canadian commitment and consider various options, including two-ship patrols instead of the staggered, three-ship approach.

Also colouring the staff's deliberations was the issue of the replacement of TG 302.3. Recent practice in the Canadian navy had been for ships to deploy for no longer than six months (for example, the NATO Standing Naval Force Atlantic deployment on the East Coast and Far East cruises on the West), with every effort being made to have all ships home for Christmas. Where a continuous presence was required, traditionally the on-station ship would be relieved by another. In this vein, planning for a follow-on deployment had begun even before the first task group had departed Halifax. Naval staffs in Ottawa and on both coasts — Maritime Command agreed that the West Coast fleet should provide the second group — spent many hours preparing various options, which were considered in their sundry permutations before 5 October when Chief of Defence Staff de Chastelain decided that the rotation, if needed, should be effected by replacing crews not ships. (He also added that the decision could be reviewed if circumstances warranted.) That decision was based ultimately on the merits of much lower cost estimates than those anticipated for what was the navy's preference — the refurbishment and rotation of a new three-ship task group — and it was received in Halifax with grudging resignation. With no end in sight to the Gulf mission, rotation was inevitable. On 17 October, Admiral George promulgated a Tasking Order under which "HMCS *Preserver*, HMCS *Huron* and HMCS *Restigouche* ships' companies will sequentially relieve *Protecteur*, *Athabaskan* and *Terra Nova*."[30] The two destroyers nominated were West Coast ships of the same classes as those in the Gulf, but *Preserver*, sister ship to *Protecteur*, was an East Coast ship. The only West Coast supply ship, *Provider*, was of a very different class, making a crew exchange impracticable. Command of the task group also was to be exchanged, with the commander and staff of the West Coast's Second Destroyer Squadron taking over from Miller. It was estimated that a month-long period was needed to complete each turnover and in-theatre workups, for January, February, and March 1991, respectively. The navy's fear was that this bureaucratic solution to a military problem, rather than accomplishing a quick, neat turnover, would result in the dismemberment of the task group and its ceasing to function as a meaningful element of the Multinational Interception Force for those three months.

The official announcement of the plan on 24 October came as Canada's involvement in the Gulf was once again the focus of public controversy. The rotation issue was rapidly overtaken on the twenty-sixth when the media responded in a furore to the new "tough talk" from Joe Clark, who said that Canada was willing to consider the use of force against Iraq if necessary and without United Nations approval. This was perceived as a shift in the government's position. Indifferent to the side issues, the task group crews — and their families back home — had all the news they wanted. It had been a challenging month. Their morale, however, was given an incredible boost with the announcement that there was indeed a stop date for OP FRICTION Phase 1.

Knowing that there was "light at the end of the tunnel," the Canadian task group looked back with a sense of pride on the accomplishments of that first month of MIF operations. They were joined by the Commander of Maritime Command, Admiral George. On 4 November, he was in the Gulf, his visit timed to coincide with a patrol turnover. He found that the three Canadian ships at sea constituted exactly half the Coalition forces then in the central Gulf. That evening, however, while Captain McClean was entertaining Vice-Admiral George at a formal dinner onboard, *Protecteur* suffered another potentially dangerous steam leak requiring immediate repairs. Two mess decks had to be vacated, and the ship proceeded to the Manamah anchorage for repairs. She did not return for duty until 9 November.

During the month of October, the Canadian navy had grown discernibly attached to MIF operations. Commodore Summers later recorded that

> Our ships' on-station availability (the highest for the major navies there) and the noticeable sense of an almost personal responsibility to intercept, challenge and board if necessary any vessel entering our assigned sectors, soon led to Canada's Navy being held up by the USN at a naval conference as the example for others to follow.[31]

It was Captain Miller's desire to maintain that elevated status. On 2 November, he submitted to Summers his programme proposal for operations until the changeovers began in the New Year. The commitment to fill two of the Charlie sectors could be met up to 13 January 1991, by lengthening the patrol cycles to fourteen days on and five off. This still would allow for the occasional extended maintenance routines for each ship and "barge days" off Manamah for *Protecteur*. He admitted that the plan was complex, but he considered it operationally sound and the best option by far to maintain the professional contribution which his task group had made to the MIF operations.

Following the swings of a mostly discouraging final week in October, Miller hoped that this plan would give his task group a fresh perspective and help them continue the pace of operations into the New Year. By the end of the month, the involvement of an expanded Canadian Forces in the Gulf, announced by Prime Minister Mulroney seven weeks earlier, was reaching fruition. On 30 October, *Athabaskan* paid an overnight visit to the port of Doha, Qatar. At a reception on board that evening, Commander Pickford represented the task group for Captain Miller, playing host to a variety of dignitaries, including General de Chastelain, Deputy Minister Fowler, Ambassador Dickenson, and emissaries from the Coalition missions in Qatar. Also present were Commodore Summers and members of his staff from the newly established Joint Headquarters ashore as well as the officers of the deployed CF-18 squadron. In a fleeting moment, the somewhat symbolic gathering united the main actors who were about to embark on a joint venture unprecedented in Canadian military history.

Notes

1 WD *Protecteur*, "Media Sitrep and Requests," 16 September 1990. (The TG PAO was embarked in *Protecteur*.)

2 WD *Athabaskan* Helicopter Air Detachment (HELAIRDET), 17 September 1990.

3 Ibid., 18 September 1990.

4 Following this, the air detachment adopted nicknames for each of the *Sea Kings*:

    404 - "Persian Pig"

    410 - "Chickenhawk," renamed in mid-January "Dusty's Dhow"

    412 - "Hormuz Harry"

    413 - "Lucky Louis"

    417 - "Big Bird"

The *Sea King* helicopters, being easily transferable, and because of their unique maintenance requirements, were considered a task group resource and not assigned permanently to either ship. For their operational employment, they could be directed by the air controllers aboard any of the three ships (or any qualified [NATO] allied warship). Certain of the aircraft tended to distinguish themselves in various ways, and in commenting on them, to emphasize the interchageability, the text will refer variously to their side numbers, nickname, and mother ship.

5 See Appendix E, "Airlift and Sealift in Persian Gulf Operations" for a comparison of the respective efforts.

6 Miller, "Interview," 30 March 1992.

7 WD CTG 302.3, "Multinational Intercept Operations - CATG Plans," 17 September 1990.

8 *The Guide*, p. 329.

9 Ibid.

10 *CPGW*, p. 51.

11 Commodore Kenneth J. Summers, "Operation FRICTION: A Personal Perspective," *Canada's Navy Annual 1991/92* (Corvus, 1992), p. 58.

12 WD CTG 302.3, 1 October 1990. The "Barber Pole" is the distinctive red and white funnel marking first worn by ships of the Royal Canadian Navy's renowned Escort Group C-3 in the Second World War. The marking has been worn since by the warships of various Canadian squadrons. *Athabaskan* and *Terra Nova*, both of Capt(N) Miller's First Canadian Destroyer Squadron, wore it in the Gulf. *Protecteur*, an auxiliary with no squadron affiliation, did not.

13 Lt(N) James Burrows, "Patrolling the Gulf," *Sentinel* 27, no. 6 (1990), p. 18.

14 WD CTG 302.3, "ASSESSREPs," 2 and 4 October 1990.

15 *Toronto Globe and Mail*, 2 and 5 October 1990.

16 Summers, "A Personal Perspective," p. 59.

17 General Sir Peter de la Billière, *Storm Command: A Personal Account of the Gulf War* (London: HarperCollins, 1992), pp. 155-56.

18 WD CTG 302.3, "Preps for MND Brief," 17 October 1990.

19 Paul Mooney, "Navy fit for Musuem: Canada scrounges to equip ships on gulf mission," *Ottawa Citizen*, 17 October 1990.

20 "Happiness is a warm Phalanx," *Hailfax Chronicle-Herald*, 20 September 1990.

21 *CPGW*, p. 62.

22 WD *Protecteur*, "QHM/CIO Tape for Families - 12 Oct 90," 12 October 1990.

23 DHist, HMCS *Protecteur* 1326-1 (AOR 509)(R2), 1 January 91, "Annual Historical Report [1990]."Annex D: "Fuel Information."

24 WD CTG 302.3, "First Time," 13 October 1990.

25 Friedman, *Desert Victory*, p. 72.

26 *The Guide*, p. 330. This was the first mention by the Security Council of a mediating role for Secretary-General Javier Pérez de Cuellar.

27 *The Kuwait Crisis: Basic Documents*, Cambridge International Document Series, vol. 1, ed. E. Lauterpacht, C.J. Greenwood, Marc Weller and Daniel Bethlehem (Cambridge: Grotius, 1991), p. 145.

28 Hiro, *Desert Shield to Desert Storm*, p. 229, quoting *Los Angeles Times*, 30 October 1990.

29 Ibid., p. 476, n. 44, quoting *Washington Post*, 31 October 1990.

30 WD CTG 302.3, MARCOMHQ, "OP FRICTION Phase Two Tasking Order," 17 October 1990.

31 Summers, "A Personal Perspective," p. 59.

CHAPTER 4

Operation SCIMITAR – Creation of the Canadian Air Task Group Middle East: August – November 1990

Prime ministerial press conferences are often held on Fridays, after the Cabinet has had time to consider the questions of the week during a final meeting. That had been the case on 10 August, when Operation FRICTION had been announced. And the same held true on 14 September, when Mr Mulroney revealed that a squadron of fighter aircraft would be sent to help protect the naval embargo. "From 12 to 18" CF-18 *Hornets* stationed at Canadian Forces Base Baden-Söllingen, Germany would be deployed as quickly as possible to join the Canadian ships inside the Gulf. As a result of these major decisions by the government, Canada suddenly became a full partner in the Coalition against Iraq, with naval and air forces placed in front-line roles as part of multinational formations.

However, the announcement concerning the CF-18s preceded the acquisition of a base of operations. When Cabinet met on 14 September, NDHQ and External Affairs had yet to find a suitable place near the Gulf for the squadron. They were considering Saudi Arabia, Bahrain, the United Arab Emirates, and Qatar. The countries which already had supplied air forces to the Coalition apparently were sharing all the available airport space in the region. Combat aircraft in the theatre already numbered about one thousand even before the Canadian offer, and France, Italy, and the Netherlands also were looking to establish air contingents. A systematic search was required to find an appropriate site. On 16 September, Ambassador Dickenson initiated contact with the several Gulf states to which he was accredited. Bahrain, recently accepted as the base of operations for the Canadian naval task group, was the obvious preference. On the nineteenth Dickenson travelled to Bahrain and met Brigadier-General Jean Boyle, commander of 1 Canadian Air Division in Germany, which was to provide the CF-18s, and Colonel Leach, fresh from his experience with Commodore Summers. The three men discussed practical questions about logistical support.

The week of 19-27 September was a whirlwind. Dickenson, Boyle, and Leach made many on the spot inspections. Because American and British forces already occupied the two Bahraini airports, they shifted their search elsewhere, with equally unsatisfactory results. It was only through enquiries to the Pentagon that they began searching in the right direction. Following a trip by General Boyle to CENTCOM's Air Component Headquarters in Riyadh, on 27 September, USAF staff officers offered airport space at Doha on the Qatar peninsula, provided that the Canadians accepted the fact that there were few facilities at the already crowded base. The various Canadian initiatives then converged. Ambassador Dickenson's diplomatic entreaties concentrated on the Qatari government. A formal, positive, reply was received on 29 September, and an agreement was ratified by the various Canadian, American, and Qatari parties on 1 October.

It had taken fourteen days to find an airport for the squadron of CF-18s. The 401st Tactical Fighter Wing of the USAF already had a squadron of twenty-four F-16 *Fighting Falcon* fighter-bombers located at Qatar, on a section of the field belonging to the Emirate of Qatar Air Force. With the arrival of the Canadians, the American unit would have to share the only hangar placed at its disposal. At first sight, it seemed that the Canadian squadron would have to function under canvas and the open sky. The verbal agreement of 29 September, however, was all that was needed to launch the deployment operation.

Operation SCIMITAR

One month before the Prime Minister's announcement, when the ships were being readied at Halifax, the J3 Plans cell at NDHQ had undertaken a study of the various augmentation options for Canadian participation. Sending a squadron of CF-18 fighters to the Saudi Arabia area had been overruled for the short-term, although investigation continued as a staff check. On 29 August, after the newly assembled NDHQ Battle Staff had reviewed the various SANDY SAFARI options, General Huddleston had formally ordered the commander of CFE, Major-General Brian L. Smith, to develop a plan for deploying an air contingent under the code-name SCIMITAR.

A special planning team at the Lahr headquarters, under the direction of the Deputy Commander of 1 Canadian Air Division, Colonel Philip Engstad, worked without a break to produce an advanced version for communication to NDHQ. It was ready by 7 September. Commodore Summers was unaware of these developments. Three days later, following the Bahrain naval cooperation conference, he proposed an expanded Canadian naval commitment, taking into consideration specific circumstances, including adequate air top cover. The planners at NDHQ made the obvious connection, and SCIMITAR easily fitted into Summers' framework of recommendations. An air defence role over the Gulf for the CF-18s would provide not only increased protection for the naval group but, more importantly, Canadian top cover for Canadian ships, as well as a reasonable response to the invitation recently made by Secretary of State Baker to NATO. It seems that these favourable considerations convinced the government that there was an opportunity for Canada to make what it would describe as a meaningful contribution.

Detaching a fighter squadron to a distant theatre for operational purposes was a first in the history of 1 Canadian Air Division. So was the concept of flying top cover for naval forces, although this was not far removed from the NATO continental air superiority role. It seemed as if by sleight of hand, therefore, that General Smith had a scheme for deploying a fighter squadron with support elements on the very day of the Prime Minister's announcement. To encompass the various factors, Operation SCIMITAR was divided into four parts: preparations, deployment, familiarization of the air group with the theatre of operations, and amalgamation with Operation FRICTION, which would mark the end of SCIMITAR. On 15 September, Lieutenant-General Huddleston confirmed Smith's plan and authorized Phase I, Preparations, at the national level. [1]

Preparation of the Air Task Group

Within days, the air contingent officially came to be named the "Canadian Air Task Group — Middle East (CATGME)." [2] The new formation was produced entirely by 4 Wing, the operational fighter formation at Baden-Söllingen, which immediately began the physical preparation of the mission-bound fighters. The eighteen CF-18s assigned to CATGME constituted a formation somewhat larger than a normal peacetime Canadian squadron. It therefore required an enlargement of 409 *Nighthawk*, commanded by Lieutenant-Colonel Edward D.K. Campbell, with elements of 421 *Red Indian* and 439 *Tiger* Squadrons, and of the accompanying services of 1 Air Maintenance Squadron.

The core air squadron would be reinforced by elements chosen from a large number of operational, logistical, and support units belonging to CFE's 3 Canadian Support Group (3 CSG) and the various base services located at Lahr and Baden-Söllingen. Because the aircraft were operationally ready as required by NATO, they needed little physical preparation other than ensuring that all planned maintenance was complete. Support was a different matter, however, and the initial phase included a preliminary stage of air transport to move necessary matériel forward from Canada to Lahr, where a considerable amount could be accumulated before the air group was deployed to an operational site. Between 20-24 September, Air Transport Group made twenty-two *Hercules* and *Boeing* cargo trips to Lahr, gathering the stocks necessary for a seven-day deployment phase ten days in advance of its commencement. The required equipment was primarily spare parts for the CF-18s and machine tools to augment those held by 4 Wing, and they came mainly from the bases at Bagotville and Cold Lake.

Personnel selection and training followed. Thirty-nine women were part of the Air Task Group of 550 persons. The administrative order included suggestions to help them to adapt to the customs of the Gulf Arab states. If they left the military base, they would have to wear dresses extending from the neck to the ankles, with sleeves to the wrists. They would have to be escorted in public and were warned never to offer their hand when meeting Arab men. Also, they could not drive cars. In previous years, women had been excluded from most of the operations in the Middle East because of such restrictions. Evolving policies, however, encouraged their presence in Operation FRICTION. The measures formulated in Operation SCIMITAR would be extended to servicewomen in the naval task group and other units as they deployed.

Since an operational site remained to be determined, it was referred to simply as "Desert Home" for the present. But it was possible to anticipate a number of the support needs required on arrival. An infrastructure of modular tents borrowed from 4 Canadian Mechanized Brigade Group at Lahr and packed on loading pallets was made available in the hangars. The air transport system, which had to include relay teams at strategic points along the route, was planned in as much detail as possible, and the Canadian liaison staff in London obtained permission to use the Royal Air Force base at Akrotiri, Cyprus. RAF Akrotiri was the ideal place to make a stopover. Wide landing strips, numerous military quarters, and familiar procedures made access to it extremely easy. Canadians had known Akrotiri for twenty-five years. They had made many stops there to resupply the Canadian contingent in Nicosia, along the demilitarized buffer zone between Turkish and Greek Cypriots, as well as numerous stopovers during weekly shuttles to supply Canadian personnel serving with other UN contingents, on the Golan Heights, in the Sinai, Lebanon, Jordan, and Damascus. When the transport aircraft maintenance teams arrived in Cyprus, as part of Operation SCIMITAR, the place was familiar to them.

At that time, the Akrotiri base was operating at the limit of its capacity. Foreign nations had to bring in their own heavy equipment for loading and unloading, as well as their own spare parts for minor repairs to the *Hercules* and *Boeing 707s*. They also were responsible for crew changes, co-ordination offices, and communications. Several mixed teams of professionals from Fighter and Air Transport Groups, therefore, had to be on location and functioning on the ground well before the first cargo destined for the Gulf arrived. It was also agreed with the RAF that Canadian personnel would not exceed 120 at peak periods and that the total would be maintained at under 80 after the first waves. On 17 September, selected members of Air Transport Group from all over Canada gathered in Lahr, where Colonel Engstad informed them of the plans and passed on his personal instructions in anticipation of their imminent deployment.

A similar system was needed at the end of the line. The air route had to be planned as a leapfrog. The initial flight had to cover the second, less familiar, segment of the air route, from Akrotiri to their final destination — Desert Home — somewhere in the Middle East, and to establish an Airlift Control Element (an organization better known by the acronym ALCE). ALCE is a well-known procedure, used to facilitate the arrival of air transport and fighter aircraft and to ensure the rapid establishment of services and controls needed for an air bridge. It includes specialized handling teams equipped with such things as an air-transportable truck that functions as a control tower and is set up soon after the first aircraft lands. ALCE progressively transforms itself into an air movement management organization, with an increasing array of strategic communications, mobile loading and unloading vehicles, and essential services to support the activity connected with massive arrivals of cargo. As the operation grows, some of the ALCE personnel and matériel may become part of the base. If not, they will be redeployed. The Desert Home ALCE was headed by Lieutenant-Colonel Donald G. Timperon, who on 19 September was tasked to be ready to deploy it on order in connection with SCIMITAR.

Reconnaissance

On Thursday 27 September, immediately after receiving word of the tentative agreement between the Canadian ambassador and the Qataris, a reconnaissance group boarded a plane in Lahr bound for Doha. They arrived late in the evening. The group was made up of twenty-one persons, including Colonel Engstad, who directed the reconnaissance both as head of the planning staff and as Commander-designate of the Air Group. On arrival, they were welcomed by members of the Qatari Ministry of the Interior. Despite the pressing situation, the Canadians were urged not to work the following day, the Muslim sabbath. Instead, an informal meeting was arranged with Colonel Jeremiah Nelson, USAF and his pilots of the "Four-O-One," during which the first links were formed between the aviators of the two countries. The first official visits to the Air Force Base of the Emirate of Qatar and the installations mounted by the USAF did not begin until Saturday, after the agreements in principle had been discussed between the Canadian representatives and the Qatari military and civilian officials.

Engstad's team soon reached the conclusion that their preliminary plan needed serious changes. After talking to the Americans in their camp, they concluded that accommodation under canvas would not be suitable. The tents borrowed from 4 Brigade were not of the double-walled type necessary in a desert. The Canadian equipment, designed for use in temperate northwest Europe, was not appropriate for conditions of stifling heat, constantly in excess of 40°C. Nor were there enough air conditioning systems. Sometimes it was ten degrees hotter inside single-walled tents than outside. Furthermore, the Doha authorities insisted that the number of persons living close to the airport must not exceed one hundred. Engstad succeeded in having this number increased to two hundred for a preliminary period, but he had to find accommodation for more than 350 others whom he wished to keep available for immediate recall.

Attention quickly shifted to an abandoned workers' camp about five kilometres from the future centre of Canadian operations. The Support Unit was given the task of establishing whether this place was healthy and practical and, of course, whether it could be acquired. They also had to devise a housing plan that included portable plywood cabins better known by the name Portakabin. The plan was finished in one night, and then they had to obtain a sufficient number of the cabins as quickly as possible. Meanwhile, a contract was negotiated for the production of ready-made offices and lodgings. These would replace the improvised installations with sturdier wood cells, which were easier to organize into work areas and were more insulated. The insulation made it possible to keep them at temperatures tolerable for personnel and electronic equipment. Lastly, to transform the workers' camp into a functioning military base, they needed plenty of carpenters, plumbers, and electricians. In the meantime, all personnel had to be booked into hotels in Doha during the first weeks. This was very expensive and time-consuming. The best rates were US$1,000 per person, per month, and there was a ten-kilometre shuttle from the city to the on-base locations. After living in hotels, the troops were not impressed with their new quarters, but by dint of hard work the camp became a renovated complex, personalized by simple decorations and cheerful wall frescoes, which artistic individuals painted during weeks of confinement imposed by the restrictions.

The name adopted for the facilities, "Canada Dry," was proposed to Colonel Engstad by a Qatari official who had lived in Vancouver and was familiar with the Canadian soft drink. It was a skilful play on words, intended to get the message across that "wet canteens" were not in fashion in Qatar. The pun was underscored on 11 October, when the Crown Prince of Qatar and Ambassador Dickenson celebrated the opening of the off-base quarters with a glass of ginger ale! Besides eventually providing accommodation for more than three hundred individuals, this camp, designated "Canada Dry One" (CD 1), housed the infirmary and headquarters as well as services that were difficult to establish inside the base. The two hundred who lived at the airport (their number would not diminish) came to envy the tenants of CD 1. The airport quarters, labelled Canada Dry 2, were set up in an open space about 2.5 kilometers from the runways and were much more exposed to airport noise. CD 2 housed several essential services, such as kitchens, water production, electricity, and repair services. Senior officers, pilots, the security company, and members of the ground crews were accommodated and fed there. It was built with locally purchased Portakabins (the "Canada" stamped on their imported frame timbers gave everyone great pride) and other Canadian-made material, almost every piece of which had to be transported from Germany by *Hercules* and *Boeing 707* cargo planes.

Engstad and his team had to reassess security systems, medical and crash emergency services, firefighting, and military police requirements. For instance, the original plan called for an infantry platoon to protect the perimeter. This was changed and the job was assigned to a company. Many questions had to be resolved: the scope of the engineering work; the need to lease or bring in a piece of heavy machinery; the extent of the plumbing and electricity; the levels of healthfulness desired for installations; the production of drinking water, which required a heavy piece of machinery for reverse osmosis; showers and laundries. The work of preparation increased with each new question. In the end, a complete base, one that was able to provide all the required technical functions, had to be as compact as possible.

The aircraft parking areas were dangerously laid out in an open field of sand at the end of the three-kilometre runway. The access ways for the CF-18s were insufficient and had to be widened with movable metal "Trackways." The creation of these secondary runways alone required many *Hercules* flights and drew heavily on the resources of Lahr, which until then had been rigorously reserved for NATO operations.

Deployment

Throughout the brief but intensive survey of Doha, Engstad had filed regular situation reports to his superiors, in order to allow activity in Germany to keep pace with the new developments. At 1 Air Division, preparations had been made for a base of operations in a desert setting. The information on resources available in the modern city of Doha made major savings a real possibility. Twenty *Hercules* loads were withdrawn from the original plan, when information reached Lahr that vehicles, water, and accommodation could be found in Qatar.

The times of D-Day and H-Hour for Phase 2 of Operation SCIMITAR were set. On Thursday, 4 October, at 0700, the first of a regular and uninterrupted stream of *Hercules* would take off from Lahr heading for Doha. The Akrotiri ALCE had to be operational by H-Hour, and the sole *Boeing 707* from 437 *Husky* Squadron at Trenton then available as an air-to-air refueller (AAR) was sent to the Mediterranean to assist the CF-18s, beginning 7 October. Twelve *Hercules* and two *Boeing* planes, as well as their numerous crews from Air Transport Group, were freed from various tasks across Canada and gathered at Lahr for the deployment. In an intricate deployment program progressing by three-hour intervals, starting at H-Hour, the pieces of the puzzle were put in place: some would stay at Akrotiri, others go to Doha, and still others carry out a continuous back-and-forth shuttle. They did not stop other than to reload matériel. Pilots and crews in rotation replaced each other at one point or another on the route according to their flying-hour limits. The air bridge lasted ten days and finally totalled seventy-nine *Hercules* and *Boeing* loads, for a sum of 700 tonnes of matériel and nearly 600 passengers.

On 7 October, it was the turn of the CF-18s to make the crossing. Under the command of Lieutenant-Colonel Campbell, eight aircraft formed the first wave to reach Akrotiri, with the help of the AAR *Boeing*, which refuelled them over Italy. Two aircraft had to stop at the American military base at Sigonella, Sicily, but they continued some hours later. The next day, they all took off from Akrotiri for Doha. The route from Cyprus, which would be followed by almost all the Canadian aircraft thereafter, passed close to Alexandria, then followed the Red Sea on the Egyptian side to just north of Medina, where the aircraft then headed east over the interior of Saudi Arabia, straight for Bahrain and Qatar. They were accompanied on all stages by the *Boeing* tanker (and later by in-flight refuellers provided by allied forces, which acted as service stations for the heavy air traffic along this route).

The morning of Monday, 8 October, the first CF-18s touched down at Qatar, twenty-three days after the prime minister's announcement. Two more waves of CF-18s crossed in the same way; first six, then four aircraft left Lahr at intervals on 10 October, arriving at Doha on the eleventh and twelfth.

Command and Control of the Air Group

As the search for a Desert Home was still in progress, Brigadier-General Boyle took a *Challenger* to Riyadh on Wednesday, 26 September. He wanted to discuss the arrival and employment of the Canadian squadron within the Coalition. Returning to Lahr, on the twenty-eighth, he sent recommendations to NDHQ concerning the command and control arrangements which he had discussed the previous day with Lieutenant-General Charles C. Horner, the United States Air Force Commander of CENTAF, the Air Force Component of Central Command.

General Boyle reported that the Canadians were received in Riyadh with a great deal of enthusiasm. The head of General Schwarzkopf's air force proposed that the CF-18s should become part of the Coalition's air forces immediately and that, since their mission was to protect the Canadian ships, they should operate from the Dhahran sector, where air patrol circuits were shared by the American, British, and Saudi air forces. Dhahran was a familiar operational setting, one in which their experience within NATO would be appreciated. After Boyle's visit to CENTAF HQ, it became clear that the CF-18s of 1 Canadian Air Division would be closely linked to the other Coalition air forces and share air defence missions covering the penetration axes along which Iraqi attackers threatened the multinational fleet in the Gulf. It was proposed as well that the Canadians establish themselves in Riyadh to be within reach of the CENTAF Operations Centre and that they take part in the process of assigning missions. France, Italy, and Great Britain also indicated their intention to set up their headquarters in Riyadh in order to have representation on the American planning teams. Boyle further suggested the assignment of three liaison officers to CENTAF headquarters, where their work would be very similar to what they had been doing in Europe.

Boyle's official message on the state of the Canadian deployment was sent as soon as he returned to Lahr. It was the first report obtained from a Canadian military source on the activities at General Schwarzkopf's headquarters in Riyadh, a full seven weeks after it was set up. [3]

Boyle's message was followed by one from Summers. Because everyone had concentrated on maritime interception operations, the subject of air-sea coordination had not rated high among the many priorities before the naval task group staff. However, having been appointed commander-designate of all Canadian Forces in the Gulf region, the commodore had become very interested in the conduct of such operations. Happily, he had at hand an up-and-running model, in the form of the Marine Corps fighters flying cover for the US Navy ships in the central Gulf, orchestrated from the flagships *Blue Ridge* and *LaSalle*. Given that the CF-18s would provide air defence to the warships enforcing the blockade, Summers came to the conclusion that a Canadian Forces version of the USN model would be easy to achieve and consistent with government policy. He therefore argued that the Air Task Group should be attached not to CENTAF, as proposed by Horner and Boyle, but to the naval air elements of Admiral Mauz's NAVCENT, which were employed in air defence immediately over the fleet. [4]

The CF-18s were the same aircraft as the *Hornets* used by the air arms of the US Navy and Marine Corps, and Doha was perfect for access to the patrol circuits under naval air control. Summers' plan was coherent. It had numerous advantages for increasing the co-ordination and logistical support of the forces, and it respected the wishes of the Canadian government. The naval and air forces could be attached to the multinational Coalition and intervene under the aegis of the United Nations. His plan encompassed the maintenance of the embargo, the protection of the fleet, and the cohesion of Canadian forces. It brought together the Canadian military forces in an easily identifiable fashion, under a mandate promulgated by the Security Council resolutions. It now became easier to work out a command and control doctrine in a situation that was totally new in the annals of Canadian operations.

When the Canadian CF-18s arrived at Doha on 8 October, they did not directly join the other Coalition air forces. They were attached instead to NAVCENT, and then Admiral Mauz assigned the squadron to Rear-Admiral Fogarty. Thus Fogarty was entrusted with the tactical employment of the two Canadian elements in the Gulf: Captain Miller's Task Group 302.3 and Colonel Engstad's CATGME. The commanders of the Canadian groups retained operational control, the authority to accept or reject, in consultation with their Canadian superiors, operational missions within the multinational force. They had to refer to national authority for any substantial change of mission.

Fogarty's USS *LaSalle* was specifically designed for the role of flagship. She was equipped with very sophisticated communications and an efficient staff, allowing her to coordinate the work of all the international elements in the Coalition placed under her control for the interception of merchant ships. The central staff divided up the responsibilities for operational sectors in accordance with a plan worked out in consultation, and they assigned the air defence Combat Air Patrol (CAP) stations providing top cover for the interdiction force. The air defence missions were part of the technical responsibility of the *Aegis* class anti-air cruiser USS *Antietam*, or in her absence the older but updated USS *England*. The staffs on board these ships exercised tactical control over the tasks of the American naval air squadrons, the air units of the US Marine Corps, and now the Canadians. [5]

The Canadian air force officers saw themselves in a setting dominated by sailors. General Boyle, who had recommended the link with CENTAF, accepted the one with NAVCENT, although his airmen would have preferred to be attached to CENTAF for professional reasons. The operational centres for the patrol sectors, the communications, the USAF tactical circuits — all were exactly what the pilots had known in Europe. Naval air operations, however, with their traditions centred on moving airports and unusual procedures, which had never been used very much by Canadians, brought with them a number of unforeseeable elements. The challenge was a sizable one for all the Coalition air forces, but they immediately recognized the extraordinary flexibility of the Canadians — a flexibility which they attributed to the unification of our forces, without being very familiar with its features.

The act of separating the operational control of the NAVCENT air forces from that of CENTAF was driven by inter-service conflicts linked to questions of tradition and prestige. Unification of the Canadian Forces had brought the sea, air, and land branches together, at least in name, twenty-five years before. But other countries' services, with forces often considerably larger and more than one operational tradition, did not take lightly the command and control arrangements which they had developed over the years. Consequently, CENTAF and NAVCENT were obliged to reach an uneasy compromise: the airspace over land would be under the control of the commander of the air component of the Coalition forces, while that over water, including the Persian Gulf itself, would be controlled by naval headquarters.

Nonetheless, a very close coordination was set up between these spheres of responsibility. [6] It was agreed that the single coordination centre of all air missions would be CENTAF, where a very sophisticated system of command, control, communications, and consultation (the C-Four, in military jargon) made possible the daily issuing of an operations order containing all the theatre's air missions. ATOs (Air Tasking Orders) assigned individual tasks to each of the 1,800 combat aircraft, including those of the naval forces. Of this number, 1,000 were for offensive missions and 800 were for air defence. [7] The Tactical Air Control Center, the Riyadh TACC, established in the Saudi Air Force headquarters, brought together representatives from each of the participating air forces in an arrangement which vaguely resembled that of a symphony orchestra. The representatives were the instrumentalists, so to speak. They sat at separate tables in a semicircle, each working at a computer, all eyes on the conductor standing on the circular stage in the middle of the room. This was where the major briefings were given, aided by two large video screens and the latest graphics and animation software. These screens were linked directly to all the main integrated systems of deployed radars. Twice a day, for what soldiers traditionally call "prayers," general meetings allowed each representative of the many staffs present to express ideas. Other basement rooms were occupied by refuelling co-ordinators, bombing analysts, intelligence cells, and other technical offices. One room was the top secret "black hole," where CENTAF prepared plans, based on intelligence, for future air missions.

The ATOs were issued electronically from this central headquarters, going out with clockwork regularity to all the operational units, who then discovered their respective and often very intertwined parts in what came to be called music sheets. The Canadian Air Group also received missions from CENTAF HQ, but only after they had been proposed to NAVCENT through Admiral Fogarty's USS *LaSalle*. Then they were routed to CENTAF's naval cell at Riyadh and integrated into the daily ATO plan, which made each mission official and adapted it to the overall context.

The small Canadian segment of CENTAF's operational orders also could be adjusted by a parallel communications network. When General Boyle visited Riyadh, he immediately saw that the established chain of communications was much too long to react quickly to needs at any level. Thanks to his recommendations, three Canadian liaison officers arrived in Riyadh on 2 October and took up positions on the international staff. Their installation at CENTAF made it possible to short-circuit the routing and allow those at both ends of the command structure to be informed faster and to react more quickly to national and operational needs. However, this direct but informal network remained subordinate to the formal Riyadh-*Blue Ridge-La Salle*-Manamah-Doha network.

CENTAF HQ was a place of feverish activity. The three Canadian officers were the primary contacts for the Air Task Group commander at Doha, assuring him that he was adequately represented during the staff conferences which distributed flight tasks in cooperation with the delegates from each country.

The Doha Base

The air group continued to report to Major-General Smith for the whole of Phase 3 of Operation SCIMITAR. Colonel Engstad therefore remained directly linked to a national commander in Germany and under him to Brigadier-General Boyle, the Commander of 1 Canadian Air Division. General Smith answered directly to General de Chastelain, Chief of Defence Staff, in Ottawa, in a manner parallel to Admiral George in Halifax, who had the same chain-of-command relationship with de Chastelain.

To make the whole system function properly, there had to be a solid foundation and a powerful infrastructure. Colonel Engstad spent his first weeks at

Doha lining up his personnel and installing his equipment so that they could operate at full power. His service unit was the main element for moving the work forward. Lieutenant-Colonel Garry Furrie's Canadian Support Unit (Qatar) (CSU[Q]) included second- and third-echelon supply. These echelons normally were provided at the base level and not integrated into the squadron. Furrie's unit contained various cells, such as transport, supply, finance, administration, medical services, and construction engineering services. These were added to the technical sections of 409 Squadron, which specialized in the immediate servicing of aircraft and fighter squadron personnel.

Furrie juggled priorities to establish Canada Dry 1 and 2 and an operations centre. Towards the end of October, he succeeded in emptying the Sheraton Gulf Hotel in Doha of Canadian personnel and bringing the teams close to their place of work. This was done progressively, week by week, while the engineers worked hard to meet a myriad of unexpected challenges. Borrowing heavy equipment from their American and Qatari neighbours, they layed foundations, built tracks and roads, and canalized waterways. They also took delivery of several dozen prefabricated accommodation cabins and erected them in order of priority.

The security of personnel in all emplacements outside the base had to be established. A 118-man infantry company — M (Mike) Company of the 3rd Battalion, Royal Canadian Regiment (RCR), from 4 Brigade in Lahr — was barely sufficient for the task. It dug defensive positions, erected fences and observation posts, and placed guards around the perimeter to control access to the base. The unit's war diary relates that the company stacked tens of thousands of sandbags and used more than five hundred rolls of barbed wire during the two months of installation. Because aircraft were not in fortified shelters, their protection posed a constant problem, necessitating continuous nighttime patrols and checks. Four *Grizzly* vehicles were brought from Canada. Armoured, armed, and fast, they were the envy of neighbours faced with similar problems. Soon, however, they were put at the service of an integrated allied patrol team. This economized the security resources of Doha Air Base.

Communications were also established in successive stages. Unfortunately, the Qatar Telephone Company took several weeks to lay its lines, and the long-range, high-frequency (HF) radio equipment brought from Canada was not equal to the task. Moreover, the volume of transmissions — military and political, Canadian and UN, and even international information relays — exceeded everyone's wildest predictions. If transmission capabilities were to be multiplied, they would have to use commercial or military satellite networks. When satellite communications systems were finally in place, and the volume of communications on all networks reached a desirable level, at the beginning of December, stability was achieved. CATGME was now ready to fulfil its obligations and occupy its rightful place within the Coalition. Other problems, though, delayed its full integration into air operations: establishing secure voice communications and fitting the Canadian CF-18s with unique naval equipment, such as Link-4 (ship-to-aircraft computer communications).

Flying Operations

With some allowance for reserves, the first group of twenty-seven pilots were divided into teams of four, sharing patrol responsibilities two aircraft at a time. Beginning on 9 October, the first pilots to arrive made familiarization flights along with Qatari Air Force *Alpha Jets*. These trials were followed up on the tenth by progressively more successful missions. Meanwhile, the pilots of 409 Squadron were busy learning the importance of the air component headquarters in Riyadh, despite the fact that they had a direct link with the cruiser *Antietam* in the Gulf. They remained in radio contact with this ship during all air missions. The network was complex and communications were extremely sophisticated.

The territorial air defense theatre of Saudi Arabia and its neighbours was divided into five overland sectors. These grouped together many defensive patrol circuits, which were occupied at all times by Coalition air force aircraft. There were also circuits occupied by the air forces of the US Navy and the US Marines. From a sector of operations in the northwest, they controlled access to the entire Gulf and to individual ships. All these circuits were supported by fleets of air refuellers, especially KC-135s and KC-10s of the USAF, KC-130s of the US Marines and VC-10s of the Royal Air Force. The fighters could could hook up to any of these in case of need. AWACS electronic surveillance aircraft and air operations control ground stations in particular sectors also had sophisticated radars, making it possible to establish a deep or vertical electronic surveillance screen.

All the US Navy's overwater circuits were within reach of Doha. They had the code-name Whiskey, derived from the radiophonic code for the letter "W", denoting their naval character. The first naval air defence circuits over the Gulf were positions Whiskey-1, Whiskey-2, and Whiskey-3, placed respectively at the north, centre, and south of the Persian Gulf (see MIF Operations map of the Gulf area). The Whiskey-2 circuit was tactically less important than Whiskey-1, because it was much farther from the borders of Iraq, but it covered in depth the area southeast of Kuwait and the Iranian shore on the east, where incursions were still possible during the first months of the Coalition's presence. The Whiskey-3 circuit, at the south of the Gulf, was in practice never taken over: it was drawn on the map for use in case of a deep enemy incursion, which was improbable but theoretically possible. It was easy to move each circuit according to the requirements of the naval controller, who communicated its centre and radius, and any other aircraft movements, either by voice radio or Link-4. Indeed, these patrol areas would be multiplied and progressively relocated as the tactical situation evolved.

As a secondary circuit, located in the centre of the Gulf, Whiskey-2 was used to initiate all new pilots to naval air operations. It had boundaries closer to Bahrain, above the naval interdiction sectors of Captain Miller's group. The progressive assumption of responsibility for Whiskey-2 during the month of October established a de facto Canadian occupation of the central Gulf.

Patrolling with the Canadians were the Marines of the 3rd MAW (Marine Air Wing). They operated with forty-eight F/A-18s from the Sheikh Isa base in Bahrain. To get to know their American teammates better, a delegation from the Canadian Air Group went to Bahrain on 12 October to discuss with them procedures and differences of equipment. Relations were cordial and some officers even knew each other from past exercises or courses taken together over the years. This was the case with Engstad. His opposite number, Colonel Manfred Risch, had been the operations officer at the US Navy's "Top Gun" Fighter Weapons School at Miramar, California, when Engstad attended it in 1977. After the Canadians had demonstrated to the coordinator of the multinational interdiction forces that they could respond adequately to enemy incursions, they were invited to take a regular part in the Whiskey-1 circuit, towards the end of October. Pairs of CF-18s did tours of duty there. At first they were accompanied by Marine Corps F/A-18s. By the end of November, however, they were on their own. At that point they had to be perfectly trained in air refuelling procedures. This was not easy for a variety of reasons, but mainly because there were many different types of tankers, some of them with nozzles incompatible with the CF-18's equipment. Pilots also had to become familiar with the operational terms and concepts of air controllers, both at sea and on land. The matter of communications was vitally important if Canadians were to gain access to the first lines of defence. Only the progressive adoption of compatible naval air systems would enable them to exercise fully their functions as defenders of the fleet.

The first encouraging news came very quickly. On 14 October, during their initial manoeuvres on the Whiskey-2 circuit, the on-station pair of Canadian pilots received a message from *Antietam* that two Iraqi jets had crossed the established warning corridor and ventured out over the sea off occupied Kuwait. This was unusual behaviour for the Iraqis, who were probably trying to assess their chances of piercing the naval defence system. The Canadians pursued the aircraft, which turned back fifteen kilometres outside their border. The CF-18 team reported the response and resumed their position, passing by the closest tanker to continue their training. The staff in *LaSalle*, following the action on radar, broke silence to congratulate the pilots for their initiative with a "Way to go, Canada!"

The Canadians, still on patrol in Whiskey-2, blocked several other attempts at Iraqi penetration beyond the warning corridor during the coming weeks of October. Their quick reactions and efficient work satisfied the air controller in USS *Antietam*, to the point where they were considered ready to replace the Marines.

For their part, the Marines were given some rest on the Whiskey-1 position, and, from that time on, they spent more time training for air-to-ground manoeuvres in preparation for a full-scale ground war.

In addition, the Canadian pilots refined quick reaction scramble techniques, in which aircraft on the ground were kept ready for launch the instant an order was received from the multinational naval force. On 7 November, the squadron was assigned the task of protecting the aircraft carrier USS *Midway* during its first entry into the Gulf. Since naval air operations were not permitted while transiting the Strait of Hormuz, the carrier was unable to provide its own top cover for the passage. The Canadian *Hornets* then were assigned CAP stations above the western approaches to the Strait until *Midway* was clear and could launch her own aircraft.

The period from mid-October to mid-December was one of tactical operational training, gradually increasing in complexity. Canadian pilots collaborated with the forces of Qatar, France (whose *Mirage* fighters also were based at Doha), Great Britain, and Saudi Arabia, as well as with the US Navy, Marine Corps, and Air Force. Formation flying was conducted with other Coalition aircraft. Many procedures were practised, including Rules of Engagement (ROE), which sometimes varied significantly from country to country and even between services. An attempt was made to standardize these rules among the Coalition air forces, but an investigation conducted by the United States Air Force after the Gulf War showed that major differences existed even between the USAF and the United States Navy on this point and were only settled by recourse to General Schwarzkopf's central authority, on 11 January 1991, a few days before the start of offensive air operations.[8]

When General Boyle visited the Doha base on 5 November, he was impressed with the changes. The Air Task Group was all set for operational command to be handed over to Commodore Summers, whose headquarters finally commenced operations on the sixth. Fifty-three days after the prime minister's announcement, Operation SCIMITAR came to an end, and the Air Task Group — Middle East became an integral part of Operation FRICTION.

Notes

1 WD NDHQ, DCDS, "Warning Order - OP SCIMITAR", 15 September 1990, gave instructions to prepare a squadron of 18 CF-18 aircraft to be sent to an unknown destination in the Middle East, in accordance with HQ CFE's plan. Specifically, it warned ATG of the need for 12 CC-130 *Hercules*, one CC-137 cargo/passenger *Boeing* and one *Boeing* tanker, which would be dedicated exclusively to Operation SCIMITAR on order.

2 The phrase "Air Task Group" is a designation without precedence in military nomenclature, "task group" being a uniquely naval designation. Its precise origins in this instance are difficult to pinpoint, but apparently they arose from a combination of factors, including the desire to tie the rationale for dispatch of the air contingent to the mission of the naval task group and to reinforce the novel concept of joint operations.

3 WD CFE, COMD 051, "CENTAF Visit Riyadh - 27 Sep 90 - OP SCIMITAR," 28 September 1990.

4 WD CTG 302.3, "Briefing Note on Canadian CF-18 Operations in the Persian Gulf Region," 29 September 1990.

5 The Marine air forces were established in the Bahraini military airport of Sheikh Isa. At that date, 3 Marine Air Wing had four F/A-18 squadrons, with a total of 48 *Hornets*. 3 MAW was eventually augmented to seven F/A-18 squadrons by the beginning of hostilities. Up to January 1991, the Hornet squadrons performed combat air patrols in a fleet defence role. No USN carriers (with their embarked air wings) were as yet on regular station within the Persian Gulf, although *Independence* (soon replaced by *Midway*) was available nearby in the Arabian Sea. During the next months the *Midway* would make an increasing number of forays into the Gulf.

6 Obviously these arrangements were not so simple. They are summarized here because it is not necessary to weigh down the discussion in technical complications, which only indirectly affected Canadian operations. For further discussion of this and other Coalition air-related subjects, see *CPGW;* Thomas A. Keaney and Eliot A. Cohen, *Gulf War Air Power Survey - Summary Report* (Washington, DC: US Government Printing Office, 1993) [hereafter cited as *GWAPS*]; Richard P. Hallion, *Storm Over Iraq: Air Power and the Gulf War* (Washington, DC: Smithsonian Institution, 1992); and James A. Winnefeld, Preston Niblack, and Dana J. Johnson, *A League of Airmen: U.S. Air Power in the Gulf War* (Santa Monica, Calif.: Rand Project Air Force, 1994).

7 The ATO for the daily operational tasks would include the codes, frequencies, authorizations, routes, and complete details of the operational teams and missions which each combat aircraft would join. This system could co-ordinate up to 3,000 missions per day. Although the US Navy and US Marine Corps had additional coordination mechanisms for their own forces, the ATOs, which formed a daily message of some 200 pages, were the only official documents which authorized air missions within the theatre. A fixed-wing aircraft could not leave the ground within the theatre of operations if it had not been authorized to do so in the ATOs. The only major exception to this rule was in the case of the Air Forces involved in PROVEN FORCE in Turkey. This force was assigned its own separate sector of operations in the northwest of Iraq. Since it was a single, mixed squadron accommodated at a single location (Encirlik), its coordination problems were much easier to resolve.

8 *GWAPS,* p. 153.

CHAPTER 5

Operation ACCORD – Creation of the Headquarters of the Canadian Forces, Middle East (HQ CANFORME): September – November 1990

Concept of Joint Command

While the naval and air groups received national attention, having been announced by Prime Minister Mulroney himself, the creation of a headquarters to supervise them garnered little publicity. Of course, there was no attempt or even need to hide its existence, but any mention of headquarters and staffing procedures generally fails to excite the imagination. Indeed, notice of the establishment of a headquarters for the newly formed Canadian Forces — Middle East (HQ CANFORME) was given in a standard DND press release and promptly ignored by the media. [1] This headquarters, however, was anything but ordinary.

In the fall of 1990, "joint" was the buzz-word on the tongues of military officers everywhere, including Canada. The concept was not a new one. It required the different elements of a nation's armed forces — army, navy, air force, marines, or whatever — to work in combination, rather than separately, to achieve a military objective. Between wars, however, the concept generally languished because inter-service rivalry for scarce defence dollars tended to heighten the differences between the elements. The Canadian unification experiment was intended, among other things, to address this very issue by integrating all elements in one common function. To this point, it has not been a success.

The Americans, on the other hand, had institutionalized a joint warfare system — the J-Staff — in peacetime. Now, General Schwarzkopf's Central Command, with its Army, Navy, Air Force, and Marine Components, was accordingly the first joint command to be operationally deployed and was a model for others to emulate. In mid-September, when Prime Minister Thatcher announced the expansion of the British commitment, she added that the individual service deployments would be combined into one operation, code-named GRANBY, to be run from a Joint Headquarters (JHQ) in England. An in-theatre commander, General Sir Peter de la Billière, subsequently was appointed to liaise with Central Command headquarters in Riyadh.

In Canada, the J-Staff had been utilized within NDHQ to help manage the twin crises which had arisen in August. The standoff at Oka finally ended when the last of the Mohawk holdouts surrendered on 26 September. As the army began its withdrawal and Operation SALON wound down, politicians and senior officers in Ottawa turned their full attention to the Kuwait crisis. The ships were about to commence operations in the central Persian Gulf, and a squadron of CF-18s stood ready to deploy from West Germany, awaiting only the identification of a suitable operating site. To date, operations FRICTION and SCIMITAR had proceeded as independent undertakings of Maritime Command and Canadian Forces Europe. The time seemed appropriate to consider coordinating the growing national commitment to the Middle East.

As soon as General de Chastelain received official word to send 409 Squadron to Doha, he announced details of the operational concept that would guide the linking of the Canadian Forces in the Persian Gulf theatre. This message, sent from NDHQ on 27 September, established the principle that all Canadian elements in the region would be placed under the authority of a single Commander, Canadian Forces — Middle East (CANFORCOMME). This general officer would be given operational command (OPCOM) of naval and air groups and all other Canadian units in the area and would be served by a joint headquarters, which would coordinate all activities under his command in order to ensure as exactly as possible the execution of Canadian policies. [2]

The territorial responsibility of headquarters covered the area bounded by the Special Duty Area theatre of operations, defined for Operation FRICTION in the Order-in-Council issued a few days earlier for the naval task group. Thus, the command did not include the Canadian troops serving in peacekeeping missions in Israel and her Arab neighbours. The responsibilities of HQ CANFORME were limited to the troops involved in the operations connected with the liberation of Kuwait.

This message from the CDS was followed the next day by a warning order from his Deputy, notifying the Commands of the main aspects of Operation ACCORD and the setting up of the joint headquarters. [3] While Operation SCIMITAR had been in preparation since 25 August, Operation ACCORD came to life with this message from General Huddleston on 28 September.

Detailed planning therefore had to follow this first warning. Those responsible had to choose the headquarters unit and staff, find them a location to become established, ensure communications and logistical support (communications are particularly important for headquarters), and transport them. A planning conference was set for Tuesday, 3 October, in Ottawa, at which all the Commands were to be represented. As local commander of Operation FRICTION, Commodore Summers was instructed to return to Ottawa within the next few days, just when his three ships were about to begin patrol operations. In his order, General de Chastelain actually appointed Summers the Commander-designate of CANFORME. It was generally accepted that the new headquarters would be set up during October, somewhere in the Middle East, probably at Riyadh, Manamah, or Doha. The remaining details — essentially everything else — had to be discussed in Ottawa in light of the recommendations coming from all quarters, and important decisions had to be made concerning the modus operandi of the joint Canadian air and sea forces in the Persian Gulf operations.

While the staffs in NDHQ scrambled for a plan to flesh out the conceptual edicts from the CDS and DCDS, there was no shortage of advice from the senior members of the air force and the navy most likely to be affected by the consequences. Fresh from his visit to Riyadh, General Boyle made three recommendations concerning his proposal for the control of the CF-18s in concert with CENTAF: one, a national commander should play a part within the higher command of the Coalition at Riyadh; two, Canadian headquarters should be located in Riyadh, if this were politically possible; and three, the Canadian Embassay in Saudi Arabia should support the commander in his dealings with other Coalition commanders. "It is my opinion," he added with conviction, "that the national joint commander would benefit greatly from being located at Riyadh. This location would provide a capability of immediately contacting the other commanders to assure the success of the mission."[4]

His message was quickly overtaken by a counter-proposal from Commodore Summers. He had spent the hours since his nomination as joint commander studying the USN model of air-sea cooperation, as well as the command relationship of NAVCENT in Bahrain with CENTCOM and CENTAF in Riyadh. He suggested that the Canadian theatre commander coordinate the scheduling of both fleet and air operations, using *Protecteur*, with her expanded command and control operations centre, as flagship alongside in Manamah. From Manamah it would be easier to coordinate Canadian efforts with the rest of the naval forces, whose major centres were not at Riyadh but on board the American ships moored in the harbour of the Bahraini capital. He could be assisted by a small liaison staff attached to CENTAF headquarters in Riyadh.[5]

Several ground-breaking decisions were made at NDHQ during the course of 3-5 October. Representatives from all Commands discussed command and control issues in a very detailed manner. They quickly agreed that the core of a land forces communications unit and a mixed, navy-air force staff would form a joint Headquarters located ashore. The communications unit was ad hoc. It was an integral part of headquarters and provided support to it, taking the shape of a type of Signals Squadron that was attached to an army brigade headquarters, but it was restructured considerably to adapt it to the particular circumstances of the mission. By 7 October, the preliminary organizational planning was complete. The inaugural date for HQ CANFORME was set for three weeks later — 28 October.

Creation of a Unit

The first stage of Operation ACCORD was selection of a location. This time (in contrast to SCIMITAR) the search was directed towards a site known in advance:

Manamah. The Bahraini government gave its agreement in principle as soon as the suggestion was made by Commodore Summers on 28 September. Visits by several Canadians to Bahrain after the beginning of the month had made Manamah a relatively familiar place. This facilitated planning for requirements. The Manamah site was confirmed during the first days of October. The main reason for its selection was that the American commander of the Multinational Interception Force, of which Canada was a member, was established in the Bahraini port. *Protecteur*, however, could not hope to house the envisioned JHQ.

Following the NDHQ deliberations, a unit of 160 persons was pieced together. Responsibility for supporting it was shared among all the Commands, mainly Mobile Command and the land elements of Communications Command, which between them provided 60 percent of the personnel and almost all the equipment. However, the staff was formed of naval and air force officers and supplied in large part by NDHQ and Maritime and Air Commands. Personnel from ninety-three different units began to gather at CFB Kingston on 13 October.

The new unit was named 90 Headquarters and Signals Squadron (90 HQ & Sigs).[6] Command was given to Major Simon Arcand, a Communications and Electronics Engineer officer, who until then had been commanding a static communications squadron at CFB Shilo in Manitoba. His deputy, Captain Vernon E. Hayes, led the Support Troop of 1 Canadian Signals Regiment in Kingston. He was recalled in haste from an exercise in Germany to coordinate the complex preparation plan. Personnel, radios, and vehicles had to be brought from many locations, some of which were at the other end of the country, and it fell to Captain Hayes and the Squadron Sergeant-Major, Chief Warrant Officer C.M. Gropp, to ensure integration into a coherent and ready unit. The task was formidable. During this time, Major Arcand went with the reconnaissance group to ascertain what could be used in Bahrain and to report any additional details that might be useful for the preparations in progress.

Reconnaissance

The reconnaissance group, which arrived in Manamah just before mid-October, assembled the key personnel who would be under the direction of Commodore Summers. Flying in from Canada were his Deputy Commander and Chief of Staff, Colonel Roméo H. Lalonde, from the Headquarters of NORAD's Canadian Region, in North Bay; the Deputy Chief of Staff for Operations, Commander Jean-Yves Forcier (formerly of the TG 302.3 staff on board HMCS *Athabaskan*), who followed Summers ashore; the Deputy Chief of Staff for Support, Lieutenant-Colonel John N. Stuart, from NDHQ transport operations; and Major Arcand.

The members of the reconnaissance party reached Manamah on different dates, according to each one's availability, but they were all on hand to start work on location by Sunday, 14 October. This advance group had to prepare for the arrival of the main body of staff and troops, due to fly in a week later, on the twenty-first. As

Stuart and Arcand tracked down the disparate elements that had to be put together to set up suitable working surroundings, they were assisted by Commander Banks of CANMARLOGDET, who had been working out of the city's Holiday Inn for the past three weeks. Although too small to perform all of the headquarters support functions, the Logistics Detachment was able to give knowledgeable advice on the services available in the capital of Bahrain and the other large modern cities of the Gulf coast.

Colonel Lalonde had to establish the modus operandi of the headquarters with Commander Forcier, his operations deputy, in order to make a quick determination of resource requirements. They had to make a detailed plan of the required communications networks and establish standard operating procedures. There were few precedents on which to draw. Canadian Forces had never applied such a concept and had little experience in setting up a joint operational headquarters. During the Second World War, General Harry Crerar, who commanded the First Canadian Army in Northwest Europe, never commanded naval or air forces. Only well into the war did the Royal Canadian Navy and Air Force establish what was then called a "combined" headquarters in Halifax, to prosecute the anti-submarine war in the Canadian Northwest Atlantic, but by then the focus of the Canadian war effort had shifted away from that particular theatre. In Korea (the historical example to which all eyes turned in the present instance), there had been no question of a joint service HQ, and the Commander of 25 Canadian Infantry Brigade had functioned within the context of a Commonwealth (Army) Division.

Nor were the postwar Canadian naval and fighter air forces linked by a common operational command. Within NATO, the forces of each army were separated into international commands, leaving Canada with few opportunities to act independently in a joint operational headquarters. The Commander, Canadian Forces Europe was not an operational commander because, in accordance with the arrangements made with NATO, the Canadian air and ground forces were formally attached to NATO operational formations and were to be controlled by them in the event of a battle.

As a result, a few officers, none of whom had much experience, had a variety of subjects to master: the definition of permanent responsibilities; the administration of logistics, finance, transport, supply, and personnel services; the place of technical and legal advice and the role of public affairs (which had taken on increased importance in recent years); and communications — internal, theatre, and strategic — with their multiple networks and different methods, capabilities, addressees, and classification levels, as well as their various rates of speed, which were often applied to a single element. The officers had to make decisions which taxed available resources and required equipment not always familiar to the members of the staff. The structure of the headquarters was sketched out in Ottawa, leaving room for any necessary adjustments during the days leading up to the departure of the troops from Kingston. Ultimately, however, everything came back to Lalonde and Forcier. The responsibility for planning rested heavily on these two men. They barely knew each other before 3 October. Now they had to "invent the wheel" in sixteen days. [7]

Colonel Engstad visited Manamah on 14 October for Commodore Summers' first meeting and reported on the progress achieved by the air task group, which had just arrived at Doha. He also took part in the discussion on the various ways of functioning. Lieutenant-Colonel Clarke Little, who had been Liaison Officer with CENTAF HQ in Riyadh for a week, informed the Canadian officers of allied procedures in the major headquarters.

Visit to Doha

On 15 October, Lalonde and Stuart took a commercial flight to Doha. There they saw first-hand that conditions were much more demanding than at Manamah. While the capital of Bahrain was a cosmopolitan and modern city, passably open to cultural and commercial exchanges, Qatar's capital was insular and isolated. Its population of 200,000 was nearly double that of Manamah, but only the international circles reflected an advanced degree of modernity. Also, Doha's requirements in national logistics would be much heavier than those of the Manamah headquarters.

After their visit with the air task group, Lalonde and Stuart were encouraged. They realized that their problems, at least as far as the erection of infrastructure was concerned, were much less serious than those faced in Doha. Their quick trip allowed them to exchange ideas with the people who had created fair living and working conditions for the air group. It was a tour de force, accomplished with very little in the way of local resources. Lalonde and Stuart came back from Qatar convinced that their plans were justified.

They also realized that travelling by commercial aircraft between Doha, Manamah, and Riyadh should have been easy but was made difficult by the Gulf countries themselves. All of them required military personnel travelling by civilian aircraft to obtain individual visas to go from one country to another. Obtaining those visas was a long and cumbersome process. To facilitate these liaison visits, Commodore Summers asked NDHQ for a military plane. It was a reasonable request, but an aircraft was hard to come by when the largest air transport effort in many years was in progress. Still, on 21 October, the DCDS ordered a CC-144 *Challenger* from 414 *Black Knight* Squadron (Fighter Group, North Bay) to serve as a command and liaison aircraft at Manamah.

Preparations in Manamah

Lieutenant-Colonel Stuart was delegated the task of setting up in Manamah. He had to be especially concerned with the physical arrangements. He needed working space for approximately 120 persons. His first move, on Saturday 13 October, was to find a local commercial agent who knew the area and could help establish contacts with Bahraini firms. These contacts would be involved in negotiating purchases and contracts. Stuart had the naval task group lawyer, Lieutenant-Commander John Maguire, help him draw up the contracts and assess the legal consequences of the transactions with local authorities. Maguire was involved in each new contract, carefully scrutinizing unfamiliar terms. As well, he had to help formalize the agreement on the status of Canadian forces in Bahrain, a document which seemed to become more complicated each time it was considered.

When Lalonde and Stuart returned from Doha on Tuesday, 16 October, the agent, Mr Rishi K. Trivedi, gave an account of the inquiries which he had made the previous day. Trivedi was a service representative for the Grey-Mackenzie Group, a large multinational shipping firm specializing in port services in the Gulf area. He presented options, some of which were quickly eliminated. Stuart and Maguire, as well as Lalonde and Forcier when they were available, already had visited some buildings that were for rent and ready for occupation, but they had made no specific recommendation. Next, they inspected a small two-storey building in the port area of Manamah. It was an uninviting place at first glance but it proved appropriate. The building was neglected and very dirty. It was in urgent need of maintenance and "hot as hell" under the October sun. But the premises were spacious and well divided. With a good cleaning and some painting, the appropriate furniture, and the installation of ventilation systems, it would make an excellent headquarters. Summers was particularly impressed by the fact that the building was near the harbour, in a quiet corner bordered by other commercial establishments and next to an accessible wharf, which could be used for an emergency evacuation by sea. The nearness of the water and the out-of-the-way location weighed in its favour. A contract between the parties, with an option to renew, was drawn up on 18 October.

There was only one problem: the Canadian officers had no money. They had to appeal to Ottawa, first to authorize the $88,000 (Cdn) required for six months' rent, and then to have it paid. The money was sent by a maze of banking transactions that circumvented NDHQ's normal financial procedures. These had to be modified quickly to meet urgent operational requirements, while maintaining strict accountability for public funds. In the new NDHQ crisis management structure, there was now a J4 Finance staff officer whose job it was to streamline the normal administrative process (see Appendix B). The result was that Colonel Stuart obtained not only what he needed to clinch the deal but also additional funds earmarked for future expenses.

Another building was found to act as barracks for the greater part of the Signals Squadron. It was a five-storey building named the *Bait al Houra*. Popularly known as The Bait, it was four kilometres from Headquarters. To everyone's surprise, the building was next to the Iraqi embassy, which had reduced but not stopped operations during the long period leading up to the war. Used to full capacity during the months the Canadians were in town, The Bait had apartments of various sizes, shared on the basis of military rank. It became a protected location, with its own guard and transport teams.

During this time, Commodore Summers met with the Bahraini Defence Staff to discuss common plans and general terms governing Canadian activities in the country. An officer of the Bahrain Armed Forces, Captain Khalifa Al-Khalifa Abdullah, was appointed to serve as interpreter and liaison officer and to provide direct communications with the senior Bahraini staff. His presence proved advantageous. Impasses with local public administration were avoided, and cordial relations were maintained at every stage of the negotiations.

Major Arcand also visited Doha, on 15 October, to make arrangements for a detachment from his unit to provide HF and VHF radio communications between Manamah and the air group. However, he had to leave the next day to join his unit in Kingston still without having established contact with them. As the only officer of the reconnaissance party to return to Canada, Arcand had to pass on recommendations concerning structure and matériel and suggest necessary changes to NDHQ.

Preparation of the Unit at CFB Kingston

The unit gathering at CFB Kingston was to be airlifted no later than the fourth week of October. It was necessary therefore that most of the troops show up by 13 October. However, this was already rather late for Captain Hayes and the base administration, which had to work out an administration and training schedule. There was precious little time to cover all the subjects related to combat. Most of those arriving at CFB Kingston were unfamiliar with the new family of 5.56 mm small arms and with the latest nuclear, biological, and chemical defence protection equipment. They needed multiple inoculations (very few escaped with fewer than four injections). They had to make wills and fill out next-of-kin notifications. And there were documents for reorganizing pay allotments to families and for terminating home base liabilities.

The deadlines proved no less exacting for home bases. They had administrative responsibilities for their members going to the Middle East. Dependent families had to be assisted in various ways to overcome the difficulties associated with the sudden departure of a spouse or parent. Base commanders assumed responsibility for the formation of aid groups; day-care; legal and financial assistance; and religious, marriage, and social counselling. Several individual cases had to be negotiated between Kingston and the home bases in the midst of numerous changes made by the various decision-making levels. These procedures were not unique to the departure of 90 Signals Squadron. However, it was the first time an ad hoc unit, coming from so many different places, had been prepared so quickly and sent off with so much efficiency. The deadline could not have been met without computers and electronic data communications.

Arrival of the HQ & Sigs Squadron at Manamah

The Headquarters and Signals Squadron finally reached Manamah in three main groups, the first of which left Trenton on Monday, 22 October. Their planned departure had to be hastily rearranged because obtaining visas from Bahrain for them proved difficult. Only twenty-five visas had reached Kingston by the twenty-second. Those who received them were designated the vanguard of the squadron without regard to their position in the unit or their need to leave early. Major Arcand himself did not obtain his visa until late in the day and finally succeeded in boarding the fifth aircraft.

A second deployment phase involving several returning *Hercules* took place on Thursday, 25 October. Included in the flights were four medium-range communications vehicles, which were intended to establish communications between Manamah and Riyadh. The two vehicles destined for Riyadh were used at Qatar, however, because the Saudi Arabian authorities refused them access to their territory, a privilege restricted to countries represented by a headquarters at Riyadh. A long-range heavy communications vehicle also was on board. That same day, a Canadian Forces *Boeing 707* took seventy-nine members of the squadron. They were the main body. This group reached Bahraini soil nineteen hours after departure from Trenton, which was nearly twenty hours fewer than it took the *Hercules* to transport the heavy equipment.

The Joint Headquarters staff who arrived with Major Arcand were a group distinct from 90 Signals Squadron. They were officers from various Commands organized within a traditional structure that brought together the staff functions of the six "J" offices. The officers making up this group acted under the command of the Chief of Staff, Colonel Lalonde, whom they met for the first time at Manamah. The preparation of the officers at Kingston had been up to the Senior Staff Officer for Operations, who was supposed to be an air force officer with the rank of lieutenant-colonel. But Air Command was unable to provide an officer of this rank. In his place, Major Jocelyn Cloutier, a pilot of 433 *Porcupine* CF-18 Squadron from Bagotville, was selected. According to Cloutier, he was chosen "to fly a fighter desk."[8]

Under the direction of Cloutier, another CF-18 pilot and two air weapons controllers shared permanent responsibility on the J3 Air desk. Their assignment was to follow the Doha air task group's operations. Unfortunately, in Kingston they did not know the means of communications at their disposal, were unfamiliar with the procedures between the Riyadh liaison officers and the operations officers in Qatar, and were unacquainted with the exact terms of the use of the Canadian aircraft in their new missions. The best these officers could do at this point was prepare themselves psychologically and search the briefings presented by NDHQ for details that might give them clues as to what they should expect.

The naval staff had a better idea of their responsibilities. Their task group had been involved in operations for some time, and they understood the interception and boarding routine, whereas the air staff had to deal with a still-evolving concept of air operations. Moreover, Lieutenant-Commander Allan Cole and his officers had previously belonged to squadron staffs at sea or naval headquarters ashore and generally had more confidence in their own experience. To them it was

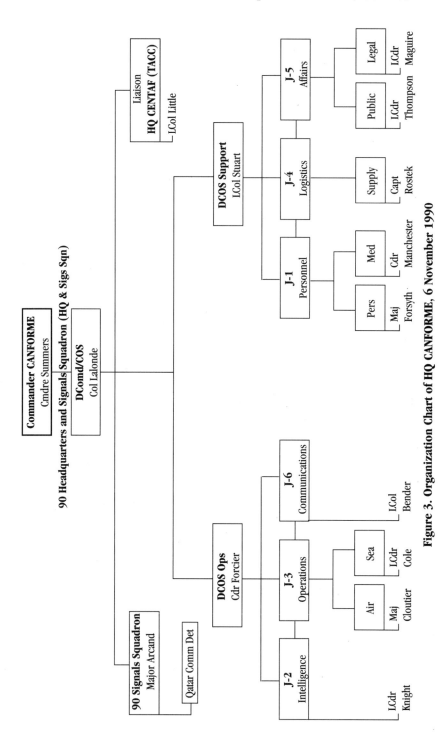

Figure 3. Organization Chart of HQ CANFORME, 6 November 1990

clear that the military environment in Bahrain would be oriented more towards naval operations because the commodore was in command and also because of the location of Joint Headquarters. Being established in Manamah, it was conspicuously close to NAVCENT, to which all the Canadian forces were attached.

Within a week of arriving, Lieutenant-Commander Darren Knight, who was in charge of the intelligence team (J2), had set up essential contacts in Bahrain with the intelligence officers on board *Blue Ridge* and *LaSalle* and with several other headquarters. Together they made up the complex and secret network of intelligence agencies involved in researching and compiling information and analyses on the Iraqi forces. By 1 November, Knight was able to deliver his first intelligence briefing to the commodore and his staff. These briefings became twice-daily events, once in the morning and once in the evening, and they continued without interruption for four and a half months. Each briefing was a compilation of current details and technical studies of evolving Iraqi operations.

The only logistical (J4) officer to arrive at Manamah before the main group was Lieutenant-Colonel Stuart, a transport officer. He was joined by two other logistical officers who were appointed to take up supply and finance functions at Headquarters. But it quickly became clear that the squadron also needed a dedicated supply officer and an air movements coordinator. The number of logistical officers for the joint establishment rose from three to five, one week after Headquarters opened for operations. The level of activity amply justified the increase. The addition of a personnel administration (J1) officer to this team brought some order to the management of individual postings to the theatre, personnel services, religious support, career and compassionate counselling, and morale boosting.

The greater the military bureaucracy, the greater the production of paper. By 6 November, the day Headquarters opened for business, 17,000 pages of documents had been produced. And the photocopying resources were insufficient! In the coming months, printers attached to the communications systems and working twenty-four hours a day produced myriad daily reports on weather; air and sea traffic; military intelligence; international liaison; national and international public information; technical instructions for equipment; and rapidly developing situations. These documents were transmitted without a break as part of current operations and had a life span of only a few hours. The result was a voluminous mass of paper made even greater by the use of computers.

Added to this staff were the three officers already on location in Manamah: the surgeon Commander Manchester (J1 Med); the military lawyer Lieutenant-Commander Maguire (J5 Legal); and the public affairs officer Lieutenant-Commander Thompson (J5 PA). The three had been posted to serve the commander of the naval task group and were transferred ashore to accompany Commodore Summers in his new functions.

They were immediately involved in negotiating the loan of the extra medical detachment on board *Protecteur* to the Bahrain Defence Forces hospital at Manamah. It was difficult for doctors and nurses to keep up their skills in surgery, anaesthesia, and postoperative care when *Protecteur's* normal medical team — a doctor and three medical assistants — was sufficient to provide necessary day-to-day care for the crews. The Command Surgeon thus recommended a temporary exchange. He had to negotiate with the country's civilian and military authorities before permission was granted for nine commissioned and non-commissioned medical officers to be landed on 1 November. This initiative benefited all parties and fostered good cooperation between the Canadians and their Bahraini hosts.

Taking Command

The arrival of the staff and personnel of the Signals Squadron solidly reinforced the Canadian presence in Bahrain. Considerable progress was made during the fourth week of October towards establishing Headquarters. But it was not enough. The initial deadline could not be met. The Signals Squadron devoted all its time to rectifying the many problems which it encountered, but the army equipment proved difficult to calibrate and was at the very limit of its capacity. The addition of satellite communications at first was little more than a palliative but became increasingly important to the joint headquarters' routine communications plan. Lieutenant-Colonel James J. Bender, Director of Communications and Electronics (Operations and Training) (DCEOT) in Ottawa, acted as NDHQ's J6 Communications and was sent on location, on 27 October, as a technical adviser to establish communications. During the next month, Bender organized and supervised the installation and progressive use of FLEETSATCOM, INMARSAT, and INTELSAT satellite systems, for faster and more direct communications by data transmission systems, telephone, and facsimile. He ended up being appointed staff officer in charge of the dual functions of J6 Communications and in command of the Signals Squadron, of which Major Arcand became the Deputy Commanding Officer.

On 6 November, a signal was sent out, informing all commands that the terms of command and control discussed during the previous month were coming into effect. The code word Ballot, issued by the Chief of the Defence Staff, gave Commodore Summers official command of the operation as of 0600. Summers had already given his first orders the previous day, so that the terms of his command would take effect on receipt of the simple code word. With this first notice, succinct instructions on command and control, communications, and rules of engagement established strict conduct guidelines, which Summers wanted obeyed.

For the first time, two distinct elements of the Canadian Forces had been brought under the baton of a single operational commander. This was a decisive moment. The mechanisms were now in place for the Canadian government to maintain close control of the actions of its military forces on the other side of the world.

Operation ACCORD: September – November 1990

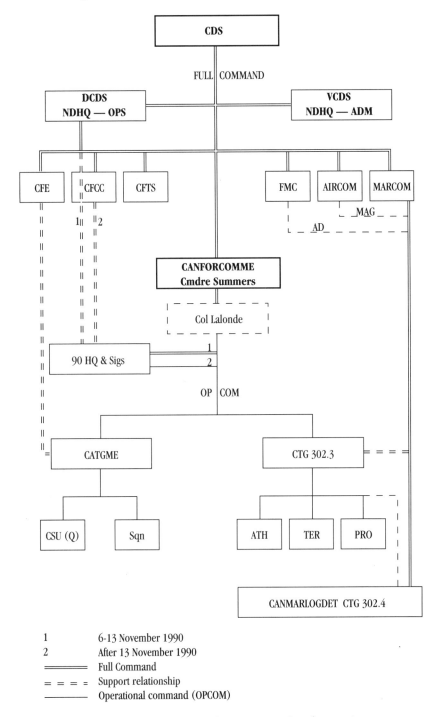

Figure 4. Command and Control of CANFORME after 6 November 1990

Notes

1   National Defence, "Establishment of Canadian Forces Headquarters in the Middle East," *Press Communiqué*, AFN 61/90, 17 October 1990.

2   WD NDHQ, CDS 188, "Command Concept for CF Operations in the Persian Gulf," 27 September 1990.

3   WD NDHQ, DCDS, "Warning Order - OP ACCORD - Dev[elopment of] JHQ for OP FRICTION," 28 September 1990.

4   WD CFE, COMD 051, "CENTAF Visit Riyadh - 27 Sep 90 - OP SCIMITAR," 28 September 1990.

5   WD CTG 302.3, "Briefing Note on Canadian CF-18 Operations in the Persian Gulf Region," 29 September 1990.

6   It is customary to give the year number to units formed for temporary missions.

7   Concurrent with the preparation of this historical narrative, the Director General of Program Evaluation (DGPE) in NDHQ undertook a separate analysis of Canadian command and control in the Gulf. See Department of National Defence [Colonel A.P. Humphreys team leader], 1258-99 (DGPE), NDHQ Program Evaluation E3/92, "Command and Control, Volume 2, A Case Study: Operation FRICTION (The Gulf Crisis)," 13 October 1993.

8   Major Jocelyn Cloutier, interview by Jean Morin, tape recording, Manamah, Bahrain, 6 March 1991.

CHAPTER 6

The Calm Before the Storm:
November – December 1990

The Wind Shifts

The activation of a Canadian HQ coincided with the announcement by President Bush on 8 November that the American contingent would be augmented by many elements from the European theatre. By moving VII (US) Corps, with all its heavy equipment, from Germany to Saudi Arabia, the American forces in the Gulf region would acquire the capacity to deal with the more numerous but much less modern Iraqi armies. Of course, it would take more than three months to move this force of nearly 200,000 troops. However, once they were in place, the Americans by themselves would be able to retake Kuwait by assault before the middle of February. This fact was noted in every capital of the world. Secretary James Baker immediately took advantage of this perception to place before the Security Council a resolution calling for the use of force against Iraq. With these elements in place, the logic of war took on a fateful momentum.

Although the Canadian position to date had favoured a naval embargo under United Nations auspices, it was clearly understood that the Americans were stealing the initiative from the UN. If it wished to retain its status, the UN had no other course than to anticipate the intended direction of the world's only superpower. Early in November, the prime minister opted to recognize the de facto American leadership. From that moment, the Canadian position took a resolutely new turn. Rather than use its influence in Washington to get the U.S. to accede to the UN's diplomatic wishes, Canada's ambassador to the UN attempted to persuade the other members of the Security Council to adopt a tougher position without initially espousing American policy as a whole.

Canada attempted to play both ends of the stick at the same time. On one end, Ambassador Fortier exercised a moderating voice in the discussions leading up to the Security Council vote. On the other, Secretary of State for External Affairs Joe Clark threw himself into a touring campaign during which he prodded his own and other countries, including those of the Gulf, to start thinking about the next military steps if the current diplomatic efforts were to have an effect. His statements (and similar ones by McKnight, the Minister of National Defence) about Canadian soldiers coming back from the Gulf "in body bags" shocked the Canadian public, who were unused to this type of rhetoric. They had an immediate effect. From mid-October to mid-November, the press reacted very strongly to Mr Clark's many pronouncements, especially to the one on 25 October, when he declared to the parliamentary committee on External Affairs and Foreign Trade that Canada might intervene even if the Security Council rejected military means.[1] Citizens as a whole suddenly became aware that Canada was involved in a campaign that could end in war. Mr Clark's work was therefore of the greatest importance in developing the Canadian position, both within Canada itself and at the Security Council. This new attitude strengthened Canadian support for the American cause. It wrapped the UN resolutions in a realistic argument and reiterated and reinforced the world body's ultimatum to Iraq.

The Canadian opposition, meanwhile, distanced itself in various ways from the government's hard line towards Iraq. Demonstrations by several groups of pacifist protesters were organized throughout the country. They wanted the government to back away from the American position.[2] Public meetings were held in Ottawa and several other cities, but they were only moderately popular. The Official Opposition in the Commons also had grave reservations about the government's initiatives. While the Liberals repeated their support of the troops in November and December, they were reluctant to give their blessing to an American offensive. Their opposition became especially fierce in mid-November, when journalists in the Gulf reported that the Canadian air force was ready to join the US Marines in an exercise near the Kuwaiti coast. In the eyes of many Canadians, this signalled the government's true intentions.

Exercise IMMINENT THUNDER

On Tuesday, 6 November, the day he officially took command, Commodore Summers was informed that CENTCOM was preparing a large-scale combined manoeuvre called IMMINENT THUNDER, which was to be carried out right in the Gulf.[3] After a week of consultations with allied commanders, Summers was in a position to give a detailed briefing on the principal reasons for Canadian participation. One of the biggest reasons was that the manoeuvre would offer a valuable opportunity for training the troops. The exercise was divided into three parts: on 15 and 16 November, CENTAF would make sorties in the direction of the advanced defensive positions near the Kuwait border; on 16 and 17 November, all allied forces detailed in CENTAF's ATO-B orders - a set of standing air tasking orders, constituting a plan for the first day of defensive operations in the event of a surprise Iraqi attack - would adopt air defence positions up to 40 percent of their planned strength; and from 17 to 21 November, the US Marines would conduct an amphibious landing, supported by the aircraft of the Marines and Navy. No other air elements would be involved.

During the first and third parts of the exercise, combat air patrols were to fly as usual. The CF-18s would have no other role than to carry out patrols on the stations which they shared with the F/A-18s of the US Navy and Marines. However, it was understood that when they returned from patrolling Whiskey-2, the CF-18s would make a short detour to the west - over the coast of Saudi territory - and simulate an enemy air force in order to exercise the air patrols of the Dhahran sector. As well, for the duration of the exercise, all sorties were to be ordered through the ATO-Ms, the special training orders for IMMINENT THUNDER which were derived from the ATO-B operational orders.

In the course of the second part of IMMINENT THUNDER, on 16 and 17 November, the Canadian CF-18s would take up positions reserved for them in Whiskey-1, according to ATO-B contingency orders. This opportunity to assume their war station (normally defended by the US Marines in the F/A-18s) came at a time when there was discussion about improving the secure voice and Link-4 communications for the CF-18s. This question attracted much attention.

Summers also gave details of a request from Admiral Fogarty that Canadian naval ships escort the hospital ship carrying the Canadian medical team. The destroyers *Athabaskan* and *Terra Nova* were to escort *Mercy* to an appropriate anchorage where it could receive medical evacuations by helicopter during a real landing. During this phase, the CF-18s were to continue providing protection for the ships in the course of their Whiskey patrols. Commodore Summers was happy with these developments because they presented rich opportunities for the further orchestration of increasingly complex missions among the members of the Coalition, whose assets were growing in numbers. He therefore recommended joining the exercise because it would allow Canadian forces to turn their hands to the type of missions that would be conducted if war were declared. He made a point of explaining that any participation would take place within the framework of the normal missions issued for DESERT SHIELD:

> Setting up this large-scale exercise, which had at first been apprehended as a somewhat provocative step, is now evaluated as a useful tool to check various operational components for a potential conflict. The participation of the Canadian Forces will be strictly limited to the exercise of our responsibilities within the context of the orders issued by ATO-B and for escorting a hospital ship.[4]

At the beginning of the exercise, however, it was discovered that the CF-18s had to take up patrol positions in Whiskey-1 from the fifteenth rather than the sixteenth, in order to replace the US Marine aircraft which had to train before taking part in the landing exercise on the seventeenth. The Canadians thus moved forward to the first line of air defence in the Gulf. They already had worked there on several occasions but under very strict American supervision. For the Canadian pilots, it was a vote of confidence in their work on Whiskey-2, a reserve patrol station which many people wrongly considered to be a training circuit without great operational importance. The move to Whiskey-1 in the north gave them a greater share of responsibilities.

On Thursday, 15 November, NDHQ was informed that during the previous evening a practice for the defence of Doha Air Base had been carried out and that a CF-18 "scramble" had responded to a notional enemy attack. The alert was issued from HQ CANFORME without being directly connected to IMMINENT THUNDER. It was the first time an alert had taken place on the Canadian network. For the personnel of CATGME, the association with the main exercise was natural, but many of them remained uncertain whether the CF-18s were actually involved in IMMINENT THUNDER. Theoretically, the Canadian missions were not a part of the Marines' landing plan, which was the focal point of the exercise. However, the use of ATO-Ms to issue orders, the unusual access to the Whiskey-1 patrol circuit, the return over the Saudi shore to simulate enemy incursions, and the alert exercises ordered by Commodore Summers - all these initiatives represented an obvious change in normal operations. At least the pilots saw themselves as full partners in IMMINENT THUNDER.

On Friday, 16 November, there were communication difficulties between *LaSalle* and Riyadh in coordinating missions due to the fact that changes were not followed up regularly in the naval cell at Riyadh. Consequently, several pairs of CF-18s were refused access to Whiskey-1 on the fifteenth by the naval coordinator because the ATO-M orders did not reflect the new mission assignments agreed to by the Marines. The Canadian pilots had to return to Whiskey-2 and wait for the Doha operations centre to clarify the situation. This took a half day of discussions. Meanwhile, journalists at Doha had got wind of the fact that Canadian pilots were involved in enemy simulation missions and that alert takeoffs had been launched without warning. All this activity was unusual, prompting the media to speak about active Canadian participation in IMMINENT THUNDER. But in public relations circles in Ottawa and Doha, Canadian participation was being described as negligible, with no real change. Reporters began to cast doubt on National Defence as a reliable source of information. Soon accusations began to pour forth that Canadian aircraft were involved in operations much more offensive in nature than had been admitted. Some feared that a more aggressive Canadian role would raise the tension in the Gulf to the degree tacitly desired by the Americans. The reality in Doha, however, was rather more prosaic. The Canadian air force finally spent nine hours on the Whiskey-1 circuit, simply replacing the Marines who had to cover the landing the next day.

On Saturday, 17 November, Colonel Engstad had to deal with the imminent transfer of control from *LaSalle* to the aircraft carrier *Midway* (which was to enter the Gulf and take command of IMMINENT THUNDER's naval operations) and the new naval air controller of the *Midway* Group, the cruiser USS *Bunker Hill*. The arrival of these two ships did not improve the poor level of communications between the Canadians and the naval cell at Riyadh. Still, the commander of CATGME said that he was very happy with the number of patrol hours he was able to spend on Whiskey-1 and that the lessons learned were quite valuable. As for the naval group, the rendezvous with *Mercy* (in the centre of area Charlie-6) brought the Canadian destroyers closer to Kuwait than they had been on any of their previous MIF patrols. From Charlie-6, they proceeded to the holding area off Al Jubayl. *Terra Nova* led the way, using her Mine Avoidance Sonar to scan the route, while *Athabaskan* hovered around the hospital ship, providing close air defence in case of attack. Once on-station, the small group remained together overnight. The next morning, 17 November, *Terra Nova* departed to the south to rendezvous with *Comfort* and then return, while *Athabaskan* maintained her close escort of the hospital ship. That afternoon the Canadian flagship made the initial radar detection of an exercise air raid. It was immediately reported through the American controlling cruiser, which alerted the CAP waiting overhead to make a successful interception. With the arrival of the second group, the two ships exchanged duties. *Athabaskan* remained with *Comfort* for the duration of the exercise, and *Terra Nova* accompanied *Mercy* to the south and resumed her MIF patrol in Charlie-1.

IMMINENT THUNDER received wide media coverage. It also provoked a short but nasty exchange in the Commons. John Brewin (NDP, Victoria), a member of the defence minister's entourage on a recent Middle Eastern tour, denounced the exercise. He maintained that Canadian participation amounted to a much more intense collaboration than had been planned for in the preparations for war. Associate Minister of National Defence Mary Collins (Capilano-Howe Sound) rose in the House to sum up the situation and explain the nature of the missions. She spoke of the "minor role" being played by the Canadians in IMMINENT THUNDER. It was limited to escorting hospital ships and maintaining combat air patrols " ... in a defensive capacity, in an air operation to test out command and control capabilities of the multinational forces which are operating in the area."[5]

It was a tempest in a teapot. IMMINENT THUNDER was already drawing to a close, and CATGME had carried out its final missions in Whiskey-1 without generating any more controversy. The landing of the Marines, scheduled for Saturday, 17 November, failed to take place because the sea was too rough. The manoeuvre was first postponed, then finally cancelled. Neither did the lack of Iraqi reaction to all this activity justify the critics' fears.

The Canadians in Doha had proven themselves capable members of the NAVCENT air defence community. One need was now clearly identified. It was imperative to obtain a secure voice and Link-4 communications system that would enable CF-18s to act on an equal footing with their American allies. The long-term effect of IMMINENT THUNDER was that it allowed the Marine F/A-18s to be progressively detached from air defence patrol missions and moved to their specialty, interdiction and close support of Marine assault formations. A study of the statistics shows that though the Marines carried out more than 30 percent of all air defence patrols in the theatre during DESERT SHIELD (4,461 sorties), this percentage fell to zero after the outbreak of hostilities, when they were replaced by US Navy fighters operating from carriers. Statistics also show that one third of the air defence patrols were carried out by non-American forces for each of the two periods, some 9,000 sorties in all.[6] The Canadians accounted for nearly 2,400 of these, including 1600 before the start of hostilities.[7] When one factors in the smaller number of Canadian aircraft available, CATGME clearly shouldered its share of the task. Furthermore, the daily report from Doha for 19 November alluded to the many additional flying hours which had been required because of the more distant deployments and training flights demanded by the exercise. Not wanting to exceed monthly ceilings, Colonel Engstad let it be known that he would have to cancel some days of operations at the end of the month.

IMMINENT THUNDER proved to be a classical case of the triumph of the implications of public relations over the substance of the manoeuvres themselves. The exercise gave a taste of things to come, both for the PR officers and the senior officers who had to take their recommendations into consideration. Although IMMINENT THUNDER did not infringe on the clearly mandated defensive posture of Canadian Forces in the Gulf, it nonetheless was a moderate and perceptible advance in Canadian preparations for war. This shift was part of a wider context which enabled the entire Coalition to prepare for offensive measures against the Iraqi invader.

Plan BROADSWORD

After President Bush's announcement on 8 November that he was sending VII Corps and several other air and naval forces to the Gulf, NDHQ became more interested in the implications which a land force would have for its order of battle. On 10 November, NDHQ staff began a rapid study of the preparation of a brigade for service in the Gulf. On 12 November, Prime Minister Mulroney made a statement to the effect that he did not consider sending ground troops an impossibility for Canada, if the United Nations made the request.[8] The next day General de Chastelain sent a message to Lieutenant-General Foster in Mobile Command (FMC), asking for a plan to prepare 4 Canadian Mechanized Brigade Group, in Lahr, to take part in a "multinational or binational" formation. The brigade was to be augmented by a third battalion of infantry and a fourth squadron in its tank regiment, and it would be equipped with combat, combat support, and logistical support reinforcements. The FMC staff was authorized to call on resources wherever they could be found in the Canadian Forces and include them as required in the plan. Foster was to present a complete option eight days later.

On Friday, 23 November, Plan BROADSWORD, drawn up in the utmost secrecy, was presented to the Chief of the Defence Staff. It included impressive details on the material and transport arrangements which would be necessary to support a 12,000-man brigade in combat for thirty days. It also included forecasts of personnel and matériel losses, which would necessitate considerable replacements and reserves. As well, it would take a period of 135 days before the formation would be ready to enter the fight somewhere in Saudi Arabia.

Plan BROADSWORD was immediately rejected, more because of the cost of implementing it than because of the timetable for deployment. The option of participating in land combat proved so onerous with respect to material losses that, as soon as it had been carefully studied, it was discarded as unaffordable and too risky for public consumption. Speculation on the anticipated cost of a ground war was the subject of intense media interest at the very time that these decisions were being made. It was obviously a subject that disturbed many Canadians. Even official military estimates, which varied greatly, agreed that Coalition casualties would be numbered in the tens of thousands. No one at the time was able to see through the gross inaccuracies of such horrifying numbers.

In any event, BROADSWORD convincingly demonstrated that sending a mechanized brigade group into battle was not within the scope of the Canadian Forces as they then existed. The navy had been criticized for the quality and number of units which it could make operational on short notice, but at least it was given the opportunity to make good the difference. The army was less fortunate. The politicians and the public were not going to get a chance to see how deficient the army really would be in full-scale combat. BROADSWORD remained classified and ended up an embarrassing footnote for the army.

Naval Operations, November - December

President Bush's decision to develop an offensive capability had little immediate effect on embargo operations, although it included a naval dimension which would drastically alter the character of the Multinational Interception Forces (MIF). From early in the crisis, Admiral Fogarty had held the front line against Iraq in the waters of the Persian Gulf. His coordination of the interception effort was backed up by a quick-reaction strike option of his own, in the form of the carrier battle group poised nearby in the Arabian Sea and the battleship on-station in the central Gulf (plus undisclosed numbers of *Tomahawk* cruise missiles carried by his cruisers and destroyers). Concurrent with the land reinforcements, the American naval presence in the Gulf region doubled in size with the addition of three more carrier battle groups, another battleship, and 40,000 embarked Marines. The new naval deployments were not fully in place until well into January, after the actual commencement of the air campaign, but the end result was the same. The MIF, which had represented a significant proportion of the naval forces in the theatre, slowly lost its authority to the enormous offensive capability of the United States Navy. Nowhere was this more evident than in the central Gulf. In November and December, the *Midway* carrier battle group made numerous excursions in this particular region.

The American president's latest announcement added to the mounting tension. The possibility of war was on everyone's mind. In mid-October, following the American buildup for DESERT SHIELD, and long before any open discussion of an offensive option, Admiral George had defined for Captain Miller the scope of the actions which he might take in the event of hostilities. These remained the guiding principles for the Canadian task group until early January:

> CTG 302.3 may place Canadian units under the tactical control of allied nations for the collective defence of friendly forces and non-combatants. The following restrictions apply:
>
> a. Offensive operations or support to allied forces conducting offensive operations are not authorized;
> b. Based on [CTG's] assessment of the threat, Canadian units must be adequately protected by either Canadian or allied forces before support is given to other nations;
> c. Canadian Task Group vessels will not operate in the Persian Gulf north of 28 degrees north or in Iranian territorial waters; and,
> d. Canadian Task Group aircraft will not operate in the airspace of Iraq, Kuwait, Jordan, Iran and Yemen.[9]

Upon notification of hostilities, the senior commanders in Ottawa and Halifax would evaluate the situation and provide further guidance as quickly as possible. Pending that, the task group would break off MIF operations for a rendezvous in the southern Gulf until circumstances were clarified.

Of more immediate interest to Miller and his officers was the recently unveiled plan for their own rotation. Planning the turnover and work-up schedules occupied much of their time during the next two months. All three ships underwent familiarization visits from the crews of the relieving ships and staff. On 6 November, the first replacements arrived, including a group for *Protecteur* led by its commanding officer-designate, Captain Dennis Cronk of *Preserver*.

As the Iraqi occupation forces in Kuwait continued their stand-off with the steadily building Coalition land and air forces in northeastern Saudi Arabia, MIF operations quickly settled into a routine. Throughout November there were no significant Iraqi challenges to the blockade in the Persian Gulf or Gulf of Oman.

Over-water training flights by the Iraqis remained steady but hardly a threat because of the constant surveillance of AWACS and Aegis. In stark contrast to the "You fly, you die" maxim of the Coalition air defence forces, Canadians sailors adopted the less threatening motto "You sail, we hail." Daily Canadian interceptions began to average in excess of twenty, while the national proportion of the MIF total steadily increased. The lull in actual boardings, which had been plaguing the Canadians since the middle of October, was briefly interrupted on 9 November. In an operation coordinated by Captain Miller, *Athabaskan* joined USS *Macdonough* in the inspection of two tugs out of Abu Dhabi bound for Umm-Qasr.

The investment made in the augmentation of *Protecteur*'s air maintenance detachment before departing Halifax began to show a return when the problem of a decreasing number of aircraft flying hours arose in early November. Unlike the air task group in Doha, which frequently rotated CF-18s from the Canadian bases in Germany, 423 Squadron had no practical way to transport replacement aircraft to the Gulf without a relieving task group. In the short term, the technicians afloat had proven equal to the task of routine maintenance, keeping even the temperamental Persian Pig on the ready roster, but a more stubborn problem was the necessity for periodic inspections. A regular maintenance routine was required on all aircraft every 500 flying hours. This was a major undertaking because this kind of maintenance had never been conducted away from home base, let alone on a ship at sea. Together the task group helicopters were averaging twelve hours' flying per day, or over 350 hours per month. Much of it was invaluable surveillance work (especially at nighttime with the FLIR). The intention to return to Halifax in the early months of 1991 partly accounted for such a terrific pace. At the beginning of November, the total number of hours remaining was just over 1,250. At that rate, this was sufficient to last until February. But the flying pace would have to pick up considerably in the event of a war.

However, there would be no replacement of ships or their embarked aircraft until at least the summer of 1991. Reacting to this information, Lieutenant-Colonel McWha, Captain Miller's senior air adviser, ordered a drastic reduction in the number of hours flown by the air detachments. Henceforth, they were to fly only when necessary. Otherwise they were to remain at alert status. Their hands were forced on 5 November, when an airframe crack was discovered on Big Bird (SK417). Ironically, it was the aircraft with the fewest remaining hours (66.6). It was grounded on the *Protecteur*, which offered the best facilities for the *Sea King* helicopters, until a metal technician from Shearwater could arrive.[10] Urgent communications passed from the task group ships at sea to Manamah and then Shearwater, resulting in the decision to begin the twenty-day periodic routine on the stricken helicopter immediately. An inspection sequence, with a February deadline, was drawn up for the remaining aircraft. With judicious scheduling, and barring the outbreak of hostilities, all five aircraft would have sufficient hours to resume flying at the accustomed rate and support task group operations well into 1992.

The last week of November was eventful. On Sunday, the twenty-fifth, dawn brought the first rainfall since the ships had left Halifax. The next day, *Protecteur* replenished USS *Wisconsin*, the first ever refuelling of an American battleship by a Canadian tanker. This was followed by the refuelling of the Dutch air defence destroyer HrMs *Witte de With* and the Aegis cruiser USS *Bunker Hill* (*Antietam*'s replacement). Also, Big Bird successfully passed a test flight on completion of her periodic inspection.

Late that same evening, *Terra Nova* intercepted the MV *Taurus*, en route to Iraq for an evacuation operation involving dredging equipment. *Protecteur*'s Persian Pig was launched to assist the destroyer's boarding party. Alternately using her FLIR and searchlight to guide the party below, the operation was completed without incident in less than half an hour. The next day, *Protecteur* intercepted MV *Gmmos Power*, a tug and barge proceeding to Iraq from Abu Dhabi. Nothing unusual was found, and she was cleared to continue. The supply ship *Protecteur* finally took her place as a boarding veteran. In his daily report for 27 November, the task group commander concluded his summary of the previous twenty-four hours by declaring that "The MIF War has been won [and the] Persian Gulf interdiction is proving very effective in upholding the UN resolutions."[11]

The jubilation did not last long. *Terra Nova*'s temperamental *Phalanx* - her security in case of missile attack - once more became unserviceable. It was all inexplicable. Captain Miller was on board the destroyer at the time, awaiting *Athabaskan*'s return from Abu Dhabi the next day, and he directed Commander Andrews to restrict his patrols to the southeast corner of area Charlie-2, the patrol area farthest from Iraq. Then shortly after midnight, 29 November, General Schwarzkopf ordered all forces throughout the region to adopt a higher degree of alert, in anticipation of a negative Iraqi reaction to the latest Security Council resolution being debated in New York.

The long-debated issue of what further measures should be taken against Iraq came to an end with a vote on Resolution 678. Passed by a margin of 12-2 (Cuba and Yemen were opposed; China abstained), it called upon Iraq to implement the earlier eleven resolutions and authorized "the states cooperating with Kuwait to use all necessary means" to uphold and implement the outstanding measures and "restore international peace and security" in the area.[12] A deadline of 15 January 1991 was set for Iraq to indicate its unconditional acceptance of the will of the United Nations.

Resolution 678 fundamentally changed the raison d'etre of the land forces from a defensive to an offensive military machine and confirmed the change in direction for Gulf naval operations signalled earlier in the month by the announcement of American naval reinforcements. As those reinforcements began to arrive, the turnaround became complete. The naval arm of the offensive option was developing teeth, and American commanders now had a mandate to discuss the anticipated operations with their Coalition partners.

NAVCENT conducted its planning for offensive maritime operations within the framework of CENTCOM's overall theatre campaign plan. The plan envisaged a four-phased operation: a strategic air campaign; air supremacy in the Kuwait Theatre of Operations (KTO); battlefield preparation; and an offensive ground assault. Each phase would have a reinforcing naval dimension. At its height, the maritime campaign would include four USN carrier battle groups in the north central Gulf (*Midway* plus three later arrivals, *Ranger, Theodore Roosevelt,* and *America*); two others, *John F. Kennedy* and *Saratoga,* would operate in the Red Sea; and two battleships (*Missouri* joining *Wisconsin*), along with a full amphibious task force of over forty ships. The two objectives of the last named were to support air strikes against Iraqi targets and threaten an assault against the Kuwaiti coast.

The bulk of this force, however, would still be en route on 15 January. Because the capacity of the Iraqis to mount a retaliatory or even a preemptive strike remained unknown, Admiral Fogarty directed his contingency planners to assure the security of his forces upon the outbreak of hostilities. Operation BASTION envisioned a fall-back of forces to a defensive posture that would give the Coalition time to set up an offensive strike capability. The central Gulf was to become the domain of the air defence cruisers. In conjunction with reinforced combat air patrols, they would establish a defensive barrier. Behind it would gather the strike units of the Arabian Gulf Battle Force (the AGBF) - the carrier battle groups and *Tomahawk* cruise missile launchers - who were well protected by close escorts. Any forces not involved in air defence or strike activities were to join the non-combatants further to the south, beyond reach of Iraqi air power. The staffs in *LaSalle* planning the operation candidly advised their Coalition partners that MIF operations would be a secondary mission during the initial execution, but they graciously invited the multinational forces to join American units under an integrated air defence umbrella in the southern Persian Gulf.

The USN commitment to the MIF and interception operations was being reordered by the contingency planning for hostilities - not only in the scope of operations but also in command structure. Preparations for an orderly transition to hostilities presaged a subtle but important transfer of US Navy operational command in the Gulf. The concentration of the immense striking power of the multiple-carrier Arabian Gulf Battle Force meant that Rear-Admiral Fogarty (as CTF 151)[13] would begin to implement BASTION but thereafter adopt a supporting role to the designated Battle Force commander, Rear-Admiral Daniel P. March (CTF 154). March was aboard USS *Midway* and would assume responsibility for the subsequent offensive operations following the entry of his force into the Gulf. But in early

December, when the draft plans were completed, the plan to exchange Fogarty for March was not widely known. At a multinational anti-air warfare coordination meeting aboard his flagship *LaSalle*, it was Admiral Fogarty who briefed the Coalition partners and discussed their participation in the proposed operations.

The response varied considerably. The most immediate and unequivocal replies came from the British and Australians. General de la Billière, commander of the British forces in the Middle East, took advantage of a rotation of senior naval staffs, planned for 3 December, to order the new commander of the British task group to develop "plans for an offensive campaign by the Navy high up the Gulf."[14] Then, on 5 December, the Australian prime minister announced that ships from the Royal Australian Navy, until now forbidden to pass through the Strait of Hormuz, would be deployed from the Gulf of Oman into the Persian Gulf for operations authorised by Resolution 678 and placed under US Navy operational command - if necessary. Within days, the Dutch government committed its task group to the support of USN operations. In mid-December, reliefs for both the Australian and Dutch naval task groups (each had essentially the same composition as the Canadian: two frigates and a supply ship) arrived in-theatre and moved almost immediately into the central Gulf from their previous operating areas, straddling respectively the southern and western approaches to the Strait of Hormuz.

At the other extreme was the reaction of the remaining members of the WEU. Coordinating their Gulf policy under the chairmanship of France, this group of Western European nations chose to maintain an independent foreign policy and specifically to refrain from any discussion of offensive operations in order not to jeopardize the possibility of a last-minute compromise. The French, Italian, and Spanish naval forces operating in the southern Gulf, joined by the combined Danish-Norwegian task group, remained assigned to MIF embargo operations.

Situated between these two camps were the Canadians and the Argentineans. The latter had relatively few political restrictions upon their operational employment, this being determined more by the limits of their air defences and the incompatability of their communications. The Canadians remained ambivalent for more complex reasons. On the technical side, connectivity was certainly not a problem, but anti-air warfare was. Unlike the British, Dutch, and Australian ships, all of which were equipped with long-range surface-to-air missiles (*Sea Dart* for the British; *Standard SM-1* for the others), the Canadian ships had no effective area air-defence systems with which to act as long-range pickets or "shotgun" close-in escorts for the strike force carriers. Also important was the domestic political dimension. The government had been thoroughly advised of the naval task group's limitations, and public opinion polls indicated that while Canadians continued to firmly support a tough stance against Saddam, they hesitated at the prospect of offensive action before all diplomatic avenues had been explored.

Nevertheless, support of the MIF effort remained a popular option, and the mandate of the task group did not change.

It was with all this in mind that in early December Captain Miller responded to the American offensive planning with plans of his own for the transition to war. Without area weapons, the Canadian ships would withdraw to the south - upon receipt of the code word "Barber Pole" - to take advantage of the protection offered by BASTION. They would escort the logistical and amphibious ships gathering in the southern Gulf, moving northward behind the strike forces only when air superiority was established. It was a far from glorious role but the only practical alternative, given the circumstances.

The naval Coalition was undergoing a transition from an MIF mentality to one more closely resembling that of the MNF ashore. The adoption of Resolution 678, which allowed the offensive option, came about because it was not entirely clear that the MIF embargo would be enough to bring Saddam to reason. Intelligence reports provided conflicting assessments of the efficacy of the United Nations action to date. There was no doubt that the blockade was virtually complete - little of any material significance was finding its way into Iraq. Still, Saddam and his regime continued to survive, and evidence was mounting that the severe rationing imposed by the Iraqi leadership probably could make existing supplies last until spring, the time of the next harvest. Unwilling to be tied to an open-ended schedule, with the cost of the deployment mounting, the Americans were anxious for resolute action.[15] But whereas USN interest in MIF operations was now decidedly secondary, there was little observable change in the scope or tempo of Canadian naval operations.

That the Canadians held a different perspective from the American MIF coordinator began to become apparent during the course of operations in November. MIF was required to inspect the tugs and barges engaged in the removal of Dutch dredging equipment from Iraq. British and Canadian searches of the first vessels on their northward journey indicated that contraband was not involved in the operation. The local (American) MIF coordinator, preoccupied with preparations for hostilities, then contended that further inspections would not be worth the effort expended. But the Canadians, supported by their Royal Navy counterparts, continued to put a high premium on the display of MIF solidarity. They insisted that all Iraq-bound merchant traffic be inspected. As a result, each interception became the subject of lengthy debate between Canadian and American staff officers on what constituted boarding criteria.

The issue came to a head in the days following the adoption of Resolution 678. Shortly after sunrise on 30 November, *Athabaskan* intercepted another tug bound for Umm-Qasr and prepared to conduct an inspection. But after confirming that there was no suspicious cargo on deck, the MIF coordinator requested that the Canadians allow the tug to proceed without boarding. Captain Miller reluctantly concurred. Then, during the night of 2-3 December, *Terra Nova* intercepted two vessels headed northwest. On the advice of the American coordinator, they were cleared without boarding, only to be inspected by HMS *Cardiff* a few hours later. Conferring with Commodore Summers, Miller confirmed that no deals had been made to let these vessels pass and that all ships were candidates for boarding on a case-by-case basis. Shortly thereafter, an opportunity to heal the developing rift was presented when *Athabaskan* and *Terra Nova* fell in alongside *Wisconsin* to take on fuel. Miller was welcomed aboard the American battleship and met one of the senior American coordinators. The two men obviously cleared the air between themselves. That evening, when *Athabaskan* intercepted the northbound tugs *Sindbad* and *Aladin*, only a brief conversation was required before the Americans agreed to the Canadians' intention to board. The two boardings were uneventful, but a principle had been established. Captain Miller's final comment on the episode was apt in more ways than one: "And so ends another chapter in the Tales of the Arabian Nights."[16]

Within days, the small fleet of dredgers began its southward return, at infrequent intervals. As dusk turned to dark on 6 December, *Athabaskan* intercepted the first two tugs outbound from Iraq. Assisted by the Persian Pig, *Athabaskan*'s boarding party conducted a full inspection of the heavily laden vessels. The Canadian officers confirmed the absence of any illegal cargo and questioned the crews, who gave them details on the increasingly desperate conditions in Iraq. This information was quickly shared with the other members of the Coalition.

During the next few days, more southbound vessels were intercepted and inspected in ones and twos by American and British ships, but the Coalition's big break came late in the morning of 11 December when *Terra Nova* intercepted the dredger-hopper (a self-propelled dredger) *Cornelis Zanen*, returning from Umm-Qasr. The destroyer's boarding party conducted a thorough inspection of the vessel. They uncovered no contraband but gleaned important intelligence concerning the remaining eleven vessels, ten tugs with barges and another dredger-hopper. They were due to depart Iraq that same day and could arrive in the central Gulf any time in the next forty-eight hours. In response, the Coalition warships heightened their surveillance effort. Shortly after dawn on 13 December, the lead vessels were located, approaching the northern extremes of the Charlie sectors. They appeared to be in two groups, one to the east led by *Toota*, and another to the west following *Gmmos Power*. The American coordinator requested that the two best-positioned MIF ships, HMS *Cardiff* and HMCS *Terra Nova*, intercept and inspect them.

Cardiff was virtually upon *Toota* (her *Lynx* helicopter had located the vessel), and she proceeded to board the tug and inspect her barge quickly and without incident. The British learned, however, that *Toota* was the only vessel making the eastern passage. The remainder were sailing in company with *Gmmos*

Power to the west. *Terra Nova* was much farther to the south, in area Charlie-2. Wishing to avoid a potentially lengthy boarding operation in the dark, Commander Andrews turned his ship to the northwest to intercept the approaching fleet.

The interception occurred early in the afternoon of 13 December, just as *Terra Nova* was crossing the boundary from area Charlie-6 into Charlie-7, the farthest point north yet for any Canadian ship. What ensued was later described by the task group commander as "a boarding frenzy." The inspection team from the Canadian destroyer was preparing to board the first of the tugs when a Royal Air Force *Nimrod* maritime patrol aircraft reported several more converging from the northwest. As Lieutenant Ian Wood led his boarding party from one tug to another, the bridge crew back in the destroyer contacted each of the approaching vessels and ordered them into position to be inspected. They reached the lead tug, *Gmmos Power*, exactly at 1400, and during the next six hours the Canadian sailors proceeded in quick order to inspect a total of eight vessels. A ninth tug was hailed but allowed to proceed because it had never entered Iraqi waters. All the tug masters were most cooperative, and no evidence of any activity contrary to UN resolutions was uncovered. *Terra Nova* returned to her patrol station in Charlie-2, holding a record that would last for the duration of the multinational interception effort: the most vessels inspected in the shortest period of time by a single ship in a single day.

Terra Nova was the only Canadian ship then at sea. *Athabaskan* was alongside in Manamah for her scheduled extended maintenance period, which had begun on 10 December and would last until the eighteenth. *Protecteur* also was in that port for 11-13 December. This time there had been no problem getting her a suitable berth. The spacious wardroom of the Canadian tanker was slated to serve as the venue for a major Coalition conference on 12 December, and Commodore Summers was proud to describe her as his "command ship." Following the first Bahrain Conference in mid-September, the Coalition naval partners had held regular monthly meetings to discuss sector allocation, but a number of problems remained in the integration of the allied and Gulf Cooperation Council (GCC) navies. This December conference was important, because for the first time since the earlier Bahrain meeting the military officers of the Gulf States were brought into the process. The meeting was judged a success. Procedures were formalized for information exchange with GCC authorities and the diversion of vessels to Gulf ports. The deliberations revolved around improving coordination of the interception effort and were put into proper focus by the opening remarks of Admiral Stanley Arthur, who had replaced Admiral Mauz as NAVCENT on 1 December. He noted that operations in the Gulf would become more complicated when the USN carriers started to make more frequent incursions.

The tenuous nature of the task group's position was underlined even as it was celebrating these latest triumphs. On the afternoon of 13 December, while her boarding party was busily inspecting the flotilla of tugs and barges, a Canadian *Sea King* delivered two technical experts aboard *Terra Nova* to inspect her troubled *Phalanx*. The first two days of extensive testing were inconclusive. The temperamental equipment obstinately refused to develop any new faults! Then on the sixteenth an unusual wind from the northwest kicked up what should have been only a moderate chop, but it was strong enough to activate the transmitter gyro stabilization malfunction, which was the source of the ship's complaints. The visiting technicians quickly rendered their verdict: replace the complete *Phalanx* weapons group, mounting and all. Unfortunately, the gravity of the situation was not immediately acknowledged by headquarters in Ottawa. The message from *Terra Nova* was misdirected, and since it was a weekend, the staff at headquarters had been reduced.

So far the naval task group had had excellent support from Canada. This particular weekend was an exception. Captain McClean, acting as task group commander, quickly conferred with Miller and Commodore Summers ashore in Manamah. They agreed that with good air and sea defences to the north, the current threat was slight and that there was no need to remove *Terra Nova* to the safety of the Bravo sectors. Still, she could not be allowed to patrol in the Charlie sectors with an unserviceable *Phalanx*. Bold action was necessary to drive the message home; so the destroyer was reassigned to patrol south of Charlie-1. That had the desired effect. By late on 17 December the logistical and movements coordination centres in NDHQ had arranged for a replacement system to be readied in Halifax and for the oversize unit (it was twenty feet high and could not be placed on its side) to be transported to the Gulf in a chartered Bristol *Belfast* cargo aircraft. Meanwhile, the naval logistical detachment in Manamah arranged for the installation work to be undertaken by the local shipyard during the destroyer's planned maintenance period beginning 24 December. This was extended until 3 January to ensure that sufficient time was available for the work. Until she could be repaired, however, *Terra Nova* carried out her patrol of what was euphemistically called "another place."

The remaining patrols for 1990 were in themselves relatively uneventful, although the tension was palpable. Almost daily *Scud* missile test firings raised expectations of an Iraqi preemptive strike at Christmas. *Athabaskan* was prepared to join the multinational boarding of the Iraqi "Peace Ship" *Ibn Khaldoon*, but that was undertaken in the Gulf of Oman by a combined American and Australian force on 26 December. *Protecteur* returned to her Charlie-1 sector on Christmas Eve from a port visit to Abu Dhabi, relieving *Terra Nova*, which proceeded into Manamah for her *Phalanx* replacement. It was to be *Protecteur*'s last patrol of the year, and the final sortie for Captain McClean and his ship's company before their planned rotation with *Preserver*'s replacement crew early in 1991. They went out in fine style. Early on 27 December *Protecteur* hailed her 500th ship, and the twenty-

DATE/TIME	CONDUCTING SHIP(S) SOLO (S) / JOINT (J)	BOARDED M/V	SUPPORTING UNITS
01 OCT., 19:26	ATHABASKAN (S)	TIPPU SULTAN	USS O'BRIEN HMS JUPITER
03 OCT., 08:05	ATHABASKAN (C) HMS BATTLEAXE	AKBAR	HMS BATTLEAXE
09 OCT., 23:00	ATHABASKAN (C) USS O'BRIEN	AKBAR	USS O'BRIEN
13 OCT., 13:33	TERRA NOVA (C) USS BARBEY	AKBAR	USS BARBEY
18 OCT., 13:36	ATHABASKAN (S)	AKBAR	USS O'BRIEN
09 NOV., 00:36	ATHABASKAN (S)	NADA	USS MACDONOUGH (ARRAISONNEMENT DU STEVEN SHAM)
26 NOV., 21:55	TERRA NOVA (S)	TAURUS	
27 NOV., 13:01	PROTECTEUR (S)	GMMOS POWER	
01 DEC., 17:24	ATHABASKAN (S)	NICE TANGO	
03 DEC., 23:25	ATHABASKAN (S)	ALADIN SINDBAD	
06 DEC., 16:52	ATHABASKAN (S)	NICE TANGO SANDRAH	
11 DEC., 12:44	TERRA NOVA (S)	CORNELIS ZANEN	
13 DEC., 14:00	TERRA NOVA (S)	GMMOS POWER MR JACKSON NADA NAASHI 4302 LADY KATHERINE CROWLEY STORM VIKKI LILLIS	RAF NIMROD HMS CARDIFF (LYNX)

Figure 5. Boardings Conducted by Canadian Warships in the Persian Gulf, October–December 1990

ninth, her last day on patrol, proved to be one of her busiest. She refuelled five Coalition warships: US Ships *Worden, Macdonough,* and *Leftwich,* HMS *Brazen,* and her own *Athabaskan.*[17]

The three Canadian ships, representing less than 10 percent of the MIF forces, had accounted for over one quarter (1,644 of 6,103) of the interceptions to date. And they were looking forward to even more. After months of development and training, the task group aircrews and boarding teams were ready to employ the new, helicopter-borne boarding technique known as VISIT (Vertical Insertion Search and Inspection Team). On Christmas Eve, under the watchful gaze of Admiral George and Brigadier-General B.D. Bowen, Commander of Maritime Air Group *Athabaskan's* team demonstrated its prowess by landing a ten-man team from two helicopters onto its fo'c's'le in one minute and fifty-five seconds. But none of the Canadian ships would have an opportunity to conduct any further boardings, let alone put their VISIT procedure into practice. As the 15 January deadline drew nearer, the embargo effort faded into the background. Because of their exclusive employment on the front line of the interception force inside the Persian Gulf, the Canadians never became involved in any of the boardings with a higher profile in the Gulf of Oman. The task group had been active in the surveillance of the two major commercial operations allowed in the Gulf within the strictures of the United Nations sanctions, the Indian relief effort, and the dredging equipment evacuation operation. All inspections which they had undertaken had been without incident. Neither warning shots nor diversions had proved necessary. In total, the Canadians accomplished twenty-two boardings: *Terra Nova* eleven; *Athabaskan* ten; and *Protecteur* one.[18]

As December 1990 came to an end, the Canadians were hardly alone any more in the central Gulf. Initial reaction to the Australian decision in early December to enter the Gulf had been to welcome the prospect of sharing the patrol workload in the Charlie sectors. But those Coalition warships which arrived at the close of the year came for a far different purpose. The American command ships *Blue Ridge* and *LaSalle* put to sea for readiness inspections. *Midway* increased her presence in the Gulf, accompanied by British, Dutch, and Australian escorts. The Canadians, continuing their interception routine, watched the buildup of the Coalition naval forces. This led the task group commander to write on 27 December: "Assessment: USN and Allied support of MIF Ops appears to be redirected towards other tasking. Are we the only ones in step?"[19]

Although Canadian naval commanders were prepared for action in the event of hostilities, for a variety of reasons they had not formalized plans to join the US-led offensive. In large part, this was due to the very success of the MIF operations. The Canadian sailors and airmen had undertaken the tasking with gusto, and the three-ship task group had contributed to the interception effort out of all proportion to their numbers. To them it was always a question of how best they could contribute to the Coalition effort. There seemed little more that they could do.

Task Group 302.3 conducts an underway replenishment (UNREP or RAS), enroute to the Gulf. From top, HMC ships *Athabaskan*, *Protecteur* and *Terra Nova*.

Craning the unserviceable *Sea King* SK404, the "Persian Pig", from *Athabaskan* to *Protecteur* for repairs, 21 September 1990.

Athabaskan's Boarding Party is lowered from Sea King SK413, "Lucky Louis", to VISIT *Protecteur*, December 1990. Note the FLIR on the helicopter's nose.

New air defence systems fitted to Canadian ships for Operation FRICTION — Gunner Denis Arsenault demonstrates the shoulder firing position of the *Javelin* Low Level Air Defence Missile, with the *Phalanx* Close-In Weapon System (CIWS) looming behind.

Athabaskan's RIB (Rigid Inflatable Boat) closes *Protecteur* for a Boarding Party exercise, while the destroyer lays off to assist.

Sailors from *Protecteur* ("Leafs") take on *Athabaskan* ("Canucks") in the Desert Sand Hockey Tournament, Manamah, 12 December 1990. (Final score: Leafs 3-Canucks 2, in overtime.)

Warrant officer D.T. Lynch directs a firefighting team during a Workups exercise aboard *Protecteur* enroute to the Gulf.

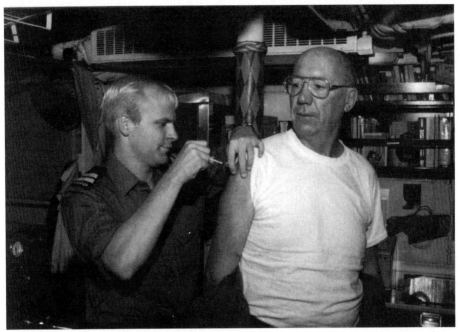

The Navy gets shot in the arm: Chief Petty Officer 2nd Class Einar Falldien receives an innoculation on board *Athabaskan* during a patrol in the Persian Gulf.

A CF-18 taxis along the Class 60 trackway laid by Canadian engineers to increase the available space at Doha airport.

The establishment of an Airlift Control Element (ALCE) requires heavy equipment. Here a K25 loader pulls away from a *Boeing* 707 during Operation SCIMITAR (8 October 1990).

Fighter pilot at Doha demonstrating the AR 5 chemical defence gear required for missions over the Gulf.

Major Dave Kendall and Captain Steve "Hillbilly" Hill after their attack on the Iraqi patrol boat. (With kind permission of David Deere, publisher of *Desert Cats*.(1991))

A CF-18 refuels from the Canadian *Boeing* 707 while on Combat Air Patrol over the Northern Gulf, 18 January 1991. Note the AIM-9 *Sidewinder* heat-seeking missile at the wing tip, the AIM-7 *Sparrow* radar-guided missile underwing, and two clearly visible external fuel tanks.

Air weapons technicians Master Corporal Réjean Boucher, with Corporals Randy Boutilier and Sue Lefebvre, load 500-pound Mark 82 bombs on CF-18s at Doha, 26 February 1991.

Camp al-Nasr (Canada Dry One) before …

… and after transformation by Canadian engineers.

Headquarters, Canadian Forces Middle East, on the waterfront in Manamah, Bahrain.

A component of the GT 185 high seas oil boom skimmer provided by Germany for Operation SPONGE being off-loaded from a CC-130 *Hercules*, 20 February 1990.

Soldiers of the Royal Canadian Regiment tending to Iraqi POWs at al-Qaysumah, 2 March 1991. Note the *Grizzly* personnel carriers in the background, which were converted for use as ambulances, with the Red Crescent painted under the front bumper.

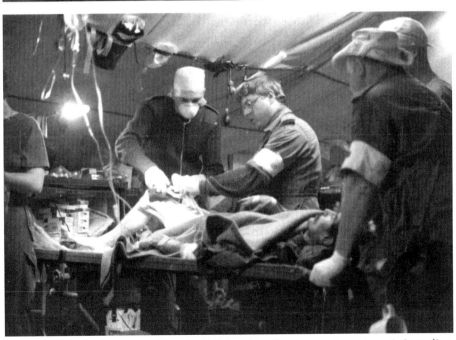

An Iraqi POW being treated by Dr. Pritchard in the "resuss" section, 1 Canadian Field Hospital, 26 February 1991.

Master Corporal Paul Mitchell works the Remote Mobile Investigator (RMI) during a bomb search exercise at Canada Dry 2, Doha, 30 January 1991.

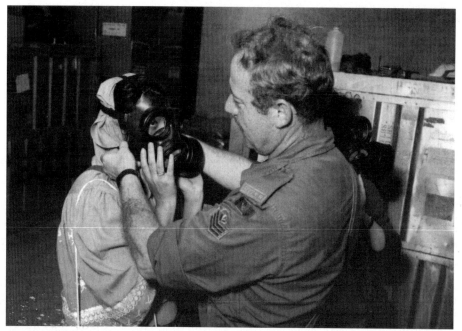

Sergeant Gilles Fortin from CANFORME HQ explains the fitting of Canadian C3 gas masks to civilians in Manamah, Bahrain, January 1991.

Signs — All over! Captain J.S. Généreux adds to the post at Doha, December 1990.

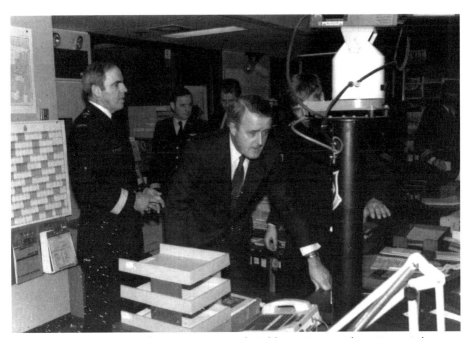

Prime Minister Brian Mulroney receives a brief from Commodore Bruce Johnston in the National Defence Operations Room, with General de Chastelain and Minister McKnight looking on, 4 February 1991.

Minister McKnight is received by His Excellency Abdulla bin Kalifa Al Thani, the Minister of the Interior for Qatar.

General de Chastelain looks through a telescope under the watchful gaze of Deputy Minister Robert Fowler, during a tour of the Doha security perimeter on 30 October 1990.

The Commander of Maritime Command, Vice Admiral Robert E.D. George (with cap), speaks with Leading Seaman Wayne Finn aboard *Protecteur* prior to a jackstay transfer to one of the Canadian destroyers.

The Commanders of Forces Mobile Command, Lieutenant-General Kent Foster (centre, hand on hip), and of Air Command, Lieutenant-General Fred Sutherland, accompanied by Colonel Lalonde on an inspection of the security troops from 1st battalion, Royal 22nd Regiment, in Doha.

15 January 1991 — Commodore Ken Summers (centre), with his Chief of Staff, Colonel Dave Bartram (left), and Commander Jean-Yves Forcier, discussing plans in the event of war.

Midnight, 17 January 1991 — Commodore Summers addresses the staff of HQ CANFORME, to alert them of the upcoming air offensive.

Captain (N) "Dusty" Miller discusses naval operations with the Deputy Chief of Defence Staff, Lieutenant-General David Huddleston, aboard *Athabaskan*.

Before their turnover and return home, the original crew of *Protecteur* gathered on the supply ship's flight deck to say "Thank you, Canada" on behalf of all those who served in the Gulf.

As Duty Tanker, *Protecteur* fuels the assault ships *Iwo Jima* (right) and *Fort McHenry* (left) of the US Marine Corps Amphibious Ready Group BRAVO in the *Ponderosa*, 1 February 1991.

Protecteur approaches US Hospital Ship *Mercy* for an underway refuelling, 27 January 1991.

They occupied stations far up in the central Gulf. *Athabaskan* and *Terra Nova* were busy conducting boardings. *Protecteur*'s services were more and more in demand. The entire Canadian naval effort was geared to the tense operating conditions on the front line of interception work. They were the police of the central Gulf, where the distinction between interception forces and the more overtly military activity of the Coalition was blurred. The transition to war seemed like the natural course of events and began to dominate discussions between Admiral Fogarty and Admiral March. Operation BASTION and the commencement of offensive operations would mean the abandonment of the central Gulf by all non-involved forces and hence the curtailing of MIF operations. The anticipated logistical force escort duties admittedly would be useful work, but they definitely would be a step back from their high-profile established in the interception operations.

Captain Miller was also facing the prospect of the sequential rotation of his ships' crews. The rotation was to start on 1 January with *Protecteur*, be followed in February with *Athabaskan* and his own task group staff, and culminate in March with *Terra Nova*. Along with necessary maintenance and work-up periods, the plan called for each of the ships in turn to be off operations for a full month. For the next three months, then, the Canadian task group commander was looking at a one-third reduction in the size of his task group and a drastic diminution in his operating flexibility. His earlier exhortation to *Terra Nova* that "Glory is fleeting but obscurity is nothing" must have come back to haunt him.

The Canadian task group ended 1990 with all three ships alongside for the first time since the beginning of October: *Terra Nova* in Manamah, with her *Phalanx* replacement progressing well; and *Athabaskan* and *Protecteur* in Dubai, the former for a planned maintenance period before the expected surge in operations in the New Year, and the latter for a turnover in her ship's company in a few days' time.

Programs for Troop Morale
During the fall of 1990, there were many ups and downs in troop morale. Sometimes these fluctuations were very obvious. At other times they were far more subtle. The moral support of the troops took on a primary importance, and the influence of public opinion was far from minimal.

During October, the creation of the air element at Qatar and pictures taken at Doha of the CF-18s in their desert decor aroused an enormous public interest. Canadians became avid followers of news from the Gulf. All the glamour and romance, however, belonged to the air force. When the naval task group reached the Gulf at the beginning of the month, the media conducting interviews on ship could not help but notice that after the initial patrols and the first boardings, the operations quickly became routine. Moreover, the burden of the heat, the repetition of the same low-intensity tasks (which seemed to stir some excitement only for the officers and combat teams on duty on the bridge), and the lack of information on the duration of the deployment - all these things tarnished the mission in the minds of many of the crew. Their intense training had raised expectations, and now these same expectations had been severely deflated.

In fact, morale on the ships was not bad around the middle of October, but a few sailors were upset and frustrated. One of them was so unhappy that he slipped a note to the influential reporter Paul Koring, who described the situation aboard *Athabaskan* as "more than simple discontent." The *Globe and Mail* picked up the story and put it on its front page. It described a situation in which there were so many complaints on board the ships that it was becoming difficult to contain them.[20] The navy was infuriated. It claimed that the story was based on hearsay and generalized from an isolated incident.

Public relations officers in the theatre and in Ottawa spent several weeks combating the negative effects of Koring's article. Their response was to repeat enthusiastic messages and direct camera crews towards Doha, where there were plenty of "sexy" air force machines to photograph. Indeed, Doha became a place of pilgrimage for Canadian cameramen, who could take enough shots to feed articles for years to come. However, despite the best efforts of public relations to regain the favour of the media, journalists continued to emphasize the isolation, disorientation, and homesickness felt by the men and women in uniform. The troops' initial enthusiasm for the mission was replaced by stoic resolution and a spirit of duty and courage. The message was clear: things were not easy in the Gulf. And the atmosphere reflected it.

The public began to show its sympathy. Televised reports mentioned "yellow ribbon" campaigns in the United States on behalf of their men and women in the middle of the Saudi desert. Canadians followed the cue from south of the border and began to write letters and send gifts to their own troops. There was a major surge in mail. Most *Hercules* and *Boeing* aircraft with leftover space were topped up with small mountains of grey postal bags. Military mailmen had never seen so much mail.

A large proportion of letters carried general addresses such as "To the Soldiers in the Gulf"; "To a Sailor aboard *Protecteur*"; "To a Canadian Airman".[21] Some letters were gentle, simple, and touching. Others were strangely moving or very personal. And still others were quite disarming, reaching into the heart of the recipients with a single word or a well-expressed idea or emotion. Of course, most of the correspondence could give only a moment's pleasure in the midst of a windfall of greetings. No one back in Canada expected a reply, but probably many quietly hoped for one.

And there were the packages - the gifts - in all shapes and sizes. Some were addressed to particular units, and others to no unit or person in particular. The gifts were of every description: aftershave lotion, perfume, underwear, toothbrushes, and sweets; board games, books, magazines, and newspapers; gift certificates for telephone calls and electronic appliances for individual and communal use; and even a wide variety of crude and funny T-shirts. The Veterans Association sent $120,000 worth of large-screen video television sets. It was a gesture of enormous generosity. The sets were distributed in a way to reach the maximum number of troops. Video rental companies shipped over hundreds of films, and other organizations provided recordings of sports events and popular television programs. The videos went a long way to relieve the hours of boredom and inactivity experienced by the troops between periods of duty.

Two of the more bizarre presents were a shipment of 125,000 condoms from a Montreal distributor, who thought that they would be effective in protecting equipment against sand and rain, and flea collars for "personal protection." Left unprotected in the desert, one's scalp was a prime target for fleas. How the condoms were used is anyone's guess, but the flea collars were forbidden for medical reasons.[22]

Once the gifts reached camp, they were opened in common areas, and everyone could dig in and choose what appealed to him or her. The troops were astonished by this cornucopia. An attempt to answer their benefactors personally proved impossible. There were simply too many letters and packages, on average several dozen per person.

All this lavish attention on the troops in the Gulf hurt the feelings of the many Canadians involved in other peacekeeping missions - in Israel, Egypt, Central America, and Africa. Many veterans had never seen a letter addressed to "A Soldier on Mission" in the course of one, two, or even three years of service abroad with the UN. Before long, however, the peacekeapers were sharing in the profusion of gifts. Hundreds and hundreds were redirected to them. Soon, large banners plastered with signatures and good wishes from all across Canada appeared in UN missions from San Salvador to Cyprus.[23] The many gifts and messages, the heartfelt encouragement and admiration, were unexpected but more than welcome.

To return to the Gulf: there were not enough walls to pin up all the children's drawings which arrived in bundles from practically every Canadian school. Thousands of greetings were mixed with an infinite variety of drawings. In many cases they featured "war art": jets machine-gunning Iraqis, ships launching missiles, puffed-up warriors who were armed to the teeth and busy breaking down walls, and naturally the red maple leaf. Obviously, the children thought that everything was Canadian - the tanks, the bombers, the *Humvees*, the artillery, the *Patriot* missiles, and the aircraft carriers. They seemed to have no idea that this stuff belonged to the Americans. Many service members found the children's confusion uneasy to bear and, at times, their violent art upsetting in its endless repetition. Many were uncomfortable with the primitive drawings of a generation bred on television violence. As parents of young children themselves, they felt sensitive to family values, a sensitivity no doubt exacerbated by the distance between themselves and their own families. The message of the drawings was clear: our children were finding in war a theme which they enjoyed. In the overflow of friendly mail, thousands of these drawings were left in their boxes.

The public's interest in the troops, especially near Christmas, gave a considerable boost to morale. The 1990 holiday season was the calm before the storm. On 21 December, General de Chastelain addressed a letter "to Canadians," thanking them for their exceptional support of the forces in the Gulf. He concluded, "You have shown that they are with us in thought despite the miles which separate us."[24]

Notes

1   See Jocelyn Coulon, "Le Canada est prêt à une offensive contre l'Irak avec ou sans le consentement des Nations unies [Canada is ready for an offensive against Iraq with or without the consent of the United Nations]," *Le Devoir* (Montréal), 26 October 1990, and Tim Harper, "War Threat 'Real', Clark Warns," *Toronto Star*, 26 October 1990; and "Preparing Canadians for the Possibility of a Gulf War," *Toronto Globe and Mail*, 27 October 1990.

2   See "Troops Out of the Gulf," *CP*, 26 November 1990; "Canadians against War in the Gulf," *Ottawa Citizen*, 27 November 1990; and "End of Arms Race," *Vancouver Sun*, 30 November 1990.

3   The distinction in the military terms should be noted here. The expression "joint" means operations which bring together elements of various *arms* (like the Canadian joint HQ) and "combined" means the contribution of elements of several *countries* in the same operation. IMMINENT THUNDER was thus both a *combined* and *joint* exercise, basically uniting the constituent elements of the forces of the United States, Saudi Arabia, Great Britain, and secondary countries in the coalition, such as the European Community and Canada. The scenario of the exercise made it possible to integrate these elements in a notional context. This helped to familiarize each of them with the procedures and tactics which would probably be used in the event of fighting - defensively, for the protection of Saudi Arabia and military sites (an eventuality still considered possible at that date); and offensively, to attack Iraqi forces in Kuwait and Iraq.

4   WD CANFORME, "Briefing - Exercise IMMINENT THUNDER," 13 November 1990.

5   Canada, House of Commons, *Debates*, 19 November 1990, pp. 15385-86.

6   *GWAPS*, p. 198.

7   WD NDHQ, " OP FRICTION Facts and Figures as of 28 Feb 91," 1 March 1991.

8   "PM Won't Rule Out Troop Move," *Toronto Globe and Mail*, 13 November 1990.

9   WD CTG 302.3, COMMARCOM, "OP FRICTION - Guidance from CDS," 19 October 1990.

10   Both the US and Royal Navies also operated *Sea King* helicopters in the Gulf, but they were attached mostly to shore units. Moreover, there were sufficient differences between the models that making use of their facilities was not a viable option.

11   WD CTG 302.3, " ASSESSREP/027/Nov," 27 November 1990.

12   *The Guide*, p. 330.

13   In preparation for operations, the USN plans called for each of the earlier American task group commanders (CTGs) to become full task force commanders (CTFs) effective 1 January 1991. Their numbering would be altered to illustrate the transition, i.e., CTG 150.1 became CTF 151, CTG 150.2 to CTF 152, etc. COMUSNAVCENT retained overall command as CTF 150.

14   de la Billière, *Storm Command*, p. 137.

15   It is doubtful if the debate on whether sanctions alone could have worked can ever be resolved. In their thorough analysis of the diplomacy of the Gulf crisis, and the influence of the embargo upon it, Freedman and Karsh, *The Gulf Conflict*, Chapter 13, "The Food Weapon," pp. 189-98, conclude that sanctions by themselves most likely would not have persuaded the Iraqi dictator to withdraw from Kuwait. The difficulty in resolving the problem is also addressed in *The Kuwait Crisis: Sanctions and Their Economic Consequences*, Cambridge International Document Series, vol. 2, ed. Daniel Bethlehem (Cambridge: Grotius, 1991), "Some Unanswered Questions," pp. xlii-xliii.

16   WD CTG 302.3, "Final SITREP - MV SINDBAD and MV ALADIN," 3 December 1990. Ironically, that

was not the end of the episode. HMS *London* boarded the same two vessels the next morning. There was an occasional lack of information exchange within the Coalition. This was the inevitable consequence of an informal command and control relationship. This example was disconcerting because it involved three of the more long-established of the NATO naval allies.

17 *Protecteur* completed sixty-four replenishments while on patrol in the central Gulf from October to December 1990. The breakdown by nations is as follows: 29 Canadian; 23 USN; 9 RN; and one each French, Dutch, and Australian.

18 Up to the outbreak of hostilities (i.e., the period of active Canadian participation), the MIF would conduct 833 boardings, of which eleven required the firing of warning shots and thirty-five resulted in diversion to a neutral port.

19 WD CTG 302.3, ASSESSREP/027/Dec," 27 December 1990.

20 Paul Koring, "Fear of War Shadows Canadian Sailors," *Toronto Globe and Mail*, 5 October 1990.

21 The volume visibly increased after 19 November, when Mr McKnight announced (National Defence *Press Release, AFN:* 68/90, 19 November 1990) that Canada Post had offered to provide letter service free of charge to the 1,700 troops stationed in the Persian Gulf. On 30 November, the Canadian Press revealed in one of its articles that the volume of mail was such that delivery was running more than three weeks behind at Trenton, where every week an average of 280,000 pieces were sent by military aircraft. This amounted to about 160 letters per person deployed in Operation FRICTION. See "Military Getting Overabundance of Mail," Regina *Leader-Post*, 30 November 1990.

22 Captain Michelle Lesieur, "L'opération Friction – les dons et les commodités dans le golfe : le maintain du moral des troupes," *Périscope*, pp. 7-9.

23 The missions in which Canada had troops in late 1990 were the following:

UNMOGIP	United Nations Military Observer Group in India and Pakistan
OSGAP	Office of the Secretary-General in Afghanistan and Pakistan
UNCMAC	United Nations Command Military Armistice Commission (Korea)
UNTSO	United Nations Truce Supervision Organization
UNDOF	United Nations Disengagement Observer Force
UNIFIL	United Nations Force in Lebanon
UNIIMOG	United Nations Iran-Iraq Military Observer Group
UNFICYP	United Nations Peace-keeping Force in Cyprus
UNOCA	United Nations Observer Group in Central America
MFO	Multinational Force and Observers
UNOVEH	Observation Mission for the Verification of the Elections in Haiti.

24 National Defence, "Letter of Thanks from the Chief of the Defence Staff to Canadians," *Communiqué*, AFN: 77/90, 21 December 1990.

CHAPTER 7

The Air War:
December 1990 – February 1991

Change of Command at Doha

The change of command from Colonel Philip Engstad to Colonel Roméo Lalonde at Doha, on 19 December, marked another step in the evolution of Canadian participation in the Coalition. As the builder of the small Canadian enclave at Doha, Colonel Engstad had met the immediate challenges. In large measure he had turned a NATO air superiority squadron into a UN naval air defence squadron-group. Colonel Lalonde, after having worked for three months in the shadow of Commodore Summers, was familiar with the military and political workings which influenced the decision-making in the Canadian command. On arrival at Qatar, Lalonde's first objective was to make the Air Group as flexible as possible in its response to directives emanating from Manamah. Also on 19 December, the commanders of 409 and 439 Squadrons changed responsibilities. Lieutenant-Colonel Ed Campbell was leaving Doha. He was being replaced by Lieutenant-Colonel Donald C. Matthews.

Colonel Campbell had trained and led his *Nighthawks* in their naval air role. Although the first weeks had been full of surprises and difficulties, the solid bonds which were created among the international elements of the Coalition had made the work of the Canadians rewarding and satisfying. Canadian pilots profited professionally from supporting the cruisers at sea and participating in the varied exercises with the air forces of the United Arab Emirates, Saudi Arabia, Qatar, France, Great Britain, and the United States. In fact, many of the pilots considered the Gulf a richer environment than Europe where, after many years, the tasks had become routine and repetitive.

The new commanding officer, Colonel Matthews, had done a thirty-day tour in Doha in October to help set up the operations cell and familiarize himself with the new setting. He visited U.S. Navy and Marine aviators and established the initial agreements to coordinate missions. Just before Commodore Summers took command of CANFORME, Matthews was officially informed that his own 439 *Tiger* Squadron was to replace 409. He then returned to Germany on 5 November to prepare his squadron.

Out of the thirty-six pilots originally forming 409 in October, nearly half came from 439 and 421 *Red Indian* Squadrons, drafted in to form Lieutenant-Colonel Campbell's one enlarged squadron. Nearly a third of the pilots from 439

Squadron already had been given to the first contingent. Half the officers now needed at Doha, therefore, were supplied by a squadron based in Canada, 416 *Lynx*.[1] Beginning almost immediately and lasting for the next five weeks, the members of *Tiger* and *Lynx* Squadrons left Baden-Söllingen and Cold Lake in small groups for Doha and formed a single squadron named the *Desert Cats*.

Given their disparate backgrounds, a flexible integration program had to be set up. It had the double task of accommodating each pilot according to his level of training and bringing him up to a common standard. Routine operational patrol flights, which began on their arrival, were not demanding on machines or reflexes, but the "red" exercises, in which one group played the enemy, pushed the new pilots to the very limit of their capabilities. They performed formation flying with different types of aircraft, instrument flying, and tactical serials in electronic warfare and at night. It was in these daily exercises, in the wide areas reserved for this purpose by CENTAF in the south-eastern sectors of Saudi Arabia, rather than in the circular operational patrols over the Gulf, that the pilots kept up their combat flight techniques. By 20 December, there remained only a few "old" *Nighthawks* on location. The *Desert Cats* felt ready to take over for the next fourteen weeks.

For some time, the *Desert Cats* had known that they had a greater chance than the *Nighthawks* of taking part in any combat. The adoption of Resolution 678 on 29 November and the constant American preparations, which had been taking place since the summer, increased the probability of a confrontation during January. NDHQ was ready to offer the government various options. After visiting General Horner at Riyadh in November, General Huddleston had been preparing briefings for the minister, which included important factors to consider in any decision to involve the CF-18s in combat missions. Beyond flying in air defence patrols, the CF-18s could escort bombers, and, if the government wished, act as bomb carriers in the course of an attack by the Coalition. The *Hornet* was one of the most versatile fighting machines in the world. Moreover, Canadian pilots, even though they often specialized in only one combat role, had undergone rigorous training in all aspects of combat duty. In the majority of cases, a refresher course would suffice to bring back the necessary skills for carrying out different missions.[2] The pilots could also be chosen for particular missions, in accordance with their respective experience.

When Colonel Matthews took up his command on 19 December, the country hoped that these military preparations would prove unnecessary. But prospects were gloomy. There were only four weeks left before the expiration of the official deadline set by the UN. Canadian authorities, in concert with their Coalition partners, took the situation seriously enough to adopt measures that were costly and full of political implications. For example, Canada decided to repatriate the families of military and diplomatic personnel in the Middle East. This caused many headaches. These families generally had no Canadian place of residence; they were not told how long they would be separated from their spouse or parent; and they had to leave without many of their personal effects.

On other fronts, United Nations contingents began defensive preparations to avoid being caught in crossfire in the demilitarized zones. They were rightfully leary of gas attacks and pro-Saddam terrorism. At the same time, a report from Amnesty International, alleging atrocities by Iraqi troops on Kuwaiti soil, created an outcry of condemnation. Public opinion, strongly influenced by Amnesty's evidence (much of which had been exaggerated, as was shown later), violently condemned the Iraqi actions.[3] With each new accusation hurled by one side or the other, the likelihood of retractions and retreat diminished. The various media, just before Christmas, were full of stories about the difficulties leading to the delay of a meeting between Foreign Minister Tariq Aziz of Iraq and the American Secretary of State James Baker. Both men took several opportunities to express their irreconcilable demands, leaving no room to manoeuvre. The only argument left was the horrible prospect of an all out war, and even it did very little to avert the confrontation.

At Doha, not only the pilots but also the ground crews were changed, according to the air force policy of a fourteen-week rotation for everyone in the Canadian Air Group. Once more the teams had to be reformed and the work setting reshaped. On the personnel administration side, the formation of a second complete contingent was more difficult because there was an insufficient pool of replacements. It became necessary to widen the search to include all the Canadian Forces. Some newly acquired integrated software, which had been put in place in the fall for operations FRICTION, SCIMITAR, and ACCORD, helped to organize and regularize the rotation of all 550 members of the Air Task Group. For the fourteen-week period, the problem of rotating personnel was extremely complex. Rotation for the other services had been planned on a six-month basis, and the matrices of their trades and qualifications were, in a general technical sense, much simpler than they were for the Air Group, with its multiple, narrowly qualified specialists. The navy and army, moreover, preferred exchanging formed units at the six month point..

As a result, the airport security infantry company was replaced by another one at the end of the fourteen weeks. Mike Company of the 3rd Battalion, RCR, was relieved at the end of December by Charlie Company of the 1st Battalion, Royal 22e Régiment, also of 4 Canadian Mechanized Brigade Group in Lahr. The "Van Doos" took up their positions in the trenches and at the guard posts, but many war preparations still had to be made. During the following weeks, with the permission of the Qatari authorities, they constructed sandbag bunkers to protect the perimeter of the base against infiltrations, individual terrorist raids, and group attacks.

War Plans

An order from General de Chastelain, on 29 November 1990, directed that attention be paid to several contingency plans in the event of hostilities. These related almost exclusively to the Air Task Group and involved the possibility of moving forward the Canadian Forces' only available *Boeing 707* in-flight refueller. According to the first war plan, code-named ENSCONCE, the refueller would go to Akrotiri and assist in the deployment of additional CF-18s to the front at the onset of hostilities. The second plan, code-named ENOBLE, identified six CF-18s and almost a hundred additional technicians. The CF-18s would replace air losses, and the technicians would augment the squadron's strength as soon as necessary. Another plan, called ENSEMBLE, following on ENSCONCE and ENOBLE, called for sending the refueller to Doha in order to assist the CF-18s in their operations. This would enable the squadron to maintain its patrols without having to be supported by allied refuellers, on which it was sometimes difficult to count. The reconnaissance took place and preliminary authorizations were given towards the middle of December, when replacement aircraft were being escorted, so that everything was ready for the change of command. From that moment, Husky One, including relief crews and ground crews, was on call.

Other plans dealt with the possibility of losses in personnel. A replacement plan, code-named ENNUI, was devised, covering up to 20 percent of all Canadian personnel in the theatre of operations. These replacements would be reinforcements on demand. A medical team led by a psychiatrist, Major Michael J. Kelly, was ready for deployment at the first critical incident.

Then there were plans to ensure an increased tempo of operations once hostilities actually began. The volume of air transport provided by ATG would be augmented under ENSILE, to allow a faster air bridge. Plan ENRICH dealt with maintenance procedures, so that they could be modified to less exacting standards through a special program known as WAMP (Wartime Air Maintenance Program). Flying hours could then be increased between mandatory periodic inspections. The Chief of Defence Staff could activate any of these new procedures and war plans by individual code word.

Communications Command also drew up an augmentation plan for its personnel. CFB Kingston became the preparation base for all personnel posted to the theatre of operations. Forty-six postings were issued on 18 December for departure on 11 January, so that the new arrivals could be on the job in Doha or Manamah by the fifteenth. Some, however, left with only minimum training. That was the case with the photographic intelligence technicians who were sent to Riyadh to join the Black Hole team in bomb damage analysis (BDA). This small group, who took with them their own light tables for air photo analysis, left in a few hours.

As soon as the Canadian bases were set up at Doha and Manamah, alert procedures were designed to recall individuals to their posts. Many exercises were conducted to adjust these measures to particular circumstances and to ensure that everyone could react properly to the signals. One procedure new to this operation was also extended to the ships at sea. The TOPP conditions (Threat-Oriented Personal Protection) demanded the wearing of NBC suits, more or less completely, in accordance with the level of alert, which was determined by the degree of probability of nuclear, biological, or chemical attack. In TOPP LOW, the protective clothing had to be kept in one's kit-bag and within reach. In TOPP MEDIUM, the suit would be worn but not hermetically sealed; the mask would be in one's pack and slung across the shoulder; and antidote syringes (HI-6 and atropine) would be kept in the mask pouch, ready to be used along with decontamination gloves and lotion. In TOPP HIGH, one had to be ready to deal with an imminent attack. The mask and suit would be worn airtight, and all measures would be taken to ensure the greatest effectiveness in a combat position in surroundings vitiated by harmful substances. The TOPP HIGH state would be declared during all enemy missile launching alerts, during every air attack alert, and at the approach of any unidentified threat to a base. WHITE, YELLOW, and RED were the warning conditions. They indicated, respectively, three states of alert: normal, intensified, and full, with respect to all types of air attack: manned aircraft, cruise missiles, and ground-to-ground ballistic missiles. A series of exercises named FLYING CARPET was conducted at Doha during December to familiarize the many new arrivals with all the latest measures. Each exercise lasted several days.

The Manamah HQ also carried out war preparation exercises. Desk personnel had to do guard duty because the military police who directed the access points were neither numerous enough nor sufficiently well trained to carry out a defence of the perimeter in a war setting. Although 90 HQ & Sigs was an army unit and had many experienced soldiers in its ranks, it was still an improvised unit, not trained in the refinements of defence planning and the construction of bunkers and control posts. These additional duties heavily taxed the staff and increased the hours of work to the point where, after some days of notional alert, they came to the conclusion that infantry would have to be called in. A platoon of the 3rd Battalion of the Royal Canadian Regiment from Baden-Söllingen arrived at the HQ on 21 January and assumed the defence of headquarters.

With war preparations taking place on all levels, the Canadian government was ready to react to any emergency that might arise in the event of war being declared. Under the direction of the Privy Council Office, an interdepartmental consultation network and a decision-making pyramid were set up (see figure 6). A committee of the leading cabinet ministers was formed to enable the government to respond to war-related needs. These structures were based in large part on the ad hoc crisis management mechanisms implemented for the Oka crisis in the summer of 1990. The prime minister officially announced the creation of the Committee of Ministers for Gulf crisis matters on 8 January, calling it the "Peace Cabinet." Journalists called it a "War Cabinet," and they used this term throughout the crisis. Whatever its name, it constituted a novel approach to government crisis management, highlighted by the fact that General de Chastelain and General Huddleston had immediate access to government consultative bodies and decision-making powers whenever required.

The Last Days Before the War
On 29 December, unknown to the world at large, President Bush told General Schwarzkopf that American forces would attack on 17 January, at 0300 local time.

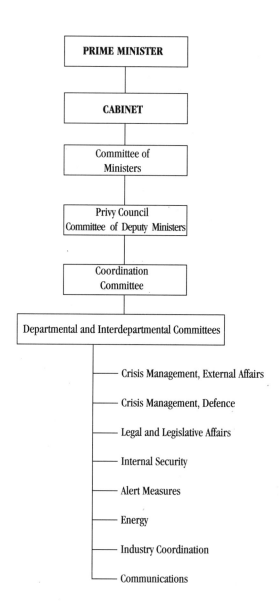

Figure 6. Governmental Crisis Management Organization for the Gulf War

In these strange circumstances, in which the start of war was predetermined, preparations unfolded with a rare degree of precision. January 15, the deadline imposed by UN Resolution 678, was considered D-Day in Canada, the day when all preparations had to be complete. Since there was little likelihood of a change in policy, preparatory measures were speeded up in a series of practical decisions and by the activation of contingency plans in accordance with a timetable that grew steadily fuller between 1 January 1991 (D Minus 15 or D-15) and D-Day.

On D-15, certain readjustments to the command and control responsibilities for the Canadian Forces in Europe, which had been decided several months previously, had major implications for the Gulf deployments. These changes were to come into effect on the last day of 1990, a choice which now appeared less judicious than originally intended. On that day, which was indeed rather late, responsibility for 1 Canadian Air Division reverted to Lieutenant-General Sutherland's Air Command in Winnipeg. Likewise, the forward elements of the army's First Division remained in Germany but now came under Mobile Command, in Saint-Hubert, Québec. As of 1 January 1991, therefore, Air Command assumed full command, with support responsibilities for the Air Group in Doha, Commodore Summers's *Challenger* at Manamah, and the *Boeing 707* in-flight refueller. Mobile Command was given similar responsibilities for the security infantry company at Doha and the Manamah platoon. Brigadier-General Banks of Communications Command retained his relationship with 90 HQ and Signals Squadron in Bahrain, and Major-General Smith kept his ties with the Canadian Support Unit in Qatar. This reorganization required new lines of communication between the units in the theatre of operations and the commands responsible for their support (see Figure 7).

The threat which hung over military personnel in the theatre of operations was no less real for civilians. On D-8, agreements were made between External Affairs and the Department of National Defence to distribute gas masks to Canadian residents who asked for them, in the countries where Canadian Forces had contingents. A staff team, including an officer and a non-commissioned officer at Manamah, managed an NBC protection program for civilians in the Gulf. On D-5, they distributed seventy masks in a single day at Manamah and taught rudimentary survival techniques to each person. In the end, External Affairs, working with non-governmental organizations such as the Red Cross, offered nearly 10,000 Model C3 masks to the threatened civilian population.

In Canada, the approach of the 15 January deadline provoked some public opposition. "NO BLOOD FOR OIL" summed up the thoughts of many who opposed the deployment of military forces to defend Western business interests in Kuwait. Pictures from Iraq showed a people who did not want war and were being pushed into it by state propaganda. On 10 January, there were marches around the Parliament buildings and National Defence Headquarters. In response to the wild speculation concerning the number of killed and wounded which both sides might suffer, Mr McKnight spoke to the media and mentioned that Canada might provide a field hospital (see Chapter 9) and send six additional fighter aircraft. On Sunday, 13 January, some 25,000 Canadians in thirty-two cities demonstrated against Canada's policy of intervention.

On D-15, the government gave tacit consent to the CF-18s taking part in escort missions in the event of hostilities, but for diplomatic reasons the announcement was withheld until the declaration of war. In the meantime, training was intensified, and NDHQ even studied the possibility of participating in bombing. Lieutenant-Colonel Matthews shared this idea with his pilots on 2 January and urged them to think in terms of imminent war.

As the countdown continued, the CF-18s were readied to carry out combat air patrol missions twenty-four hours a day on the Whiskey-1 circuit. Six aircraft with the highest number of elapsed flying hours returned to Germany and were replaced by aircraft from 4 Wing, which had been freshly inspected and overhauled. They were accompanied to the Gulf by Husky One, the *Boeing* tanker commanded by Major Robert M. Prystai. They arrived for training on D-7. On D-5, the Air Group established operational routines for AAR manoeuvres without radio contact, which became easier with practice. The air refueller even carried out training missions with up to eight pairs of CF-18s. Air traffic over the Gulf was so heavy at times that aircraft had to line up to be refuelled. The CF-18s could also be refuelled by allied tanker models, such as the USAF KC-135s, recently refitted with Navy-compatible probes and drogues (which the CF-18 used). On D-1, authorization was officially given to the CF-18s to receive fuel from RAF and US Navy tankers. By then, the Gulf countries were giving free access to all Gulf and Shell Oil fuel distribution points. This made refuelling much easier to administer.

Once the intensive training with Husky One proved satisfactory, General de Chastelain gave the signal "ENOBLE," on 11 January, sending the refueller to Akrotiri to join up with the additional six CF-18s. The group left Cyprus at 0600 on D-2. With their arrival at Doha, the number of Canadian fighters increased to twenty-four and the escort mission was completed. Then everything fell into place. The *Boeing* officially came under the operational command of Commodore Summers; the wartime refuelling operation ENSEMBLE was activated; training flights were interrupted; and patrol missions on the circuits were increased in anticipation of surprise attacks before D-Day.

Particularly strenuous efforts were made to correct the deficiencies that still existed in tactical air communications. During the last days of December the pressure of the international situation forced the Canadians to improve their position in the air. On D-16, the CF-18s once again were vectored in pursuit of Iraqi aircraft venturing beyond the territorial limit of Kuwait. However, Canadian communications, which were efficient but less advanced than those of the Americans, slowed down their intervention. In peacetime, seconds lost were not vital, but in wartime every second would be crucial to the protection of the ships. The time had come to provide the CF-18s with the best equipment possible.

The Link-4 system was obtained by special diplomatic and military representations made in Ottawa and Washington. After a month of discussions, the American digital data receivers were installed at the beginning of the new year. The first Canadian plane flew with the Link-4 on D-2. By the evening of the same day, 13 January, all the Canadian aircraft had been equipped with it, to the great satisfaction of the pilots. In addition, the WSC-3 naval satellite communications system was obtained from Halifax and installed in the new Canadian Control Centre at Doha, creating a direct link to the anti-aircraft cruisers at sea. These improvements allowed the CF-18s to be placed on proper alert within NAVCENT.

Many missions were conducted during the next two days to allow the pilots to use the new Link-4 sets in various circumstances and to train the ground crews in degrees of operational intensity to which they were unaccustomed. Short missions were carried out over Saudi Arabian territory to familiarize pilots with flight procedures and to check communications with ground and air stations. The armaments on the aircraft were also changed. The number of short-range missiles (AIM-9 *Sidewinder* units, with a range of approximately ten miles) was increased from two to four, and the number of long-range missiles (AIM-7 *Sparrow* units, with a range of approximately sixty miles) was decreased from four to three.

All Canadian fighter aircraft were armed by 2100 Zulu (Greenwich Mean Time) on D-3. The day before D-Day, an unusual note was sent to the *Desert Cats* from the Deputy Commander of USCENTAF at Riyadh. Major-General Thomas R. Olsen congratulated the Canadian Air Group for having placed all its aircraft on a war footing, noting that they were the first formation in the theatre to be completely ready for the next day.

The Final Countdown

In the midst of mounting speculation on all sides, D-Day and D+1 passed in the Gulf without any major incidents. The hours ticked by backwards in the preparatory countdown plans, until 0759 on 16 January (2359 on the fifteenth in the eastern part of North America). This marked the end of the forty-six-day period of grace which the United Nations had granted Iraq. At 1600 local time, the entire headquarters personnel at Manamah were recalled to their offices and told to remain there until further orders; at 2200 orders were issued to take pyridostigmine bromide pills to guard against the effects of toxic gases.

A little after midnight, Commodore Summers called all the joint headquarters personnel together in the canteen and announced that in a few hours the Coalition would strike. During the day he had learned that night attacks would inaugurate the assault on Iraq. A Canadian Forces film team, which was passing through, videotaped Summers as he addressed all ranks who were present: "Like it or not, Ladies and Gentlemen, we're going to be involved in something in the very, very near future."[4] It was an unforgettable moment.

Prime Minister Mulroney had received two calls from President Bush on 16 January. The first one was in the morning and warned that the attack was in preparation and that more details would be made available during the day. The second call came late in the afternoon and confirmed that the attack was going to take place in two hours. Mulroney was still trying to obtain a mandate from Parliament when the first attacks were announced on television, just before 1900. The Coalition offensive had been launched. Canada was taking a defensive role as authorized by the prime minister himself, without parliamentary approval. The need for a motion of support seemed to have disappeared, but the debate went on uninterrupted. While Canadian naval and air forces were operating in their areas of responsibility, the House continued to discuss whether it was appropriate for Canada to become militarily involved. Having further recourse to the executive powers of the Cabinet, the prime minister addressed the House after the fighting had begun and authorized the CF-18s to take part in air escort missions beyond the borders of Kuwait as soon as General de Chastelain considered it a favourable time to do so.[5] The House debated these decisions for several days and voted 217 to 47 in favour of them, on 22 January.

Interestingly, Prime Minister Mulroney committed Canadian troops to the Gulf War without having the same kind of support enjoyed by President Bush, who had to deal with a Senate dominated by the Democratic Party. The Canadian House of Commons was the last legislative body of any Coalition country to authorize its executive's operational action, and it did so five days after the start of the conflict which had been foreseen almost fifty days earlier.

The Canadian government differed from its Coalition partners in another important respect. Joe Clark, Secretary of State for External Affairs, did not close the Iraqi embassy in Ottawa. Canada remained one of the few Coalition countries which retained diplomatic links with Iraq while taking part in a war against it.

Hostilities

On D-1, Commodore Summers received the order from General de Chastelain to transfer tactical control of the operational groups to the Coalition commanders. Admiral Arthur, in his NAVCENT flagship, USS *Blue Ridge*, thus became the authorized controller of both the Air Group and the Naval Task Group for all tactical operations (see Figures 7 and 8). At 1430 local time, on 16 January, the cruiser at sea ordered the launching of the CF-18s on alert at Doha. Dispersed at the ready, they took only an impressive six to eight minutes to become airborne.

From the moment the CF-18s assumed the patrols on Whiskey-1, the US Marines were freed to prepare in secret for the first round of night bombing. Husky One began its routine of three four-hour sorties per day. By joining the Coalition refueller pool, it maximized the employment of aircraft and flying hours. However, before too long, Husky One needed its first spare parts. Fortunately, these were available from a first-line reserve, which had been brought along with specialist

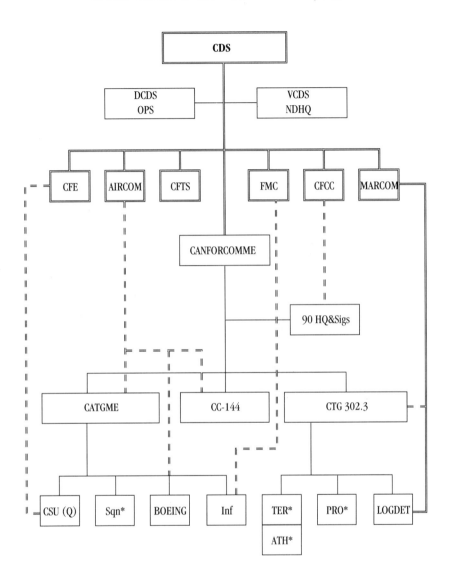

Figure 7. Command and Control of CANFORME, 14 January 1991

technicians. But these breakdowns were a warning that using a single aircraft for more than twelve flying hours per day without second-line support might be too demanding. As for the CF-18s, the number of available flying hours per month had just jumped from 860 to 1,010, as a result of the increase in their numbers from eighteen to twenty-four (a little more than forty hours per aircraft per month, an average which had been maintained and only occasionally exceeded since the beginning of the missions). This increase was substantial but still fell short of the ideal of uninterrupted operations. Operations had to be planned within these limits as long as Canada was not at war. In wartime, flying hours could be increased if circumstances warranted and resources permitted.

At 2300, the battle staff was called to the Canadian Control Centre at the Doha airfield. They were told that offensive operations were about to begin. The first wave was a carefully coordinated attack, using air- and sea-launched cruise missiles, commencing at 0250. Shortly thereafter, F-117 *Stealth Fighters* began their systematic destruction of Baghdad, undetected by Iraqi radar. Even before their precision bombing began, the Canadian HQ had adopted TOPP MEDIUM alert.

The SHIELD had turned into a STORM. On board the carrier USS *Midway*, Major Jocelyn Cloutier was on duty with the naval air staff in its operations room when the air offensive began. He had been detached on 5 January from his position on the air staff at the Manamah headquarters to act as a liaison officer on board Admiral March's Arabian Gulf Battle Force flagship, and he had a duty shift with the naval air staff in its operations room. Because of the way the tours of duty worked out, Major Cloutier was tasked to issue the code word for Warning Red - Weapons Free, the authorization for the units afloat to open fire at will to protect the fleet against enemy counterattacks. At the end of the watch, as Cloutier later recalled, Admiral March returned his salute and joked, "If things turn out badly, I can always say it was the Canadians who started it ..."[6] By 0600 (2200 EST), the first night of the DESERT STORM air war had ended. Out of 2,388 air sorties made in three main attack waves, only three Coalition planes were lost: one each from the United States, Britain, and Kuwait .

Air Superiority Operations
I: Defensive Patrols

Air operations over the whole front had been divided into four major classes. First, the Coalition struck at Iraq's major command and control centres. The conventional cruise missile and F-117 *Stealth Fighter* attacks on Baghdad were part of a campaign to sow confusion, cause a loss of confidence in the government, and considerably reduce Iraqi military capabilities. Second, the Coalition had to achieve air superiority in the Kuwait theatre. Its aim was to neutralise the effect of Iraq's air force and anti-aircraft missiles. The Iraqi integrated air defence network was, indeed, dismembered in the first hour of the war. The achievement of local air superiority was followed by attacks on airports and anti-aircraft defence centres. In third place came battlefield preparation. The

Coalition attacked troop concentrations and the nerve centres of the Iraqi communications and transport systems. Their goal was to prevent reinforcements from advancing and Iraq's land, naval, and strategic forces from functioning at full strength. Fourth, the Coalition had to provide close support for the ground forces. The use of the air force had to be coordinated with any land battles as they developed, but except for some raids by special forces, these battles would take place later.[7]

Communications centres, headquarters, air defence radar systems, and missile sites were the main targets during the opening days of the air war. Before systematically destroying the enemy's forces, however, it was necessary to make sure that he could not make a breakthrough with his own strike force. Protection of Saudi soil and military resources were also concerns, and the air defence patrols carried out by the Canadians were a major ingredient in maintaining air superiority.

Throughout this activity, the CF-18s kept their stations on the Whiskey-1 position. They completed nearly 100 patrol flying hours during the first day of war, which meant that they would break the monthly ceiling of flying hours in ten days. The pilots at the controls were close to the action. They saw with their own eyes the *Tomahawk* missiles and then the rush of attackers who threw themselves at their targets inside Kuwait and Iraq. Their role was to defend the Coalition fleet against counterattacks which might come from certain well-identified airfields in Iraq and Kuwait. Their task was to intercept any unidentified aircraft from the north. The Canadians were assisted by the air defence cruisers, which were acting as air controllers. These cruisers could penetrate the horizon, day or night, much more deeply than any aircraft on-board sensor. Using powerful radars as well as the data transmission link-ups, they were able to obtain electronic images produced by the complete network of AWACS and ground stations. Thanks to the newly acquired Link-4 display system, a digital image animated and filtered by the cruiser provided the CF-18s with details pertinent to their sector of immediate interest.

The hundreds of aircraft which carried out their attack missions in accordance with the CENTAF Air Tasking Orders were to return to their bases by well-identified corridors. Procedures had been established to minimize the chances of collision or confusion. The Canadian pilots, on their patrol circuits, knew these corridors and kept them under surveillance. Returning aircraft were also equipped with specially programmed Identification Friend-or-Foe (IFF) transmitters, which automatically answered a signal (known as a "squawk" in the pilots' jargon). The IFF transmitter worked very much like a password. Once the returning aircraft had identified themselves to the pilots on patrol circuits, they were allowed to return to their home bases; if they had been hit, they were directed to the nearest base, or, if short of fuel, to the circuits of the refuelling tankers.

During that first night, however, there were numerous incidents of navigational error, pilots losing their way, making emergency landings, flying outside the corridors and returning via the defensive patrol circuits. F-16s, F-14s, F/A-18s, and A-6s came back as if seized by panic after being scalded by Iraqi surface-to-air guns and missiles used en masse, almost blindly, to defend towns and airports which were under attack. Many Coalition pilots were stunned by the phantasmagoric rain of anti-aircraft artillery fire (the notorious Triple-A) and surface-to-air missiles (SAMs), which could be seen at a distance of over 100 kilometres at night. Their electronic detectors registered numerous shafts of radar illumination looking for targets.[8] In all the excitement, when the whole horizon was throbbing with violent action, many aircraft returned at dizzying speeds and failed to give their identification message. Some passed through at full speed, performing violent manoeuvres to avoid the patrollers, acting like Iraqis ready to use their *Exocet* missiles. This was when the rules of engagement came into play.

Rules of engagement originate with each national government. They are based on international laws governing air traffic and contain instructions applying to pre-war situations, such as the embargo against Iraq, and to wartime itself. These directives, whose legal aspects are sometimes complicated, have to be reduced to a notebook of simple instructions for the pilots, which can be stored in the cockpit or memorized. The rules of engagement required the pilots to visually identify the unknown aircraft (a bogey) and determine whether it was an enemy (a bandit).

To visually identify an aircraft diving towards one at a combined speed approaching Mach 2 (that is, by nearly a kilometre every two seconds) is a difficult and dangerous task. One has to get into position to "escort" the intruder, which is the only way to see the aircraft and identify the model and its distinctive signs. It is also necessary to watch the unidentified aircraft's electronic weapons. The bogey can make a move which immediately identifies it as hostile if it directs a missile guiding beam toward the defender. The air controller on the cruiser, or the pilot himself, can declare the unidentified aircraft to be hostile if they believe they are being threatened, or that the resource which they are protecting is being threatened. This decision has to be made within a few seconds. When it has to be made at night, the difficulty is multiplied.

Canadian pilots were tested early and often that first night of fighting. Each shift had to deal with serious incidents in which identification of an aircraft heading south had to be made without the help of a squawk, perhaps because of a defective device or because a nervous pilot forgot to activate the mechanism. On several occasions, the defenders had sufficient reason to use their weapons, but they kept themselves in check and continued on course. They put themselves at great risk while conducting "non-cooperative target recognition," a procedure which makes it possible to identify an oncoming plane by its unique electronic characteristics. To intercept those who were coming back from hell, sometimes one had to manoeuvre just as violently to be able to get a good look at the aircraft and identify the emblem or number on the airframe by light. Some pilots used an incredible manoeuvre. They put on their air brakes while turning on their afterburner jets and lit up the aircraft flying next to them.[9] The pilots came back sweaty and exhausted but never made a single mistake. The *Desert Cats* showed in one night that they were goalkeepers of great skill.

Husky One also was on task during the night, when two returning F-14s from the aircraft carrier USS *Ranger* called for an emergency refuelling. They were the first of the renowned *Tomcats* to refuel from the Canadian *Boeing 707* but would not be the last.

Canadians were involved in other aspects of the air offensive, too. Several were part of the NATO AWACS group, which continued to watch for Iraqi air movements on the Turkish frontier. Some twenty other Canadians served with this type of aircraft in Turkey and Saudi Arabia, attached to 552 AWACS Wing. They were not part of NATO but of 28 Air Division of the USAF. Canadians thus found themselves involved, in one sector or another, in all facets of airborne control of air operations in DESERT STORM. One postwar report claims that "Canadians were members of AWACS crews in 35 out of the 36 victories over enemy aircraft."[10]

The first night of bombing was a huge success. The Iraqis were not able to mount a counterattack because their nerve centres had been pounded so heavily and accurately. The Coalition had established local air superiority. The next phase was to carry out a systematic destruction of Iraqi defences, in accordance with a list of target priorities that was open to adjustment as the results came in. The night of 16-17 January was a first punch that stunned the Iraqis into a state of ineffectiveness, from which they never recovered. They were able to mount on average only twenty-five combat aircraft sorties per day for the next ten days. Then they fled to Iran.

Later on 17 January, ENRICH, the plan authorizing wartime maintenance procedures for the aircraft in the theatre, was activated. This measure facilitated operational management of the aircraft and regulated mission planning. In anticipation of a follow-on to ENOBLE, NDHQ ordered the dispatch of six additional CF-18s from CFB Bagotville to Lahr, so that they would be in a position to respond immediately to a call for reinforcements or replacements. The aircraft from the Bagotville wing were chosen because they had recently been given a complete overhaul. As well, 433 *Porcupine* Squadron had been chosen by Fighter Group Headquarters to replace the *Desert Cats* at the end of March, in tandem with the 421 *Red Indians* of 1 Canadian Air Division at Baden-Söllingen.

After the first day of the air war, operations stabilized considerably, passing from the intense and unforeseeable to the sustained and systematic. Their progress was punctuated only by the numerous alerts of *Scud* missile attacks, which were falling at a disquieting rate throughout the theatre. At this point, it was not known what effect they would have on the war's outcome. Also unknown were their numbers and targets. For months, the intelligence services had been admitting that Iraq might have nuclear or chemical warheads for these rockets, which were simple, almost crude in design but impressive in size and range. Since the base at Doha was within the eastern arc of these missiles (and in fact on the same ballistic flight path as Jubayl, Dhahran, and Manamah), the Canadian Air Group had to react to every alert in the sector. Air raid warning RED and the consequent TOPP HIGH condition were declared some twenty-one times before the end of DESERT STORM, although Doha appears never to have been the object of an attack.

At Manamah headquarters, all personnel were recalled to the Gray-Mackenzie building in the afternoon of 15 January. They slept in sleeping bags and folding cots. Two days later, the first RED alert took place. Everyone, including those on relief, put on their suits, masks, rubber boots, and gloves and thoroughly checked each other's fastener seals. Barely recognizable, they went to the stairs, making polite and unaccustomed gestures to one another. Each person carried a rifle and an empty bag cross-slung. Their walk was strange, and they stared behind glassy goggles. Everything happened as if it were an exercise, except that they were shorter of breath, their gestures were more nervous, and their voices were louder, somewhat forced to reassure their comrades. They met in the ground floor rooms, prepared with sandbags and waterproof sheetings, and waited for instructions over the loudspeakers. Those who were on duty stayed at their posts and passed on any messages which they received about the unfolding situation.

These alerts left very vivid impressions. One participant summed up the atmosphere well by admitting: "At the beginning, we all secretly had the impression that our names were written on a bomb." After the first experiences, tensions lessened. People spoke of the infinitesimal probability of a direct hit, and most recovered a more balanced perspective, which their intense training had skewed to a certain degree. Each *Scud* which turned out not to have a chemical warhead reduced the level of anxiety. Improved technical means made it possible to be more accurate about the point of impact and real threat. Just a few days after the initial alerts, fear of a *Scud* no longer had the same effect. It was then decided to react more cautiously. Each threat was assessed with greater precision, and full alerts were avoided when deemed excessive in relation to the nature of the attack. Even when explosions were clearly heard from the Dhahran region, some days later, the degree of nervousness at Manamah never reached the level experienced during the opening bombardment of Iraq.

Some pilots were in a position to inform their compatriots about the flight paths of the *Scud* missiles. From Whiskey-1, Captain Marcus Walton followed the trajectory of one enemy rocket and the successive launching of three *Patriot* missiles, one of which seemed to strike the *Scud* squarely, reducing it to incandescent fragments.[11] The spectacle was fascinating. For the defenders on air patrol, the sacrifice of the *Patriot* units was not without its symbolism, reminding them of the seriousness of the responsibilities which they themselves shouldered in the night sky.

The fleet in the Persian Gulf had grown rapidly. A second and a third carrier - USS *Ranger* and USS *Theodore Roosevelt* - joined the flagship *Midway* and those ships of the Arabian Gulf Battle Force which were within range of air operations. Together, these three carriers had about fifty F/A-18s, some forty F-14 *Tomcat* aircraft, fifty A-6E *Intruder* bombers, and smaller numbers of assorted tankers, electronic warfare aircraft, and a compact AWACS, the E-2C *Hawkeye*. With this flying and floating armada, the *Desert Cats* suddenly found themselves in the midst of an impressive array of naval aircraft.

This had not been the case up to 19 January. Before then, the Canadians had been virtually alone on the Whiskey-1 station, sometimes providing up to five aircraft at a time. However, they did not have enough aircraft to maintain that rate for too long. The augmentation of naval air elements (the *Tomcat* planes were long-range air fighters) allowed the Canadians to reduce their hours of responsibility on Whiskey-1 to the point where they could offer their services to the forces in Saudi Arabia.

II: Sweep and Escort

The F-16C squadron of 401 Wing USAF at Doha lost three of its aircraft in quick succession to bombing missions during the first days of the war. Despite the great reduction in the capabilities of the Iraqi anti-aircraft networks, additional close support was needed to suppress the remaining point defences. As a result of the progressive training they had begun on 7 January, the prime minister's immediate authorization for escort missions as of the morning of the seventeenth, and the reduction of their responsibility for Whiskey-1, the Canadians were ready to assist by the twentieth.

By taking on an offensive counter-air commitment, the Canadian squadron could carry out two types of mission: sweeps and close escort. There were few differences between them. The bombers were not equipped with defensive armament, and in particular, they were too heavily loaded to be able to manoeuvre in an air battle. The sweep missions gave the fighters a sector of responsibility where they were to arrive ahead of the bombers and prepare security for their arrival and departure. These were often called "Migsweeps" because of their prey, Soviet built *MiG* fighters. The escorts accompanied the bombers to and from the target, keeping at a distance of five to thirty kilometres. The air defenders' responsibility was to prevent enemy fighters from hitting the bombers with their fire, and to confirm the positions of ground-based anti-aircraft missiles.

The bombers were directed to a specific target or a "killbox" - an area thirty miles square - and told to wait for further instructions. The air controllers aboard the AWACS, with the help of those in the JSTARS (Joint Surveillance Target Attack Radar System) and ABCCC (Air-Borne Command and Control Center) aircraft,[12] orchestrated the final details according to the developing tactical situation. The complete attacking group typically included four waves of eight F-16 bombers, four wingers to defend each wave of bombers (normally F-15s but also CF-18s), and the F-4 *Phantom* Wild Weasel suppresser, which was armed both with powerful electronic receiver-emitters and missiles whose function was to locate and destroy radar stations and ground-based missile sites.

The two functions of sweep and escort combined elements of offence and defence. Like hunting dogs, the CF-18s' mission was to flush out the enemy, either by forcing Iraqi defensive fighters to take off, in which case the CF-18s would confront them, or by provoking illumination of the enemy's missile guidance radar, which electronic counter-measures aircraft would attack and neutralize as the bomber flew to its mission. There was little that they could do about Triple-A artillery. It was everywhere and not connected to radar systems. And information on Iraq's SAMs had to be gathered on a mission-to-mission basis because they were mobile. Defensive tactics also varied according to whether the bombing took place at high or low altitude. Most of it was carried out at high altitude. The anti-aircraft protection provided by the Canadian squadron covered all altitudes where an enemy fighter might show up.

Two escort missions were planned for 20 January. Captain Jeffrey G. Beckett and Captain David D. Stone were leaders of two teams of four, each of which was to accompany eight F-16s on a bombing mission. Their objective was Jalibah, on the banks of the Euphrates, some 150 kilometres inside Iraq.

After studying the terrain in great detail and memorizing the mission codes, each pilot was given his weather and intelligence briefings at his unit. Then the section leaders made conference calls to coordinate their actions beforehand. They left Doha in formation, topped up from Husky One just behind the start line, and joined the eight bombers of 401 Wing and the other mission escorts at the rendezvous point. Then the formations shook themselves out, the air defenders deploying in their teams of two about fifteen kilometres in front of the bombers and keeping their distance from one another.

Before they could penetrate Iraqi territory, the ABCCC controller informed Beckett that the mission was cancelled because unfavourable weather made it impossible to observe enemy targets. All the aircraft immediately returned to base. In the afternoon, it was Stone's turn to be sent back to Doha with his team, this time because the F-16s could not obtain in-flight fuel before crossing the border. Following these two cancellations, an unfortunate controversy arose over Canada's alleged involvement in offensive counter-air missions.

At the regular, late-afternoon briefing given by the commander in the Gulf, the CANFORME briefer alluded to the fact that Canadian aircraft had taken part in sweep and escort missions with American bombers. This marked the first time since the Korean war that Canadian aircraft had been involved in offensive air combat.[13] However, the briefer did not give any results of the missions, and failed to mention that they had been cancelled before the aircraft had crossed the border. (Military staff are reluctant to give complete information that could reveal operational procedures.) News that the missions of 20 January had been aborted only came to the surface at the noontime daily briefing in Ottawa, when the briefers were confronted with information provided by journalists in Doha. It was too late to correct the morning radio and television reports and put an end to the speculation. The reporters in Manamah and Doha were criticized by their editors in Canada for having provided false information and were shocked to realize that they had fed the speculation. To Commodore Summers, the term "mission accomplished" was accurate because the Canadian CF-18s had carried out what they had been asked to do. The NDHQ spokespersons patiently explained over and over again the problems they had to face in protecting information on war operations. But the journalists, frustrated in their attempts to satisfy a public hungry for information on the bombing campaign, were hostile to the explanations.

On 24 January, the commanding officer of the *Desert Cats*, Lieutenant-Colonel Matthews, finally became a leader of a team of four fighters able to carry out an escort mission to completion. Although no Iraqi fighters rose to the challenge, the first few offensive missions clearly demonstrated that several dangers remained. SAMs showed up at places where they were not expected. After being moved on the ground, they attacked combat groups which were not under the immediate protection of the Wild Weasels. Alerted by the warning flashes (called "spikes"), which appeared on the cockpit panel, the pilots carried out effective evasive manoeuvres. But on-board electronic devices could not detect anti-aircraft artillery shells, and a distressing number of Coalition aircraft on low- and mid-level missions fell victim to Triple-A fire. Moreover, wary of the Coalition anti-radiation missiles, some Iraqi defenders were firing their missiles blind, without initial radar direction. The probability of their hitting a high-altitude target, however, was remote. Some Canadian pilots experienced a sinking feeling when they saw a trail of smoke climbing from the ground in their direction. Fortunately, these missiles levelled off too low, but the experience was nonetheless a vivid one.

At this stage, the Canadian Air Group expected to make contact with the enemy during the offensive counter-air missions in the Dhahran sector. However, it was in the Gulf itself, where missions on the Whiskey patrols were still going on, that Canada finally opened fire on an enemy target.

In the early hours of 30 January, the Hornet 13 team of Captain Stephen P. Hill and his winger, Major David W. Kendall, were patrolling the new Whiskey-4 circuit, which had just been laid out further north after the recent successes against the Iraqi navy (see Chapter 8). At about 0200 they received an unusual message from their controller aboard the USS *Mobile Bay*: "Would you like to strake a boat?"[14] The controller then explained that a team of A-6 *Intruders* had attacked a group of Iraqi fast missile-carrying ships making for the safety of an Iranian port. Two had been engaged, the first with two laser-guided bombs and the other with an ordinary iron bomb which had immobilized it and set it on fire. But the A-6s had exhausted their ammunition and been obliged to retire. The controller added that a third ship of the *TNC-45* type (a fast attack ship carrying four *Exocet* missiles) had taken flight and at that moment was heading north-northwest at a speed of thirty knots to regain the Bubiyan channel. It was necessary to delay this ship until another A-6 could be sent to attack it.

The Canadians were the closest and Hill accepted the mission. At a distance of thirty kilometres from the sector, Hill and Kendall were instructed to visually identify the ship before attacking it. They could see its outline, thanks to a brilliant moon, but even after making a second pass and launching flares, the two Canadian pilots could not positively identify the ship as Iraqi. At that moment an E-2C *Hawkeye* intervened to confirm that there were no allied ships in the area and that it was indeed the enemy. The controller added that during previous engagements there had been no evidence that anti-aircraft fire or radar had been used by this ship. The *Hawkeye*, acting as airborne coordinator, authorized the attack.

Hill and Kendall flew into the night, emptying their 20 mm *Vulcan* cannon at the ship, one after the other. Several rounds hit the target. During another pass, they considered trying to hit the ship with a heat-seeking missile, but the heat was not sufficient to catch the sensor of the AIM-9 *Sidewinder*. An attempt was then made to use a larger AIM-7 *Sparrow* missile, which carries its own integrated radar system and has a recognized (but limited) capability against surface targets. After Kendall's had failed to acquire the target, Hill's aiming device locked on the ship. He decided to fire, releasing the *Sparrow* so that it would continue to follow the target by itself. However, probably confused by an effect known as "ground clutter," it dropped into the sea fifteen metres behind the forty-metre-long ship, which continued zigzagging on its tactical escape. Kendall and Hill went back to Husky One to refuel before returning to Doha. They were immediately replaced on circuit Whiskey-4 because their two-hour tour of duty had ended.

These engagements were part of the Battle of Bubiyan, a thirteen-hour naval air engagement, which ended with the complete destruction of the Iraqi navy. An official review determined that the first group of A-6s, flanked by F/A-18s, had hit three enemy ships and that the Canadian aircraft had caused irreparable damage to a fourth ship. It was of the *OSA* type, rather than a *TNC-45*, and was later seen in an Iranian port. Some days later, the Hornet 13 team received official credit from NAVCENT for helping to destroy that warship.[15]

Pilots Hill and Kendall were introduced to the press at the end of the day to mark "the first shot" by Canadians in the Gulf War. According to a tradition that became popular in the Second World War, Hill was authorized to paint a picture of a crossed-out patrol boat on his aircraft (side number 1884613). Of all the CF-18s that saw service in the Gulf, this was the only aircraft credited with an official victory.

To Colonel Lalonde, not everything was going well at the beginning of February. There was an increase in taskings, and there were new delays in sending two additional aircraft to increase the squadron from twenty-four to twenty-six *Hornets*, as promised on 21 January. The reserves were shrinking, and replacements would not arrive until 8 February. Lalonde was particularly concerned about the sweep and escort missions. The reports from the pilots were disquieting. Each day they mentioned dangerous experiences which the enemy ground defences put them through. The radar detectors in the CF-18 cockpits jumped from one type of SAM to another, registering serious and even lethal levels. This indicated that a missile was chasing them and that impact was imminent. The pilots were forced to carry out evasive manoeuvres, the last chance to break contact before ejecting. The chances of a blue-on-blue accident were increasing because the volume of air traffic crossing the border was larger than ever. Lalonde asked Commodore Summers to have the sweep and escort missions reconsidered, given the reduction of the Iraqi Air Force to almost nothing. What was left was fleeing to Iran. He also intended to restrict flying hours, which could not be kept to the 1,010 hours per month authorized at the beginning of the war, 1,578 hours having been flown in January. The way things were going, this total, too, would be widely exceeded before the end of the first half of February.

Even the relative safety of the combat patrol missions was put at risk when the more northerly Whiskey-4 circuit, exposed to ground-to-air missile systems from the shores of Kuwait, definitely replaced Whiskey-1. New patrols were carried out in Sector 5, as well, north of Dhahran and very close to Iraqi territory. These circuits were more than 600 kilometres from Doha and required both additional fuel and extra flying hours. This heightened the need for coordination, especially since Husky One had been grounded on 30 January, due to a hydraulic problem, after sixteen consecutive days of operations. Refuelling of the CF-18s had to take place almost at random, with tankers of any type. Also, communications for the CF-18s in the Dhahran sector were poor. Although they were now equipped to function in the naval setting, they did not have USAF *Havequick* secure voice radios.

However, Colonel Lalonde's request to reduce the escort missions was publicly refused by General de Chastelain. He answered from Ottawa that there was no question, for the moment, of reducing missions of this type and that flying hours were not a problem. Oddly enough, de Chastelain also refused Lalonde's request that the CF-18s be allowed to jettison their exterior fuel tanks, citing costs. It therefore fell to Lieutenant-General Huddleston, who represented the Canadian Forces in the televised meetings of the combined Defence and External Affairs Committees, to reconcile the seemingly contradictory positions of General de Chastelain and Colonel Lalonde. He stressed that the force had to be flexible when dealing with an enemy and that agility in command must allow for progressive change. Though air defence patrols had been very important until recently, circumstances had changed and other operations would now take their place. "We are in a tactical context," he said. "We are flexible. Circumstances have changed. We must adapt."[16]

Despite Colonel Lalonde's fears, the bombing escorts continued throughout almost the whole of February, not only with the American F-16s but also with RAF *Tornado* aircraft. Fortunately, their usual low-altitude bombing missions had been modified to take place at high altitudes, thus assuring more protection against missiles and artillery. The Canadians penetrated to about 150 kilometres southeast of Baghdad, accompanying British aircraft in their attacks on the fortified aircraft shelters of As Salman and Jalibah. During the entire month, they did not come into contact with any enemy aircraft. However, they were constantly harassed by anti-aircraft artillery and missiles. The Iraqis seemed to have an endless supply of both, which allowed them to put on impressive and dangerous displays of fireworks.

Battlefield Preparation Operations

Since November, the options presented by the Department of National Defence to the government had always included the possibility of conducting interdiction bombing within the borders of Kuwait and Iraq. There was nothing to stop CF-18s from carrying and dropping bombs. Their medium weight prevented them from hauling the same tonnage of bombs as a light bomber, such as the carrier-borne A-6 *Intruder*, which could carry 15,000 pounds of ordnance. The naval air *Intruder* was not a fighter, however, precisely because of its mass (naval air pilots call it the "cement truck"). The CF-18, equipped with two tons of armament (eight 500-pound bombs) and the proper instruments for high- and low-level bombing, was manoeuvrable enough to be a full member of the fighter class.

Moreover, the CF-18 pilot training courses at Cold Lake included a significant phase on bombing, and all qualified CF-18 pilots had to have the skills both for fighter and ground-attack missions. The Air Division in Germany retained this dual role until June 1990, when it reduced the low-level air-to-ground commitment in order to improve its performance in the air-to-air role. That did not mean, however, that Canada ceased to recognize the *Hornet*'s ability as a bomber. In fact, the CF-18s retained a core air-to-ground function as a secondary capability for NATO. As a result, the more experienced pilots, such as the team leaders in the *Desert Cats* squadron, had solid experience of low-altitude air-to-ground operations (for interdiction behind enemy lines or in close support of allied land forces) when they arrived in the Gulf.

When Lieutenant-Colonel Matthews took command of the *Desert Cats*, on 19 December, he thought that the bombing role might be given back to the unit, although the minister had given no indication to date that that was a plausible option. Because of political circumstances, therefore, Matthews had to confine preparations to reviewing operational theory in the classroom. The first estimates called for seven days' notice to carry out physical preparations and training.

Things changed on 14 February. On that day, Air Command Headquarters in Winnipeg began to work on the details of a bombing campaign, as well as a public relations campaign on behalf of the government that would explain and defend what might be an unpopular decision. Everything was conducted in secrecy. Any action prior to an announcement would tip off the throng of Canadian reporters in Doha, and the government's hand would be forced. Two days later, Lieutenant-General Sutherland visited the theatre of operations, made an inspection tour of the Doha airfield, and discussed the arrangements for handling bombs. Commodore Summers, reassured by his recommendations, confirmed to General Boyle in Lahr that the plan could be put in motion as early as 23 February, if the signal were given immediately. Sufficient training would be completed by the twenty-second. On the negative side, Summers told Boyle that twelve sorties per day would mean an increase in the number of flying hours to more than 1,800 per month, a ceiling that could be easily exceeded despite the most accurate planning.

The Manamah headquarters determined that three levels of bombing could be maintained with the resources available: twelve, sixteen and twenty-four sorties per day. The NDHQ staff summarized the situation for Defence Minister McKnight on 19 February and awaited a decision by the government. Also, preliminary orders for the operation were authorized by Ottawa and promulgated by Air Command, which identified parameters for transporting basic loads of bombs: 89 tons for a first level of activity and 218 tons for a third-level effort.

On 20 February, at the very moment when the Minister of National Defence was making his public announcement, General de Chastelain issued a FLASH executive order. It reached Doha 30 minutes later, authorizing all preparations for the operation. This meant two things - training flights could be scheduled for the pilots who had been prevented from carrying out notional or practice bombing missions before the government's announcement, and ammunition could be transported from Lahr.

However, there was something odd about Mr. McKnight's announcement. He said that "well-trained" Canadian pilots would join those of nine other Coalition countries in ground attacks.[17] Back in Doha, Lieutenant-Colonel Matthews had a more realistic picture of the situation. His pilots had been trained in Europe for low-level missions. But the Coalition was not NATO, and Iraq was not Europe. The Coalition was hitting Iraq with high-altitude bombing, and Canadian pilots were not well trained in that area. Matthews therefore insisted that any bombing be done by instrument navigation, without pilots having to visually locate their targets. There were two reasons for this: first, the cloud ceilings were too low (the weather in the Gulf was very bad during these weeks); and second, the bombing would be more accurate. In any event, the lack of training nullified any other option. Matthews was not particularly happy with this state of affairs. He had known for two weeks about these missions, but had been unable to prepare his pilots.

On 20 February, the Air Operations Centre in Winnipeg issued orders to the Canadian Air Group and sent weapons experts and ammunition technicians to the theatre of operations. NDHQ intervened at this precise moment, however, to decree that transport priority must remain with Operation SCALPEL, the deployment of the field hospital, which required numerous planned flights. Bomb transport remained a second priority, but arrangements with Akrotiri airport were concluded quickly, so that as soon as the *Hercules* were ready, they could begin to make stopovers en route to Doha.

Exploring the availability of ammunition in the theatre, the chief of staff at the Manamah headquarters, Colonel David Bartram, in concert with the liaison officer at Riyadh, discussed the possibility of obtaining a loan of bombs from the Americans. General Horner agreed to place bombs at their disposal, in order to overcome the problems caused by the Canadians' "limited capability" of transporting bombs by air. The date of 26 February was mentioned as the most likely for the mission to begin.

Colonel Lalonde also initiated discussions with the commander of 401 Wing. Colonel Nelson was delighted that the Canadians would join them on bombing missions and had received the news of General Horner's offer of ammunition. Nelson immediately gave his unconditional support and offered his own, unguided, Mark 82 bombs to arm the CF-18s. Lalonde accepted them without hesitation.

Meanwhile, the liaison officer in Riyadh provided the *Desert Cats* with the latest information on CENTAF's arrangements for the Coalition ground assault, which was expected to be launched within the next few days. The new Whiskey-8 MITCHELL air defence circuit pushed the patrollers still further north, close to Bubiyan Island, on a path which covered the whole of the tactical land theatre. New combat air patrols were designed to support the ground manoeuvres, too, and coordinate the very heavy bomber traffic going forward over Saudi Arabia to the "killboxes," which served as the targeting framework in Kuwait and Iraq. And, in addition, there were refueller circuits, massed in very large numbers in the forward areas.

On 22 February, the CFE Operations Centre issued the recently completed air transport plan IRON SABRE.[18] Major-General Smith planned to sustain operations at a medium level of between eight and sixteen sorties a day, for thirty-two days. A *Boeing 707* flight and four *Hercules* would conduct a continuous transport shuttle.

Also on 22 February, Commodore Summers gave his final instructions to Colonel Lalonde on the bombing missions. The Air Group was not to provide low-level close support of ground troops, unless there was an emergency or the danger of inflicting casualties on friendly forces was very low. Each team understood clearly that if they apprehended a blue-on-blue danger, or if identification of the target was uncertain, the mission was to be aborted.

The first *Boeing* arrived that night. Colonel Lalonde reported that the process of unpacking and providing secure storage at Doha could not be finished in time to arm the aircraft with Canadian bombs. Their first mission would have to wait until 25 February. However, the first four missions could be carried out as early as the twenty-third with American bombs and hand-picked pilots. And Lalonde still believed that twenty-four missions could commence on the twenty-sixth.

On 23 February, Colonel Lalonde was ahead of schedule. His pilots were ready for eight bombing missions the next day. Besides using the USAF's bombs, he had received an offer of 1000-pound laser-guided bombs from the US Navy. They could be dropped in "buddy bomb" fashion, guided by a LANTIRN-equipped American aircraft. The offer was confirmed in a message from Admiral March the next day, identifying sixteen high-precision bombs for specific targets. Although the offer was accepted, these bombs did not reach Doha before the end of the war.

On 24 February, G-day, the beginning of the ground attack, Captain Beckett, one of the most experienced pilots in the squadron, led the first group into enemy territory. His team, Talon 01, dropped thirty-two Mark 82 500-pound bombs on the designated target, a concentration of artillery in southern Kuwait, at about 1000. They were followed by a second team of four led by Captain Stephen R. Forsythe. They bombed the same target at about 1530. By the twenty-fifth, Lahr had established a resupply routine of more than thirty tons per day, thanks to the use of fifty-bomb loading ramps in the *Boeing*. Since things were going so well, it was decided to drop only Mark 82 bombs. Neither Canadian-made CRV-7 rockets nor CBU cluster bombs would be used.

The pilots of the *Desert Cats* carried out fifty-six bombing missions between 24 and 28 February 1991. The Canadian fighter-bombers were guided by USAF AWACS and ABCCCs and assisted by JSTARS aircraft, which could locate and follow the enemy's movements if conditions were appropriate.[19] Their objectives were mostly artillery concentrations or vehicle convoys. Studies have shown that bombs released on the aim of the on-board ground radar lock generally burst within a 75-metre radius of the target, with varying degrees of precision, depending on prevailing wind conditions. But it was impossible to determine the actual results of the Canadian bombing because enemy ground troops were withdrawing and the situation was changing from hour to hour. A formal Bomb Damage Assessment (BDA) was pointless.

The Canadian bombing effort was only one small part of the Coalition air interdiction plan, but it freed other, better-equipped air forces to provide close support to the ground assault. In fact, the Doha-based *Hornet* aircraft provided a Canadian presence across the full range of Coalition air action against Iraq.

Throughout this activity, the CF-18s maintained one core mission - the air defence of the fleet. Although Iraqi capabilities were decreasing rapidly, they remained capable of striking at ships at sea. Any attack would have been humiliating for the Coalition cause. According to the *Gulf War Air Power Survey*, the "Coalition shared more widely the mission of controlling the air."[20] And the Canadians bore the brunt of fleet defence during the critical period of 16-19 January, the transition to war, when Iraq's pre-emptive or counterattack intentions were unknown but a very real threat. This period was also marked by the sudden departure of the Marine F/A-18s and the progressive arrival of USN F-14s and F/A-18s to take over combat air patrol duties.

Thereafter, the multi-role capabilities of the CF-18 allowed the Canadians to progress to higher-profile areas, first to sweep and escort and then to bomb. Each role had its complicating factors and dangers, and each brought its rewards. Deploying the panoply of instruments available to him as orchestra leader in Riyadh, Lieutenant-General Horner directed all facets of the air effort, and the Canadian *Hornet* aircraft played their part in perfect harmony.

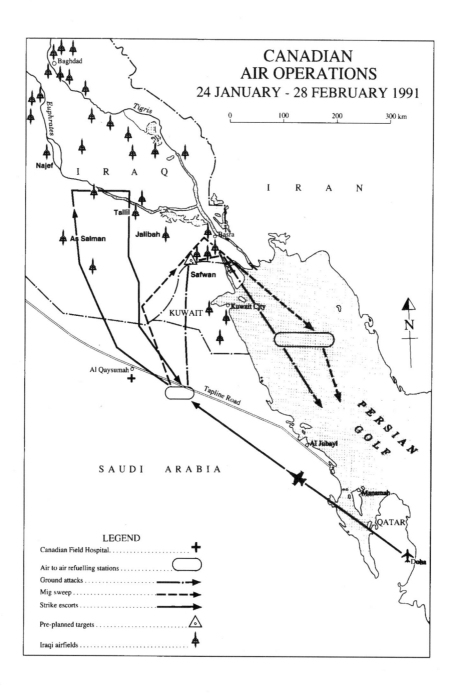

CANADIAN
AIR OPERATIONS
24 JANUARY - 28 FEBRUARY 1991

0   100   200   300 km

Baghdad

Euphrates

Tigris

Najef

I   R   A   Q

Tallil

Jalibah   Basra

As Salman

Safwan

Kuwait City

KUWAIT

Al Qaysumah

Tapline Road

SAUDI   ARABIA

Al Jubayl

I   R   A   N

N

P E R S I A N
G U L F

Manamah

QATAR

Doha

LEGEND
Canadian Field Hospital. . . . . +
Air to air refuelling stations . . . .
Ground attacks . . . .
Mig sweep . . . .
Strike escorts . . . .
Pre-planned targets . . . .
Iraqi airfields . . . .

Notes

1   Lieutenant-Colonel Donald C. Matthews, "Squadron Commander," *Canadian Defence Quarterly* (June 1992), p. 40. At Baden, the remainders of 409 and 439 Squadrons were amalgamated with the third operational squadron of 4 Wing, 421 *Red Indian* Squadron, which served as the training unit for pilots and ground crews before they left for the Gulf. 421 Squadron was called HIT for *Hawks*, *Indians* and *Tigers*. Up to the end of October, it was seriously considered as a replacement for 409, but a decision was made for a 439/416 combination, based on technical considerations and cadre options. Officers, non-commissioned officers, and corporals had to be withdrawn from 421 and 416 squadrons and the base services at Lahr and Baden to fill out 439.

2   The exception was in air-to-ground (bombing) missions. These had been practised in Germany until the beginning of March 1990, only months before the Gulf crisis, but after that date 1 Air Division withdrew from this role to devote itself exclusively to air-to-air assignments. 416 Squadron from Cold Lake was more familiar with bombing because Cold Lake was equipped with the best bombing ranges and was the home of the air weapons instruction school.

3   "Iraq's Occupation of Kuwait: Excerpts from Amnesty International's Report (19 December 1990)", *The Gulf War Reader*, pp. 157-160. The Canadian Broadcasting Corporation's *5th Estate* later determined that Amnesty International had reported information of dubious authenticity, seemingly produced by propaganda originating from the Kuwait government in exile.

4   National, Defence, *A Cry of Bugles: The Canadian Forces in the Persian Gulf*, CAT #31-0548 (video, 93 min.).

5   *Debates*, 16 January 1991, p. 17164.

6   Cloutier, "Interview," 6 March 1991.

7   Several major works review the strategic theory used by the air force during these first hours. One may consult among other sources: *CPGW*, *Storm Over Iraq*, *Gulf War Air Power Survey*, and *A League of Airmen*.

8   The numerous, type ZSU 23mm, quick-firing anti-aircraft guns had practical ceilings of 2,500 metres. The 57mm guns were effective at over 4,000 metres. Some 57mm (S60), 85mm (KS-12), 100mm (KS-19), and even 130mm (KS-30) anti-aircraft guns could present a considerable threat to aircraft up to altitudes of 30,000 feet - even 40,000 feet. SA-2, SA-3, and SA-6 missiles, which were the main anti-aircraft threat at high altitudes, had a range of about twenty-five kilometres. The HAWK missiles, concentrated around choice targets, covered a radius of forty kilometres. SA-8, SA-9, ROLAND and SA-13 missiles, with shorter ranges, were also a danger. SA-7 missiles, which were shoulder-held and could be carried anywhere, were particularly dangerous during low-altitude bombing because they could strike at a distance of up to four kilometres.

9   The CF-18s which were sent from Germany to the Gulf were not equipped with spotlights to illuminate an unidentified aircraft at night. This was done in NORAD interception manoeuvres in America, where narrow beam lights were used to light up the Soviet *Bear* planes, which patrolled the length of the northern Canadian coast. Without these powerful lights, it was extremely difficult to positively recognize an aircraft as friend or foe. Lights were installed on the CF-18s a few days after the beginning of hostilities, greatly reducing tension on the patrol positions. The CF-18 pilots also learned to turn these lights on when an unidentified plane approached. This informed the approaching aircraft that a friendly defending plane wanted its identification. Avoidance manoeuvres were immediately reduced in frequency and speed.

10   Dorge, "The Eye of the Storm," pp. 8-10.

11   *Desert Cats: The Canadian Fighter Squadron in the Gulf War*, ed. Captain David Deere (Stoney Creek, Ont: Fortress Publications), p. 30.

12 The JSTARs were recently modified USAF *Boeing 707* aircraft (there were only two available for use in-theatre). Each one had an experimental radar capable of identifying concentrations of moving vehicles. The ABCCCs were embarked in specially modified USAF C-130 *Hercules*.

13 National Defence, "CF-18 Participation to Sweep and Escort Missions." *News Release*, AFN: 04/91, 21 January 1991.

14 *Desert Cats*, p. 32.

15 *CPGW*, p. 266; and Robert J. Schneller Jr. (USN Historical Center), "Persian Gulf Turkey Shoot: The Destruction of the Iraqi Naval Forces during Operation Desert Storm," (paper presented to the Society for Military History, May 1993).

16 *Minutes of Proceedings and Evidence of the Standing Committee on External Affairs and International Trade*, Issue No 85; and *Minutes of the Proceedings and Evidence of the Standing Committee on National Defence and Veterans Affairs*, Issue No 44, 5 February 1991, p. 8.

17 National Defence, "CF-18 Air-to-Ground Attack Role Authorized," *News Release*, AFN: 10/91, 20 February 1991.

18 At one point, serious consideration had been given to using HMCS *Provider*, the West Coast naval supply ship, to sealift the IRON SABRE ordnance, but the shortened implementation time made this impractical.

19 Beginning on the evening of 25 February, the general withdrawal of the Iraqi forces produced concentrations at bottlenecks. As a result of these developments, incidents took place, such as the one along the Kuwait-Basra road a little north of Mutla (called by the world press the "Highway of Death"). Nearly 1,400 vehicles of all sorts were destroyed there. Other concentrations also occurred at Hawr al Hammar, further north, and at Basra. These were the targets which were chosen as priorities by the air controllers, as the bombing control line advanced to keep well ahead of the moving land forces. The Canadians did not take part in these large battles.

20 *GWAPS*, p. 197.

The Naval War –
The Combat Logistics Force:
January – February 1991

Origins of the CLF

Divorced from the frantic activity to prepare the air task group for its wartime roles, the Canadian naval task group entered the New Year of 1991 still very much dedicated to Multinational Interception Force operations. From his vantage point at the headquarters in Bahrain, however, Commodore Summers recognized that continued support of the MIF option was increasingly impractical and that the Canadian task group was out of step with the march to the offensive. Summers was concerned that his task group would not have a meaningful role in the forthcoming operations. Moreover, it was unlikely to remain as an identifiable unit. When the Canadian navy was last at war, off Korea from 1950 to 1955, its destroyers had done great service but never as a recognizable Canadian task group. Instead they had been allocated to Commonwealth and USN task groups as required. After the war, this had been seen as having diluted the political, if not operational, impact that the navy could have made. [1]

Consequently, keeping Task Group 302.3 together throughout its Gulf deployment had become practically an article of faith for Canadian naval planners. The essential unity of the task group had been achieved without difficulty under the loose coordination and cooperation principles of MIF operations, as practised with Admiral Fogarty's Middle East Force staff in *LaSalle*. But the tighter command and control essential to successful combat operations, in particular the principle of unity of command, suggested that Americans would control the battle groups being formed around the USN carriers. Operational responsibility for the offensive shifted to Admiral March in *Midway*, but the staff of his Arabian Gulf Battle Force was unaware of the earlier, ill-defined arrangements for the escort of the hospital ships and other auxiliaries. March's staff simply assumed that the Canadian task group would join the British, Dutch, and Australians in the close escort of the carriers and take their assignments from the Americans. Summers feared accordingly that, once the combat equipment limitations of the two Canadian destroyers (specifically their lack of area air defence weapons) were appreciated, each would be relegated to a different carrier group for mundane "planeguard" duties. (A frigate or helicopter always trailed in the wake of a carrier during flight operations, ready to rescue the crews of any aircraft lost overboard during the tricky launch and recovery sequence - a vital but routine task.) For her part, *Protecteur* would be lost in the rear echelon, one of many "tanker bottoms."

Near the end of December, *Midway* returned to the central Gulf, and Commodore Summers took the opportunity to call on Admiral March to discuss Canadian involvement in the Battle Force operations. Accompanying the Canadian theatre commander to the meeting on New Year's Day, 1991 were his senior advisers on naval and air operations. While Summers conversed with March, Commander Forcier and Major Cloutier gave their "sales pitch" to the USN staff on the respective roles of the Canadian naval and air task groups during hostilities. The consultations proved timely and of mutual benefit to the allies, although their true import was not immediately apparent.

In the short term, the Canadian destroyers were saved from the obscurity of planeguard and used to solve a different problem for American planners. Each of the four carrier battle groups comprising the Battle Force was to be accompanied by its own fuel, ammunition, stores, and food replenishment vessels. These were to be consolidated in one large Combat Logistics Force (CLF) in the southern Gulf, the only place where they could avoid congestion and ensure their own security in the early days of hostilities. For the same reasons, and to ensure the resupply of their own warships attached to the American battle groups, the British, Dutch, and Australians also planned to send their supply ships to the CLF. As requirements arose, designated vessels would be dispatched from the southern Gulf to the appropriate Battle Group. However, the lightly armed supply ships would require some protection of their own, both in their holding area and in transit. Even with all of the warships at their disposal, the Americans were hard pressed to divert frigates from escorting the carriers. It was a higher priority. They finally did agree, however, that the Canadian destroyers would escort the Combat Logistics Force in its holding area in the low threat environment of the southern Gulf, a task well within their capability. This would free USN warships for direct support of the carriers.

As for the air task group, little change was foreseen in its combat air patrol employment, but Major Cloutier was able to make an important arrangement with his American hosts. From their base in Doha, Colonel Engstad and Colonel Lalonde had long advocated establishing a direct link with the American flagship staff, which would close the Doha-Manamah-Riyadh-Aegis cruiser planning and tasking loop. Anticipating a greater volume of activity in the northern Gulf skies with the arrival of the four carriers, as well as direct American tactical control over the Canadians during hostilities, Cloutier advocated a close liaison with the air planning staff aboard the new flagship. By the time Commodore Summers' delegation departed,

Admiral March had agreed that two Canadian staff officers - one air and one navy - would embark in *Midway* to serve with the flagship staff as of 5 January.

The Americans seemed more interested in the Canadian air force, and saw the naval liaison position as a reciprocal measure. Ironically, it was to be of greater consequence than the air force. The USN staffs expected little of the Canadian logistical escort, other than to keep the forces safe in the backwaters of the southern Gulf. But the law of unintended consequences was in play, and circumstances were to combine in favour of a very meaningful role for the Canadians in the forthcoming war against Iraq.

Major Cloutier, the air officer, joined the carrier's air group staff to coordinate the CAP stationing of the Doha-based *Hornet* aircraft. The importance of his position fluctuated according to the changing deployment of the CF-18s. The naval liaison officer nominated by Commodore Summers was Lieutenant-Commander Greg Romanow. As Captain Miller's senior operations officer, he had an intimate knowledge of Canadian intentions. He was attached to the staff of the designated Battle Force Anti-Surface Warfare Commander. An American, this commander was responsible for all operations by surface ships in the Gulf. Among his various tasks were the coordination of offensive action in the northern Gulf against Iraqi surface vessels and the occupied oil platforms and the provision of fleet defence for the Coalition naval forces, which included responsibility for the security of the Combat Logistics Force.[2] Because the Canadian task group provided the only escorts for the CLF, the Canadian officer on the Battle Group staff was given the minor responsibility of coordinating their stationing requirements.

But Romanow's responsibilities were hardly minor. He had to keep tabs on the whereabouts of the Coalition tankers assigned to the CLF and, in planning the logistical force operations in the southern Gulf, found it necessary to track the movements not only of the American logistical units but also of the multinational embargo forces.

At the same time, the remaining members of the Multinational Interception Force were not oblivious to the drift towards war in early January 1991. The monthly MIF planning meeting was scheduled for 9 January, aboard HMAS *Success*. It was anticipated that the agenda would gravitate to the troubling subject of the role of the MIF in the event of war. Once hostilities began, MIF operations would be superfluous - there would be no Iraq-bound merchant traffic while offensive operations were underway - and alternate tasks had to be determined.

The WEU members usually held a closed session in advance of any MIF meeting to coordinate their policy before joining the wider MIF forum. In the course of their preliminary meeting on 8 January, they agreed that their present political instructions would allow them to undertake certain "support operations" as long as their numbers were not directly involved in offensive operations and did not operate beyond the geographic confines of the southern Gulf. An officer to coordinate such activity with the USN still had to be identified. The senior British naval officer was the prime candidate, but his ships were committed to "direct" operations. Although the French were nominally chairing the WEU effort, their one warship in the Gulf, the small but well-armed frigate *Doudart de Lagrée*, lacked a good communications interoperability with the Americans. The same held true for other, similar sized vessels of the WEU. Thus, the WEU officers arrived at the MIF coordination meeting on 9 January with good intentions but significant limitations.

The moment was ripe for the Canadians and they seized it. During the days following his New Year's talks with Admiral March, armed with further details provided by Romanow, Commodore Summers' thinking on the Canadian war role had evolved to the point where he believed that his naval task group could form the nucleus of a multinational replenishment task group. At the MIF coordination session, the plan for a Combined (*vice* Combat) Logistics Force was presented by Lieutenant-Commander Romanow, as the representative of both Commodore Summers, the Canadian theatre commander, and Admiral March, the American Battle Force commander. With the implied blessing of the USN, the concept practically sold itself to the participants. In addition to the Americans, the Canadians, Australians, Dutch, and British already had committed forces to the CLF. For the remaining countries, joining the CLF offered greater security to their supply vessels or at the very least a chance to escort CLF ships, a task which could easily be rationalized as a support function. Best of all, it was a genuine alternative to sitting idly by while history was unfolding. When it came time to decide upon a coordinator for the CLF, the Canadians were the obvious candidates. Romanow's liaison duties aboard the carrier already incorporated much of the required staff work, and *Athabaskan*'s upgraded radio fit guaranteed excellent communications connectivity between the Canadian and American flagships.

Returning to *Midway*, Romanow persuaded Admiral March to confirm the CLF's change of scope. With March's recommendation firmly in place, the wartime role of the Canadian task group underwent an important transformation. Captain Miller was elevated to subordinate Warfare Commander in his own right - "UNREP Sierra" (naval parlance denoting command of the underway replenishment area) - the only non-USN officer accorded such status. [3] As 10 January drew to a close, his daily report categorically declared that his task group's MIF operations were secondary to concentrating on the replenishment group escort requirements, with himself - CTG 302.3 - as the allied MNF coordinator.

While awaiting the replies assuring Coalition participation, the task group staff officers had to work quickly to put together a plan to run the CLF. USN and allied warships were taking up their BASTION stations. *Midway* was scheduled to re-enter the Gulf on 12 January and *Ranger* on the fifteenth. By the morning of 11 January, a day and a half after the MIF conference, the Canadians had established a protected area in the southern Gulf. Naming it the Ponderossa, they put out the call:

"The largest parking lot in the Persian Gulf is about to start up business." [4] The designated Coalition logistical vessels began to arrive, slowly at first. The pace quickened considerably during the two days leading up to the UN deadline. However, the Canadians could only muster two escorts - their own destroyers. By themselves, these were clearly insufficient to handle both the security of the Ponderosa and the escort of the vessels to and from the battle groups operating to the north.

Miller's problems were aggravated by the inconvenient but necessary withdrawal of *Athabaskan* into Dubai for the critical days of 11-14 January. The flagship had to offload her RIM-7E *Sea Sparrow* point defence missiles and replace them with an upgraded model, a slightly modified version of the same AIM-7M *Sparrow* carried by the CF-18 *Hornet* aircraft. This was another sign of the navy's continuing concern for the task group's air defence capability and the determination to set it right. With his alternate command ship *Protecteur* also indisposed - she was on her way to the Gulf of Oman to continue workups - Captain Miller and his staff transferred to the cramped quarters of the smaller *Terra Nova* to oversee establishment of the Ponderosa.

The Canadian task group commander's recent elevation in status brought with it diplomatic as well as operational obligations. In trying to coordinate combat operations with the other Coalition members, Miller was drawn back into the interplay between the MIF and MNF forces, but from a different perspective. It was now a Canadian officer, formerly of the MIF and now of the MNF, who had to rationalize the expanded participation of the Coalition partners. On 12 January, UNREP Sierra began to exercise his newfound responsibility for much of the southern Gulf. Still uninformed of his allies' intentions, Captain Miller sent out a direct and urgent plea for more escorts. Recognizing that each member of the Coalition had its own political, geographic, and even equipment restrictions, he promised to incorporate their concerns in any plan. First, though, they had to communicate their concerns. Directed specifically at the WEU allies was Miller's assurance that national requirements regarding MIF patrol sectors would be incorporated into the corresponding CLF areas.

The British, Dutch, and Australians were unable to assist. They had assigned their tankers to the CLF, but their destroyers and frigates were committed to carrier escort tasks. Other commanders, still anxious to get in on the action, convinced their home governments that there were no entangling commitments and finally began to join the force. In short order the Danish-Norwegian task group committed its two ships, HDMS *Olfert Fischer* and KVS *Andennes*, and the Italians offered two of their frigates, ITS *Zeffiro* and *Libeccio*. Both task group commanders indicated that their designated ships could help patrol the CLF protection area, adjacent to the southern Gulf interception points (the Bravo areas), in the course of their MIF operations. The offers were gratefully accepted, but they only partially solved one of Captain Miller's two requirements: he still needed escorts to range farther afield. In his daily report for 13 January, he noted ruefully: "It's working but [I'm] not sure why." [5]

There remained a shortage of escorts free to cover those assignments less clearly labelled "support," and the Canadians had to assume the additional taskings alone. The unavailability of more capable destroyers and an enthusiastically broad interpretation of their mandate led to the bizarre spectacle of *Terra Nova* departing Ponderosa to rendezvous with USS *Ranger* in the Gulf of Oman, on 15 January, and escort her and her battle group through Silkworm Alley to their central Gulf operating area. Before her smaller sister ship could return, *Athabaskan* was ordered away from Ponderosa early on the fifteenth. She went north to *Midway*'s operating area for the first of many southbound escorts. On this occasion she escorted the American ammunition ship *Kiska* and the Australian tanker *Success*. While *Terra Nova* and *Athabaskan* were absent, Captain Miller had little choice but to leave the protection of the remaining supply ships to the WEU forces operating in the immediate vicinity of the CLF area, despite the fact that they had been denied permission by their national authorities to participate actively in escort operations. His fears were borne out when *Athabaskan* returned in the afternoon of the fifteenth to find that the Italian frigates had moved on to new MIF assignments in the Gulf of Oman. The Danes and Norwegians had remained on the scene, but their adjacent Bravo-2 sector was unfortunately located to the east of Ponderosa, far removed from the expected thrust of an Iraqi attack.

Frequent pleas for more capable escorts were finally answered with the arrival of the American destroyer *Harry W. Hill*, on 16 January. Its job was to provide an air defence cover for Ponderosa. Eventually the Argentineans, Spanish, and even the British would join, but in some ways the most welcome addition to the escort fold was the French ship *Jean de Vienne*, effective the morning before the expiry of the UN deadline (0800, 15 January). This ship, newly arrived in the Gulf, was a large, modern, well-equipped destroyer, and came without any significant restrictions on her employment. Admiral Bonnot, the French regional commander, freely assigned her to Captain Miller for his tactical control. Bonnot was the only force commander to make such a practical move. [6] The *Jean de Vienne* was just what Miller needed to round out his escort force. As soon as the French destroyer reported for duty, she was assigned to assist *Terra Nova* on yet another transit of the Strait of Hormuz. Their mission was to rendezvous in the Gulf of Oman with a squadron of American amphibious assault ships. Hostilities were imminent.

As the watches turned over in the three Canadian ships in the normally quiet time after midnight, on 17 January, all three crews were roused and each person was administered a tablet of pyrodestigmine-bromide, a drug to counter exposure to nerve gas. As a further precaution against chemical attack, everyone was ordered to carry their special chemical protection garb at all times. Two hours

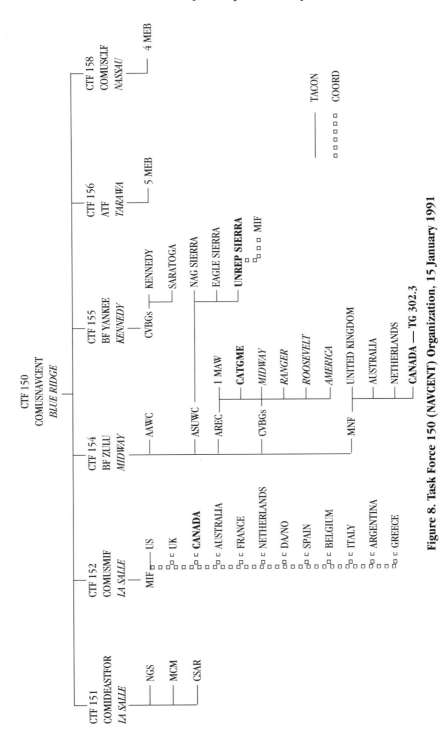

Figure 8. Task Force 150 (NAVCENT) Organization, 15 January 1991

185

later, the radar screens lit up with seemingly endless Link-11 tracks. They were illuminating waves of *Tomahawk* cruise missiles and carrier strike aircraft, all heading up the Gulf.

New Frontiers for the Canadian Navy

Involvement in hostilities was a new and sobering experience. Few members of the Canadian task group could claim to have been alive when their fleet had last been at war, let alone offer their own experiences of actual combat. Still, the beginning of the bombing campaign was anticlimactic after the frantic activity of the preceding seven days. The tension of the previous weeks evaporated and was replaced momentarily by a fear of the unknown terrors that had been unleashed. Then, as the anticipated Iraqi counterattack failed to materialize and news of the overwhelming success of the Coalition air strikes came in, the men and women of the task group settled into a routine. They had spent their entire adult lives preparing for war. A grim determination bordering on satisfaction filled the atmosphere. That was the sentiment expressed in *Athabaskan*'s contribution to a family tape the following day: "A few folks are wondering about their New Year's resolution to quit smoking and feel their timing may be a bit off. Of course our main concern is to do our job so we can help resolve this conflict quickly." [7]

It proved to be a very different war from the one for which the Canadian navy had prepared, at once familiar yet strange. True, there was the intense activity of carrier battle groups operating in a restricted space. It reminded one of the TEAMWORK exercises in the Norwegian Vestfjord, with the Canadian task group commander exercising a prominent warfare responsibility. But that had been in an anti-submarine role. There were no enemy submarines in the Gulf. Coordinating the movements of a loosely bound multinational logistical force was a new departure, but Captain Miller and his staff officers adapted quickly and confidently, drawing upon their years of training to pioneer innovative operational solutions to fit their newfound obligations.

On a different level, there was something of the western frontier to the Combat Logistics Force. For example, the very name Ponderosa (after the Cartwright ranch of the popular 1960s television series *Bonanza*) conjured up the image of a ranch-on-the-sea, where the heavily laden supply ships, not unlike fattening cattle, were safely corralled, waiting to be driven to the carrier market. Nearby were the escorts riding "shotgun." The metaphor was sometimes mixed with references to the "Pachyderm Palace," [8] an allusion to the large and clumsy auxiliary vessels.

The Combat Logistics Force had hit its stride just in time. Its success, combined with the vital air defence patrols flown by the Canadian *Hornet* planes over the northern Gulf, prompted Admiral March to send a message of congratulations to Commodore Summers in recognition of the Canadian contribution to the first day of naval operations:

Ken, Dusty is doing a superb job with the CLF Box. I was particularly impressed with the speed with which he got defenses organized ... The Canadian FA-18 folks have really filled the holes in our fleet air defense posture effectively. Their can do attitude is great. You certainly have an outstanding team. Thanks for your support. Warm regards, Dan.[9]

The crystal clarity of the "significantly brighter sunrise" of 17 January, as Commodore Summers coined it,[10] brought with it some order to the CLF operations. The recalcitrant allies gradually received permission to come on side and lend assistance, although they still could not participate to the extent Miller would have liked. The situation may have stabilized, but it was no less complex. The stream of escort demands had not slackened; it only became more regular. Military logistical ships and other auxiliaries continued to arrive in the Gulf of Oman and required escort through the Strait of Hormuz either to Ponderosa or direct to the carrier operating area. A press release explaining the Canadian role later described the diversity of the replenishment effort:

> For a huge, multinational naval force such as that in the Gulf, food is but one of the hundreds of different supplies needed every day to ensure continued operation. Ammunition — bullets, cannon shells, missiles, rockets and bombs; fuel — oil, jet fuel, hydraulic fluid, lubricants; spare parts — tires, clamps, nuts and bolts, circuits and wiring, tubes and computer chips; and even letters from home: these are but a fraction of the supplies needed each day by the allied fleet and provided by the logistics force.[11]

The pace of operations meant a constant demand for resupply. Every two days, one carrier alone took about 1.5 million gallons of aviation gas for its airplanes and required 300 vertical hoist lifts of ammunition for bombing sorties. On 17 January there were two carriers operating in the central Gulf; within days there was a third; and by mid-February there was a fourth, each one conducting an average of seventy sorties every day. [12] Their attendant screening ships, plus the destroyers and frigates, which extended the Coalition reach into the northern Gulf, needed to be refuelled at least once a week, with even more frequent top-ups preferred.

By the very fact of its existence the CLF presented a paradox. The problem was how to come to grips with the threat. Ponderosa had been established in the southern Gulf precisely because the likelihood of a direct Iraqi attack was remote. It was well beyond *Scud* missile range, and any *Osa* patrol boats and *Mirage* aircraft would have several rings of surface and air defences to penetrate before attempting an *Exocet* missile strike. Concerns focussed accordingly on nuisance attacks, potentially as dangerous as direct full-scale attack and in many ways more difficult to guard against.

In fact, the confined waters of the Persian Gulf were chock-full of floating targets. The heavily laden and poorly manoeuvrable supply ships were especially vulnerable. Attacks could take several forms. The drifting mine was the most deadly menace to surface ships. There existed ample evidence of their use by Saddam's forces. Storm waves had broken some loose from fields laid off the Kuwaiti coast, but others had been deliberately released, an action outlawed under international law (see map for "Drifting Mine Danger Area"). There also existed the possibility of suicide attacks by small civilian aircraft, able to fire antitank rocket-propelled grenades (RPGs) or spray poison gas in the fashion of a crop duster. To be sure, the likelihood of this ever happening was almost nil because of a significant reduction in commercial air traffic in the Gulf and the restrictions throughout the Arab world in general on private ownership of aircraft. But there were other dangers. Ponderosa was in the midst of several major oilfields, and a constant eye had to be kept on commercial helicopters resupplying the drilling rigs. Dhows, small traditional vessels used for fishing and coastal trade, presented a similar problem. It would be easy to arm their crews with portable weapons such as RPGs. The threat was not unrealistic. During the Tanker War, the Iranian Republican Guard had launched attacks from dhows and high speed "cigar" boats. [13] The commander of the Argentine task group, Capitán Rosenthal, later described the particular problem they posed:

> [Translation:] To distinguish between peaceful but ignorant fishermen, smugglers anxious not to come into contact with any form of authority, honest and upright masters of coastal trading vessels, and possible terrorists conducting clandestine operations, gave a lesson in showing the degree to which a commander at sea is in charge of the destiny of so many people. [14]

Given the expanse of the CLF protection area, and the shortage of escorts, Miller found it a constant struggle to keep abreast of the dhows' movements, and therefore placed a high premium on the employment of patrols. Again the big Canadian *Sea King* helicopters proved quite versatile. They were able to remain airborne longer than the smaller aircraft operated by the rest of the Coalition, and their FLIR was especially helpful at night against targets too small for effective radar detection. The effort to identify and warn away intruders was fairly successful until the end of January, when Arab fishermen suddenly seemed determined to resume their traditional livelihood in the area.

All this coincided with the Battle of Khafji, 29-31 January. This was an Iraqi probe down the Saudi coast that included an assault by commandoes embarked in small boats. The Khafji seaborne attack was effectively broken up by British and American naval helicopters, but it reminded commanders everywhere of the very real dangers of these nuisance attacks. From 30 January to 1 February, Captain Miller felt compelled on four different occasions to authorize the use of machine-gun warning fire to divert dhows: from *Athabaskan*, which fired the first shots by the Canadian navy in the Gulf; *Olfert Fischer*; USS *Horne*; and finally from *Protecteur*'s SK413, Lucky Louis. The last named accomplished a double first - the first shots fired in anger from a Canadian *Sea King* and by a female crew member, the airborne sensor operator, Master Corporal Karin Lehmann. Fortunately, the forces protecting Ponderosa never had to resort to harsher action. The problem was never satisfactorily resolved, but the terrorist threat never manifested itself either. Anyway, the problem was left behind when the logistical force was moved in mid-February to a new operating area.

Until then, the nearby presence of the United Arab Emirates was both a boon and the source of some frustration to those charged with the protection of Ponderosa. The forces operating in the southern Gulf enjoyed access to the large, modern facilities of the ports of Dubai, Abu Dhabi, Jebel Ali, and Sharjah, without experiencing *Protecteur*'s problems at Manamah. These ports greatly eased the supply, maintenance, and shore leave requirements of the Coalition warships. The huge fuelling depot of Jebel Ali was only a half day transit from Ponderosa, and all the ports were within easy helicopter range for regular mail and critical spares pickups. When the Bahrain airport was closed to all non-operational traffic, the Canadian naval logistical airhead finally had to change location, and Dubai was the obvious choice. Its deep-water port already had been selected as the site from which to conduct the in-theatre crew rotations and coincident maintenance periods for the three ships of the naval task group. It now became the focal point of the Canadian naval logistical effort in the Gulf. While maintaining his primary offices in Manamah to support the Canadian Middle East Headquarters, Commander Banks established a sub-detachment in Dubai. Under its direction, *Athabaskan*'s *Sea Sparrow* missiles were replaced, and emergency repairs to a critical boiler room pump in *Terra Nova* were expedited, in mid-February. During the war, *Protecteur* put in for two major storing periods of several days apiece (plus one barge day off-shore). The time was used to begin the lengthy installation of an additional air conditioning plant for the supply ship and to undertake major helicopter repairs not possible at sea, such as the final replacement of the Persian Pig's troublesome main gear box. Despite local customs and the threat of terrorism, the Canadians found their new forward operating base a most pleasant and accommodating port of call.

In operational matters, however, integration of Arab armed forces in the southern Gulf with the Coalition was virtually non-existent. Although United Arab

Emirate patrol boats regularly passed near the Ponderosa, they made no apparent effort to dissuade the dhow traffic through the area, and on occasion their own actions were open to misinterpretation as a possible threat. There were several alarming incidents in which Coalition helicopters had to take evasive action when "locked-up" by fire control radars from the Emirate garrisons on the nearby island of Sir Abu Nu'Ayr. And then, just as the dhow incidents in early-February had everyone's nerves on edge, Emirate *Mirage* fighter aircraft began unannounced drills over the island. Fearful of the increasing probability of some sort of incident, an exasperated Captain Miller requested Admiral March intervene. In due course the American embassy in Abu Dhabi opened a liaison channel with the Emirate Navy, but it was only on 14 February that the Americans reported the UAE Navy had directed its units to communicate with the CLF commander for the purpose of cooperation - even as the logistical force was in the process of vacating the Ponderosa for operations elsewhere.

Of course, not all of Captain Miller's security concerns were tied to the Ponderosa. Nearly a hundred miles lay between the holding area in the southern Gulf and the carrier operating area to the north. For the protection of the supply ships while in transit, Captain Miller instituted a daily "train" schedule. Each evening a northbound and a southbound procession of auxiliaries would depart with their escort; one from Ponderosa and one from the carrier area, heading for each other. The trip would be made overnight, allowing for the added safety of darkness and full daylight for the replenishment operations scheduled the next day at either end.

Essentially small convoys, the trains were crucial in bringing some order to the constant shuttle between the two areas, especially given the small number of escorts. But shepherding the train proved to be a far from simple task. Limits on MIF employment were complicated by language barriers and a reluctance on the part of some of the supply ships to submit to the unfamiliar multinational escort. Moreover, it was often difficult to get the mostly civilian masters (the auxiliaries of most navies have minimal regular navy crew) to conform to strict rendezvous and stationing assignments. They were accustomed to operating independently. This prompted the operations officer in *Terra Nova* to report to the Canadian flagship on the progress of one mission: "Finally have ___ moving in the right direction ... This is like pulling teeth. Will submit requisition for whip and cattle prod soonest." [15]

Their casual attitude was in large part a consequence of the failure of the Iraqis to mount a credible naval or terrorist threat. But the possibility could not be ignored. The risks attendant to passage in the area were underlined during the evening of 12 February, when a Danish registered merchant vessel, MV *Arktis Sun*, sailing independently from Damman for Dubai, raised a distress call that she had been boarded by pirates who had made off with a large sum of money and some classified material. The vessel's position was just to the northwest of the Ponderosa. Within minutes *Terra Nova* (passing close at hand with that day's northbound train) and a helicopter from *Protecteur* arrived to assist. Neither found any trace of the attackers. Following questioning of the master in Dubai by Danish officers from *Olfert Fischer*, the incident was determined to have been a hoax. Still, no chances could be taken.

Although none of the incidents ever amounted to anything, the prompt responses indicated that the protection of Ponderosa and the trains was effective and probably appropriate to the level of threat. Although the receding danger allowed ever larger groups of supply ships to proceed with fewer escorts, Miller and his staff were continually balancing tasking requirements against escort availability. To factor in all the elements of the complex matrix, the Canadian staff officers aboard the two flagships developed an arrangement whereby the American Surface Warfare Commander would issue daily intentions (penned by Romanow, the Canadian liaison officer). From these intentions, UNREP Sierra (Captain Miller, through his operations officer, Lieutenant-Commander Jimmy Hayes) would take the appropriate sections for translation into his own instructions. However, the pace of events was often so swift that by the time the formal instructions message was received in the destination ships, it had been overtaken by events. Only a combination of perseverance, the liberal use of satellite telephone, and occasionally a sense of humour, made it work.

Even with the support of the other Coalition partners, Miller's own Task Group 302.3 was the workhorse of the CLF. Escorts came and went; new units were rotated; port visits were continued; and on occasion other national taskings were undertaken. Only the two Canadian destroyers remained constantly on the scene, except for *Terra Nova*'s two-day stint in Dubai, 10-12 February. In the course of operations, the CLF required 106 escort taskings, thirty-five of which were undertaken by the two Canadian destroyers. For *Protecteur*'s part, once she had completed her work-ups, she assumed the regular role of duty tanker - ready to fuel any passing warships on thirty minutes notice - and occasionally acted as guard ship in the absence of the destroyers. These duties were punctuated only by stopovers in Dubai to take on stores.

By 19 January, the third day of hostilities, the logistical force had swollen to almost its anticipated strength. Captain Miller was coordinating the activity of some ten escorts and twenty auxiliaries. Two days later, on the twenty-first, his report of the naval situation gave an apt description of the CLF's multinational character and variety of operations. Summarized with the comment that "CLF ops were low intensity today, it recounted:

> [Air] strikes continue against targets in Iraq. [Iraqi] air and naval response remains minimal. *Ath[abaskan]* and *Ter[ra Nova]* remained in the CLF area ... *Pro[tecteur]* conducted RAS with *Brazen*, *Almirante Brown* and *Spiro*. *Olna* conducted RAS

ESCORTS		AUXILIARIES	AMPHIBS
MNF	**MIF**		
HMCS ATHABASKAN*	HDMS OLF. FISCHER*	HMCS PROTECTEUR*	*PHIBRON 5:*
TERRA NOVA*	KVS ANDENNES*	HrMs ZUIDERKRUIS*	OKINAWA
FNS J. DE VIENNE*	ITS LIBECCIO*	HMAS SUCCESS	FT McHENRY
HMS BRAZEN	ZEFFIRO*	RFA ORANGELEAF	DURHAM
BRILLIANT	FNS DOU. DE LAGREE	OLNA*	OGDEN
EXETER	COMDT BORY	FORT GRANGE	CAYUGA
ARA ALM. BROWN*	SPS NUMANCIA	SIR BEDEVERE	
SPIRO*		SIR PERCIVALE	TRIPOLI
USS HARRY W. HILL*		ITS STROMBOLI*	
HORNE*		VESUVIUS*	
FORD		SAN MARCO*	
FRAN. HAMMOND		USS KANSAS CITY*	
FIFE		KISKA*	
WORDEN		SHASTA*	
HALYBURTON		SPICA*	
		ACADIA*	
		NITRO*	
		MOUNT HOOD*	
		HASSAYAMPA*	
		PASSUMPSIC*	
		KILAUEA*	
		PLATTE*	
		SAN DIEGO*	
		NIAGARA FALLS	
		SACRAMENTO	
		MV COURIER*	
		RANGER*	
		ROVER*	
		OREGON STAR	

Figure 9. MIF/MNF Units Variously under the Coordination of CTG 302.3 for CLF Operations ("Ponderosa", 12 January – 14 February 1991) (* indicate regular)

with *Okinawa*, *Durham* and *Ogden*. *Success* conducted RAS in the vicinity of the CV Op Area with *RK Turner*, *Caron*, *Sacramento* and *Sydney*. *Olfert Fischer* escorted *Zuiderkruis* to and from Jebal Ali. *Jean de Vienne* escorted *Orangeleaf* to *LaSalle* for a RAS and then on to *Argus*. *Brazen*, *HW Hill*, *Terra Nova* and *Athabaskan* patrolled the CLF area ... *Lib[eccio]* returned to the CLF area and then departed for the [Gulf of Oman] for national tasking ... WEU ships *Numancia* and *Doudart de Lagrée* patrolled the eastern side of the CLF protection area. *Ter[ra Nova]* departed the CLF area at approx 1200Z to go to the CV area to escort *Kansas City* and *Spica* back to the CLF area. *Zuiderkruis* departed the CLF area at approx [1700Z] under escort of *Almirante Brown* and *Spiro*. *Numancia* departed the CLF area at approx [1800Z] en route the CV Op Area to RV with *Sacramento* and escort her to the vicinity of the CLF Box for a CONSOL RAS with the *Star of Oregon* AM 22 Jan. [16]

Some problems of equipment incompatibility and unfamiliarity with procedures were encountered, but they were overcome as the multinational force became comfortable working in close proximity over an extended period. The permutations of taskings against the availability of ships occasionally made for some interesting combinations. The degree to which Miller could press the Coalition was demonstrated on 10 February, when he prevailed upon the only available tanker, the British ship *Olna*, to pass fuel to the Argentinean ships *Almirante Brown* and *Spiro*, its old Falklands adversaries. HMS *Exeter* "screened" the operation from a distance.

Commodore Summers' vision of a multinational replenishment group had been realized. Participation in, and command of, the CLF was a task tailor-made for the Canadian naval task group. They had expressed a desire for an identifiable role, and there was a need for a separate logistical force. But nothing was preordained. Despite the extensive upgrades prior to deployment, neither Canadian destroyer could rightfully claim a spot in the defensive lines to the north, though they did credible service as escorts in the reduced threat area of the southern waters. To the credit of the Canadian navy must go the fact that each of its three ships in the Gulf had something specific to offer the Coalition. *Athabaskan* was fitted out as a command flagship for a task group, with a staff well-versed in coordinating NATO alliance operations. In *Terra Nova* Captain Miller had under his direct control a hardworking escort with which to encourage greater participation from the other partners. And *Protecteur*'s pre-war experience as the central Gulf MIF supply ship made her a natural model for the logistical force.

On a different level, the Americans, preoccupied with the move to the offensive, were quite happy to pass the southern escort role to a proven ally. For his part, the Canadian UNREP Sierra recognized the importance of the image of Coalition solidarity and was responsive to the sensitivities of the Multinational Interception Force. Most MIF members were handicapped by the political restrictions on their operating areas and their less sophisticated communications suites. The only ones who could operate on a close tactical level with the USN - the British, Australians and Dutch - were already doing just that and were involved in the battle force operations to the north. Somehow, Miller had been able to square the circle of MIF affiliation with the CLF.

The logistical force's coordination role was also a godsend closer to home, where the Canadian government had a circle of its own to square. Opposition critics and various peace groups charged that by participating in the offensive against Iraq, Canada was reduced in status to nothing more than an American lackey. The inescapable fact of American military leadership was difficult to reconcile with the official position that Canada was responding to a United Nations call to arms. Explaining the nuances was difficult, as Minister McKnight discovered when he appeared before the Standing Committee of National Defence and Veterans Affairs (SCNDVA) on 31 January. He was confronted directly by Mr Warren Allmand (Liberal - Notre-Dame-de-Grâce), who claimed: "[T]he assignment and the coordination of roles seem to be under the control of the United States and not under the control of the United Nations ... Obviously it is not a UN operation." The defence minister proudly pointed to the CLF and countered:

> [You] and I disagree on whether this is a UN operation ... The collaborating nations have joined together to enforce United Nations resolutions, some 12 United Nations resolutions ... Canada, when hostilities commenced, placed its assets and personnel under the tactical control of the overall commander. That happens to be in this case *U.S. General Schwarzkopf* ... Captain Dusty Miller of the Canadian navy ... is in tactical command of the combat logistics group, which is made up of assets of some eleven nations ...
>
> The moral responsibility, the moral operating authority and the legal operating authority for the Canadian forces are that of the United Nations resolutions, in this case particularly 660 and 678. [17]

Despite its logic, the message did not catch on with the media, whose tone was both jingoistic and disparaging of the national effort. The story of the Canadian role in the Combat Logistics Force went virtually unreported in Canada for several reasons. At first, the military was reluctant even to admit the existence of its new role. For reasons of security, it did not wish to draw unwanted attention to a vital supply concentration area. But once its existence was acknowledged, it was difficult to arouse interest in the mundane routine of what was essentially a sideshow of a sideshow. The world was mesmerized by the "Star Wars" spectacle of the air war. Several official pronunciations - a detailed brief by Commodore Summers on 20 January, the official NDHQ press release on the twenty-eighth, and the minister's testimony before the Standing Committee on the thirty-first - had little effect. Moreover, reporters were hardly encouraged by the Canadian navy. One example will suffice. A *Twin Otter* aircraft chartered out of Abu Dhabi by a group of journalists from the Halifax CTV affiliate approached Ponderosa several times, trying to get footage of the task group in action, but was repeatedly warned away on the suspicion that it might be a terrorist aircraft! DESERT STORM was a visual experience. No footage meant no story. Rebuffed, the film crews returned to the more telegenic task of counting *Hornet* sorties from the comfort of their Doha hotels overlooking the airfield.

For all its successes, the CLF was not without its problems. Ponderosa never became the anticipated focal point for all logistical activity in the Gulf and that complicated Miller's task. Dispersion of elements of the force to the control of other commanders throughout the Gulf worked against bringing some order and regularity to CLF's activities and made Miller's efforts occasionally appear reactive and disjointed. Frequent assertions of support and admiration from others for the job he was doing could not paper over the fact that Captain Miller was constantly battling his Coalition partners for scarce resources. The trend towards decentralization was fostered by the increasing security of the central Gulf and the irresistible desire of operational commanders to have their resupply forces close at hand. From the very beginning, those few American supply ships with a good self-defence capability, such as the fast combat support ships *Sacramento* and *Kansas City*, were retained in the central area to provide ready fuel to the carriers and their escorts. Each one was equipped with *Sea Sparrow* and *Phalanx*. For the first intensive days of operations, even the 1950s-vintage *Hassayampa* was stationed nearby, ready to surge to the strike box when called by Strike Sierra. As the pace settled, *Hassayampa* returned to Ponderosa and took her place from time to time in the train. But, as confidence increased in Coalition air superiority, more and more of the precious oilers extended their stays in the central Gulf to sustain the carrier operations, returning to the logistical force area only for their own replenishment.

Support of the aircraft carriers was not the only task to pull logistical force ships from Miller's control. As operations pushed into the northern Gulf (known as the NAG, or Northern Arabian [Persian] Gulf), it became necessary to replenish the ten to fifteen ships of the American, British, Australian, and Dutch navies on station there, in a fashion reminiscent of *Protecteur*'s MIF Operations role as the

Chuckwagon. Once a week two or three American supply ships, each one of which was loaded with fuel, ammunition, or food, would make the three-day "NAG Swing". They were occasionally augmented by the Dutch *Zuiderkruis* and the British *Olna* to fulfil any specific national requirements. Ironically, although *Protecteur* had better self-defence armament than either the Dutch or the British ships, it never undertook the NAG Swing because there were no Canadian ships in the northern Gulf. The earlier loss of her Mine Avoidance Sonar was also a factor, although none of the other tankers had one either.

The days of the Ponderosa were numbered by the arrival of the USN Amphibious Task Force (ATF) in early February. The few assault ships in the Gulf up to that time had worked out of Ponderosa in close liaison with Captain Miller, but the new group of some forty ships established a separate "'gator holding area" north of Dubai. Although not especially troubling in itself, this was contrary to the original intention of the CLF. And further difficulties arose when the new group would go off without warning on manoeuvres, invariably through Ponderosa and usually at night. This increased the chances of collision, much to Miller's distress.

By late January, the British already had established their own separate supply ship holding area southeast of Qatar. *Olna* remained with the CLF for the next two weeks, but the two Royal Navy frigates previously available to Miller were siphoned away to protect the other half-dozen British auxiliaries in their new location. The ostensible reason for the move was to shorten the supply lines to the British forces dispersed throughout the Gulf. In fact, it seems that while relations between Miller and Commodore Christopher Craig were genuinely good, the intent of the British task group commander was not so much to get away from the CLF as from the WEU, so that he could enjoy the greater freedom of action that came with physical separation from the restricted European group.

Unrest was also developing among the Europeans. At the fifth WEU Naval Forum convened in Paris on 30 January, the French delegation complained on behalf of its in-theatre forces that being a CTG or coordinator with no ships was not very interesting. This was an obvious reference to the diminished role of the interception force and the gradual secondment of the European warships to the expanding requirements of the Canadian-led logistical support escort role. In response to the pressure from home for a more active part in the command of the CLF, the captain of the Italian *Zeffiro*, acting as WEU coordinator, visited the Canadian task group commander aboard his flagship and discussed the possibilities for continued WEU cooperation. Captain Miller employed his considerable diplomatic skills to persuade his guest that it would be difficult to duplicate the organizational structure elsewhere. The meeting culminated with a tour of *Athabaskan*'s Operations Room. Miller showed the Italian captain the room's banks of communications gear and rows of radar displays depicting the full span of current activity throughout the Gulf, all of which was available to the Canadians on their Link and radio channels. Reporting back to his confreres and superiors, the Italian reaffirmed the existing cooperation principles between the WEU Group and CTG 302.3 and ended by expressing his great satisfaction at being part of the group.

The problem was one of perception. Far removed from the Gulf, sceptical observers had difficulty in appreciating the bustle of the rear-area activity. Even those close to the action could hold unrealistic views of the war because they were not privy to the high-technology command and control networks. As the Italian commander had discovered, the Canadians were tapped into a whole different level of the conflict. The French captain of *Jean de Vienne*, however, was more insistent than his Italian comrade. He went so far as to suggest that perhaps it was time that he assumed the coordination responsibility. Captain Miller made a quick visit to the French ship for "a liaison coordination meeting," on 3 February. He compared *Jean de Vienne* to *Athabaskan* and forced the French commander to admit that his ship had neither the staff nor the communications to take on the task of CLF. *Athabaskan* might be older, but she was obviously the most capable command ship in the multinational forces.

February brought two pleasant pieces of news for the ships' crews. The first concerned crew rotation for the destroyers, which had been postponed indefinitely with the eruption of war. *Protecteur* had already undergone the procedure, and *Huron* had sailed from Esquimalt for Halifax, where her crew would train before flying to their new ship in the Gulf. The West Coast destroyer reached Halifax on 27 January and awaited developments. By then, a growing appreciation of Captain Miller's new logistical force responsibilities had provoked a reevaluation of the stalled rotation plan. If the Canadian navy wished to continue the CLF coordination role, it had to maintain *Athabaskan*'s level of command and control. Miller already had demonstrated to his several Coalition partners that few allied destroyers could boast an equivalent fit. But the same was true of *Protecteur*. Despite all the upgrades which enabled her to act as an alternate command ship for the Canadian task group, it was not equipped to the same degree as *Athabaskan* and therefore could not exercise the same level of command and control over the more complex operations of the large multinational group. Moreover, the planned replacement of crews only would require *Athabaskan* to depart from Ponderosa for two to three weeks, depriving the task group commander of his flagship for that period. If the command and control exercised from *Athabaskan* could not be passed directly to another, similarly equipped Canadian ship, Commodore Summers feared that he would have no alternative but to transfer this responsibility to another nation. To make things even worse, there was no guarantee that Canada would regain this role once the rotation was completed. The settling of the air war into what promised to be a prolonged campaign ultimately decided the issue. On 31 January, General de Chastelain gave the long-awaited order to recommence the rotation process, but in vastly different fashion. All previous rotation plans were cancelled, and MARCOM was ordered to take immediate action to prepare and deploy HMC Ships *Huron* and *Restigouche* to relieve *Athabaskan* and *Terra Nova*, which would return to Halifax by mid-May.[18]

The replacement crews of the two West Coast destroyers already were well advanced in their preparatory training, but nothing had been done to the ships themselves. Work got underway immediately in the Ship Repair Units in Halifax (for *Huron*) and Esquimalt (for *Restigouche*), at an estimated cost of $25-30 million. The money was to come out of funds set aside for the planned FRICTION Phase III preparation of the destroyers *Nipigon* and *Annapolis*, due for rotation in the upcoming summer. *Huron* was ready within three weeks and sailed from Halifax the morning of Sunday, 24 February, just as the ground offensive was getting underway. Because the work on *Restigouche* was not completed until after hostilities had ceased, she did not make for the Gulf. Eventually, she filled the Canadian position in the Standing Naval Force Atlantic, to compensate for the demands which FRICTION had made on the Atlantic fleet.

In the meantime, for those crews still in the Gulf, their return to Halifax was delayed but now fixed with some certainty. Any remaining disappointment was quickly offset by the second piece of news: notification of expanded benefits, foremost of which was an allowance of $600 tax free per person per month, irrespective of rank, to compensate for the extra risk of war, and an extension of the deadline for filing 1990 income tax returns until 31 October. As one newspaper observed, Canadians serving in the Gulf "scored a victory over a more traditional enemy ... the tax man".[19]

That news came at an opportune moment. The Canadian naval deployment had been on an emotional roller-coaster since day one. A downturn was about to begin. As the second week of hostilities drew to a close, it became apparent that the quick knockout victory promised by the proponents of air power had failed to materialize. Admittedly, from the point of view of the navy, the air force had met many of its aims. The enemy had not been able to make any significant demonstration against the armada ranged in the Gulf. The few attempted sorties by the Iraqi air force had been turned back or the aircraft even destroyed while still on the ground. Thereafter, it remained hunkered down in hardened shelters or busy flying to Iran. For its part, the main Iraqi naval fleet had been sunk or badly damaged by Coalition air forces. The only real naval action in the traditional sense had occurred in the week of 21 January, following the appointment of the Commander of Carrier Group 7 as Anti-Surface Warfare Commander. Rear-Admiral Ronald J. Zlatoper was embarked in *Ranger* and to speed up the tempo of the maritime campaign he devised a more aggressive, so-called "rollback" plan to neutralize Iraqi forces in the northern Gulf.[20] Under his direction the Kuwaiti island of Qaruh was liberated on 24 January, and Free Kuwaiti forces operating from American frigates regained control of the offshore oil drilling platforms.[21] On 29

January, the quick defeat of the Iraqi light seaborne forces in the assault on Khafji underscored the demise of the Iraqi navy. The official American record noted: "By 2 February, all 13 Iraqi surface craft capable of delivering anti-ship missiles had been destroyed or disabled, and the Iraqi naval force was considered combat ineffective." [22] Six days later, Admiral Arthur in NAVCENT declared that the Coalition controlled the waters of the northern Persian Gulf. But the elimination of the Iraqi threat to Coalition shipping in the Gulf had been accomplished slowly and at arm's length from the main surface fleet. Except to the pilots flying missions over Iraq and Kuwait, the war effort seemed to be stagnating.

That mood was reflected in the Ponderosa, where CLF operations were winding down. The activation of Operation DESERT TURNPIKE (see below); MIF escort port visit schedules; the departure of the Royal Navy ships; and *Terra Nova*'s engineering defect - all combined to reduce the available supply of warships. Also, the bad weather, which had extended the air campaign, was slowing the repositioning of VII (US) Corps westward into the Arabian desert. The Saudis, acutely aware of the approaching month of Ramadan, were growing increasingly impatient for the launch of the land offensive. So were the media pools. They were tired of rehashing events often staged for their benefit. There was an urgent need to inject some life into the Coalition campaign, and all quarters looked anxiously to the next phase of operations.

Changing Directions: The Shift North and the DESERT TURNPIKE

Admiral March and General Schwarzkopf met on 2 February to discuss the integration of a full-scale amphibious assault, code-named Operation DESERT SABRE. It was to be part of the ground campaign, set for launch in three weeks, on 21 February. They came to the regrettable, but necessary conclusion that an extended timetable of preparations would preclude direct naval and Marine participation. The problem was that the offshore Iraqi minefields were larger and more sophisticated than expected, and clearing them would be a lengthy but necessary project before any shore bombardments and landings could begin. The admiral estimated that it would be at least twenty-eight days - into early March - before the first Marine could set foot on a Kuwaiti beach.

Still, there were advantages in allowing overt preparations to continue. General Schwarzkopf was counting on the naval forces in the northern Gulf to keep significant Iraqi forces tied down to the east, facing seaward, and away from the primary thrust which would come from the southwest. At the same time, Admiral March argued that further delays in the air and ground campaigns might make a seaborne assault necessary. An amphibious demonstration by the Marines off the Kuwaiti coast, then, promised the best opportunity to bring the navy into the action. To lend the demonstration credibility, March ordered planning to begin on Operation SLASH - a large-scale raid on Faylakah Island, overlooking the mouth of

Kuwait harbour. The attack window was set for the few days after the moonless night of 15 February, when the tides would be favourable.

To proceed with the operation it was necessary to redistribute the naval forces throughout the Gulf. The anti-surface rollback operations were complete and security of the Gulf assured, save for the danger posed by both laid and drifting mines in the northwest sector. Inshore operations off the coast of Kuwait got underway when USN and RN minesweepers, held in reserve in the south, were moved forward. They cleared paths first for the battleships *Wisconsin* and *Missouri*, which began shore bombardment of Iraqi positions, and then for the Marines' assault ships. The ATF had arrived in the Gulf, fresh from a full-scale rehearsal off the coast of southern Oman. They were ready for action.

The arrival in the Gulf on 14 February of a fourth aircraft carrier, USS *America*, presaged the new phase in the naval war. The biggest element of the reorganization was the shift of the carrier operating area some hundred miles northwest, farther up the Gulf, bringing the carriers within 150 miles of Faylakah. This allowed the A-6s and F/A-18s to dispense with time-consuming in-air refuelling and freed the carriers' deck cycle for more purely offensive sorties. Rumours that a shift north was impending had been rife since late January. Because they lacked more solid information but knew that any implementation would be rapid, all ships had to be prepared to move without delay to their new stations. Late on 12 February, Captain Miller learned that the change was imminent. He immediately appreciated the impact that a further displacement from the carriers would have on his logistical force operations. Doubling the hundred-mile length of the train would make even a one-way trip take the better part of a day and increase the strain on his ability to fulfil the escort taskings. What was worse, it would encourage even less reliance on the southern Gulf holding area, and the gradual erosion of Canadian control of the logistical concentration in Ponderosa would become a landslide. And what of the continued participation of the MIF escorts, many of whom were pressing their operational limits?

But Miller had no need to fret. In a month of CLF operations the two solitudes of the naval Coalition had come closer in their thinking. Having gained an appreciation from Romanow of the intricacies of Miller's tasks, the American battle force staff had anticipated his problem and sought to circumvent it. A major element of their new plan was the logical extension of what had become the de facto arrangement: as the carriers shifted north, so too would the CLF, and it would be fully amalgamated with the carrier operating area, occupying its southern quarter in a new sector to be known as "Virginia City." Escorts in screening stations would flank the whole of the larger area. From another perspective, the Coalition forces for the most part were satisfied by the favourable progress of the war and content they could remain distanced from the "direct" offensive activity by their "support" role. The commanders at sea were able to gain quick acquiescence from their home governments for an extension of their CLF operations to the north. With little or no delay, the French, Argentinean, Italian, and Spanish warships upon which Miller had been relying joined the Canadians in Virginia City.

On 13 February, the day before the shift was implemented, *Athabaskan* was on an escort mission in the vicinity of the carriers, and *Terra Nova* joined the northbound, evening train. Instead of returning with the southbound group as planned, *Terra Nova* was ordered to remain with the carriers, while *Athabaskan* conducted the return train and oversaw the CLF segment of the shift. By the time the flagship arrived, very few ships remained in Ponderosa. Acting as guard ship, *Protecteur* already had entrusted their safety to USS *Ford*, the American ship assigned to remain as the local air defence coordinator in the south. In Captain Miller's words, Ponderosa was now "extant but dormant". With nothing to hold them back, *Athabaskan* and *Protecteur* took their leave of Ponderosa and turned their bows north, *Protecteur* slowing en route only long enough to fuel *Comfort* and *Mercy* before proceeding to the new horizons of Virginia City.

Miller was excited at the prospect of a return to his old Charlie sector stomping grounds; nevertheless, he was uneasy about his new terms of reference. The major rationale for his position as UNREP Sierra had vanished overnight. Incorporation of the CLF into the carrier operating area meant that daily trains and a separate protection zone were no longer necessary. As soon as his flagship brought him to the central Gulf in the afternoon of 14 February, Miller made for *Midway*. He was joined by Commodore Summers, and the two men had a meeting with Admiral March to discuss the future of the logistical force. To their relief, they found that the American commander was still keen on having the Canadians act as the middlemen of the Coalition.

Combining the carrier and logistical force operating areas allowed a more economic distribution of the valuable escort forces. Under the new arrangement, the multinational forces of UNREP Sierra would assume the screening positions around the southern half of the carrier area, close to the new CLF Box. Miller no longer had to provide a separate protection, and his northern flank was more than adequately covered. Furthermore, his ships freed several of the better-equipped missile shooters to shift farther north into the Gulf, where their presence extended the air defence umbrella to include the minesweepers and battleships as they conducted their inshore operations and the ATF massed to the north of the carriers.

Other elements of the new plan further reduced the demands on Miller's escort forces. The southern Gulf was secure enough to limit the use of escorts to specially designated vessels, such as ammunition transports, on their infrequent trips through the area. UNREP Sierra's new task would be to assign escorts north of the major shipping routes to Ad Damman and Jubayl. Coalition warships were roaming even the northern Gulf with relative impunity. However, until the amphibious assault took place, there was little need for non-military traffic. The CLF defence responsibilities were expected to be static and relatively threat free.

To his surprise, Captain Miller learned that his responsibilities continued to involve the southern Gulf. He was given a role in the newly-activated DESERT TURNPIKE, a controlled highway for merchant shipping through the Gulf. The flow of ships quickly resumed once the threat of Iraqi retaliation diminished to practically zero. In any event, the ferrying of VII Corps from Europe and the regular sustainment of the land forces occupied the Coalition navy. Commerical vessels were allowed to proceed on their own, under caution, in much the same fashion as they had during DESERT SHIELD. Soon there were reports of incidents of piracy and terrorism. Although they never amounted to anything, they were enough to give pause to shipping firms and masters only too aware of the legacy of the Tanker War, and lead them to demand more visible protection. What they got was Coalition control of shipping.

DESERT TURNPIKE was intended to reassure commercial vessels without placing further demands on the few Coalition escorts. It would have been impossible to convoy the immense volume of merchant traffic in the Gulf. Nor did the tactical situation warrant the close escort of shipping destined for south and central Gulf ports. Instead, picket ships were deployed at several points along a convenient route. They provided mine advisories, threat updates, and assistance if the need arose. USN warships took charge of checkpoints Alpha (in the Gulf of Oman) and Charlie (in the vicinity of Ponderosa). UNREP Sierra was responsible for checkpoints Bravo (at the western end of the Strait of Hormuz, usually filled by the *Olfert Fischer* and the *Andennes* of the WEU), and Delta (north of Qatar, near Virginia City). From this last point, the ships would disperse to the nearby ports of Manamah, Ad Damman, and Jubayl or continue farther north under close escort provided by UNREP Sierra. The assignment of checkpoints Alpha and Charlie to the USN was a tactful gesture to ensure that incoming traffic was initially received by an American warship and thereafter never out of VHF radio range of an English voice. Other non-English speaking Coalition partners continued the valuable work of filling the intervening gaps, without having to risk misunderstandings because of language difficulties.

Fogarty activated Operation DESERT TURNPIKE on 27 January. Miller at first deferred accepting coordination responsibilities, because he was pre-occupied with the impending escort demands of the carriers moving north. The new operation was immediately popular among the WEU group, however. For those few warships whose national leaders still prevented their move north to Virginia City, TURNPIKE offered an option for continued membership in the Coalition.

Indeed, Miller had set the stage for TURNPIKE. In mid-January, the widely differing views on the necessity for offensive action strained the unity of the naval Coalition, which the US so desperately needed to retain intact for diplomatic purposes. By drawing other Coalition navies into the CLF protection scheme, the Canadians provided links between the divergent needs of the Coalition partners and helped to channel support from them for DESERT TURNPIKE.

The move north to Virginia City added another dimension to Canadian involvement in the TURNPIKE. As soon as the logistical ships changed location, the southern checkpoint keepers became the lonely outposts of the Coalition effort. In the process, they lost their convenient replenishment sources. It fell to Miller to organize a weekly SAG Swing along the lines of the earlier NAG Swing. That experience had yielded some important lessons. However tactically undesirable, the procession of Coalition supply ships across the northern waters was unavoidable. Despite the principle of NATO standardization, compatibility problems had arisen among the different navies operating there, particularly in the case of different American and British JP5 (aviation gas) refuelling couplings. [23] Single-product or national supply ships could not be rationalized for the secondary tasking in the south. There was now a need for multi-product supply vessels.

With all this in mind, Captain MIller sought a candidate for the southern Gulf circuit and recalled that *Protecteur* had proven immune from the compatibility problems in earlier MIF operations in the central Gulf. In fact, she was known to have amassed a private collection of couplings, many of which were fashioned in the ship's machine shops and tagged according to customer. As a multi-product platform, she was one of the few Coalition supply ships designed to carry both types of fuel (distillate for ships and JP5 for aircraft), as well as ammunition and food. She had plentiful storerooms to stock any special items of national interest, and she could meet virtually any supply needs. With her recently fitted self-defence capability she could travel anywhere with relative fearlessness. Captain Cronk picked up McClean's mantle, and his replacement crew encountered no problems doing a changeover in an active theatre. The turnover and work-ups had necessitated her absence from operations for only a week in mid-January, and in the month since joining the CLF, the Chuckwagon had completed thirty-eight replenishments, covering the spectrum of the Coalition forces. She was the obvious candidate to supply the multinational warships at the TURNPIKE checkpoints. Shortly after arriving in Virginia City, Captain Miller ordered *Protecteur* to prepare for the three day SAG Swing, code-named Outrider, beginning on 17 February.

While *Protecteur* went about her preparations for the Outrider circuit, *Athabaskan* and *Terra Nova* settled into their new homes. Virginia City was a noticeable change from Ponderosa. Demand for escort protection was reduced, and the incoming replies from his Coalition partners revealed to Captain Miller that restrictions on operating limits had been loosened considerably. The result was an increased flexibility in their taskings. The new screening arrangements were relatively static in nature. Because there was no train to organize and all the sectors had been assigned, there were fewer tasking orders, and even those that existed, such as the weekly ammunition ship shuttle, were far less intense. Integration in the new area, which was close to the active carrier flight zone, required closer coordination of UNREP Sierra's air assets (helicopters were still employed for mine searches and logistical transfers); otherwise it promised to be a period of routine operations.

This was closer to the style of warfare for which the Canadian fleet had prepared. All about them was a modern battle force in action. In her screening sector on the southeastern flank of the carrier area, off the Iranian coast, *Terra Nova* was well positioned to observe the seemingly endless parade of the floating airfields turning northwest into the prevailing winds for the start of their launch and recovery sequences. Then, on 16 February, she was ordered out of her sector to rendezvous with *Mercy* east of Qatar, to escort the hospital ship to Bahrain for a demonstration of her casualty clearing system. Aboard the flagship, meanwhile, the combat teams practised their naval gunfire support (NGFS) drills and waited anxiously for *Athabaskan* to get the call to support an amphibious landing alongside the American battleships. The crew was eager to use the ship's medium-calibre 5-inch gun. Captain Miller recognized that his range of options had widened. His report of 15 February confidently predicted that CLF operations in the new area would be challenging and of a distinctly different flavour from that of previous CLF ops. [24]

However, there were many false starts in Coalition preparations for the seaborne assault. The amphibious demonstration suffered a severe setback early in the morning of 18 February, when two key American ships struck mines in quick succession, while clearing a path to Kuwait for the raid on Faylakah. The first was *Tripoli*, the command ship for the mine-clearing operation. Even with a thirty-foot gash in her bow, the assault carrier was large enough to be able to contain the damage and continue supervising the clearing effort for another three days. The deception of DESERT SABRE was maintained, although Operation SLASH itself was to be abandoned. Within three hours of the strike against *Tripoli*, USS *Princeton*, a cruiser providing air defence cover for the sweeping force, fell victim to a mine. It detonated on the shallow seabed only a few metres below the ship, and the resulting explosion was powerful enough to lift the stern of the 9000-ton cruiser nearly out of the water. She was not immediately holed. But the violent heaving action was aggravated by the detonation of a second, "sympathetic" mine off her starboard beam. This explosion literally twisted the ship, causing at least two major cracks across her decks. The most severe was in a critical spot forty feet from the stern. Immobile and in danger of her quarterdeck breaking off, *Princeton* had to be repaired in dry dock. A civilian salvage tug was chartered to take her to Dubai. Non-combatant vessels could not travel alone that far north in the Gulf; so it fell to UNREP Sierra to provide an escort.

Satisfied that the screening of Virginia City could be accomplished without his constant presence in the immediate vicinity, Captain Miller decided that his own flagship, with her special mine-searching, bow-mounted sonar and her helicopters, was the best available ship for the duty. There was only one hitch: although the Canadians had the most flexible operating limits among the CLF, *Athabaskan* remained forbidden to operate past 28 degrees north (the northern extreme of the carrier operating area). *Princeton* was some seventy miles beyond that. Permission to conduct the mission required higher, national authorization.

Commodore Summers had just disembarked from *Athabaskan* when the request for assistance was received. The three ships of the task group (as well as the Doha air group) had been awarded Canadian Forces Unit Commendations in recognition of their embargo enforcement efforts the previous fall. Summers was making the rounds to present the distinguishing pennants in person. Following a brief ceremony on the flagship's flight deck, he was off to visit *Terra Nova*, standing off Bahrain with *Mercy*, and would meet *Protecteur* in Manamah the next day when she completed her Outrider swing.

Naturally, it took some time to relay the request for national authorization, first to Summers and then to Ottawa. Confident that the required approval would be obtained, *Athabaskan* left to join the salvage tug. Carefully picking a route that avoided previous mine sightings, the ship pushed its way beyond the parallel of the Kuwaiti border into waters traversed by few Coalition ships. Just before sunset on 19 Febraury, *Athabaskan* came upon *Princeton*. The crippled cruiser was taken under tow and began its 300-mile journey down the length of the Gulf to safety, at an agonizing pace of barely seven knots.

Any greater speed would have risked aggravating the damage to *Princeton*'s hull. The following sea, a condition normally desired by sailors, continued to work on the cruiser's stern structure, and worsening weather on the twentieth threatened to shear off her quarterdeck. Captain Edward Hontz of *Princeton* reassessed the situation and came to the conclusion that the vessel was unlikely to reach Dubai. At noon that day, the three ships changed course for the safety of Bahrain. Twelve tense hours later, just after midnight on 21 February, the tiny flotilla finally arrived in Manamah harbour. *Princeton*'s agonizing progress had been followed anxiously by every sailor in the Gulf. They knew only too well the danger of her situation and the chance that a random mine could put them in a similar predicament. By virtue of her proximity, *Athabaskan* had developed a particular empathy with the stricken ship. Before taking leave, the destroyer's crew sent over a special cargo of "suitable libations" - a bottle of Canadian beer for each sailor in *Princeton*. In his thanks, Captain Hontz paid special tribute to the Canadians:

> [W]e owe a debt of gratitude for the superb professionalism of those who extracted us from the minefield and delivered us to safe haven … [and] to HMCS *Athabaskan* for leading the way

from [the Northern Arabian Gulf] to Bahrain and even more so
for the seventeen cases of beer you sent over by helo today.

Thanks also to everyone who helped bolster our morale
with congratulatory messages. Next time send beer like
Athabaskan!! [25]

Once all three Canadian ships were back in Virginia City, the two destroyers resumed the routine of sector patrols. For *Protecteur*, the freshly completed replenishment circuit was such a success that it was immediately ordered to embark on a second SAG Swing, dubbed Outrider II, from 22 to 25 February. Miller made longer range plans to undertake the runs on a weekly basis for the foreseeable future. The two destroyers had been looking forward to the end of the month for an opportunity to put in to port for much-needed repairs. Both ships had been at sea essentially since early January, except for quick emergency stopovers for *Athabaskan*'s missile changeout, 12-14 January, and *Terra Nova*'s engineering repairs, 10-12 February. In peacetime it was not uncommon for ships to spend four to five weeks on exercise between port calls. *Athabaskan*, however, was approaching nearly fifty continuous sea days, under the far more demanding conditions of wartime operations. Equipment and personnel were in need of a respite. Hopes were nonetheless dashed because most of the other CLF escorts were announcing plans for their own port visits. Faced once more with a shortage of escorts, Miller was forced to take up the slack with his own ships. The opportunities alongside were accordingly postponed until sometime in March.

It was just as well. Once again plans were overtaken by events. On Friday morning, 22 February, President Bush issued his "final ultimatum" to Saddam Hussein: he had "until noon Saturday to do what he must do - begin his immediate and unconditional withdrawal from Kuwait." [26] When it expired without appropriate reply, the battleships and amphibious task force moved close to the Kuwaiti coast. The long-awaited ground offensive began that night. Keeping the amphibious deception until the end, *Missouri* fired the first broadsides of the bombardment at 2200 on 23 February.

Earlier in the day, the American hospital ships were also brought out of their southern holding area and readied for casualties. After consultation with General de Chastelain, Commodore Summers ordered the medical team in *Protecteur* to augment their comrades already embarked in *Mercy*. The transfer was accomplished that same afternoon, when the tanker topped up both hospital ships before setting off on her second circuit of the southern checkpoints. The next day, *Comfort* was ordered to move on to Jubayl, and Captain Miller was requested to provide an escort for her journey to the front.

Once again, Commander Pickford's *Athabaskan* was the best of the available choices. In a virtual repetition of the scenario practised long ago in

Exercise IMMINENT THUNDER, the Canadian flagship joined a floating American hospital. On 24 February, they began their northward progress. They were soon in the area of drifting mines, but the passage was uneventful and they arrived off Jubayl at sunset that evening. While awaiting further orders, the hospital ship went to anchor about fifteen miles offshore amongst some small islets, and *Athabaskan* continued her patrol, on the watch for drifting mines and terrorist activity.

The ground battle raged a hundred miles to the north. Coalition casualties were unexpectedly light, and *Comfort* remained at anchor during the twenty-fifth. The quiet of the ship's surroundings was broken only by a call to UNREP Sierra from HMS *Brilliant*, on patrol in the carrier operating area forty miles to the east. She had located what looked like a mine and required an underwater demolition team to dispose of it. When the task group had sailed from Halifax seven months before, each of the ships had its own Explosives Ordnance Disposal (EOD) team aboard for just this kind of emergency. This was a call to action for *Athabaskan*'s squad. Within minutes a Royal Navy *Sea King* arrived to take Lieutenant Jay Frew and Master Seaman Arthur Mulack to the British frigate. It was impossible to verify the mine from the air; so Mulack was lowered into the water for a closer investigation. To his surprise, he discovered that the mine was actually garbage in a blue bag with three protrusions. It was a very good facsimile of a mine. Despite constant warnings to Coalition ships against dropping garbage over the side, the practice had persisted, and the majority of mine sightings, especially among large concentrations of ships in the carrier and logistical force operating areas, had proven false. To make sure that no other Coalition crew was fooled by this bag of garbage, it was sunk by machine gun fire from the helicopter before the Canadians were returned to their ship.

The holding area for *Athabaskan* and *Comfort* was on the same *Scud* flight trajectory as Jubayl and Dhahran. During the night of 25-26 February, the crews of the two ships witnessed particularly heavy Iraqi attacks before they withdrew from Kuwait. The first alert of the evening was about 2030. The *Scud* was quickly assessed as of little immediate threat to the ships and outside the range of *Athabaskan*'s *Sea Sparrow*. It passed safely over with little notice. Shortly after, however, they learned that that *Scud* had killed twenty-eight and wounded another ninety-eight members of a US Army Quartermaster Detachment, in a warehouse turned barracks in Dhahran. [27] It was to be the deadliest *Scud* attack of the entire war. When the next alert was sounded soon after 0100, the response was somewhat brisker. The Action Stations alarm sounded throughout *Athabaskan*. Everyone in the Operations Room stared at their scopes as the reported Link track of the missile closed upon their position. This missile too passed overhead, only three and a half miles to the west of their position, but still too high to be engaged by the *Sea Sparrow*. It was shot down by a longer range *Patriot* missile from Dhahran. [28]

Sitting off Jubayl came to an end - thankfully - when Comfort was ordered to move to a position off Khafji. The pretext of the amphibious demonstration off the coast was finally played out. The 5th MEB offloaded on 26 February to act as a reserve for the Marines advancing up the coast, and a hospital ship was required as far north as safely possible. As *Athabaskan* stood down from action stations, *Comfort* weighed anchor, and the pair struck course due north, making away from the coast and the drifting mines. Still, they made good time. By dawn, they were already halfway to their objective when the ubiquitous Persian Pig, scouting ahead, reported an oil slick extending beyond sight to the north and west. This was their intended path to Khafji. The slick was probably drifting down from damaged oil platforms to the north. The engines of any ship sucking up the oily water mixture into its intakes would quickly jam. By mid-morning they dared proceed no further. Instead of the scheduled turn west to Khafji, Commander Pickford decided that there was no alternative but for *Athabaskan* to lead her charge away to the east in an even larger sweep.

Circumnavigating the extensive oilfields was to add over ninety miles to the passage, which meant that they could not reach their objective before nightfall, and that to get there they would have to skirt the unswept southern edge of a known Iraqi minefield. When sunset arrived, there were still twenty perilous miles to go. The Persian Pig did one last search ahead before it became too dark to visually identify mines. Then it was up to *Athabaskan*'s mine avoidance sonar to confirm that the path was clear. Four nerve-racking hours later the two ships safely reached the new holding area. *Comfort* anchored near the amphibians of 5th MEB, who were already there. Having completed the passage, *Athabaskan* surpassed her own previous record (while escorting *Princeton*) for the farthest point north reached by any Canadian ship during the deployment.

The destroyer's work was far from over. *Athabaskan* began the slow patrol back and forth to the north, which she would continue for the next three days, watching for any mines bearing down upon the larger vessels. It was a monotonous task, made all the more oppressive by the thick smoke blowing in from the extensive oilfield fires, set by the retreating Iraqis in nearby Kuwait. Offshore visibility in the pungent haze was reduced at times to less than half a mile, and the smoke caused several cases of nausea and respiratory discomfort to the sailors working topside. As an oily grime slowly built up on the ship's superstructure, access to the upper decks was restricted, and all personnel who had duties outside were required to wear surgical masks.

Protecteur was barely halfway through her second Outrider circuit when the ground assault began, forcing the cancellation of her planned Dubai maintenance period in favour of returning to the CLF. She had to be ready should the logistical force be called in to support action off the coast of Kuwait. The supply ship returned to find Virginia City under the capable supervision of Commander Andrews, who was operating from *Terra Nova*'s patrol sector on the eastern flank of the carrier operating area. Otherwise, little had changed and they remained far removed from the action ashore. *Protecteur* spent her time preparing for a third, and what proved to be final, swing of the DESERT TURNPIKE. Her weekly visits had become quite popular with the multinational ships on picket duty. She was certainly the right supply ship for the role. *Protecteur* had serviced warships from ten of the twelve Coalition navies (the exceptions being the Australians and the newly arrived Belgians) without experiencing any compatibility problems.[29] The crowning moments had been the replenishments of the American frigates *Halyburton*, at Checkpoint Charlie, and *Francis Hammond*, in the Gulf of Oman. Both had been complicated operations, involving the simultaneous transfer by span wire of two types of fuel and palletized stores at the same time. Additional loads were slung across by helicopter. Each replenishment took little more than an hour, a brisk enough pace for any such operation, and earned *Protecteur* the praise of the American captains.

Aboard *Terra Nova*, the electronics technicians had rigged an antenna for CNN broadcasts, which gave the crew an advantage not shared by many other ships. They were able to keep up with the latest developments of the rapidly progressing Coalition offensive into Iraq and Kuwait. But even that could hardly prepare them for the astounding news early on 28 February that a ceasefire was taking effect at 0800. One hundred hours after Coalition soldiers began crossing the Kuwaiti frontier; six weeks and one day since the first bombs of DESERT STORM fell on Baghdad; seven months after the invasion which precipitated the embargo against Iraq - the liberation of Kuwait was complete.

Elation was soon overtaken by reality. The effort to amass the armada had taxed the resources of each of the participating navies, which were anxious to attend to pressing matters elsewhere. On the one hand, the minesweeping effort to clear a path first into Kuwait harbour and then to make the northern Gulf safe once again for commercial traffic was only just beginning. On the other hand, the disengagement of the other naval forces was to occur much faster than anyone anticipated and with little plan for the future. The abrupt and almost anti-climactic end to the naval war found all three Canadian ships absorbed in logistical force operations. As the battle force reverted to a defensive posture and almost immediately began to disperse, there was a virtual stampede southward. Until the confusing situation and the status of the Multinational Interception Force were clarified, Captain Miller ordered his own task group to proceed to Dubai for a well-earned break and the opportunity at last to catch up on badly needed maintenance.

At 0800 on 2 March, Commodore Summers reclaimed tactical control of Task Group 302.3 from Admiral March. One by one, the three ships completed their various commitments and converged on Dubai. At the appointed hour, *Terra Nova* departed the nearly deserted Virginia City. The previous afternoon, *Athabaskan* had turned over custody of *Comfort* to a Dutch frigate and started on her southward passage. *Protecteur* was the only Canadian ship with outstanding business. Having advanced and accelerated the Outrider III schedule, she fuelled USS *Francis Hammond*, the Checkpoint Alpha picket, on the afternoon of 2 March. The commitment to DESERT TURNPIKE was finished. The supply ship turned west into a beautiful Persian Gulf sunset for the return transit through Silkworm Alley.

As dawn broke on 3 March, the trio of Canadian ships assembled in the approaches off Dubai and made their entrance into the southern Gulf port. Many had been their meetings at sea. They were proud to have fulfilled their commanders' ambition of operating throughout the deployment as an identifiable national task group. Now they were together in the same port for the first time since *Athabaskan* and *Terra Nova* had sailed from Bahrain as novices on the Charlie sector patrols, five short months ago. During that brief but hectic period, they had undergone a lifetime of experiences.

A return to some sort of interception force seemed the most likely future for multinational naval operations in the Gulf. Under that regime, logistics had been a national responsibility, and UNREP Sierra was suddenly out of a job. Late on 2 March, as Captain Miller's flagship was passing the old Ponderosa, where it had all begun, he promulgated his final UNREP Sierra instructions, concluding with a summary of his appreciation of the cooperative effort:

> [I]t has been an honour and privilege to have worked with such a professional group of navies. Given the diversity of languages/ communications/ helos and JP5 connectors, the ease of meshing the Combat Logistic Force for escort and fuelling tasks has been nothing less than outstanding. Thank you all for your support ... Have a safe and speedy voyage home. Bravo Zulu [well done] Pachyderms and Keepers. [30]

The final verdict on the Combat Logistics Force arrived a few days later, in a message from Admiral March, commander of the Arabian Gulf Battle Force:

> Dusty, the job you performed as the trail boss of the Ponderosa ... was nothing short of magnificent. You took on a job not considered very glamorous but one as important as any in the Battle Force ... Your force rode shotgun over the herd with a tenacity and zeal that were a pleasure to observe ... and the entire Battle Force and I are grateful you performed [the task] so well. I'd sail the trail with you anytime ... [signed] Dan. [31]

Notes

1   This theme is explored further in RAdm (ret'd) F.W Crickard and LCdr R.H. Gimblett, "The Navy as an Instrument of Middle Power Foreign Policy: Canada in Korea 1950 and the Persian Gulf 1990," *Maritime Forces in Global Security: Comparative Views of Maritime Strategy as We Approach the 21st Century*, ed. Ann L. Griffiths and Peter T. Haydon (Halifax, NS: Dalhousie University Centre for Foreign Policy Studies, 1995), pp. 327-42.

2   *CPGW*, p. 260.

3   Ibid.

4   WD CTG 302.3, "Combat Logistics Force Box," 11 January 1991.

5   Ibid., "ASSESSREP/013/JAN," 13 January 1991.

6   *Jean de Vienne*'s experiences with the CLF are related by her Commanding Officer, Capitaine de vaisseau Guy de Chauliac, "L'enclos des pachydermes", in *Marine et Guerre du Golfe: août 1990 - août 1991. Une année d'opérations navales au Moyen-Orient* ([Paris:] Addin, 1992), pp. 114-19. He does not refer to the Canadian coordinating role but to his "integration with an American naval force".

7   WD *Athabaskan*, "Dateline ATHABASKAN 18 Jan," 18 January 1991. Every day, each of the ships submitted a short paragraph on the previous day's activities to the task group Public Affairs Officer. This officer combined them into a prepared taped text and made it available on a special public hot line number in Halifax. The intent was to keep the crews' families informed.

8   Interestingly enough, it was this latter term, rather than the frontier, which seems to have caught the fascination of the non-North Americans. See Chauliac, "L'enclos des pachydermes."

9   Retransmitted in WD CANFORCOMME, "Kudos," 18 January 1991.

10   WD CANFORCOMME, "SITREP - 074/Jan 91," 17 January 1991.

11   National Defence, "Canada Controls Combat Logistic Force in the Gulf", *News Release/ Communiqué*, AFN: 05/91, 28 January 1991.

12   Hallion, *Storm Over Iraq*, p. 255. He cites 18,100 fixed-wing sorties from six carriers in forty-three days but notes that "the average number of theatre-strike sorties that a carrier launched in the war was only 18.82 per day ..." The rest were divided among such duties as CAP, SUCAP (anti-Surface Air Patrol), AAR, CSAR (Combat Search and Rescue), and the like.

13   Cordesman and Wagner, *Lessons of Modern War,* vol. 2, pp. 285-87 and 531. They conclude that the "relatively low-grade revolutionary force ... illustrated that unconventional war can be a major naval threat."

14   Capitán Eduardo Alfredo Rosenthal, "La Armada Argentina en el Golfo Pérsico", *Boletin del Centro Naval [Argentina]*, 109, no 763 (Winter 1991), p. 264.

15   WD *Terra Nova*, "TACSIG 003," 02 February 1991.

16   WD CTG 302.3, "ASSESSREP/021/JAN," 21 January 1991.

17   *Minutes of the Proceedings and Evidence of the Standing Committee on National Defence and Veterans Affairs*, Issue No 43, 31 January 1991, pp. 6-8.

18   WD NDHQ, CDS, "FRICTION III Rotation Plans," 31 January 1991.

19   "Armed forces get extra pay," *Regina Leader-Post*, 1 February 1991.

20   Schneller, "Persian Gulf Turkey Shoot," pp. 15-16.

21   Ibid., pp. 21-22.

22   *CPGW*, p. 267.

23 In an attempt to overcome the immediate problem, the British auxiliary repair ship, RFA *Diligence*, was ordered to manufacture adapter couplings, and Miller (as UNREP Sierra) was enlisted to distribute them amongst the American tankers. When dispatching the new coupling to *Hassayampa*, Miller included a covering message on how to recognize the part: "It's big. It's made of brass. It probably runs on steam. It must be British."

24 WD CTG 302.3, "ASSESSREP/015/FEB," 15 February 1991.

25 D.P. Langlais, "408 Bottles of Beer", USNI *Proceedings*, December 1991 (Vol 117/12/1,066), p. 71.

26 Quoted in *Gulf War Reader*, p. 350.

27 Atkinson, *Crusade*, pp. 418-20; and General H. Norman Schwarzkopf and Peter Petre, *The Autobiography: It Doesn't Take a Hero* (New York: Bantam, 1992), pp. 460-61.

28 Debate continues as to the effectiveness of the *Patriot* missile against the Iraqi *Scud*. See David F. Bond, "Army Scales Back Assessments of Patriot's Success in Gulf War," in *Aviation Week & Space Technology*, 136, no. 15 (13 April 1992), p. 64. Citing a report conducted by the US Government Accounting Office, Bond suggests that "the success rate could not be higher than 15%-25% and might be as low as zero." Atkinson, *Crusade*, pp. 416-18, contains a discussion of the issue, describing it as a "surveillance range gate error", which was corrected by a subsequent software update.

29 Excluding four replenishments conducted for work-ups "training," *Protecteur* made seventy wartime replenishments of vessels from ten different nations. The breakdown by nation is as follows: 28 USN; 14 Canadian; 8 Argentinean; 5 Norwegian; 4 Danish; 4 Spanish; 3 RN; 2 French; and one each from Italy and the Netherlands. The only two Coalition navies not fuelled during the war were the Australian, which had their own tanker, and Belgian, which arrived late. The total includes Consolidation Replenishments (CONSOLs and CONREPs - respectively, underway refuellings and bulk stores transfers from US Naval Ships; the stores were not for Canadian use but for further transfer to USN ships). The CONSOLs were Protecteur's sole wartime supply of fuel; it was provided free of charge by Saudi Arabia (through the USN) for distribution within the Coalition.

30 WD CTG 302.3, "Daily UNREP Sierra Intentions - 016 Feb 91," 02 March 1991. "Bravo Zulu" is a derivation from a naval tactical signal meaning "Well done."

31 Quoted in Commodore D.E. Miller and Sharon Hobson, *The Persian Excursion: The Canadian Navy in the Gulf War* (Toronto: Canadian Institute of Strategic Studies, 1995), p. 212.

Operation SCALPEL – 1 Canadian Field Hospital: January – March 1991

Medical Resource Requirements

During the months leading up to hostilities, politicians, media pundits, and military staffs debated the likely number of military and civilian casualties in any full-scale war between an overly armed Iraq and the thirty countries of the Coalition. Widely different estimates, ranging from the most thoroughly researched to the most intuitive, were published by numerous sources. The only constant in all these speculations was that any confrontation would produce horrifying results because of the proliferation of weapons and the accumulation of forces on each side. Although the social and medical assistance measures provided by many countries and international agencies were numerous, they were insufficient to cope with the expected number of casualties.

From August to January, many countries made great efforts to prepare health services that would be able to handle an immense wave of civilian and military wounded. Hospitals as far away as Munich and Seattle made plans to place beds at the disposal of those wounded in the Gulf and offered specialized services for the treatment of wounds caused by nuclear radiation, neurotoxic gases, and "war germs," such as anthrax and botulism.[1] A worldwide evacuation network already had been set up before the first blows were exchanged (see Chapter 10, Operation UNARMED WARRIOR). But because of the time factor, which weighed so heavily in the medical equation, very few people believed that these measures would even come close to being adequate.

To meet the needs of Canadians as well as other Coalition forces, *Protecteur* had been equipped with a ten-member medical team in August. This team of surgeons and laboratory and radiological technicians was sent to the Bahraini Defence Forces Hospital at Manamah on 1 November, as soon as local arrangements could be made. Attachment to an active hospital prior to hostilities gave them an opportunity to work that was unavailable on board the supply ship. They returned to Canada, however, with the rotation of *Protecteur*'s crew at the beginning of January, and their replacements were put on board ship in anticipation of hostilities. Another, nine-person medical team was sent to the American hospital ship *Mercy* in September.

They were relieved by another nine-person team in January 1991. As soon as the CANFORME headquarters was set up, a medical staff (J1 Med) was employed to work out evacuation plans and specific programs for Canadian personnel, in collaboration with the other Coalition countries. As of mid-January, forty-four persons connected with the medical profession were in the theatre of operations. They were divided among three main centres but were to serve fewer than 2,000 Canadians.[2] Three supplementary agreements on the provision of medical services had been reached. The first was with the Bahraini Defence Forces Hospital at Manamah, and covered medical care beyond what the HQ CANFORME infirmary could provide. The second was with the USN, so that sailors could be evacuated to the hospital ships *Mercy* and *Comfort* if the need went beyond *Protecteur*'s resources. And the third concerned Doha. In addition to the medical team that was integral to CATGME, the Canadians could be admitted to the USAF's hospital attached to 401 Wing. Since the Canadians were not exposed to front-line fighting, except for the CF-18 pilots on their air patrols and some other individual cases, these resources were considered sufficient.

Several other nations, particularly those which expected to be involved in the ground fighting, however, figured that their medical needs would be much greater. Estimates of casualties differed according to the sources, but the statistics for each estimate took into consideration the high-intensity fighting expected in an assault on Kuwait and Iraq. Even without considering Iraq's supposed nuclear, biological, and chemical weapons, their impressive defences prepared along the Kuwait perimeter made it difficult to envisage a breakthrough without considerable losses on both sides. These defences included a panoply of minefields, anti-tank ditches, hidden and protected anti-armour defensive positions equipped with tanks, and concentrations of powerful artillery and infantry crossfire.

The American and British governments, therefore, made plans that included augmented medical organizations at all levels of command in their armed forces. Nearly 10 percent of American personnel in the Gulf were associated with medical services. A joint international medical strategy was established to employ mobile field hospitals and hospital ships, which would provide emergency treatment to victims as close as possible to the battle lines and organize the rapid evacuation of the wounded to local hospitals and ultimately their own country. Because even the temporary burial of "infidels" in Muslim soil was not allowed, a portion of the medical evacuation network was identified to deal with the recovery and repatriation of the remains of the dead.

British Needs

To support their armoured division, the British had three main field hospitals (numbers 22 and 32 at Al Qaysumah, and 33 at Jubayl), as well as a general hospital at Riyadh and their own 100-bed hospital ship, the Royal Navy's Fleet Auxiliary *Argus*, for a total of roughly 1,850 hospital beds in the theatre. Since the estimates indicated that there would be more wounded, both enemy and allied, than there were beds for them, General de la Billière anticipated a shortfall in the order of 600 beds. And he wanted more teams of surgeons deployed near the land combat lines. The Defence Minister in London appealed in November for medical volunteers from the Reserves and the Territorial Army to join 1 (British) Armoured Division.

The government of the United Kingdom also issued an international request for medical personnel and equipment of various types that could be integrated into the medical system. Romania, Norway, and Singapore offered separate hospitals of various dimensions, and Sweden, Belgium, Denmark, and the Netherlands promised surgical teams for hospitals already in existence. Thirty-three (33) Field Hospital, a 600-bed facility that was partly under canvas and relatively far in the rear at Jubayl, benefited from the international reinforcements in the areas of specialized care and national evacuation. The Riyadh hospital and third-line detachments at Dhahran and Tabuk and at sea on board the *Argus* also benefited indirectly from these foreign contributions. However, by the end of December, the situation had not changed significantly because the additional elements were still not operational, and several countries were experiencing considerable problems in sending their personnel and equipment to Saudi Arabia.

The UN deadline of 15 January was approaching at a dizzying speed for the headquarters of British Forces Middle East, and the government in London was insisting that the arrangements called for by the International Red Cross and the Geneva Convention should be implemented for the treatment of Iraqi prisoners. On the last day of 1990, after informal discussions which had gone on at several levels, the British High Commission in Ottawa officially requested the Canadian government to consider sending a surgical hospital to help make up the identified shortfall of 600 beds for the needs of wounded prisoners of war. During the course of the New Year holiday, in consultation with the representatives of the J1 Medical, J4 Logistical, Transport, Supply, and Finance cells, and several Canadian headquarters and bases, the NDHQ J3 Plans cell ran an initial staff check, as part of the main data collection preparatory to making a decision. A briefing to the high command by Commodore Johnston on 2 January set out the possibilities of using the Canadian Forces' only surgical field hospital, which was permanently lodged at CFB Petawawa, for such a mission.

At that point, Canada did not have the appropriate size of field hospital to fulfil the British request. 1 Field Surgical Hospital (1 FSH), part of the Canadian Forces Hospital and Medical Supply System (CFHMSS), was rather small and its personnel and equipment had been reduced to a minimum. Its modular tenting complex included two modern mobile surgical centres providing advanced second- and third-line treatment for the quick resuscitation and stabilization of patients prior to evacuation to permanent hospitals. The Field Hospital had existed in various forms since 1967. But it only had some sixty beds. Although it had never been used for critical surgical operations, it had served as an infirmary for formations on manoeuvres, and all its technical devices and operational procedures for massive or serious surgery had been put to the test by realistic exercises. Still, the Field Hospital was an awkward resource to mobilize, requiring considerable augmentation of personnel and equipment from other organizations to put it into operation.

The hospital had only thirty-four personnel immediately available. The rest, some 190 individuals, were designated to fill national emergency functions in the event that the hospital was actually deployed. Such postings obviously would force these people to leave their usual place of work, at bases, stations, units, and hospitals throughout Canada, and would necessitate internal reorganizations of functions and even the temporary employment of civilians. The price of these replacements was quickly estimated at $21,000 per day. The Surgeon General of the Canadian Forces, Major-General Jean Benoît, nonetheless saw the activation of this unit as a partial response to the needs of the British, and General de Chastelain agreed to continue with preparations and present them to the government as an option. On 4 January, he assigned Lieutenant-General Foster to continue contingency planning. If the hospital were sent, it would be placed under Mobile Command, which had used it in the past and had a staff aware of the requirements of such land operations. Foster was granted a ceiling of 500 individuals to expand the unit and was to draw up a plan to be presented to NDHQ on 9 January, with a view to obtaining a political decision the next day. The name given the operation was a sharp one: SCALPEL.

Canadian Military Planning

The army staff once again was given the task of preparing a plan in great haste to send Canadian land forces to the Gulf. The planning considerations for SCALPEL called for a "medical treatment centre" not exceeding 500 personnel to be assembled and deployed to Saudi Arabia for use 100 to 200 miles behind the front lines. An assembly and preparation period of fourteen days at Petawawa and deployment over twenty days were given as parameters. The plan also allowed seven days for acclimatization in Saudi Arabia. The hospital should be ready to provide care for its first patients six weeks after the commencement of its mission.

Details were sought immediately from the British Defence Ministry on Operation GRANBY, outlining the overall deployment of British forces in the Gulf, since the hospital would be inserted into a system of supply, transport, and operational links, each detail of which could have implications for the composition of the unit. The medical staff of Mobile Command, under the leadership of the Command Surgeon, Colonel Jean-Marie Rouleau, had to settle thorny questions of technical compatibility with the British Medical Services, which included clinical aspects as well as practices in fields as specialized as pharmacology, radiology, and anaesthesia. The level of communication that this planning demanded of the many participating agencies was impossible to reach at such a distance. A reconnaissance team had to be formed as quickly as possible to go to London, Lahr, Jubayl, and Manamah and settle hundreds of matters. Six officers with various specialties were chosen. However, NDHQ could not authorize their departure before 10 January, for want of political direction.

In a report published in October 1990, barely ten weeks before the British request, the Auditor General of Canada, Mr Kenneth Dye, recognized that current deficiencies in the Canadian Forces limited their ability to provide complete and continuous medical support in wartime. "It aims rather to respond to peacetime requirements," he concluded.[3] The deficiencies of which he spoke had been known for a long time and miracle solutions did not exist.

In the present situation, the need to recruit highly specialized medical personnel was arguably the worst problem. In January 1991, there were nine surgeons and nine anaesthetists in the (Regular) Canadian Forces. Not a single Reservist surgeon or anaesthetist volunteered to go to the Gulf. They all had large practices requiring their presence. At the very best, a few might replace those who had left the military hospitals, on a part-time basis. Of the nine regulars available, one surgeon and one anaesthetist were attached to each of *Protecteur* and *Mercy*, and replacements for each of these four people were therefore required in January. Another member of each professional group remained in permanent reserve in Canada to be shared among the four hospitals where the Canadian Forces usually performed surgery (Ottawa, Halifax, Cold Lake, and Valcartier). Since they had to work in tandem, the four remaining surgeons and anaesthetists later joined the field hospital. The situation for the general practioners and nurses, although less tense, was still difficult. In addition, medical assistants, whose trade in combat situations had no equivalent in the civilian medical profession, could not be replaced by Reservists without intense training in field exercises and service with combat formations. It was obvious, then, that sending the field hospital taxed these professions to the absolute limit. With one blow, it drained the Canadian military medical system.

Mobile Command's Plan SCALPEL immediately made other problems apparent. Since the hospital had to be relatively independent of direct Canadian resupply and support, it had to be provided with additional transport and special equipment necessary to adapt it to desert surroundings. In its present form, the hospital would not have enough personnel to operate around the clock in a war setting and maintain realistic shift schedules. The prospect of having to operate in nuclear, biological, and chemical warfare conditions also added complications, some of which were insoluble. By the time the plan was presented to NDHQ on 9 January, Mobile Command had added considerably to the bill, proposing to go beyond the 500-person ceiling granted by General de Chastelain and to increase the number of pieces of equipment to some 250 vehicles and trailers.

Nonetheless, the new army plan to provide a field hospital that was complete, independent, and equal to the task was well received at NDHQ. Even though it proved impossible to obtain the political decision that was hoped for on 10 January, General de Chastelain authorized the reconnaissance team to establish contacts in London and Lahr, with the staffs at Manamah and Doha and with the British Divisional Support Group. Meanwhile, the Department of External Affairs and the embassy in Riyadh prepared the ground diplomatically to enable the interdepartmental committee to recommend the decision to Cabinet.

Reconnaissance

The designated commander of 1 Canadian Field Hospital (1 CFH) was Lieutenant-Colonel Joseph Kotlarz. He worked in clinical medicine at NDHQ and was commander of the Petawawa field hospital as a secondary duty. He was to meet the military medical authorities and discuss with them in detail the technical contribution Canada could make to its mission. Just as important as determining the employment of the medical teams were the logistical requirements for implementing the deployment. Command of the reconnaissance, therefore, fell to the Commander of Canadian Forces Base Petawawa and Deputy Commander of the Special Service Force resident there, Colonel Christopher R. Wellwood.

The division of responsibilities among all the agencies was not an easy matter to settle. Wellwood knew from experience that there could be a gulf between what was promised in London and what proved feasible on the ground in wartime, when priorities could be upset in a matter of seconds. That was why the reconnaissance group, which left in January, first went to London, where contacts already had been set up between the Canadian Defence Liaison Staff and the British Ministry of Defence. The draft memorandum of agreement defined the respective responsibilities for support and cooperation, on which a start had been made, and anticipated the main problems that would have to be addressed before the group visited the sites.

This kind of agreement is always complicated because it must summarize one country's undertakings with another in an almost contractual way. For example, a memorandum of intent between Bahrain and Canada was the subject of a signing ceremony on 16 January at Manamah, three months after the Canadians had arrived in that country. However cordial and favourable the atmosphere, lengthy negotiations were needed between the diplomatic and military services of the two countries before an agreement could be concluded. On the other hand, negotiated understandings with Qatar and Saudi Arabia were never signed despite the constant efforts of Ottawa, Doha, and Riyadh. The arrangement between Great Britain and Canada was signed on 13 March, after the text had been approved on 20 February. In the early stages of the discussions, Colonel Wellwood could only draw up informal agreements with London, not knowing whether the desired expression of contractual obligations between the respective governments would follow. He therefore left for his tour of the Gulf with invitations that were genuine but lacked the force of a signed document.

The Canadian personnel and equipment were to arrive at Jubayl, Saudi Arabia, one of the busiest seaports and airports in the Arabian peninsula since the start of logistical operations for DESERT SHIELD and GRANBY. It was the location of the British Support Group land transport centre, where combat supplies and large stores of ammunition, POL (petroleum, oil, and lubricants), food, spare parts, and all sorts of other military and even medical supplies for the various forces were stored and transshipped. In December, General de la Billière had obtained a change in affiliation of his armoured division, joining it to VII Corps from MARCENT (Marine Component Central Command, deployed south of Kuwait). The resupply lines had to be redrawn, but the British commander decided to keep Jubayl as his logistical centre rather than move his stocks to a location closer to the division's new attack position further west in the desert.

Arriving in Jubayl on 12 January, Colonel Wellwood was met by Lieutenant-Colonel Stuart from CANFORME headquarters. They discussed Canadian plans, then met General de la Billière and Brigadier R.H. Hardy, Chief of Land Medical Operations. During these discussions it became clear that the immediate need was for at least one deployable surgical centre which could join 33 British Field Hospital at Jubayl. This centre would stay at Jubayl until all the Canadian personnel had been trained and then be deployed to the forward lines as an integral part of 1 Canadian Field Hospital.

They also discussed available British resources and agreed that the Canadian forces would be supported in large part by the British as soon as the Canadians set foot on Saudi soil.[4] However, Wellwood urged that the hospital be as autonomous as possible and be equipped by a Canadian source. The Canadian Field Hospital needed Canadian supplies. Any mix-ups might be costly. For example, Colonel Kotlarz discovered that British stretcher handles failed to meet NATO specifications and that their ends would have to be cut off to make them usable as medical bed support. This type of technical incompatibility could have tragic consequences in the heat of the action. The case of the stretcher handles was only one of hundreds of details awaiting adjustment.

Jubayl's sea-port and airport were modern, very large, and superbly organized. They were able to take shipment of the Field Hospital. At the same time, though, the hospital had to be set up according to a tight timetable that would coordinate both its initial unloading and its transportation out of the port's temporary storage areas. The main part of the hospital's equipment would have to be transported by civilian ship, and it would have to be resupplied regularly by Canadian *Hercules* or *Boeings*. Canadian personnel would be brought to the theatre in chartered aircraft just before taking delivery of the equipment at the port. Responsibility for coordinating the port services with the timetables for the Canadian arrivals fell to Colonel Stuart. On the appointed day, he had to have at his disposal unloading teams, who could drive convoys as soon as they touched down from the "roll on / roll off" (RO/RO) transport ship. All personnel would live in temporary shelters while the hospital itself would be moved to the forward positions, about 400 kilometres along the Tapline road. This was the same road the Americans were using to mass their XVIII and VII Corps as they prepared to attack Kuwait and Iraq.

Colonel Wellwood met Commodore Summers at Manamah on the morning of 16 January. They discussed plans for the immediate dispatch of the first two surgical teams, each of which comprised two surgeons and about sixty personnel. These teams would have to be transported with all their mobile equipment, including about ten trucks, by Canadian aircraft from Trenton, and one team would have to be in place in less than thirteen days. Since the hospital was to be placed under the operational command of Commodore Summers, all the details concerning its establishment would have to be integrated into CANFORME's general logistical support plan for the theatre. As soon as agreement was reached on arrangements, the reconnaissance report, a document one inch thick, was sent by facsimile to Saint-Hubert and retransmitted to NDHQ.

It was Colonel Wellwood's intention to return directly to Canada on the evening of the sixteenth. Fortunately, he had had the foresight to fax ahead the results of his reconnaissance. The *Hercules* which left Doha at midnight local time was recalled by the Riyadh air controller and forced to return and await further instructions. Hostilities had begun, and the flight corridors had to be kept free for the Coalition's fighters and bombers. The reconnaissance group had to wait three days in Manamah for the air controller to authorize the comings and goings of the transports in isolated corridors. They finally returned to Canada via Cyprus and Lahr on 20 January. In the meantime, the personnel of 1 CFH had reached Petawawa two days earlier and were waiting impatiently for fresh news on their unexpected mission.

Political Decisions

Despite the departure of the reconnaissance group on 10 January, it took the government until the sixteenth to give an official answer to the United Kingdom's request for medical personnel and equipment. Defence Minister McKnight had allowed the media to understand that the British request was a formal one and that it was being given serious consideration by the Canadian government. But Ottawa did not declare itself officially until Saddam Hussein refused to modify his position, and the Security Council assumed full powers to carry out the provisions of the ultimatum contained in Resolution 678. With this in mind, Canada fell resolutely in step with the Coalition after the deadline of midnight, 15 January.

A few hours before the Coalition attacked Iraq, Mr McKnight revealed to the public in a press conference that, following Great Britain's request, the Canadian government had authorized the deployment of 1 Canadian Field Hospital. This 100-bed medical establishment enabled the Coalition to provide more adequately for the Geneva Convention's requirements for the treatment of captured war wounded. The press release also declared that the hospital would be deployed in two sections: the first was a forward surgical centre made up of two teams of surgeons, who were to arrive in Saudi Arabia towards the end of the month; the second section was the rest of the hospital and a second surgical centre, which would be ready in fifty days. The hospital would fly the Canadian flag. It would be under the national command of Commodore Summers, and tactical control would be given to the commander of the British forces in the theatre. The deployment of the hospital had been approved by the Saudi Arabian government, which had expressed its appreciation to the government of Canada.[5]

Preparations at Petawawa

Mr McKnight's announcement finally launched Operation SCALPEL. Of course, secret preparations had been underway well in advance of his press release. Even before the plan was presented to Ottawa on 9 January, Mobile Command had issued internal warning orders concerning matériel and personnel. Laboratory technicians, medical assistants, nurses and doctors were taken off strength for the mission. A large number of administrators and logisticians were added to the specialists and medical technicians. Together they formed a unit put together with the greatest care and adapted to expected operational needs. As the plan unfolded, 536 persons and 246 vehicles and trailers were taken from across Canada and hastily assembled at CFB Petawawa.

Training had begun according to a plan produced during the preceding days by the three officers and thirty non-commissioned members and soldiers permanently posted to the Field Surgical Hospital. Courses and exercises began as soon as the personnel arrived, and they were given the highest priority so that the first surgical team would be able to leave on 24 January 1991.

In anticipation of Ottawa's approval, the Surgeon General recommended the rapid purchase of equipment and proposed operational posting policies for medical personnel coming from other commands. By 14 January, plans already included the use of a Danish transport, MV *Arnold Maersk*. It was scheduled to arrive in Halifax, where it would load hospital vehicles, trailers, and containerized matériel. A large proportion of this equipment had to be transported by rail or road to Halifax, between the 22 and 25 January. Everything was to be on board by the twenty-eighth.

Personnel had to be prepared with courses and exercises covering the use of weapons, NBC defence matériel, and field medical procedures, which some people had not used since basic training. The radiologists, nurses, and doctors had to renew their familiarity with the arrangement of the modular tents for triage of the wounded and their systematic progression from one treatment tent to the next under combat conditions. These exercises took place at Petawawa within a tight timetable. Several resident units helped by participating in realistic exercises and recreating a desert environment in the metre of snow that covered the training areas!

First Advanced Surgical Group

The first two surgical teams prepared themselves quickly, since they had to leave almost immediately. Colonel Claude Auger, a surgeon from the Halifax Medical Centre, was appointed the officer in charge of 1 Advanced Surgical Group (1 ASG). The seventy-five members of the hospital's first surgical centre included two surgeons, two anaesthetists, several doctors, medical assistants, nurses, technicians, and support personnel.

Although Colonel Auger was higher in rank than the commanding officer of the hospital, he did not exercise official command. He had been appointed surgeon in a posting where a major would normally have been required, but there were no remaining surgeons at the rank of major in the Canadian Forces. It was agreed in advance that Lieutenant-Colonel Kotlarz would have command of the hospital, that working relationships would be completely professional for the specialists, and that Colonel Kotlarz would be in charge of administration and discipline.

The rapid deployment of 1 ASG meant that Colonel Auger had to take this first group to Jubayl without the advantage of having with him someone who had "seen the ground" and taken part in the support agreements. Several of his personnel did not know one another beforehand, and some of them were performing functions they had never carried out, even in training. The week at Petawawa had improved this situation, but, all the same, the plan still called for a month of preliminary training and familiarization with combat surgery methods at Jubayl, where the team was to join 33 Field Hospital before moving close to the combat sectors along the Iraqi border.

On 24 January, the members of the first surgical group and their fifteen vehicles boarded ten *Hercules*. By long stages they made the trip from Trenton, Ontario to Jubayl, Saudi Arabia. Arriving thirty-six hours later, the Canadians passed through the British transit camp "Blackadder" and registered with the military administration of BRITFORME (British Forces Middle East) Command, after which they were brought to Camp Al Zamil in Jubayl, close to 33 British Field Hospital, to acclimatize themselves to their new surroundings.

The complete Canadian group was on the ground with all its equipment by 29 January. After an initial rest, which was considerably disturbed by further inoculations,[6] the phased familiarization with British medical techniques began. Operating room techniques were reviewed for surgeons, nurses, and medical assistants. It was necessary to become immediately acquainted with different medicines, new instruments, some of which were obsolete, and methods that had been practised only for the first time in Petawawa. Canadian equipment was simply unloaded and inspected at this point.

The new arrivals were integrated into the 33 Field Hospital rotation teams and inserted into the day and night shifts. The modest numbers of injured were mostly due to traffic accidents, because of the large convoys from Jubayl to the west, which were in full progress. There were also victims of weapons accidents, some of which had tragic results.

Still, the Canadians found that their talents were being underutilized. The original plan was to await the arrival of the complete Canadian hospital at Jubayl before moving forward to Al Qaysumah, but Colonel Auger suggested that 1 Surgical Group move to the forward position as soon as it was ready. Auger had his reasons. Canadian personnel had the technical training and were qualified to take on the task. Supervisors were disappointed at being integrated so haphazardly with the British of 33 Field Hospital, when all along they had hoped to work as an independent Canadian team. Also, the need for surgical teams in the forward hospitals was beginning to increase. Although the number of wounded was low, everyone anticipated a dramatic rise in casualty rates once the ground war began in earnest. Therefore, it would be best for the Canadian surgical centre to deploy as quickly as possible. Colonel Auger discussed this option with Brigadier Hardy, and the two of them came to the conclusion that the Canadian surgical group could be used more advantageously with 32 Field Hospital.

Colonel Auger contacted Commodore Summers and NDHQ to discuss this new option. He was authorized to carry out a reconnaissance at Al Qaysumah and, if circumstances allowed, to prepare for the quick dispatch of 1 Surgical Group within the next few days. Auger made the 400-kilometre trip from Jubayl to Al Qaysumah on 3 February, in a small convoy inserted into the rolling flow of men and equipment heading west, as if they were on a gigantic conveyor belt. Dumping its load at or near the front lines in the west, the "conveyor belt" was empty on its return to the ports in the east.

Auger was given a pleasant reception by the Commanding Officer of 32 Field Hospital, Colonel Peter Lynch, a Reserve cardiologist. It soon became obvious that this forward position did not have all of the logistical support promised by the authorities in London. But the two of them worked out a plan of cooperation by which the Canadian surgical group would be joined to the tent network of 32 Field Hospital's triage area. This appealed to Colonel Auger because it allowed him to preserve the integrity and independence of his team. He returned to Jubayl on 4 February, having decided to move to the front. The Surgical Group had enough transport to carry all its own equipment, but it was necessary to wait a few days for the British Transport Corps to obtain a vehicle for the personnel. On 8 February, a convoy of nine trucks and a bus started out.

As soon as the Canadian surgical group arrived, it squeezed itself inside the protective sand berms around 32 Field Hospital. Tents were erected for accommodation and an operating room. In front of the operating room was a common triage room and a "resuscitation" room,[7] and behind it there was a post-operative recovery room, as doctrine prescribed. From there, the patient would be returned to the British hospital. The Canadian module was attached to the hospital by two canvas corridors. It provided post-operative care and treatment and pre-evacuation preparations. Theoretically, the Surgical Group was able to have the operating table always occupied. At least this was its potential from the moment it was set up on the morning of 13 February.

Meanwhile, tactical control of the Canadian Surgical Group passed on 9 February from Commodore Summers to Brigadier Hardy. Lieutenant-General Foster, Commander of Mobile Command, reviewed the arrangements made by Colonel Auger

The 1st Canadian Field Hospital
Disposition in al Qaysumah

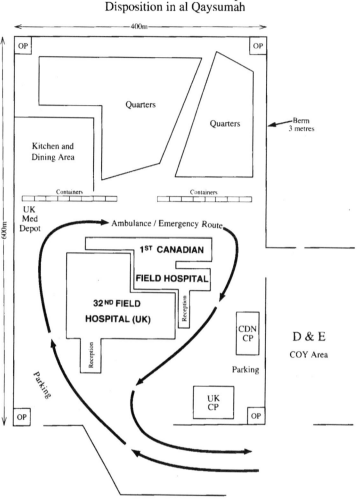

The 1st Canadian Field Hospital shared a position with the 32nd (UK) Field Hospital in al Qaysumah, Saudi Arabia. The two Canadian advanced surgical centers were joined to the British hospital without being amalgamated with it, until the arrival of the main body of the hospital on February 25th. This way the Canadian surgical centers received the wounded from the 32nd Hospital triage and could provide care either in the ressucitation section or through their three operating rooms. Patients were then evacuated through the 32nd Field Hospital or returned to their frontline unit. The construction of the 1st Canadian Field Hospital was not terminated and the whole array of services planned for the hospital were not provided before the end of the war on 28 February 1991.

when he visited him at Al Qaysumah on 11 February, as part of a general tour of FMC troop dispositions in the Gulf. He noted that the Canadian medical troops wanted to be used as effectively as possible. Four days later, on 15 February, General de la Billière came to inspect 32 British Field Hospital. He took advantage of the opportunity to visit the Canadian surgical group attached to the hospital. By chance he arrived while the surgical team was treating a trauma case. In the course of the visit, he noted that the Canadians' modern equipment complemented the simpler yet quite practical equipment of the British hospital. And he discussed the possibility of 1 Canadian Field Hospital, with its integral transport, accompanying the British armoured division assault — a task, which, though reserved for 22 Field Hospital, could be performed quite efficiently and effectively by 1 Canadian Field Hospital. In any event, as General de la Billière wrote in his memoirs, "22 Field Hospital, which had been standing with all its equipment packed in containers north of Qaysumah expecting to hurry north through the breach to a new site inside Iraq, never had to move."[8]

Even before the rudimentary hospital structures had been completed, the weather changed. The wind rose and it grew colder. Soon, sandstorms were followed by torrential downpours, and the thick mud did nothing to improve the first wartime experiences of the Canadian medical personnel. Nor did the colour of the sky leave them much to cheer about in the coming days. The noise of the bombing to the north, arriving from across the expanses of sand, clearly and frequently, reminded everyone that a powerful enemy was going to ground only one and a half times the range of a gun from their own compound.

Second Advanced Surgical Group

The second surgical group of two operating teams left Petawawa on 13 February. They had received two weeks of thorough training. This time the troops flew to Lahr in chartered aircraft and then joined the *Hercules*, which were loaded with their equipment. Each load of equipment was taken over by the troops who were going with it. This second surgical group also had double the equipment of the first. For instance, 1 Surgical Group was handicapped by the fact that it had no X-ray table. This was an oversight that was not repeated the second time around. With so much new equipment about to arrive, it was easy to predict that the embryonic hospital would grow considerably.

Two (2) Advanced Surgical Group (2 ASG) only stayed at Jubayl long enough to register with the British forces, receive theatre inoculations, and visit 33 Field Hospital. This time there was no training stage. As soon as the equipment was ready for the road and transport could be obtained from the British Transport Corps, the convoy was organized to go to Al Qaysumah. Tired from a long trip (their acclimatization was made difficult by *Scud* alerts, which took place soon after their arrival[9]) and sore from injections, they reached British 32 Field Hospital on the evening of 18 February.

The weather immediately began to deteriorate once again. Two (2) Surgical Group had just finished erecting its tents when there was a violent rainfall.

It flooded the accommodation areas, creating the kind of thick mud that seems to accompany military operations everywhere, even in the desert.[10] Tents were shaken by persistent winds, forcing the new arrivals to lash everything down firmly for fear of seeing the canvass shelters carried off. Several days were spent digging drainage ditches and repairing tents. Fatigue got the better of them.

As soon as they were installed, the surgeons of the two groups set to work on the wounded who began to arrive at 32 Field Hospital in increasing numbers. Soldiers suffered from accidents, traumas, burns, fractures, and lacerations. They arrived by road and air evacuation from 1 Division. Even though 1 Division did not begin its offensive until the morning of 24 February, the number of casualties arriving at the three hospitals at Al Qaysumah was still substantial. Considerable experience was gained from the first cases, especially in triage and resuscitation, two functions which were not practiced in a normal hospital setting. The team, which had been preparing mentally for a month, began to develop its skills and confidence in the means at its disposal.

The Main Group

The field surgical hospital at Petawawa could be deployed by air - at least in theory. But there was no longer any question of moving it in this manner after it had been modified on 15 January to become the impressive 1 Canadian Field Hospital. Because of the mobile and self-contained character of its new configuration, 1 CFH was a cumbersome formation that just managed to transport itself on wheels. It needed 150 trucks and fifty trailers, as well as fifty-nine containers filled with medical supplies and Canadian spare parts.

Transporting all of this by air would have required hundreds of *Hercules* flights. The cost was unacceptable. The only alternative was to charter a RO/RO vehicle transport ship to move the more than 1,700 tons of the equipment (see Appendix E). It was a tour de force to assemble vehicles and equipment at Petawawa, prepare them for rail and sea transport, and route them to Halifax. The whole process began on 23 January, seven days after the Minister's announcement. The *Arnold Maersk* was scheduled to depart from Halifax on 28 January in order to ensure delivery to Jubayl by late February. The Saudi Arabian military port authorities reportedly gave no extensions.

What makes up a Field Hospital? One (1) CFH was divided into a headquarters and three main companies: treatment company; service company; and infantry company. Headquarters had seventy personnel. It included the command cell and a signals troop, made up of thirty-five signallers. Most of the headquarters personnel arrived with the main group, but an administrative and signals vanguard accompanied 1 Surgical Group and remained at Jubayl to prepare for the arrival of the remaining members. The HQ also contained the military operations planning cell and the platoons providing the troop and patient administrative services.

Treatment Company was the operational core of the hospital. It had a strength of 164, in five platoons. Surgery Platoon, made up of four 16-person surgical teams, was essentially composed of the two surgery groups already deployed. Resuscitation Platoon had triage, pre-op, and post-op sections. A Clinical Support Platoon was made up of pharmacy, laboratory, and radiology sections. The Ward Platoon had five intensive care teams, a dentist, and a specialist in internal medicine. The operating room and intensive care nurses and bedside workers formed the fifth group.

Service Company, made up of 156 persons, supported the rest of the hospital. It included the supply, transport, and maintenance platoons. The necessary logistical services were grouped together in this company and included the specialized services of pharmaceutical supplies, medical supplies, and technical maintenance, as well as kitchens, water services, garages, quartermaster stores, and hygienic, sanitation, and dietary services. The Canadian Field Hospital had everything found in non-mobile field hospitals, plus the ability to follow the advance of the combat formation to which it was attached. In these manoeuvres, Service Company established a temporary base which acted as a *pied à terre* during moves.

An infantry company, Charles Company of the 1st Battalion, Royal Canadian Regiment of London, Ontario, was 120 strong. Its job was to protect the field hospital, provide manpower, and guard wounded prisoners. This company was a great help in actually handling the wounded and fulfilling security tasks. Several members ended up wearing the distinctive red cross of stretcher-bearers, nurse's aides, and hospital hands.

However, the employment of an infantry company aroused a degree of controversy. On the one hand, it was supplied by Mobile Command to provide active protection for the hospital and to be ready to fight if needed. On the other hand, NDHQ made the point that, according to the Geneva Convention, a company of infantry assigned to a hospital could not use its weapons to defend the hospital as if it were an occupied position. Commodore Summers, who was given the final decision, ordered the heavy weapons withdrawn with their ammunitions and left under guard of the National Support Element at Jubayl. The company had a red cross and crescent painted on its *Grizzly* vehicles and placed them at the disposal of the hospital for use as armoured ambulances. They were never used as such, but the soldiers of the RCR often acted as stretcher bearers and were used in a prisoner-of-war camp several kilometres from the hospital, where they performed guard duty, searched prisoners, and lent a hand to a British infantry unit in charge of controlling a camp whose population was to reach 6,000 by the end of the war.

The arrival of the main hospital group was timed to coincide with that of the equipment, so that troops could take delivery of the vehicles and cargo as soon as they arrived in port. This type of carefully timed operation took place repeatedly at all the Gulf ports. The American and British armed forces had to carry out their unloadings with no less synchronization, deploying their units and reuniting them with their equipment as quickly as possible. The Coalition could not afford clogged ports. The Canadian operation was not helped by several readjustments of dates and the uncertainty over whether Jubayl or Damman would be the point of arrival. This was due to the large oil slicks threatening the Saudi coast. In any event, *Arnold Maersk* arrived within the allowable period, on 19 February.

During the next few days, three *Boeing* flights brought the ranks of the hospital to completion. The arrival procedures had to be carried out with a group now numbering nearly 400, but the reception team was well experienced. Everything went much faster and more efficiently than the reception of the two surgical groups. This time the troops were not travelling in the noisy *Hercules* and were arriving in better shape. Colonel Stuart had made arrangements so that in the first hours after the ship had docked in Saudi Arabia, a group of drivers and handlers from the hospital would unload all the cargo for a designated camp, obtain additional transport from the British Transport Corps, and set out for Al Qaysumah. Obviously, given the speed with which the loading had taken place at Petawawa, things were not always clearly numbered and placed in the proper order. The material had to be reorganized to allow the immediate deployment of prioritary materials once they arrived at 32 Field Hospital.

Al Qaysumah

On 25 February, a seventy-eight-vehicle convoy of the main group left early in the morning and reached Al Qaysumah in the afternoon. They found the two advanced surgical groups well installed, despite their losing fight against rain and wind. The tents were still wet and battered, and much more work was needed to drain off the accumulated pools of water. The first elements of Service Company were given a warm reception. Their quartermaster trucks were full of much needed but previously missing articles and tanks of clean water. More tents were erected. Several were outside the restricting berms of 32 Field Hospital. The British military engineers lent a hand with their bulldozers and constructed new sand berms around the Canadian Service Company camp, two kilometres to the south. The Royal Canadian Regiment security company was also outside, pressed against the outer wall of the sand embankment, because there was no room inside for its personnel and *Grizzly* vehicles. The transition was eased by the arrival of Lieutenant-Colonel Kotlarz on 19 February. He took over the management of resources and the coordination of efforts.

From 25 February on, one could speak of a real hospital at Al Qaysumah rather than just two surgical groups. Being grafted onto an existing organization, 1 CFH was almost immediately available for duty.

They had arrived just in time. The Coalition ground offensive had hit its stride, having commenced the previous day. On the eastern flank of the VII Corps thrust, 1 British Armoured Division formed the hinge of the army swinging north into Iraq before turning east across central Kuwait to encircle the Republican Guards Divisions.[11] But the methodical breach of the prepared defences did not produce the battle of attrition anticipated by each side. Much has been written elsewhere about the overwhelming Coalition advance against a collapsing enemy. Resistance, however, was far from minimal. The psychological effect exercised by the Republican Guard, fighting what turned out to be a defensive withdrawal to protect retreating armour, was not insignificant. XVIII and VII Corps did not hit the enemy with the resounding thud that was expected. They inflicted and received significantly fewer casualties than had been anticipated.

By 26 February the advancing British Division was discovering more and more wounded, mostly Iraqi survivors of the preparatory bombings for the ground attack. They were dirty and emaciated, with wounds several days old and unattended, already subject to suppurating infections. Given enough first-aid treatment to keep them alive, they were evacuated in large numbers by ambulance and helicopter to Coalition hospitals. Triage was carried out to decide each one's route through the medical chain. After concentrating its technology on hitting the Iraqis hard, the Coalition was now deploying its best techniques to saving the lives of those who could be treated.

Patients were sent to the resuscitation sections of the two hospitals according to a priority system. As soon as they arrived, they were stripped of their soiled clothes, searched by the guards, examined by the doctor on duty, and sent for medical or nursing care. Some needed radiology, laboratory work, or examination by a specialist or surgeon. Most of the wounded had not eaten for several days, and some had been unconscious or only semiconscious for a long time. Selected Kuwaitis acted as interpreters. They interrogated the wounded in their own language, asking them questions on their battlefield experience and the pain they were feeling. Answers were relayed to medical personnel, who used them to make diagnoses. The interpreters also translated identity documents found among the personal effects of the wounded, in order to keep accurate records of their stay in hospital. Surgery was performed on about 10 percent of them. The rest were bandaged, cleaned, sewn up, and plastered. In most cases, these simple measures, accompanied by good meals, were enough to restore their strength, so that they could be sent under escort to the British prisoner-of-war-camp, where other medical personnel would conduct secondary, follow-up care. A small number were evacuated to the third- or fourth-line American or British hospitals.

Although some of the wounded were in terrible shape, their stained bandages hiding horrible wounds, their numbers fortunately did not exceed the hospitals' capacity. What the doctors feared most was being forced to conduct hurry-up procedures because of an overwhelming influx of casualties. Haste always provides an opening for infection and sometimes makes irrevocable decisions necessary. None of this happened at Al Qaysumah. The surgeons were able to give all patients whatever time it took to complete the appropriate procedures. Some operations proved to be very lengthy, especially because of the dirt and the compounding effects of shock upon the patient. Triage and movement of cases through the hospital up to evacuation generally took place in an atmosphere of calm deliberation.

On Friday, 1 March, the day after the fighting stopped, a seriously wounded Iraqi soldier arrived at the Canadian hospital. He had received shell fragments to his head, his nose had been almost completely blown off by an explosion, his right arm was considerably lacerated and infected, and his whole right side was riddled with holes from shell fragments. Surgeons Lieutenant-Colonel Ian Anderson and Major Barry Armstrong and orthopaedic surgeon Major Charles Buckley, assisted by an otorhinolaryngologist from 32 Field Hospital, spent nine hours cleaning and suturing his wounds to save him. They even opened his cranium to take out metal and bone fragments, which had penetrated up to three centimetres into the right and left frontal lobes of his brain. The patient was conscious and lucid before the operation, however, despite an infection which had had five days to spread. He had been left for dead by his fellows at the bottom of a trench and was discovered when British troops inspected the ground. Few believed that he would pull through, but the surgeons noted in their diagnosis that the patient had resisted his wounds extremely well, perhaps because of the nighttime cold, which had retarded the putrefaction of the wounds. Surgeon Buckley saw the patient again in Jubayl some days later when he was being given skin grafts to his arm. He was on the way to recovery. In more pressing circumstances, it would have been necessary to amputate his right arm without waiting. This would have had serious consequences for the patient. He would have been handicapped for life and at an extreme social disadvantage, because Muslim custom forbids the use of the left hand to perform certain actions.

Dr Buckley had also been involved in another serious case a few days earlier. A lieutenant of the Royal Regiment of Fusiliers had been evacuated to Al Qaysumah on the afternoon of 26 February. Two British *Warrior* armoured troop-carrying vehicles had been hit by *Maverick* missiles from two American A-10 *Thunderbolt* aircraft. The misdirected fire had killed nine soldiers and injured eleven others, including the lieutenant, who was seriously wounded in both legs. A lengthy surgical operation, in which the Canadian orthopaedic surgeon took part, did not succeed in saving the lieutenant's legs, which had to be amputated. Surgeon Buckley and the British lieutenant kept in touch with each other, however. Having met in these tragic circumstances at Al Qaysumah, their paths crossed again in Canada two years later, when the former fusilier took a trip to this country.

The End of the War
When Captain E.R. Crane reached Al Qaysumah on 27 February with the remainders of his signals troop - the last of the Field Hospital complement to deploy - he was afraid that he had arrived a little late. The intelligence briefings were describing a much faster advance than originally expected by the Coalition armies. All objectives

had been reached with almost incredible speed. However, during the afternoon, he could not know that it would be all over the next morning. Crane settled down for the night after reviewing with his non-commissioned members their plans to begin setting up new communications systems very early the following day. When he awoke, he learned that the operation was over and new instructions were to follow.

The hospital's Operations Officer wasted no time in returning some of the still unloaded stocks to Jubayl. The trucks retraced their steps over the 400-kilometre route which they had taken only the day before and unloaded their equipment on the same spot where they had picked it up! The surprising end of the war did not slow down the pace of operations; it was simply redirected in the opposite direction. The tents were struck with the same energy as they had been erected, without the news having had a real chance to sink in.

In recognition of the victory, the Commanding Officer of 32 Field Hospital made arrangements for his unit, which had been deployed for some months, to stand down on 2 March. For that one day, Canadian personnel replaced the British in the treatment rooms and took over all duties. To the Canadians, this was their reward. And it was the only day when 1 CFH worked at full capacity. They dealt with all the wounded and performed all the operations. The triage and resuscitation sections finally ended their work as a family. They treated eighty-two patients, the same number of patients as on all previous days combined. Thereafter casualties grew fewer in number. The British resumed control and 1 Canadian Field Hospital ceased operations on 3 March 1991.

Many now hoped that the hospital would be sent to Kuwait to provide medical support during the cleanup. They found it hard to bear that such a team might be dissolved without having worked to its full capacity. They were, however, to be disappointed. After waiting some ten days for a decision to be made, it was learned that 1 Canadian Field Hospital would not be needed in Kuwait. The medical personnel in greatest demand in Canada accordingly returned within a few days. The main group left on two chartered *Boeing 747* planes, on 19 and 21 March, and the last of the hospital personnel departed Jubayl on 3 April. A merchant ship returned the Canadian equipment to Montréal.

For the first time since the Second World War, the Canadian army had established a battlefield hospital. Operation SCALPEL's greatest moment was the one full day of activity for 1 Canadian Field Hospital. The fact that its capacity was never used to the fullest was one of those vagaries of war. Losses on both sides due to combat proved to be far fewer than the most dire predictions. It is estimated that 205,500 Iraqis died in 1991 from the effects of the war.[12] Of that number, 56,000 military personnel and 3,500 civilians succumbed directly; 35,000 deaths were caused by the effects of violence following the war; and 111,000 were caused by the war's delayed effects on public health. In comparison, the number of American lives lost was 390. Of these, 148 were killed in action. There were no Canadian dead or wounded in the course of the fighting.

Notes

1   See "Area Hospitals for Wounded," *Ottawa Citizen*, 13 January 1991.

2   Cdr Margaret Cavanagh, "Aperçu du soutien médical dans le conflit du Golfe Persique [Survey of Medical Support in the Persian Gulf Conflict]," *Medicus* (Winter 91/92), pp. 10-12.

3   Kenneth M. Dye, *Report of the Auditor-General of Canada to the House of Commons: Financial Year Ending 31 March 1990* (Ministry of Supply and Services Canada, 1990), 23, pp. 596-606.

4   Support responsibilities were usually shared between the Canadians and British, so that resupply of water, rations, fuel, blood, and bandages was provided by the British at the third-line level. It was understood that it was also their responsibility to provide engineering and bomb disposal services as required. Assistance included messes, accommodation, and local procurement. Transport for the deployment and preparation of the site was a British responsibility. On the other hand, Canadian responsibilities included water tanks, electric generators, coolers for air conditioning, and other equipment for torrid climates, as well as medium- and long-distance communications to Manamah HQ and the national strategic network.

5   National Defence, "The Department of National Defence is Deploying a Field Hospital in the Persian Gulf," *Press Release*, AFN: 03/91, 16 January 1991.

6   Most had received multiple inoculations only a few days before emplaning. In-theatre they received injections against the plague and anthrax, contagious infections likely to be spread by biological weapons. Like all personnel in the theatre, they took doses every twelve hours of the antibiotic doxycycline (of the tetracycline family) and every eight hours of pyridostigmine bromide (against the effects of neurotoxic or neuroplegic gases). The secondary effects of these many medications, although generally mild, had a severe impact on some individuals, who suffered weaknesses and pains for up to forty-eight hours.
    Pyridostigmine bromide caused a major controversy after the war when several people who had taken it complained of significant secondary effects, such as memory loss, general malaise, and chronic weakness. The treatment of the victims of "Gulf War syndrome" was the subject of serious research in the United States. The results of this research had not been accepted as conclusive by the time of the preparation of this manuscript.

7   The term "resuscitation" applied to all care administered to wounded patients not requiring anaesthesia on arrival. The resuscitation room was not a place to restore to life patients who seemed to have lost it, as the normal use of the word might suggest. For example, radiology and non-operative care were located in the "resuscitation room."

8   de la Billière, *Storm Command*, p. 290.

9   During the night of 16 February, a *Scud* hit the port of Jubayl, about 800 metres from the headquarters of the British Support Group. There were reportedly 500 tons of explosives awaiting transport piled on the wharf 300 or 400 metres from the point of impact. The debris of another *Scud* crashed on the fifteenth at Hafar al Batin, twenty-three kilometres from al Qaysumah. Several Canadians went to the site to bring back souvenirs in the form of small pieces of twisted metal from *Scud* debris.

10 The thick mud was due to the fact that, to create berms around the hospitals to protect them against shell bursts, direct fire, and blasts from explosives, it had been necessary to scrape and pile up the surface sand with a bulldozer. Under the sand was hard earth, which took on the consistency of paste when it was mixed with rainwater. The effect of finding oneself in that sort of mud was strange to newcomers, who had imagined the grainy sand one found on beaches. Relying on that expectation, several people had left their heavy boots at home to lighten their baggage.

11 Among the tanks of 1 (BR) Armoured Division were the troop led by Canadian exchange officer Captain Steve McCluskey. See his "View From the Turret," *Legion* 67, no 7 (February 1993), pp. 6-10.

12 See B. Dapointe, "A Case Study in Estimating Casualties from War and its Aftermath: The 1991 Persian Gulf War," summary published in *Medicine and War: International Concerns on War and Other Social Violence* 9, no. 4 (October-December 1993), p. 367.

CHAPTER 10

Related Operations

Operation SPONGE

One event which had a major impact on some of the operations in January and February, chiefly those relating to sea transport, was the deliberate spilling of oil into the Persian Gulf. The Iraqis began dynamiting the Kuwait Oil Company's offshore wells on 17 January, the first day of the Allied air attacks. They also released oil from sea terminals on 19 January. Slicks began to appear on the twenty-first. The Pentagon reported on the twenty-sixth that oil was burning at several points in the Gulf and that refineries in the area of Kuwait City had been set on fire. This was Iraq's version of "environmental terrorism."[1] They opened valves at Sea Island, sixteen kilometers offshore from Mina al Ahmadi, and at Mina al Bakr, an extension into the sea of the large Iraqi al Faw oil pipeline terminal (see MIF Operations map), spreading millions of gallons of oil. They positioned tankers so that their contents would pour into the waters of the northern Gulf, where the Shatt al'Arab waterway creates a constant counterclockwise current. The Iraqis then planned to set fire to the oil on the surface of the Gulf, with the aim of blocking naval shipping and preventing the U.S. Marines from disembarking on the beaches of Kuwait. On 27 January, the spill was estimated to be twelve million barrels, or three and a half times the Mexican spill of 1979.[2]

Because of contrary winds, the oil slick did not move as quickly as anticipated toward the beaches of the southwestern Gulf, where the currents were bound to take it. Nevertheless, by 28 January the slick had advanced 100 kilometers southward, beyond the borders of Kuwait, reaching Khafji. By that time, several private and government agencies had alerted the world community to the fact that Saudi Arabia needed help to save the beaches between Khafji and Dhahran.The numerous bays, vast expanses of shallow water, and grassy swamps along this 300-kilometre stretch of coast had valuable wildlife reserves, which were home to white-tailed eagles, herons, flamingos, and cormorants, as well as several marine species vitally important to the food chain.

Three local agencies shared the task of slowing down the advance of the slick. The large Saudi Arabian oil company Aramco used boats and booms to prevent the oil from moving toward the beaches, but it did not have enough equipment. The Royal Commission for Jubayl and Yanbu and the Saudi agency MEPA

(Meteorological and Environmental Protection Administration) used all their staff and resources, but to no great effect. They needed reinforcements.

Help came in the form of companies specializing in cleaning up accidental oil spills. Among these were several American companies which had gained considerable experience from the *Exxon Valdez* accident in Alaska in March 1989. A few of them did not wait for an invitation to join the contractors and ecological activists already at the scene. Fortunately, the overall rate of the spill was slowed down by a remarkably successful aerial bombardment of Sea Island on 28 January, which knocked out the pumping station and halted any further spilling at that location. On 2 February, in light of more accurate data, the estimates of spillage were cut in half to some 4-6 million barrels.[3]

On 27 January, the Department of National Defence received a request to prepare a briefing on the oil spill for a meeting of the Government Planning Committee, scheduled for the twenty-ninth. Following this briefing, it was decided that a team of Canadian experts would go to the Gulf to evaluate the situation. That same day, when he appeared before the parliamentary subcommittee on External Affairs and International Trade, Secretary of State Joe Clark committed the government to help Saudi Arabia.[4] Accordingly, Lieutenant-Colonel J.A. Séguin of the Military Plans Coordination Directorate at NDHQ was chosen to escort seven people who would visit Bahrain and several other Gulf countries. Headed by Mr Sam Baird of Environment Canada, the group included representatives of Energy, Mines and Resources Canada, the Coast Guard, and DND. They left Trenton on 2 February and returned on the thirteenth.

On their recommendation, the Canadian government agreed to support several initiatives to be undertaken by various departments and private agencies. For example, under the coordination of Environment Canada, a computerized cartography system monitored the expansion of the spill and charted the threat it posed to the giant desalination plants. A number of experts also gave advice regarding booms, powerful pumps, and oil.[5] Much of this equipment was transported by Canadian Forces aircraft, which were already scheduled to leave Trenton and Lahr for the Gulf to supply Operation FRICTION.

The main problem in the field was the coordination of all the international agencies involved in the cleanup. The rush to save the coastline was so great that the government of Saudi Arabia was not able to draw up proper contracts and define responsibilities. Confusion and wasteful duplication threatened the rescue effort. Canada's response came in the person of Lieutenant-Commander Al Cole. From the Maritime Operations desk at the Manamah Headquarters, he was an advisor to Commodore Summers on all matters concerning the recently devised Operation SPONGE. Visiting throughout the Gulf, Cole acted as a useful liaison between the various environmental groups. He was able to report on 10 February that the volume of oil in the slick was less than originally feared and that the spill was lighter and easier to clean up than at first reported, despite the extensive damages. There is many a slip twixt cup and lip, however. The disaster remained "the worst oil spill in history" up to that time.

National interest in Operation SPONGE was aroused with the appearance on the scene of Jose Carreiro, a bird rescue expert from the Canadian Wildlife Service. He arrived in Manamah by *Hercules* on 12 February, bringing with him two trailers full of specialized equipment to catch, clean, and disinfect birds. In addition to contributing his own labour, he planned to instruct the local authorities on the proper methods of saving birds in oil slicks. Bahrain television paid tribute to Carreiro's dedication, and his efforts captured the interest of the international media. A second special assignment was announced when equipment belonging to the Canadian Coast Guard was shipped from CFB Trenton in eight *Hercules* aircraft between 11-13 February. The commanding officer of 2 Air Movements Unit (2 AMU), Major Mark Matheson, stated that this shipment was one of the most difficult loads in his experience: "The equipment was heavy, unwieldy and bulky. My people have bruises to prove it."[6]

Meanwhile, Germany asked Canada for assistance in airlifting some large equipment to Bahrain. After some discussion involving Ambassador Dickenson, Canadian *Hercules* aircraft transported 20,000 feet of booms and two ten-ton GT-185 oil skimmers from the Norholz military base in Germany to Manamah, on 16 and 17 February.

When the war ended, the Canadian government was still discussing the idea of sending more equipment to clean up the shore, but reports arriving from the Gulf indicated that the rapid international intervention from the outset of the crisis had lessened the degree of damage to marine life. By then an international plan to preserve the ecology of the Persian Gulf was firmly in place. But there was another problem. Over 700 oil wells in Kuwait were sabotaged in January and February 1991, and many Canadian companies, mostly from Western Canada, played a very active role in putting out the fires there. This extremely difficult operation took eight months instead of the four or five years initially estimated, thanks mostly to new technologies.[7] Cleanup of the side effects of the disaster in Kuwait is still going on.[8]

Operation UNARMED WARRIOR

Another purely humanitarian operation was the provision of medical personnel to help evacuate casualties from the Gulf. Casualties were airlifted to three main locations, two in Germany and one in the United Kingdom, which were organized to carry out triage of patients on arrival, give them on-site care, and complete their evacuation to European hospitals. Since late December, U.S. Forces in Europe had been seeking additional ambulance transport. On 2 January, the Commander in Chief of the U.S. Forces in Europe asked General Smith in Lahr for help, in the process reminding him that Canadian casualties, too, would be handled by the European evacuation system.

After considering this request, NDHQ decided that Canadian personnel would assist a U.S. evacuation battalion in transporting casualties between the Ramstein base, the location of one of the aeromedical staging facilities, and hospitals in the region. Major-General Smith's Headquarters in Lahr assumed responsibility for the operation beginning 10 January. Dubbed UNARMED WARRIOR, 4 Canadian Medical Group was formed specially for it. It was supported primarily by 4 Field Ambulance and 4 Service Battalion, both of which were integral units of 4 Canadian Mechanized Brigade Group. Lieutenant-Colonel Pat Ceresia, Deputy to the Command Surgeon of Canadian Forces in Europe, was put in charge of the 175 people who made up this tailor-made organization.[9]

Four (4) Canadian Medical Group functioned primarily as an evacuation company. It served under the tactical control of 7 Medical Command of the U.S. Army in Europe and was under the direction of 421 (U.S.) Evacuation Battalion at Ramstein. In addition to commanding the Canadian group, Colonel Ceresia was assistant commanding officer to U.S. Colonel Norman Shaefer of the Aeromedical Staging Facility. A number of Canadians served in this organization, several of them in the treatment rooms set up in the huge air base hangars. These converted facilities could accommodate 250 patients at a time and handle between 2,500 and 3,000 patients a day. They provided intensive care, psychiatric care, and pharmaceutical services, and arranged the transportation of patients to the appropriate hospitals in the region.

The Canadian road evacuation group was equipped to provide up to 154 spaces at a time for stretcher patients or walking wounded and move them on board seven multipurpose buses equipped with movable stretchers and oxygen mask systems. Medical teams were assigned to these buses to provide care during transport. The Canadians also provided ten high-quality Mercedes Benz *Unimog* ambulances and two one-and-a-quarter-ton field ambulances. Using these resources, Canadians evacuated 244 patients before 15 February. This was a significant proportion of the casualties transported by road. They continued to do important work throughout the ground war, especially when the number of casualties arriving at Ramstein peaked on 3 March with 200 arrivals. Because Canadian ambulances were considered to be excellent, they were the first choice for transporting casualties whose condition did not require air transport.

The Ramstein evacuation services remained in operation for six months. The Canadians, however, returned to CFB Lahr between 4 and 9 March, after seven weeks of service. With the end of the war, other NATO forces assumed responsibility for the provision of medical services.

Operation UNCLENCHED FIST

The Canadian Forces in Europe were involved in another operation to support the U.S. Forces in Europe engaged in Operation DESERT STORM. In response to a request to move munitions from storage points on U.S. bases to the Morbach railway station, forty kilometres east of Trier, Germany, Canada made available nine thirty-five-ton tractor trailers to 50 Munitions Maintenance Squadron of the U.S. Army in Europe. These munitions were transported mainly from the Hahn base, where Canadian military truckers stayed throughout the war, but some were moved from Ramstein, Spangdahlen, and Bitburg. Dubbed Operation UNCLENCHED FIST, it was authorized at the outset of hostilities, on 17 January, and continued until 1 March. From 1 to 8 March, the direction of the movement of munitions was reversed. Unsent munitions were returned to their original storage facilities. By the end of the operation, Canadian trucks had transported some 10,000 tons of munitions.

Operation NECESSITY

In the absence of Ambassador Dickenson, the Canadian Embassy in Kuwait had been staffed by Mr Bill Bowden and other officers of the Canadian diplomatic service, from 1 August until they had to leave on 19 October, because of pressure by the Iraqi military.[10] The Embassy was reopened at the end of the war. On 1 March, the ambassador boarded Commodore Summers' *Challenger* and returned to Kuwait City from his secondary post in Manamah. Dickenson and Summers landed at the capital's devastated airport and obtained a British escort. It was the only way to negotiate the heavily damaged streets. When they reached the Embassy, they found signs of a break-in but little damage. Commodore Summers used his revolver to smash the thick glass of the front door when no one could find another way of entering. The building was then inspected by an accompanying explosives and ammunition disposal team, and the Embassy was officially reopened the same day. In a brief ceremony, the Canadian flag was hoisted in the presence of many Kuwaiti passers-by, who stopped to give profuse thanks to the Canadians. This was a moving moment for Ambassador Dickenson. He had gone on vacation just a few hours before the invasion. He had tried to return to his post, but had been refused re-entry. During his thirty weeks of waiting, he often wondered what he would find on his return.[11]

Electricity, sewage, and telephone service had been cut all over the city. To carry out urgent repairs to the Embassy, the military were the obvious choice. When Commodore Summers returned to Manamah on the evening of 1 March, he ordered technicians from 1 Canadian Field Hospital to go by road from Jubayl to Kuwait City with their workshop trucks and commence necessary repairs to the Embassy and the Ambassador's residence. The task, called Operation NECESSITY, lasted for a month.

The initial cleanup on 3 March restored some degree of order to the Embassy rooms, which had apparently been visited several times by the Iraqis and left in what the Ambassador drily described as "a bit of a mess." Generators restored light. They were a godsend because during the day the smoke from the oil wells and the forced interruption of municipal services kept the city in semidarkness. Running water was next. Soon groups of construction engineering soldiers were busy making a number of repairs. The consular assistant to the Ambassador stayed in Kuwait City to maintain Canada's diplomatic presence. The military helped him reestablish contact with the city's international community by putting vehicles in running order, restoring communications, and providing security for meetings.

During the first days of reoccupation, soldiers guarding the Embassy were involved in a "rescue." A Kuwaiti family approached a Reserve signals corporal on guard and asked him to come and get a young Iraqi soldier who was hiding at their home. They wanted to protect him from bands of Kuwaitis bent on reprisals. Corporal Kevin Samson, accompanied by a military police officer, was driven to the Kuwaitis' home to bring back the young soldier, who was happy to surrender to "NATO" troops, as he had wished. He was then escorted to the British Embassy, where a protected assembly point for prisoners was maintained. He was the only prisoner captured by Canadians during the Gulf War.

On 7 March, the detachment from 1 CFH returned to Jubayl and was replaced by staff from the Department of External Affairs. They gradually brought the Embassy back into service. Engineers involved in Operation MAGNOLIA (see Chapter 11) gave additional assistance within the framework of Operation NECESSITY. They removed mines and searched for dangerous munitions in Kuwait City in April. Canada was one of the last nations to vacate its embassy in Kuwait and among the first three to return at the end of the war.

Safwan

Two days after visiting the Embassy, Commodore Summers was Canada's military representative at the Safwan Conference. It took place on 3 March 1991 in a tent in the desert where the 1st (U.S.) Infantry Division had halted its advance. Its purpose was to negotiate the terms of Iraq's surrender to the Coalition. Lieutenant-General Sultan Hashim Ahmad, Deputy Chief of Staff of the Iraqi Ministry of Defence, and Lieutenant-General Salah Abud Mahmoud, commander of the now defunct III (Iraq) Army Corps, acted as Saddam Hussein's representatives. Representatives of the main Coalition nations attended this conference, but, apart from some interventions by Lieutenant-General Prince Khalid of Saudi Arabia, only General Schwarzkopf spoke in an official capcity.

The day before the meeting, the UN Security Council had passed Resolution 686. It called on Iraq to comply with provisions concerning the treatment of Kuwaiti hostages, prisoners of war, security measures, and temporary agreements on the ceasefire to be reached between the military representatives of the Coalition and Iraq. Accordingly, Schwarzkopf, Khalid, Ahmad, and Mahmoud discussed lines of demarcation between forces, procedures for exchanging the 60,000 Iraqi prisoners for some forty Coalition prisoners, and arrangements which would prevent clashes in the immediate future. General Schwarzkopf took pains to make clear that these were only temporary lines, subject to discussion by political authorities. There was no question of defining new international boundaries.

The meeting lasted for three hours and was attended by forty people. It followed a precise order, and a dignified tone was maintained. General Schwarzkopf insisted that Iraqi representatives should not be humiliated. But they were. When Schwarzkopf revealed his troops' positions, the Iraqis blushed at the map he showed them. They could hardly believe that Coalition forces had covered so much distance in so short a time. In fact, they were so poorly informed that General Ahmad had to ask General Schwarzkopf his name when he arrived for the meeting.[12] Trying to control their reactions, they went from surprise to surprise as they saw how badly they had been defeated.

By chance, Commodore Summers was seated directly behind General Schwarzkopf. He was able to hear the conversation clearly. When the Iraqis reported that two Italian pilots were among the prisoners, he passed a note to the head of the Italian delegation, Major-General Mario Arpino, who was relieved to hear the news.[13] In all, the five Coalition countries with missing personnel were informed of their status: seventeen Americans, twelve Britons, nine Saudis, two Italians, and one Kuwaiti. Exchanges would be made in the next few days. The official agreement between Iraq and the UN was concluded in Resolution 687, passed on 3 April 1991, which laid down final reconciliation measures (see Chapter 11).

Although General Schwarzkopf had the upper hand in these negotiations, perhaps to a degree unheard of for a winning general in modern history, he committed one big blunder that later led him to exclaim through clenched teeth: "I was suckered!"[14] He gave General Ahmad permission for Iraqi forces to use helicopters over their national territory. This concession allowed the Iraqi military to crush the Kurds in the north and the Shi'ites in the south. Both peoples suffered greatly from Schwarzkopf's decision. However, in his defence, one must keep in mind that he had never set himself the goal of overthrowing Saddam Hussein's government. His mission from President Bush was to bring about as total a defeat as possible of Iraqi forces in Kuwait and to drive them back inside their own borders. No territorial ambitions or hidden goals of the Western powers lay behind the border crossing. Schwarzkopf pursued this mission ferociously until he was halted in his tracks by presidential authority on the morning of 28 February 1991.

Safwan, a bare landing strip just inside the Iraqi border, directly north of Kuwait City, marked the completion of this mission. The desert was littered with thousands of vehicles and tanks and the skeletal remains of downed aircraft, bearing dramatic witness to the Coalition victory. Flying over the surrounding desert, in particular the Mutla Hill battlefield just north of Kuwait City, Summers was overwhelmed by the extent of the losses. Fascinated, he returned to the area, so that he could go over it on foot and take pictures. He said later that the destruction was something that he would never forget.[15]

Notes

1   Rae Corelli, "The End of Illusion," *Maclean's*, 4 February 1991, pp. 26-28.

2   The initial spills immediately suggested that they would be tens of times greater than the *Exxon Valdez*, estimated at 10.8 million gallons or 257,000 barrels (a barrel contains forty-two U.S. gallons). The Ciudad del Carmen spill from 3 July 1979 to 24 March 1980 was in the order of 140 million gallons or 3.3 million barrels. See Thomas Y. Canby, "After the Storm," *National Geographic* 180, no. 2 (August 1991), pp. 2-35. See also Michael McKinnon and Peter Vive. *Tides of War : Ecodisaster in the Gulf* (London: Boxtree, 1991).

3   A later calculation in *Oil Spill Intelligence Report* [An International Newsletter from Cutter Information Corp] 15 (26 March 1992) put the figure at 5.8 million barrels. According to the most accurate estimates, fifteen to twenty-two times more crude oil was spilled in the Gulf than by the *Exxon Valdez* in Alaska. Since the circumstances were different, however, it would be wrong to compare the extent of the disaster on the basis of this scale alone. An important factor in this equation is the type of oil spilled. The Persian Gulf oil was not as thick as that carried by the *Exxon Valdez* and was thus more prone to evaporate.

4   *Minutes of Proceedings and Evidence of the Standing Committee on External Affairs and International Trade*, Issue No 82; and *Minutes of Proceedings and Evidence of the Standing Committee on National Defence and Veterans Affairs*, Issue No 41, 29 January 1991, pp. 6-7.

5   Manon Cornellier, "Des experts canadiens aideront le Bahreïn à contrer la marée noire," *Le Devoir* (Montréal), 9 February 1991.

6   Capt Renée Mactaggart, "Airforce Green," *ATG Newsletter*, 1 (1991), pp. 8-9.

7   Some wells did not catch fire. Instead, they spilled their oil in huge slicks that grew week by week to eventually form over 200 lakes of crude oil, the largest of which covered thirty-six square kilometres. When Coalition troops recaptured this ground, six million barrels of oil a day were burning or spilling from damaged wells. An estimated 3% of Kuwait's reserves were lost to Iraqi acts of destruction, but Kuwait regained its normal output level in 1993 and was even criticized by OPEC for exceeding its quotas for most of the year. In September 1993, Kuwait was producing 2.16 million barrels a day for world markets. These figures show that the equivalent of less than three days' output was spilled into the waters of the Gulf. The fires of Kuwait, on the other hand, probably caused losses in the order of 600 million barrels of oil, or 25 billion gallons.

8   Four main companies shared the task of putting out the fires of Kuwait, of which *Safety Boss* was from western Canada.

9   "The Gulf War: Ramstein AFB," in *4 Field Ambulance: Outstanding Support in Peace and War* (Lahr: Demmer, 1992), pp. 79-91.

10 Coulon, *La dernière croisade*, Chapter 2, "Siège de l'ambassade." pp. 25-30.

11 Ralph Coleman, "Canadian Flag Flies Again in Kuwait", *Ottawa Citizen*, 21 June 1991.

12 Schwarzkopf, *It Doesn't Take a Hero*, p. 484.

13 Coulon, pp. 141-42.

14 de la Billière, *Storm Command*, p. 318.

15 Commodore Summers, interview by Hal Lawrence, H Lawrence & Associates, Oak Bay and Esquimalt, BC, 14-15 July 1992. Used with permission.

CHAPTER 11

Disengagement and Return

The end of hostilities marked a sharp reversal of priorities. It would take time for them to filter down to the lowest levels of the military hierarchy. When President Bush declared that the fighting would stop on 28 February at 0800 local time, many could hardly believe their ears. The president's "hundred-hour war" was ending just when a number of logistical systems were coming into play. Within VII (U.S.) Corps, for example, units in the rear kept up their momentum for several days after the ceasefire. It could not be reversed or even stopped. At the front, the sudden halt brought on general torpor, and soldiers crashed with fatigue after running on adrenalin for several days. Skirmishes continued for three days, mainly because of lack of information on the Iraqi side. The news spread very quickly, however, among Coalition forces. On 3 March, after the Safwan conference, the question uttered in chorus by nearly a million Coalition soldiers was: "When are we leaving?"

Operation SCABBARD

This question was much discussed among Canadians. The joint headquarters staff in Manamah had known about the ceasefire for at least a day before it happened. Interestingly, general plans for a withdrawal, known as Operation SCABBARD, had been in preparation since 21 February. Seven days later, Commodore Summers was sent additional staff from Canada to assist headquarters. Their one goal would be to close down everything, following appropriate procedures. Lieutenant-Colonel J.R. Hinse, a logistical officer from NDHQ, brought a team of some twenty officers and NCOs to oversee the closing of the books and the in-theatre disposal of non-recoverable matériel and to devise a coherent plan for the gradual return of personnel to Europe and Canada. On his team was an air transport control group in direct liaison with Ottawa, Trenton, and Lahr. They were to plan cargo and personnel flights beginning in the first week of March.

Defence Minister McKnight and General de Chastelain also went to the theatre of operations to thank members of the Canadian military. On 7 March, at the port of Dubai, Mr McKnight informed the crews of the three Canadian vessels that their mission was over and they were free to leave. The two men then toured all the other locations where Canadian units were stationed, in Manamah, Doha, and

Jubayl. In answer to the one question on everyone's mind, "When can we go home?" the answer was always the same: "As soon as possible!" In the afternoon, McKnight and de Chastelain met the entire Joint Staff, including the two liaison officers on board *Midway*, and were given an extensive briefing. This was the beginning of the end of the Canadian presence in Bahrain. The team from Ottawa, which had arrived a few days before, took charge of administrative measures and the few special operations still requiring attention. In the meantime, the staff members completed their service, wrote their final reports, and packed their kitbags. The CF-18s left for Germany the same week, with the last flight but one out of Doha on 9 March,[1] and the ships of TG 302.3 sailed from Dubai on the twelfth.

Personnel came home several different ways. Most took chartered aircraft in the second and third weeks of March. In Canada they were given a warm welcome. Families and the general public alike showed up at airports to thank the returning troops for their service. Impressive ceremonies were organized in Ottawa, Toronto, and other large Canadian cities.[2] In Halifax, it seemed that the entire city was in the port on the morning of Sunday, 7 April, to celebrate the return of the three Canadian warships from their 226-day odyssey. At 1000 on 16 April 1991, the Manamah Headquarters officially closed, and the next day the last flight of personnel, including Commodore Summers, reached Ottawa, where their arrival was greeted with impressive ceremony. Operation FRICTION had lasted 248 days.

Military representatives of all ranks were given a joyful welcome by a great many Canadian municipalities. Across the country, people were relieved that Canada had been able to make a meaningful contribution to the Gulf war, without suffering a single death or injury due to hostilities and without losing any of our planes, ships, or military equipment in battle. Some commentators pointed out how remarkably fortunate it was that despite the Oka crisis and Operation FRICTION, the Canadian Forces did not suffer any losses in combat in 1990-91. For the vast majority of Canadians, this was the only measure of success, and it was achieved by the careful deliberations of the Mulroney cabinet and the professionalism of the Canadian military. For a brief period in the political life of a nation, the thorny problems of the hot summer of 1990 were forgotten. Operation FRICTION ended in harmony. No shadow marred the joy of homecoming.

Operation AXE

While the first of the homecoming celebrations were taking place in Canada, the Coalition remained busy on the recent battlefield. And Canada had its role to play in the postwar operations.

With the approach of the ground assault by Coalition forces, the Joint Headquarters had acquired the services of an army staff team to monitor the battle and keep the commanding officer apprised of the progress of the various Coalition army corps. This team of three officers from Mobile Command arrived in Manamah only a few days before G-Day. One of them, Lieutenant-Colonel David Chupick, was dispatched at once to Riyadh to be seconded to the Joint Staff at HQ BRITFORME. Chupick observed how the situation was unfolding hour by hour at the front, and relayed this information to HQ CANFORME in Manamah.

These army officers, together with Lieutenant-Colonel Bender, were the chief actors in an operation which took place a few days after the war. They set out to recover arms and equipment abandoned by the Iraqis on the battlefield. Their initial search in the Kuwaiti desert, known as Operation AXE I, was not very fruitful, however. Unexploded munitions made the terrain highly dangerous. Traffic by vehicle and on foot was reduced to a minimum. The U.S. and British services insisted that the spoils of war be gathered immediately in controlled enclosures to prevent collectors from scavenging in the desert. The Coalition found loaded weapons, damaged explosives, and clever booby traps which claimed the limbs of many. The Canadian group eventually acquired various items and sent them to Canada. They were studied by intelligence services and then used for training purposes.

A group of researchers from National Defence travelled to Kuwait in April, in the course of Operation AXE II, to discuss information concerning the types of weapons used and the war's one great revelation about weapons technology. Like all scientists who followed the fighting in the Persian Gulf, the National Defence researchers concluded that so-called force-multiplying technologies acted in the way the name suggests. From now on, any assessment of hostile forces facing each other prior to battle would have to take such multipliers into account: advanced electronic systems used in weapons sighting; communications; air, sea, and topographical navigation; plane- and satellite-based air observation and surveillance systems; and stealth systems. The U.S. and a few other advanced nations used these technologies to great and devastating effect, multiplying the force of their arms well beyond the actual number of weapons they possessed. Iraq neither possessed nor fully comprehended such multipliers. Consequently, their vast array of weaponry, while impressive on paper, was quickly destroyed.

The overall military conclusion drawn from the Gulf war was that countries that do not develop their own war technologies are not very adept at using them and are at a distinct disadvantage on the battlefield against those countries that do develop their own weapons systems and know how to use them to the fullest. To buy a foreign technology is to make oneself dependent on the nation exporting it. By virtue of the very fact that it was able to produce the technology, the exporting nation can better control its limits. The exporter always ensures that it can defeat its client. This example is very clearly illustrated by the Iraqi Air Force. Even though it had modern aircraft and complex systems, it did not have the technological depth to make them perform at maximum capacity. They simply did not have the multipliers that could have increased their air force's capabilities. Canada could not - cannot - afford to ignore this lesson.

Operation MAGNOLIA

Once the bulk of the FRICTION forces had completed their disengagement and returned to Canada, having learned valuable lessons in joint warfare, in a certain sense Canadian military operations reverted to their more traditional pattern. On the one hand, 1 Canadian Field Hospital was not deemed necessary to help Kuwait get back on its feet. On the other hand, the country was littered with munitions, mines, and explosives that threatened the population wherever they went. The cities and desert were bristling with all sorts of bombs that had failed to explode on impact or were left behind by the fighters because they weighed too much or simply because they were no longer needed. Someone remarked that 20 percent of all munitions used in the Gulf war had not worked. This is not supported by any solid statistics, but clearly a high proportion of explosive devices simply failed to go off when launched. Artillery shells, tank shells, bombs, mines, rockets, and grenades of every description are all booby traps for a public ill-informed about the hazards they represent. Kuwait desperately needed help to rid itself of all this unexploded material.

This was one of the conclusions reached by General de Chastelain when he visited Kuwait in early March. He returned to Ottawa with the clear message that soldiers, not children, should collect the explosives.

On 11 March, NDHQ directed Commodore Summers to establish contacts with Kuwaiti authorities and determine precise requirements for assistance. For its part, Mobile Command had anticipated NDHQ's directive to Summers. As early as 8 March, following his own tour of the Gulf, Lieutenant-General Foster had drawn up a plan to provide a Canadian contingent for reconstruction. It was called Operation SAPPER and would consist mainly of engineering troops. A very favourable report by Ambassador Dickenson convinced the minister that he should send a reinforced team to Kuwait City for explosive ordnance disposal (EOD). General Huddleston in Ottawa urged Summers to assemble such a team from resources already in the theatre. An initial reconnaissance concluded that a troop of engineers qualified in EOD could be integrated directly into an international organization named "Task Force Freedom." Headed by the U.S. Army, it was working to clean up Kuwait and restore normal conditions. This information reached the Deputy Chief of the Defence Staff on Wednesday, 13 March. He immediately gave orders for Operation MAGNOLIA. Major Malcolm G. "Mac" Fraser, an engineering officer newly arrived on the Manamah HQ staff, became the officer in charge of the Canadian operation.

The following Sunday, twenty-three sappers from Manamah, Doha, and Jubayl began clearing Kuwait City of mines. Their first two tasks were to help handle Egyptian Army artillery shells and organize sectoral rapid intervention EOD teams. Four three-person teams joined Egyptian troops to clean up Sector 10 of the BRAVO zone, an area of about twenty-five square kilometres south of the city. It consisted mainly of an industrial park but also included a racecourse and stables, a hospital, Kuwaiti military barracks, and large numbers of ammunition depots. Sergeant Charlie Ralph of 4 Combat Engineer Regiment (4 CER) in Lahr calculated that the job would take a couple of weeks.[3] (Ralph was to be mentioned in dispatches for his services in Kuwait and was to die a year later in the former Yugoslavia, doing the same type of work.) His men found hundreds of tonnes of ammunition, including dangerous bomblets dropped from the air by Coalition aircraft, strewn over vast stretches of ground.[4] They found corpses and even the carcasses of horses tortured and killed by the Iraqis. They also had to go into dangerous hiding places that might have been booby-trapped. Fortunately, there were no victims.

Commodore Summers visited the engineers on 27 March and was able to judge for himself the harsh conditions in which they had to work. In addition to the constant danger, the heat was stifling and the air was thick with oil particles. On 8 April, after three weeks of work in Sector 10, the troop packed up and returned to Manamah. A merchant ship brought back the vehicles and matériel, and a chartered plane carried the Operation MAGNOLIA team on 17 April 1991, all its members being sound in mind and body.

The end of Operation MAGNOLIA, however, did not mean the end of Canadian collaboration in rebuilding Kuwait and clearing it of mines. Indeed, some of the engineers' colleagues already had received orders to leave for Kuwait.

Operation RECORD (UNIKOM)
On 3 April 1991, the Security Council adopted Resolution 687, confirming the ceasefire between Iraq and the Coalition agreed upon a month earlier at Safwan. It was the fullest, most detailed resolution ever passed by the Security Council. Referring to the thirteen previous resolutions relating to the liberation of Kuwait, it set forth nine principal clauses covering the following subjects:

A. Confirmation of the existing borders between Iraq and Kuwait and their inviolability (paragraphs 1 to 4)
B. Creation of a demilitarized zone and a UN observer mission to identify and report any hostile actions observed along this border (paragraphs 5 and 6)
C. A list of measures regarding the possession, production and verification of Iraq's biological, chemical, and nuclear weapons (paragraphs 7 to 14)
D. Measures taken to restore the property of Kuwaiti citizens (paragraph 15)
E. Measures applying to the discharge of Iraq's liabilities toward other countries, including the creation of a commission to manage a fund set up by Iraq to pay legitimate claims against it (paragraphs 16 to 19)
F. Measures relating to maintaining an international embargo against Iraq until the conditions in the liability clauses stated earlier are fulfilled (paragraphs 20 to 29)

G. Measures relating to the free return to their own country of citizens of Kuwait and nationals of other countries whose fate is unknown (paragraphs 30 and 31)

H. The requirement that Iraq renounce terrorism (paragraph 32)

I. Final provisions regarding the ceasefire agreement between Iraq and Kuwait (paragraphs 33 and 34).

This resolution was followed on 5 April by a report of the Secretary General to the Security Council on the proposed provisions for establishing the United Nations Iraq-Kuwait Observation Mission (UNIKOM), which was to maintain a demilitarized zone between the two countries along their common border. It was a band of territory extending ten kilometres into Iraq and five kilometres into Kuwait and comprising a total of 3,500 sq. km.. It took 1,400 military and civilian personnel under UN colours to clear this area of mines and set observation posts that were to be constantly occupied to oversee the ceasefire, monitor movements between the two countries, and report incidents.

This was a terrible task because of the dangers involved and the working conditions, which included savage summer temperatures. Thirty-three countries were asked to supply personnel, and many participants had to be sent from other UN missions. Among the first contingents to arrive were those diverted from UNFICYP (Cyprus), which provided infantry companies from Austria and Norway, and from UNIFIL (Lebanon), which sent infantry troops from Ghana, Fiji, and Nepal. The Norwegian and Swedish logistical unit also came from Lebanon. Military observers were in high demand to fill the 300 positions. The most favoured were those officers already familiar with UN methods, since they would be better prepared to make a good start in their new mission as objective observers. Command of UNIKOM was entrusted to Major-General G.G. Greindl, a Norwegian officer with lengthy experience in commanding UN missions, especially in Cyprus. He was appointed Chief Military Observer (CMO). In its final form, the mission comprised a headquarters with civilian and military personnel for communications and administration, a helicopter sub-unit, five infantry companies, and logistical, medical, and engineering units.

As soon as the Chief Military Observer was appointed, Major Mac Fraser went to Kuwait and took up a temporary position as military engineering advisor on General Greindl's international staff. On 19 April, Canadian Lieutenant-Colonel Michael G. McKeon, another engineer, became the deputy chief of operations of the UNIKOM HQ, which settled in the squash courts of a Kuwait City hotel while waiting to move closer to the borders. At the time, nothing better could be found to accommodate the UNHQ. The preferred option was a ravaged hospital in the Iraqi border town of Umm Qasr, but it would take a year to put it back into working order.

Disengagement and Return

On 8 April, Canada indicated that it could provide the embryonic UNIKOM with a preliminary contingent for reconnaissance, consisting of ten observers and about forty engineers. Mobile Command already had chosen a detachment of 1 Combat Engineer Regiment from Chilliwack, British Columbia for the task, and Operation RECORD was officially expanded on 16 April to include the entire Engineer Regiment. The vanguard of 154 troops from the Regiment left on 23 April and was followed by the main group of 136 on the twenty-ninth. One of the terms of the ceasefire of 12 April said that once UNIKOM was established, the withdrawal of troops from Operation DESERT STORM would be completed by 8 May 1991. By 5 May, the Canadian contingent of UNIKOM was operational and ready to take over responsibility from the U.S. 3rd Armoured Division, which had occupied the demilitarized zone since the end of the Gulf war. In anticipation of the changeover, work preparing the observation posts was begun 2 May.

As an engineering unit, 1 CER remained under the command of its CO, Major Richard E. Isabelle. Its duties fell into two main categories. Its primary function was military engineering with an emphasis on mine removal, EOD, and clearing roads in the demilitarized zone. Its secondary function was construction engineering. This included setting up observation posts, huts, and dormitories in the desert, building helicopter landing pads, and providing safe parking for ground transport. Naturally, the two functions went hand in hand. The observation points became oases in the desert. At first, only their immediate surroundings and the roads connecting the posts were free of mines. The regiment was to oversee the maintenance of over 3,000 km of roads and tracks connecting all points in the demilitarized line.

Then there was work to be done at the hospital in Umm Qasr. It was supposed to house UNIKOM HQ, but its restoration required materials that were often in short supply. This caused numerous delays. Matters became even more complicated when children, women, and workers were taken to the former hospital for treatment of injuries caused by explosive devices on the ground. But the hospital was hardly a hospital, and it was virtually impossible to attend to these hapless victims. The UN sent medical detachments from a Norwegian field hospital to deal with these civilian casualties.

Also in Umm Qasr was an Iraqi naval base. The UN decided to use it as a camp. Since the hospital and the camp were inside the demilitarized zone, they were suitable places for housing support troops. Known as "Camp Khor," it took a full year to complete. This was where Canadian engineers from the third contingent finally settled, in April 1992. From April 1991 to April 1992, however, they lived at Doha, Kuwait (not to be confused with Doha, Qatar), just south of Kuwait City. From there they commuted to the demilitarized zone to do their work. Eventually, the teams worked in weekly rotation, going from one post to the next in a bid to cope with the boredom of routine.

By 22 May, a month and a half after 1 CER had arrived, fourteen of the eighteen observation points figuring in General Greindl's plans were occupied by observers, and by 3 June, ninety-seven incidents within the demilitarized zone had been reported. The regiment's work was expected to be nearly completed by August. Until then, the oil wells would continue to burn and spread their foul smell and smoke, which had to be endured day and night in addition to the extreme desert temperatures of the summer tour. On the worst days, the thermometer rose to 60°C. Such appalling heat posed a real threat to the workers, who had to perform their tasks non-stop for several hours at a time. They worked at mine disposal, drove tractors, graders, and bulldozers, and did carpentry, plumbing, and electrical work in observation posts. They had to drink six to twelve litres of water a day because they perspired so much. However, it was so hot, their clothes were always dry! Temperatures of 40°C came to be considered normal. Sandstorms added to the danger, since the strong winds blew stray ammunition back into places already cleared by the engineers.

On 7 June 1991, the Canadians had to recover the corpse of a Kuwaiti serviceman killed in the demilitarized zone. Several times they had to replace the signposts along cleared roads, which had been removed by patrols from one side or the other for the sake of the construction material they contained. All basic tasks were performed. Later in June, it was decided that the contingent of engineers scheduled to replace 1 CER would be reduced to a squadron of about one hundred.

In early October, then, the Chilliwack regiment was relieved by eighty-eight members of 59 Squadron, from 5 CER at CFB Valcartier. This sub-unit would continue the EOD work already under way. Despite the disposal of over 10,000 explosive devices, an estimated 600,000 anti-tank mines still remained in the demilitarized zone.

The Iraqis, meanwhile, were anxious to recover some of these devices and paid people to venture into the forbidden sectors to bring them back. Dozens of people died or were injured trying to earn the equivalent of a few dollars in this trade. Canada continued to provide observer officers for the demilitarized line between Kuwait and Iraq, but they were gradually replaced by civilian police. In April 1992, 59 Squadron was replaced by 29 Squadron from 2 CER in Petawawa. Then 29 Squadron was replaced by another squadron, also from Petawawa. The Canadian engineers completed their work in December 1992, and the second squadron of fifty people returned to Petawawa. Canadian military observers are still posted in the demilitarized zone in 1996.

Operation ASSIST

The postwar disturbances in Iraq did not bring about the political overthrow of the dictator Saddam Hussein. Long kept in check, ethnic and religious revolts exploded when Saddam's forces of coercion were decimated by setbacks in combat. Saddam's capacity to resist these movements should not be attributed solely to his ruthless determination to stay in power. There was a general desire among the Iraqis to maintain his regime. It was fuelled by a fear that Iraq would turn into another Lebanon, fragmented by overly powerful minorities. Indeed, despite the crippling attacks inflicted by the Coalition, five Iraqi divisions had been able to retreat from the hell of Kuwait and join the twenty-one divisions that had been kept in reserve and remained practically untouched. Together these twenty-six divisions cruelly and effectively enabled Saddam to regain full control of the situation. By the end of March 1991, four weeks after Kuwait was retaken, Shi'ite subversive groups in the south had been isolated in the huge swamps of Mesopotamia, and one and a half million Kurdish refugees in the north had fled to the mountains above the Tigris, most of them heading towards Iran and the rest in the direction of the Turkish border.

The United States, supported by the United Nations, prohibited the use of fixed wing aircraft by the Iraqi government but did precious little to support the Shi'ites and the Kurds in their revolt. On both counts, the Americans and the UN were subjected to harsh international criticism. Sadly, the Coalition's decisive defeat of Iraq could not be translated into toppling Saddam from power. As a result, his opposition was left to fend for itself, and did poorly on the battlefield. The only thing the West could offer was a gesture of moral support. Whole peoples were being torn apart. The United Nations was especially sensitive to the lot of the Kurds and had, indeed, strongly denounced the use of gas by Iraq in the anti-Kurd repressions of 1988. Turkey was another problem. As a Western partner, it had to be protected from a tidal wave of displaced humanity that might destabilize its domestic politics and compromise its future.

On 5 April, the UN passed Resolution 688. It called for humanitarian aid for Iraq's oppressed minorities. The U.S. administration had remained aloof from the politicking in support of the resolution, but its passage created a political climate that Congress was unable to resist.[5] In response to the Kurdish nightmare and the UN initiative, the White House launched two operations. PROVIDE COMFORT, unveiled on 6 April, was to supply food and survival requirements to refugees, and SAFE HAVEN, beginning on the sixteenth, was to create protected enclaves in northern Iraq. By ultimately supporting a humanitarian aid operation far greater than the airlift to save Berlin in the late 1940s, the U.S. absolved itself of all charges of macchiavellianism in the conduct of the Gulf war. Under the leadership of the UN, NATO, and the European Community, the airlift to the Kurds was clearly dissociated from any covert attempt to overthrow the authority of the Iraqi Government, which had been firmly restored by early April. Although it cannot be denied that the two projects were conducted within definite political and strategic contexts, Operations PROVIDE COMFORT and SAFE HAVEN remained an unprecedented superpower enterprise combining military muscle with humanitarian generosity.

It was in this very same spirit that Canada took part in the airlift. Ottawa responded immediately to Resolution 688 by offering its strategic transport capabilities. On 9 April, the government's Crisis Management Committee decided that the humanitarian aid sent by the Canadian International Development Agency (CIDA) and the Red Cross would be carried by aircraft from Air Transport Group. Prime Minister Mulroney's announcement of Friday, 12 April, substantially increased the scope of the plans then being discussed. He committed $7.5M worth of aid to refugees on the Turkish side and $800,000 to those on the Iranian side. At this point, all activities relating to Canadian efforts to help Kurdish refugees were combined into one operation, code-named ASSIST.

The airlift phase of the Canadian operation in fact had begun on 11 April with the dispatch of an Armed Forces *Boeing 707* containing "400 family-size tents, 3,000 blankets, 1,500 20-litre jerrycans, 1,000 cooking sets, four mobile field kitchens, and water purification tablets."[6] It flew to the airport of Diyarbakir, a provincial capital in eastern Turkey, where the international Task Force was concentrated. It was followed on 14 April by two *Hercules* from Trenton carrying matériel and equipment for an airlift control element (ALCE) of forty-seven people. From their Incirlik base, these two *Hercules*, served by four crews qualified in tactical flight, began to shuttle rescue materials by parachute.[7] They joined a multinational force which numbered over fifty *Hercules* and dozens of C-141 *Starlifter* and C-5A *Galaxy* aircraft. As of 18 April, each Canadian *Hercules* flew two missions per day into the mountains, dropping up to sixteen parachutes each time. By 2 May they had delivered almost 400 tonnes of goods in the high valleys between summits of up to 3,000 metres. At the same time, the German Red Cross was involved in another air transport operation within the framework of ASSIST. During the period 12-23 April, six ATG missions carried 200 tonnes of material from Lahr to Tehran for distribution to refugees who had fled towards Iran.

NDHQ delegated most coordination responsibilities to Major-General Smith at CFE HQ. On 13 April, he sent two liaison officers to Incirlik to contact U.S. forces involved in Operation PROVIDE COMFORT and discuss intervention options for medical personnel. They concluded that Canada would provide the same ambulances it had deployed at Ramstein for Operation UNARMED WARRIOR and any additional medical personnel at its disposal. Lieutenant-Colonel Leslie Dubinsky, commanding 4 Field Ambulance in Germany, was designated to provide humanitarian aid to refugees along the border between Turkey and Iraq, commencing the following week.[8] From 18 to 21 April, three USAF C-5A *Galaxy* planes and one C-141 *Starlifter* transported the Canadian evacuation company to Incirlik. The company consisted of sixty-two people and forty vehicles, including trucks, jeeps, and ambulances.

On arrival, Dubinsky left by plane for Silopi, the closest airport to the advance field positions. He had to identify in detail the tasks that would be performed by his two evacuation platoons. In the meantime, Major Allan Darch, a doctor and company commander with 4 Field Ambulance, assumed responsibility for the unit and formed a road convoy to go from the air base at Incirlik, on the shores of the Mediterranean, to Silopi, very close to the border between Turkey and Iraq. It took twenty-eight hours to complete the journey of 750 kilometres. Darch rejoined his commanding officer on 24 April. If this "mother of all road trips" was any indication, the operation was going to be quite a challenge.[9]

Civilian international aid groups from Silopi already had been deployed in rescue posts, just north of the border, to provide care to the refugees who came down from the mountains to the camps. These sanctuaries were protected by international troops and offered food, clothing, medication, and general care in ever-growing quantities. The refugees were in terrible condition. A large proportion of them were suffering from diarrhoea, dehydration, and various diseases brought on by poor hygiene, lack of clean water, and weakness due to cold and hunger. Families had been uprooted and torn apart, and, in many cases, children were missing. The refugees approached the camps cautiously. They had been promised help and protection from the Iraqi troops that had devastated their homes and pursued them to the foot of the mountain, but relations between Turkey and the Kurds were strained because Kurdish extremist groups, such as the Kurdish Workers' Separatist Party (PKK), laid claim to "Kurdistan," the traditional homeland of the Kurds situated on territory in Turkey, Iraq, and Iran. Recent clashes between the Turks and the Kurds had made the Turks less than pleased to see large movements of Kurds towards their border with Iraq, where a mass exodus might increase social pressure inside Turkey. After receiving care in Turkey, the Kurds returned to Iraqi territory to live in protected enclaves.

On arrival at Silopi, Dubinsky's original plans had to be changed immediately. Instead of forming two almost identical evacuation platoons, he organized four different groups, each one having a distinct role. First, Captain Michel Petit brought a group to Yekmal, 150 kilometers from Silopi, where one of the twelve refugee camps on the Turkish side was located. They joined *Médecins sans frontières* and established a clinic under canvas where they treated the neediest of the 100,000 refugees who wound up there.

Lieutenant-Colonel Dubinsky led a group inside Iraq to an abandoned hospital in the locality of Zhako. Under the protection of U.S. Marines, and in cooperation with a French military medical team, they worked in indescribable conditions to restore a minimum level of hygiene and organization to the hospital. The handful of doctors and nurses, who had remained at the hospital when Iraqi troops had arrived, had no water or electricity. There were no kitchen or laundry facilities. They were unable to give anything remotely resembling medical care to the dozens of sick and dying patients. Dubinsky's group restored hope. Refugees began to pour in within a few days of their arrival. During the weeks that followed, Zhako became the regional emergency measures centre for assisting refugees inside Iraq and the first hospital in the region to perform surgery.[10] Indeed, the Zhako hospital was up and running before Operation SAFE HAVEN was fully under way.

For his part, Major Darch was at the head of a group deployed by helicopter to the remote villages of Yesilova and Uzumlu. He set up his tents in the midst of myriad dangers, ranging from mines laid haphazardly in territory that had recently been the scene of conflict, to poisonous snakes, to threats against his group by local factions. He had the good fortune to be protected by U.S. and British troops stationed at appropriate points. Darch was in charge of five examination tables at a time, as if he were involved in combat medicine. Nurses performed all sorts of medical procedures under his supervision. Patients queued up around the tents from morning to evening, and work did not stop until nightfall. Some of the injuries were serious. Medication was very precious and had to be doled out carefully. Illicit trade, envy, and theft became big problems for Darch and his beleaguered staff.

The fourth and final group was headed first by Captain David Wilcox and then Captain J.R. Brisebois. They were located at Kani Masi. From there Canadian ambulances evacuated patients to more distant hospitals in the north. Because of local conditions, ambulance drivers often performed medical interventions. Treating casualties took priority over transporting them.

The massive deployment of international military force within the framework of SAFE HAVEN was a deciding factor in stopping the exodus from Iraq. On 20 May, international troops entered the provincial capital of Dahuk in the north of Iraq, marking a new stage in international aid. As refugees returned to protected camps inside Iraq, medical needs in Turkey diminished, and 4 Field Ambulance was redeployed. The 120 Canadians involved at Incirlik and in the Silopi area were back in Lahr by June 1991.

Operations FLAG and BARRIER

The immediate aftermath of hostilities, when Iraq seemed to have been virtually destroyed, led the Canadian government to determine that its contribution to the Multinational Interception Force did not require the continued commitment of a full task group. Nor was it necessary to continue the ship-crew rotations. On 12 March, Task Group 302.3 - including the recently re-crewed *Protecteur* - sailed from Dubai and exited the Strait of Hormuz. For *Athabaskan*, it was the first time in nearly six months that she had been out of the Persian Gulf. Her sister ship and replacement, *Huron*, already halfway across the Atlantic, was ordered to put into Gibraltar, take on certain special FRICTION stores and equipment from the task group as it passed, and await further instructions.

It soon became apparent, however, that Saddam Hussein was going to implement the terms of Resolution 687 only with the greatest reluctance. As the Coalition's land and air forces departed, it found it necessary to maintain a visible naval presence in the area. It had to be vigilant against further aggressive Iraqi action and continue the imposition of sanctions as the only practical means of encouraging compliance with the ceasefire terms. Sidelined during the course of hostilities, the MIF was suddenly returned to the forefront of activity.

Accordingly, *Huron* was ordered to the Gulf. It was to join the resurgent MIF and assist the Department of External Affairs in reestablishing a Canadian diplomatic presence in the region. The code name for the operation, until then known as FRICTION II, was changed to Operation FLAG.[11] *Huron* passed through the Suez Canal on 14 April and arrived in Manamah ten days later. During the next two months, it conducted three patrols in support of the MIF but found "simply [identifying] and [tracking] what little peaceful merchant shipping braved the unsure waters of the Gulf"[12] a relatively uneventful exercise.

Excitement was to be found elsewhere. On 3 June, *Huron* responded to a distress call from a Polish freighter and conducted a dramatic helicopter evacuation of a crew member who had suffered a heart attack. At the end of her third patrol, in the forenoon of 20 June, *Huron* entered the 2,000 yard-wide mine-swept channel leading to Kuwait City, arriving that afternoon without incident. She remained alongside for the next two days, giving her crew ample opportunity to tour the war-torn country and offer the services of their ship - especially the galley and the hot showers - to the engineers of the Operation RECORD contingent, who were still without proper facilities of their own.

The end of their stay in the Gulf was at hand. On 7 June, *Huron* had hosted the fourth postwar MIF commanders conference. The consensus was that the MIF embargo in the Persian Gulf was an expensive and impractical employment of naval resources. It was decided that the mine-sweeping effort of the combined WEU (now bolstered by German and Japanese forces) would continue and that an American carrier battle group would maintain a presence in the central Gulf. Apart from that, the United Nations would be petitioned to concentrate inspection efforts in the Red Sea approaches to Aqaba, the only real port of entry for cargo bound for Iraq, a task existing Coalition forces were already capable of handling.

In the light of these decisions, the presence of a Canadian destroyer was no longer necessary. The crew, too, were anxious to return home. Ever since their departure in early January, their deployment had been beset by the never-ending uncertainties of a continually changing mission. Fear for the safety of their families in Victoria was also a factor. In striking contrast to the overwhelming support from elsewhere in the nation, opposition by a local so-called peace element manifested itself in crude threats against the dependents of the crew.[13]

On 27 June, *Huron* passed through the Strait of Hormuz, outward bound for the last time. Since there were no plans to replace her, she undertook the long journey home, across the Indian and Pacific oceans, in effect circumnavigating the globe. HMCS *Huron* arrived in Esquimalt to a thunderous reception from families and friends, on 2 August 1991, a fitting commemoration of the first anniversary of Iraq's invasion of Kuwait.

But that was not to be the end of Canadian naval involvement in operations against Iraq. As recommended at the June 1991 MIF conference, the focus of Coalition embargo efforts shifted to the Red Sea in the autumn, but support for the embargo soon declined. By February 1992, only Australia and France remained on station with the United States Navy. The situation changed when the United Nations Security Council called for a renewed effort to enforce Resolutions 661 and 665. In response, the Canadian government agreed to dispatch another warship. Code-named Operation BARRIER, the task fell to *Restigouche*, a West Coast destroyer and sister ship to *Terra Nova*. With her FRICTION II upgrade equipment still intact, the *Restigouche* sailed from Esquimalt on 24 February 1992, passed through the Panama Canal on 14 March and the Suez Canal on 18 April, and joined MIF operations on the twenty-first.

Supported by a scaled-down version of the CANMARLOGDET, in Safaga, Egypt, *Restigouche* very quickly settled into the busy MIF routine of inspecting all shipping proceeding into Aqaba. Without exception, the ships boarded by the Canadians were cooperative, but a thorough search of holds and containers often took hours in the sweltering heat. A typical day would include two or three inspections. On one occasion, nine were undertaken.[14] Like *Huron* before her, *Restigouche* was also tasked to support Canadian diplomatic efforts in the area, and she became the first Canadian warship to make official port calls to Saudi Arabia (Jiddah, 4-7 May) and Israel (Haifa, 4-14 June).

Restigouche's last day of operations with the Multinational Interception Force was 4 July 1992. To mark Canada's 125th anniversary, the crew completed its 125th (and last) boarding inspection of the deployment. For the return journey, *Restigouche* also circumnavigated the globe, stopping for fuel in Colombo, Singapore, Guam, and Pearl Harbor. She arrived in Esquimalt on 21 August 1992, and the Canadian naval support for operations against Iraq were over.[15]

Operation FORUM (UNSCOM)
Clause C of Resolution 687 of 3 April established a United Nations Special Commission (UNSCOM) for the inspection, enumeration, and elimination of Iraq's weapons of mass destruction. By May 1991, multinational inspection teams were in place. They were given a mandate to locate all sites involved in the production of chemical and biological weapons and components for nuclear weapons. Canada was a member of this commission, contributing some twenty civilian and military experts in the verification and destruction of such weapons. Most of the Canadian members worked at Al Muthanna, near Baghdad, which had a stockpile of shells filled with harmful chemicals. But several were part of the team that inspected nuclear material production centres, bacteria production laboratories, missile sites, and even so-called superguns.

Iraq's chemical weapons production centre had laboratories for the industrial production of neurotoxic agents and mustard gas. Team members found these substances in thousands of warheads, including about thirty *Scud* missiles. Hundreds of tonnes of these products were packed into enough barrels to cover some 150 sq km. In addition, the ground was littered with bombs which had "wept" after being heated by the sun. They also discovered that the extremely potent Sarin was the most commonly used neurotoxic substance at Al Muthanna.

Canadians took part in three expeditions to this depot in 1991. During the first visit in June, they assessed the work required to decontaminate the place. They returned in September and destroyed those munitions not loaded with harmful substances, and, from October to December, they completed the decontamination. Several accidents occurred during this work. In one of them, an Iraqi was sprayed with toxic material when a shell exploded. He immediately lost consciousness and had to be given high doses of atropine and other medication in hospital. His colleagues' quick reaction saved his life.

Naturally, this type of accident did not reassure the inspectors. They had to go into overheated warehouses where munitions were sometimes in an advanced state of deterioration. Compounding the problem was the fact that Al Muthanna had been heavily shelled by Coalition forces during the war, and the damage caused by those bombardments created uncertainty as to the stability of the weapons and the chemicals used in their production. Sometimes individual containers broke, and ruined and overstocked buildings threatened to collapse. Wearing their protective clothing and gas masks, the inspectors approached the stocks with detectors, which occasionally showed sudden readings of dangerous concentrations. They had to take samples of the substances, analyse them, and decide on the best methods for disposing of the material. Master Warrant Officer Brian Brown, an instructor with the NBC School at CFB Borden, Ontario, served on a team of two which had to determine the relative danger posed by the munitions. He summed up his impressions by saying that despite his many years of experience, he acquired new and unique knowledge during his time at Al Muthanna and that the level of tension he felt decreased as his experience increased.[16] The expertise of the Defence Research Establishment at Suffield, Alberta also proved valuable for developing techniques for destroying these munitions. Dr Peter Lockwood, Chief of the Biomedical Defence Section, was a safety officer for two important projects at Al Muthanna. His job was to identify, sample, transport, and destroy substances in as safe a manner as possible for the inspectors.

Several Canadians were involved in one nerve-racking incident. Captain J.J. Mansfield and four colleagues were members of a forty-person inspection team taken prisoner by the Iraqis on 24 September 1991, after a team member discovered classified documents relating to arms production in a Baghdad building formerly used as headquarters for the nuclear research program. They were held captive for four days. It took ninety-six hours of international negotiations to convince the Iraqis that the documents had to stay with the inspectors. The five Canadians belonging to this group were released without having been mistreated. The material they had found was considered very important for analysing the full scope of Iraq's nuclear program.[17] Following this and other, similar incidents, the UN passed Security Council Resolution 715, on 11 October 1991, declaring the entire Iraqi military industry under the complete control of the UN.[18] Site inspections have continued in Iraq since that time, and twelve members of the Canadian Forces have remained on call to help multinational teams inspect and neutralize Iraq's chemical, biological, nuclear, and long range weapons. On average, two Canadians at a time are working within the framework of Operation FORUM, which is in its fourth year.

The Gulf war was not in vain. The Coalition victory over Saddam has allowed the UN to conduct a thorough campaign to destroy the dictator's many weapons of mass destruction.

Notes

1   One of the *Hornet* aircraft had been cannibalized for spares during the air war and had to be left behind, in the care of the American squadron remaining in Doha. A Canadian maintenance crew from Baden-Söllingen eventually returned with the required parts to make the aircraft serviceable, and it was flown back to Germany on 23 March.

2   On 19 March, a grand ceremony called WELCOME HOME was held in Ottawa to mark the return of a representative group of Canadian Forces personnel. The same day, three representatives of the forces were at Toronto's Maple Leaf Gardens for a special ceremony. On 8 April, six representatives accompanied by the CF Central Band were invited to open the Toronto Blue Jays baseball season, and one of them threw the first ball. The City of Toronto also paid homage to the Canadian military by organizing a welcome parade down its main streets on 29 April. The leading commanders and representative troops took part. And ceremonies were held across the country. Canadians even took part in the huge parade in New York to salute General Schwarzkopf and thank the U.S. military. Lastly, on 22 June, the first "Gulf and Kuwait 1990-1991" medals were issued on Parliament Hill to forty-two members of all trades and ranks. This ceremony was the main event of "National Armed Forces Day." See "National Armed Forces Day - 22 June 1991," *DND News Release*, AFN:21/91, 18 June 1991.

3   Major M.G. Fraser, "Prelude to Op Magnolia," *UBIQUE* No 38 (January 1992), pp. 5-6; and Captain K.J. Mills, "Op Magnolia," ibid., pp. 7-8.

4   Bomblets are either small explosive devices packed inside bombs dropped by aircraft or shells launched by multiple rocket launchers. These bomblets scatter over the ground and are exploded by various mechanisms, either by contact or as time bombs. Engineering soldiers fear them because they often malfunction and explode unexpectedly. They call these bomblets "baseballs of death" because they look vaguely like hardballs or softballs. Bomblets are all the more cruel because they attract children. A large number of them died or were horribly wounded by these devices in Kuwait, and some were victims even years afterward. The accident rate for Canadians was very low. Only one Canadian engineer was maimed by them: a Reserve master corporal lost two fingers and a thumb in January 1993. However, in the first ten months after hostilities ended, mine removal in Kuwait claimed eighty-four victims. There is a simple explanation for this. Canadians were significantly better trained than workers from other countries. An engineering soldier from Scarborough revealed that some Third World workers used ten-foot poles to handle mines, and a number them died as a result. See Bill Fairbairn, "Stepping Into the Minefield," *Legion* (August 1993), pp. 17-19.

5   See Dannreuther, *The Gulf Conflict*, pp. 64-67. The initiative for the resolution of 5 April 1991 came from France and then the United Kingdom. The record demonstrates that President Bush was gradually won over, in response to the momentum generated by events. However, Resolution 688 was not passed unanimously by the Security Council, on which Canada no longer sat. Cuba, Yemen, and Zimbabwe opposed it, and China and India abstained. They were reluctant to give the UN and the West the right to interfere in the internal affairs of a nation, however much it might be at fault.

6   Capt Renée Mactaggart, "Strategic & Tactical Missions of Mercy," *ATG Newsletter* 3, no. 2 (Fall 1991), pp. 15-18.

7   The crews came from 429 *Bison* and 436 *Elephant* squadrons at Trenton and 435 *Chinthe* at Edmonton. See Capt Mike Allen, "Feeding the Hungry," *AirForce* 15, no. 3 (Fall 1991), pp. 34-35.

8   Government of Canada, "Canadian Forces provide humanitarian aid for Iraqi refugees," *News Release*, 15 April 1991. See also *4 Field Ambulance — Outstanding Support in Peace and War* (Lahr, 1992), pp. 84-92.

9 Capt Brett Boudreau, "Refugee Relief," *Sentinel* 27, no. 4 (1991), pp. 2-5.

10 Ibid., "Hospital from Hell," *Sentinel* 27, no. 4 (1991), pp. 2-5; and LCol Les Dubinsky, "Medics make the difference in Kurdish refugee camps," *Der Kanadier*, (29 May 1991), pp. 1, 4.

11 National Defence, "The Deployment of HMCS *Huron* to the Persian Gulf," *News Release*, AFN:14/91, 26 March 1991.

12 DHist, DHN: 1325-1, *HMCS HURON [UIC 7712] Annual Historical Report, 1991*, 13 February 1992.

13 "Harassment: Navy officer's wife finds body bag dumped on lawn," *Vancouver Sun*, 21 January 1991.

14 Lt(N) Andrew Liebmann, "Patrolling the Red Sea," *Sentinel* 28, no. 6 (Dec 1992/ Jan 1993), pp. 2-4.

15 At the time of *Restigouche*'s deployment, none of the new frigates were ready for operations; nor were any of the DDH-280 class any longer available, because *Huron* was preparing to join *Athabaskan* and their sisters for the TRUMP refit. Newly commissioned Canadian Patrol Frigates finally appeared in the Persian Gulf in 1995, when HMCS *Fredericton* (FFH-337) visited Kuwait City, Abu Dhabi, and Dubai in March, and HMCS *Calgary* (FFH-335) arrived in the fall to join a reconstituted MIF.

16 Capt Brett Boudreau, "The most dangerous place in the world," *Sentinel* 28, no.2 (1992), pp. 2-6.

17 Capt JoJo Mansfield, "Trapped in Baghdad!" *Sentinel* 28, no. 2 (1992), p. 6. The four Canadians accompanying Capt Mansfield were Warrant Officer Tom Stuart, Warrant Officer Steve Gordon, Sergeant Brock Durette, and Master Corporal Paul Mitchell. They were combat engineers from the Canadian Forces in Europe.

18 Coulon, *La dernière croisade*, Chapter 17, "Une boîte de Pandore," p. 166.

Afterword

The summer of 1990 caught Canada and the rest of the Western world unprepared for Iraq's invasion of Kuwait. The collapse of communism in eastern Europe and the end of the bipolar world held the promise of a less hostile future in a new world order. Keeping in step with other military forces in the West, Canadian Forces were busy adapting to changes brought about by "the peace dividend." Moreover, attention in Canada was turned for the moment to internal security when the troubles at Oka threatened an escalation of the military intervention. Saddam's conquest of Kuwait came at this critical juncture in national and world affairs. The results of Canada's participation in the Coalition tell us a great deal about the "Canadian way of war."

The national response to the crisis in the Persian Gulf in 1990-91 had everything to do with continuing Canada's self-ascribed role of "middle power." For the fifth time in its military history, Canada dispatched an overseas expeditionary force. The expeditions to the Boer War, the two world wars, and Korea were undertaken during the half century when the middle power role was emerging and being defined. Forty years after Korea, with that status entrenched but untested in war, the force dispatched to the Persian Gulf was significant for its departures from the "model" experience.

Although naval forces had been the first in action in both the Second World War and Korea, and thousands of Canadians had been in the air force in both world wars, the army had hitherto predominated in every overseas conflict. The Gulf deployment was marked by the absence of a sizeable ground force, leaving the navy and air force to take centre stage for the first time. On each of the four previous occasions, major adjustments were required to the existing military establishments, which were basically the product of theoretical constructs fashioned in peacetime. Nor was there the traditional call for "volunteer" enlistment in large-scale contingents: all Canadian forces sent to the Persian Gulf were regular serving units, the ad hoc nature of 90 Signals and Headquarters Squadron and of 1 Canadian Field Hospital notwithstanding. And in the past, the appointment of national theatre commanders had always devolved on single-service representatives with offices established close to the allied councils. This was not the case in the Gulf war. Commodore Summers' mission was constituted in a Joint Headquarters that was located far from the centre of power in the Coalition capital of Riyadh.

Finally, there was no traditional postwar occupation force. Instead, Canada participated in a peacekeeping contingent. This fulfilled the prediction General de Chastelain made at the start of the crisis. As it turned out, Canadian Forces assumed an important role in the UNIKOM mission to patrol the demilitarized zone between Iraq and Kuwait. But even the peacekeeping involvement, familiar as it had become over the years, was also a departure from the past. The Gulf crisis encouraged the United Nations to undertake a broader role in the management of world affairs. In a bold departure from previous missions, Canada supported UN intervention in the internal affairs of another country: it helped to supply humanitarian aid for displaced Kurdish refugees and joined weapons inspection teams inside Iraq.

The initial intent that the forces deployed in the Persian Gulf would act as a joint force was as ill-founded as it was ultimately unnecessary. The legacy of forty-five years of armed peace - in Canada's case, the last twenty-five of them as an integrated force - was a mixed one. The strength in numbers philosophy of collective security arrangements, such as NATO and NORAD, kept Canada's defence budget expenditures relatively low. However, participation in these alliances maintained both a degree of specialization within each of Canada's air, land, and sea forces and of interdependency with sister services of other nations. For all the flexibility which each traditional service of the armed forces was able to display, their discrete commitments left them poorly prepared to cooperate with each other in national joint operations. For example, neither equipment nor procedures allowed the CF-18s to provide direct air support to the Canadian task group. Consequently, the Joint Headquarters in Manamah was not used on the operational level - tactical control (TACON) of all elements was assigned to American and British commanders - but as an in-theatre tool for national commanders in Ottawa to manage the level of participation.

Canadian forces were governed by a paradox. They were unable to operate jointly as a national force despite the promises of a quarter century of unification; but each individual service was admirably prepared to combine with similar forces from allied nations. Hence, the navy joined the multinational embargo and later the logistics protection force; the air force flew defensive patrols over American carriers and escorted offensive missions into Iraq; the field hospital was part of a British medical facility; and dozens of Canadians served on exchange duties as integral members of deployed allied (NATO, American, British, and French) units. Despite the limitations of years of single-service commitments and budgetary neglect, Canadian forces proved remarkably versatile. The air force operated effectively in a naval air defence environment and changed roles several times during the short span of the actual combat. And the command and control capabilities in the Canadian ships allowed the task group commander to exercise an important wartime coordination function over allied forces.

Afterword

Coalition warfare allows member nations a greater degree of independence than strictly defined alliance requirements, a fact not lost on Canadian commanders as they struggled to maintain a recognizable Canadian identity in the Coalition. And it was a mighty struggle. There were only three Canadian ships among the hundreds of Coalition naval vessels; only twenty-four bombers among the thousands of Coalition aircraft; and there was only one Canadian field hospital. To make matters even more difficult, their small headquarters was not in the Saudi capital. All told, Canada had an in-theatre personnel strength never exceeding 2,700 men and women. Canadian Forces should have been lost amid the half million men and women under arms. But they were not, because Canadian commanders insisted on national control over their troops' employment. Even when tactical control was extended to foreign commanders, it was done on the understanding that there were specific limitations, a sort of "TACON with a veto." Certainly, Canadian units could have operated just as effectively, if not more so in some cases, under the direct command of American or British Coalition commanders. They could have conducted operations quietly and anonymously, as just another flag on the board, but to what national advantage? At stake was Canada's acquired status as a middle power. Although there existed strong impulses to yield to American management, senior officials at External Affairs and National Defence exhibited a rare unanimity of purpose. They were determined to make a meaningful contribution to the Coalition, one that would add to the Coalition's superiority over Iraq and support the middle-of-the-road Canadian policy on a resolution to the crisis. Canadian commanders in the theatre accordingly exploited every opportunity to assure Canada's distinctive role in the conflict.

Rating Canada's participation in the war against Iraq is therefore difficult. It defies quantification in the traditional military sense of crossing swords with an enemy and inflicting and suffering casualties. It is clear that the will of the Canadian people, brought to bear on daily government decisions with the help of modern polling techniques, was not insignificant in the search for criteria other than the iron vessel, which measures only blood, to find worth. Only once did a Canadian unit serving in the Gulf meet an opposing Iraqi force, when the team of Captain Hill and Major Kendall strafed a fleeing Iraqi patrol boat. Beyond that, the only other type of offensive operation undertaken was the CF-18's bombing role - in itself a rather detached form of warfare - and given the post-war reassessment of Iraqi casualties, it is unlikely that even those missions inflicted many casualties.

That is not to imply that Canadian forces did not expect, or were not prepared, to take on the enemy. Five short months before the launch of DESERT STORM, National Defence Headquarters conducted a survey of the different SANDY SAFARI scenarios in which Canada might participate. At the time of the survey, though, no military officer, politician, or think-tank expert could have predicted Canada's role in the Coalition of nations that was to repel Saddam's forces and inflict such enormous damage on his military infrastructure. Canada's armed forces were structured and trained for a North Atlantic or continental European threat. But in the end, considering the forces at play, it may not be that surprising that each element of the Canadian Forces deployed in the Gulf war, albeit for its own reasons, functioned so well in a non-traditional fashion. The navy task group commander organized the protection of a loosely bound multinational logistical force. The air force flew protective cover for allied naval forces. The army set up a state-of-the-art field hospital.

None of these truly excited the interest or earned the gratitude of Canada's Coalition partners. Theatre commanders and diplomats in New York certainly appreciated Canada's participation in the Coalition, but, since the end of operations against Iraq, the not inconsequential Canadian contribution has been studiously ignored. Mainstream American, British, and French accounts of the conflict make only passing (if any) reference to Canada's role in the Coalition victory.[1]

The obvious reason for Canada's postwar banishment to obscurity in official histories of the Gulf war is that perceptions are extremely important to one's status within a coalition. The problem of "quantifiable accountability" was sensed by Canadian military commanders as the conflict progressed. But attempts to redefine our participation in terms more meaningful to the major Coalition partners only served to detract from the value of the Canadian effort. Confusion attended the escalation of the CF-18 role from defensive combat air patrols to frontline sweep and escort and finally to bombing missions. The logistical protection force chased an enemy that failed to materialize. And the Canadian armed forces were unable to put together a mechanized brigade group.

On a more basic level, there was the cost of the deployment. The total cost of all Canadian Forces operations in the Gulf region was $682 million (calculated in September 1991). With the addition of foreign aid expenditures made through the Department of External Affairs, the total was probably closer to $1 billion. When one considers how onerous a burden that was on a recession-threatened economy, Canada contributed more than its fair share to the costs of the Coalition.[2] However, a nation's participation in a war cannot be judged solely by budgetary allotments. Judgment must be made on the depth and quality of the logistical and personnel support it gave to its deployed forces. In the case of Canada, this support was slight. Luck played too big a part in the fact that the CPF and TRUMP programmes provided ready equipment for the naval task group and that the CF-18s involved in the war did not require just a few more spare parts.

In the end, though, the Canadian government got exactly what it wanted: an active but limited participation in the Coalition that was conducted at arm's length from direct American control, and to a degree to which a middle power with a limited defence budget can realistically aspire in the expensive high-technology business of modern war. Playing their assigned roles, the Canadian Forces in the

Gulf performed admirably, providing their government with a credible military presence in support of the policies of the Cabinet at home and our ambassador at the United Nations.

Operation FRICTION was a defining moment for the Canadian Forces. While it remains to be seen how postwar events will unfold over the long term, the national military effort of 1990-91 was a fitting testament to the professionalism and dedication of the Canadian Forces at all levels. Behind the senior decision-makers were thousands of junior officers, sailors, soldiers, and airmen, who performed their duties quietly and effectively, enabling their commanders to make commitments they knew would be fulfilled.

In the end, it was a meaningful contribution.

Notes

1 Prior to this volume, there has been only one full-length Canadian treatment of the Gulf war, Coulon's *La dernière croisade : La guerre du Golfe et le rôle caché du Canada*. Coulon's work is generally positive, but its publication in French undoubtedly limited the size of its audience and the extent of its impact on public opinion.

2 Katsuaki L. Terasawa and William R. Gates, "Burden-Sharing in the Persian Gulf: Lessons Learned and Implications for the Future," *Defense Analysis* 9, no. 2 (August 1993), pp. 171-95.

Appendices

Canadian Forces Rank Insignia

General Officers
Officiers généraux

Army/Air Force	General	Lieutenant-general	Major-general	Brigadier-general
Armée/Aviation	général	lieutenant-général	major-général	brigadier-général
Navy	Admiral	Vice-Admiral	Rear-Admiral	Commodore
Marine	amiral	vice-amiral	contre-amiral	commodore

Junior Officers
Officiers subalternes

Army/Air Force	Captain	Lieutenant	Second-Lieutenant
Armée/Aviation	capitaine	lieutenant	sous-lieutenant
Navy	Lieutenant (N)	Sub-Lieutenant	Acting Sub-Lieutenant
Marine	lieutenant (M)	sous-lieutenant	sous-lieutenant intérimaire

Army/Air Force	Chief Warrant Officer	Master Warrant Officer	Warrant Officer
Armée/Aviation	adjudant-chef	adjudant-maître	adjudant
Navy	Chief Petty Officer 1st class	Chief Petty Officer 2nd class	Petty Officer 1st class
Marine	premier maître de 1re classe	premier maître de 2e classe	maître de 1re classe

OFFICER RANKS / SIGNES DISTINCTIFS DES GRADES D'OFFICIER

Senior Officers
Officiers
supérieurs

Army/Air Force	Colonel	Lieutenant-Colonel	Major
Armée/Aviation	colonel	lieutenant-colonel	major
Navy	Captain (N)	Commander	Lieutenant-Commander
Marine	capitaine (M)	commander	lieutenant-commander

Subordinate Officers
Officiers subordonnés

Army/Air Force	Officer Cadet
Armée/Aviation	élève-officier
Navy	Naval Cadet
Marine	élève-officier

NCM RANKS / SIGNES DISTINCTIFS PERSONNEL NON-OFFICIER

Army/Air Force	Sergeant	Master Corporal	Corporal	Private
Armée/Aviation	sergent	caporal-chef	caporal	soldat
Navy	Petty Officer 2nd class	Master Seaman	Leading Seaman	Able Seaman
Marine	maître de 2ᵉ classe	matelot-chef	matelot de 1ʳᵉ classe	matelot de 2ᵉ classe

Ship Equipment Upgrades for Operation FRICTION

SYSTEM/WEAPON	SHIP(S) FITTED	FROM	USE	REPLACED	DESCRIPTION
Phalanx CIWS (Close-In Weapons System)	ALL	CPF/ TRUMP	AAW	ATH/TER-Mortars PRO-New	Automatic self-defence system designed to engage fast moving air targets within one mile of the ship. It fires a 20mm high density round at a rate of 3000 rounds/min. It works on the principle of the radar tracking the target and guiding the bullets to the target. It is capable of tracking multiple targets simultaneously.
HARPOON	TER	CPF	ASUW	ASROC	A subsonic, active radar homing, fire-and-forget anti-ship missile, there is no update of the target enroute. It has a range in excess of 60nm and one hit is estimated to disable most ships.
SRBOC (Super-Rapid-Blooming Offboard Chaff)	PRO[1]	STOCK	AAW		Several canisters mounted in multiple mortar launchers. Chaff effectively creates a false radar image of the ship at a set distance away. SRBOC is deployed at the very last minute to seduce incoming anti-ship missiles away from the ship.
SHIELD	ATH PRO	CPF	AAW		Shield consists of a number of short range rockets fired out of tubes. The rockets carry either infra-red or chaff decoys for anti-ship missile defence. It can be deployed in either a seduction or distraction role.
KESTREL	PRO	STOCK[2]	EW		Broadband ESM receiver with an instantaneous bearing capability and a very high probability of intercept, allowing the ship to detect the emissions of ship, missile, or aircraft radars. They are equipped with separate automatic computer operated threat library.
ALR-76	ATH	STOCK[3]	EW		Broadband ESM receiver with characteristics similar to Kestrel.
DLF-2 (Rubber Duck)	TER	NEW	AAW		A passive, inflatable decoy system which is dropped off the ship in a canister. It is designed to decoy a missile away from the ship.

1   Already fitted in *Terra Nova*.
2   Kestrel was in the process of being procured for fitting in all Canadian AORs.
3   The ALR-76 had been removed from surplus CP-121 *Tracker* aircraft up for disposal.

SYSTEM/WEAPON	SHIP(S) FITTED	FROM	USE	REPLACED	DESCRIPTION
40MM BOFFIN (BOFORS)	ALL	STOCK	AAW/ ASUW		A manually trained and aimed weapon, it has a range of 5000 meters and fires a tracer round with a proximity fuse at a rate of 120 rounds/min. It is effective against small manoeuvrable ships and slow flying aircraft.
.50 cal MG	ALL	STOCK	AAW/ ASUW		A fast firing (450 rounds/min) heavy calibre machine gun which is manually aimed. It has a range of 1500 meters (against a small fast moving target) and employs a tracer round.
JAVELIN	ALL	NEW	AAW	BLOWPIPE	A shoulder launched, optically guided short range missile system, with a range of three kilometres, used against fast moving air targets.
INMARSAT	ALL	NEW	COMM		A commercial satellite communications system, it offers the ships worldwide communications via satellite and the commercial telephone system. When used in conjunction with STU III, capable of handling secure voice and facsimile communications.
SATCOM/DAMA (Demand Assigned Multiple Access Satellite Communications)	ALL	STOCK/ NEW	COMM		SATCOM is a military satellite communication system (USN FLEETSAT) capable of handling secure voice and teletype communications. DAMA offers the flexibility of multi-channel simultaneous transmissions.
JOTS (Joint Operational Tactical System)	ALL	STOCK	C²		A command decision aid capable of automatic or manual updating of high interest targets.
ADLIPS (Automated Data-Link Plotting System)	PRO⁴	STOCK	C²		A computer operated system for the plotting of radar information and which allows for the exchange of information with other ships on a computer-to-computer basis via Link 11.
Spectra-Scan 3000 MAS (Mine Avoidance Sonar)	ALL⁵	NEW	MCM		A Canadian developed sonar (C-Tech, located in Cornwall, Ont), it is a short range, high frequency set with a 360-degree scanning capability with a maximum range of 4000 yds and minimum range of 200 yds.
HYPERFIX	ATH TER	STOCK⁶	MCM		A medium range, extremely accurate electronic positioning system. It is used in the coastal areas of the Gulf for very precise navigation.

4 Already fitted in *Terra Nova, Athabaskan* had a different (CSS-280) system.
5 Fitted in all, bur subsequently lost from *Protecteur* (see later text).
6 Had been purchased for fitting in Canadian MCM vessels.

Sea King Equipment Upgrades for Operation FRICTION

SYSTEM/WEAPON	FROM	USE	DESCRIPTION
FLIR 2000 (Forward Looking Infrared)	NEW	ASUW	A thermal imaging system to enhance night surveillance capability.
STABILIZED BINOCULARS (FUJINON Model S1040)	NEW	ASUW	Gyro-stabilized binoculars used to identify surface contacts at extended ranges.
GPS (Global Positioning System)	NEW	ASUW	A worldwide day/night all weather navigation system which uses satellite information to calculate accurate positions.
HAVEQUICK	NEW	COMM	UHF secure voice radio.
ALQ-144/ M130 (Infrared Countermeasures)	NEW/ STOCK	ASE	Protects against infrared heat-seeking missiles; in conjunction with the M130 flare dispense system, decoys incoming infrared missiles away from the helicopter.
APR-39 (Radar Warning Receiver)	STOCK	ASE	A passive omni-directional radar receiver used to warn aircrew of radar controlled missile threats.
ALE-37 (CHAFF Dispensing System)	STOCK	ASE	Dispenses CHAFF to deceive incoming radar guided missiles.
LWR (Laser Warning Receiver)	NEW	ASE	Detects and alerts aircrew of laser energy being directed at the helicopter.
NVG (Night Vision Goggles)	NEW	ASUW	An image intensification device which amplifies ambient light to allow visual detection and identification at night.
C-9 LMG (Light Machine Gun)	STOCK	ASUW/ASE	Provides a self-defence capability.

Airlift and Sealift in Persian Gulf Operations

OPERATION	AIRLIFT (TONS)	SEALIFT (TONS)	TOTAL
FRICTION	3,000	245.3	3,245.3
SCIMITAR	1,500	-	1,500
ACCORD	100	-	100
SCALPEL	485.7	1,740.7	2,226.4
SPONGE	111.2	-	111.2
IRON SABRE	228.3	-	228.3
NATO SUPPORT	191.2	-	191.2
TOTAL	5,616.4	1,986.0	7,602.4
DESERT SHIELD / DESERT STORM TOTAL	486,500	2,845,000	3,331,500
RECORD	175	-	175
ASSIST	582.5	-	582.5
AXE	12.5	-	12.5
TOTAL	770	-	770

Honours and Awards – Persian Gulf 1990–1991

Order of Canada - Officer
General John A.J.G.D de Chastelain
(Awarded for service as CDS, including involvment in Gulf War operations)

Meritorious Service Cross
Lieutenant-General David Huddleston
Commodore Kenneth J. Summers
Colonel Roméo H. Lalonde
Captain (N) Duncan E. Miller
Major Richard Eugène Isabelle
Mr William Bowden
Mr Mohammed Jaafar
Mr Eoin MacDonald

Meritorious Service Cross (to foreign nationals)
General Colin L. Powell (USA)
Vice-Admiral H. Mauz (USN)
Lieutenant-General C. Horner (USAF)
Lieutenant-General Sir Peter de la Billière

Meritorious Service Medal
Colonel Philip Christopher Engstad
Colonel Michael G. O'Brien
Colonel William Hiram Minnis
Lieutenant-Colonel Donald Charles Matthews
Major Joseph Armand Pierre Rochefort
Captain Jeffrey Gordon Beckett
Captain George Kenneth Campbell
Chief Petty Officer Second Class David George Ashley
Master Warrant Officer Robert James Bissett
Master Warrant Officer George Allison Leach

Chief Petty Officer Second Class Mary Nanette Wilson
Sergeant Wade Greeley
Master Corporal J.C. Wight
Mr Albert Bamboukian
Mr Britton Mockbridge
Mr Ron Waugh
Ms Sharon Waugh

Mentions-in-Despatches
Rear-Admiral Bruce Johnston
Colonel David W. Bartram
Commander Stuart Douglas Andrews
Commander Jean-Yves Forcier
Lieutenant-Colonel John Noel Stuart
Lieutenant-Colonel Dennis James Roberts
Lieutenant-Commander James Terrance Hewitt
Major Richard Daniel Kelly
Major D.W. Kendall
Captain S.P. Hill
Master Warrant Officer F. Churchill
Chief Petty Officer Second Class H. Cooper
Chief Petty Officer Second Class I.D. Corkum
Master Warrant Officer D.W. Downard
Master Warrant Officer J.R. Palmer
Warrant Officer Collin Afflect
Warrant Officer J.G.M.A. Bolduc
Sergeant D.L. Chiasson
Sergeant J.W.M. Gauthier
Sergeant C. Ralph

CDS Commendations
Commodore James Archibald King
Captain(N) Gregory Evan Jarvis
Commander Robert George Allen
Commander Michael Henry Jellinek
Lieutenant-Colonel Lawrence Albert McWha
Commander Jerry Peacocke
Commander William Joseph Poole
Commander Pierre Thiffault
Lieutenant-Commander Richard John Dickinson
Major Anthony Glynne Hines

Lieutenant-Commander Darren W. Knight
Lieutenant-Commander John Alfred Westlake
Captain Linda Bossi
Lieutenant (N) Bruce William Belliveau
Captain John Frederick Peckitt
Chief Petty Officer Second Class Serge Jean-Marie Joncas
Chief Petty Officer Second Class Jack Richard McMullen
Master Warrant Officer Gary Myers
Warrant Officer Edmund James Condon
Warrant Officer Bernard Lawrence McCarthy
Warrant Officer Pius Gerard McIntyre
Warrant Officer Joseph Wayne Parsons
Warrant Officer W.V.L. Leclair
Sergeant Mark O'Connor
Master Corporal Randy S. Shepherd
Master Corporal Gary Joseph Vienneau
Corporal Jerome Fitzherbert
Corporal Pauline Joyce Giese
Corporal Ronald J. Gignac
Corporal Jonathan Victor Steele
Corporal Chester Edson Warner

CF Medallion
Mrs Maria Brûlotte
Mr Robert Harry Keddy
Mr Peter Smedley
Mr D.G. Elphick
Mr W.H. Eastwood

Gulf and Kuwait, 1990-1991, Medal
All Canadian Forces members who served within the limits of the Canadian Forces Middle East (CANFORME) Special Duty Area, or who were otherwise specially involved in Operation FRICTION, were awarded a campaign medal struck to acknowledge their service. The face (obverse) of the medal is a profile of the Queen of Canada with the inscription "Elizabeth II Dei Gratia Regina". The reverse bears the inscription "The Gulf and Kuwait 1990-1991 - Le Golfe et Kuwait 1990-1991", surrounded by a wreath of laurel with a maple leaf centred at the base. The associated ribbon is made up of seven coloured bands. In the centre, a band of yellow sand represents the desert. Six other bands represent (two each, moving outwards) the navy (navy blue), the army (scarlet), and the air force (sky blue) which all contributed to the

multinational force. Members serving in the theatre during hostilities wear a clasp to the medal.

Some 4,660 medals were struck following the operations of 1990-1991. In ddition to military personnel, eleven civilians from the public service received the Gulf and Kuwait 1990-1991 medal: from Chief Research and Development, D.N. Benson, C.G. Coffey, Dr J. Ho, A.B. Markov, D.H. Saint, and M.R. Spence; from the Ship Repair Unit (Atlantic), G.L. Publicover, J.L. Gratto, N. Halliday, and W. MacKinlay; from the Naval Engineering Unit (Atlantic), A.F. McGrath; and the civilian artist involved in the Canadian Forces Civilian Artist Program (CAFCAP), Ted Zuber.

The first Gulf and Kuwait 1990-1991 campaign medals were presented by the Governor-General of Canada, His Excellency Raymond Hnatyshyn, to 42 representatives of the Canadian Forces, on 22 June 1991, in the course of a ceremony on Parliament Hill.

Battle Honours - "Persian Gulf 1990-1991"
HMCS *Protecteur*
HMCS *Athabaskan*
HMCS *Terra Nova*
423 Helicopter Anti-Submarine Squadron
439 Tactical Fighter Squadron

Honorary Distinction (by CDS)
416 Tactical Fighter Squadron
437 Transport Squadron

Unit Commendations
HMCS *Protecteur*
HMCS *Athabaskan*
HMCS *Terra Nova*
409 Tactical Fighter Squadron
Company "M", 3rd Batallion, Royal Canadian Regiment
2 Air Movements Unit
Ship Repair Unit Atlantic
Naval Engineering Unit Atlantic
416 Tactical Fighter Squadron
439 Tactical Fighter Squadron
423 Helicopter Anti-Submarine Squadron
CF Crypto Maintenance Unit (Ottawa)
1 Combat Engineer Regiment (for UNIKOM)

FOREIGN AWARDS

Bronze Star Medal (United States)
Commodore Kenneth J. Summers
Lieutenant-Colonel John MacNeil
Major Brian W. Travis
Major Kevin A. Moher

Meritorious Service Medal (United States)
Major Robert T. Jensen

Air Medal (United States)
Major Pierre J. Beauchamp
Captain Bjorn H. Helby
Captain James T. Rolfe

Joint Service Commendation Medal (United States)
Captain J.J.L. Serge Pelletier

Medal of Bahrain
Commodore Kenneth J. Summers
Colonel David W. Bartram
Lieutenant-Colonel John Noel Stuart
Lieutenant-Colonel James Bender
Commander David Banks

Medal of Kuwait
Commodore Kenneth J. Summers
Commodore Duncan E. Miller
Colonel Roméo Lalonde

Kuwait Liberation Medal
The Kuwait Liberation Medal was offered by Saudi Arabia to all members of all allied armed forces serving in the theatre, and accepted by Canada on behalf of serving members. The wearing of a second medal for exactly the same service being "contrary to national honours policy", however, each qualified person has received the medal, but without permission to "mount or wear in conjunction with official orders, decorations and medals."

Bibliography

This bibliography represents the major unclassified sources referred to in the preparation of this narrative. Citations are made in the language of origin. The authors also had full access to available unit reports, war diaries, and message traffic, and conducted interviews with many participants. Although many of these sources remain classified, they have been cited where appropriate in the text. Valuable resources open to researchers at the Directorate of History are *Annual Historical Reports* (by unit) and "Iraq-Kuwait Press Roundup" files, prepared during Operation FRICTION by the Director General of Public Affairs in NDHQ.

Two important sources not listed below are the journals of the Canadian Forces, *Sentinel* and *Sentinelle* and the newspaper *Der Kanadier*. Before being cancelled for budgetary reasons in 1994, they carried numerous articles on the operations of the Canadian Forces. As well, the official Press Releases, Communiqués, and Backgounders of various government departments are not listed; nor, in general, are newspaper or magazine articles. All these and further details may be found in the chapter endnotes.

Primary Sources

Canada. Cabinet de Premier ministre. «Notes pour une conférence de presse du Premier ministre Mulroney, Tribune de la presse nationale, 10 août 1990».

Canada. Cabinet de Premier ministre. «Notes pour une conférence de presse du Premier ministre Mulroney, Tribune de la presse nationale, 14 septembre 1990».

Canada. Chambre des communes. *Débats* [var., septembre 1990 - mars 1991].

Canada. Chambre des communes. *Procès-verbaux et témoignages du Comité permanent des Affaires étrangères et du Commerce extérieur* [var., janvier - février 1991].

Canada. Chambre des communes. *Procès-verbaux et témoignages du Comité permanent de la Défense nationale et des affaires des Anciens combattants* [var., septembre 1990 - mars 1991].

Canada. Défense nationale. *Liste des officiers des Forces canadiennes (Forces régulière)* [A-AD-224-001/AF-001]. Ottawa: Ministre des Approvisionnements et Services du Canada, 1990, 1991.

Canada. Department of National Defence. *Canadian Forces Officers List (Regular)* [A-AD-224-001/AF-001]. Ottawa: Ministry of Supply and Services Canada, 1990, 1991.

Canada. House of Commons. *Debates* [var., September 1990 - March 1991].

Canada. House of Commons. *Minutes of Proceedings and Evidence of the Standing Committee on External Affairs and International Trade* [var., January - February 1991].

Bibliography

Canada. House of Commons. *Minutes of Proceedings and Evidence of the Standing Committee on National Defence and Veterans Affairs* [var., September 1990 - March 1991].

Canada. Office of the Prime Minister. "Speaking Notes for Prime Minister Brian Mulroney Press Conference, National Press Theatre, 10 August 1990."

Canada. Office of the Prime Minister. "Speaking Notes for Prime Minister Brian Mulroney Press Conference, National Press Theatre, 14 September 1990."

Comité International de la Croix-Rouge. *Les Conventions de Genève du 12 août 1949.* Genève: Comité International de la Croix-Rouge, 1977.

Comité International de la Croix-Rouge. *Les Protocoles additionnels aux Conventions de Genève du 12 août 1949.* Genève: Comité International de la Croix-Rouge, 1977.

Dye, Kenneth M. *Rapport du vérificateur général du Canada à la Chambre des communes : exercice financier clos le 31 mars 1990.* Ottawa: Ministre des Approvisionnements et Services du Canada, 1990.

Dye, Kenneth M. *Report of the Auditor-General of Canada to the House of Commons: Financial Year ending 31 March 1990.* Ottawa: Ministry of Supply and Services Canada, 1990.

International Comittee of the Red Cross. *The Geneva Conventions of August 12 1949.* Geneva: International Committee of the Red Cross, 1977.

International Committee of the Red Cross. *Protocols Additional to the Geneva Conventions of 12 August 1949.* Geneva: International Commitee of the Red Cross, 1977.

United Nations. *Resolutions of the Security Council of the United Nations, 1990-1991.*

Secondary Sources

4 Field Ambulance: Outstanding Support in Peace and War. Lahr: Demmer, 1992.

Arnett, Peter. *Live from the Battlefield: From Vietnam to Baghdad, 35 Years in the World's War Zones.* New York: Simon & Schuster, 1994.

Atkinson, Rick. *Crusade: The Untold Story of the Persian Gulf War.* Boston: Houghton Mifflin Company, 1993.

Bethlehem, D.L., ed. *The Kuwait Crisis: Sanctions and Their Economic Conseuqences.* Cambridge International Documents Series, vol. 2. Cambridge: Grotius, 1991.

Blackwell, Major James (US Army, retd). *Thunder in the Desert: The Strategy and Tactics of the Persian Gulf War.* New York: Bantam Books, 1991.

Blair, Colonel Arthur H. (US Army, retd). *At War in the Gulf: A Chronology.* College Station, Texas: Texas A & M University Press, 1992.

Blanchette, Major Richard V. *Qatar : 1er Bataillon, Compagnie C, Royal 22e Régiment; décembre 90 - mars 91.* [publication privée].

Bland, Douglas. *The Administration of Defence Policy in Canada 1947 to 1985.* Kingston: Ronald P. Frye, 1987.

Boulden, Jane, and David Cox. *The Guide to Canadian Policies on Arms Control,*

Bibliography

Disarmament, Defence and Conflict Resolution, 1991 and *1992* (short title: *The Guide, [year]*). Ottawa: Canadian Institute for International Peace and Security, 1991 and 1992.

Boulden, Jane, et David Cox. *Guide sur les politiques canadiennes relatives à la limitation des armements, au désarmement, à la défense et à la solution des conflits, 1991* et *1992* (titre court: *Le Guide, [date]*). Institut canadien pour la paix et la sécurité internationales : Ottawa, 1991.

Braybrook, Roy. *F/A-18 Hornet*. London: Osprey, 1991.

Canada. Department of National Defence [Colonel A.P. Humphreys, team leader]. 1258-99 (DGPE), NDHQ Program Evaluation E3/92, "Command and Control, Volume 2, A Case Study: Operation FRICTION (The Gulf Crisis)," 13 October 1993.

Canada. Secrétariat du Conseil du Trésor [Stephen Tsang coordonnateur]. «OPERATION FRICTION : La remise en état de trois navires de guerre à destination du golfe Persique. Un exemple de succès de gestion du matériel». Ottawa: Ministre des Approvisionnements et Services du Canada, septembre 1991.

Canada. Treasury Board Secretariat [Stephen Tsang coordinator]. "OPERATION FRICTION: Refitting Three War Ships for the Persian Gulf - A Success Story in Materiel Management." Ottawa: Ministry of Supply and Services Canada, September 1991.

Canby, Thomas Y. "After the Storm." *National Geographic* 180, no. 2 (August 1991): 2-35.

Careless, J.M.S. "Frontierism, Metropolitanism and Canadian History." In *Approaches to Canadian History*, ed. by Ramsay Cook. Toronto: University of Toronto Press, 1967.

Carhart, Tom. *Iron Soldiers; How America's First Armored Division Crushed Iraq's Elite Republican Guard*. New York: Pocket Books, 1994.

Cohen, Roger, and Claudio Gatti. *In the Eye of the Storm: The Life of General H. Norman Schwarzkopf*. New York: Farrar, Straus and Giroux, 1991.

Cordesman, Anthony H., and Abraham R. Wagner. *The Lessons of Modern War*. Vol. 2, *The Iran-Iraq War*. Boulder, Colorado: Westview, 1990.

Coulon, Jocelyn (avec la collaboration de Yvan Cliche). *La dernière croisade : La guerre du Golfe et le rôle caché du Canada*. Montréal: Méridien, 1992.

Craig, Commodore C.J.S. (RN). "Desert Shield / Desert Storm - The Right Flank." *The Naval Review* 80, no. 1 (January 1992): 3-7; and 80, no. 2 (Spring 1992): p. 156 ("Addendum").

Crickard, Rear-Admiral (retd) Fred W., and Lieutenant-Commander Richard H. Gimblett. "The Navy as an Instrument of Middle Power Foreign Policy: Canada in Korea 1950 and the Persian Gulf 1990." In *Maritime Forces in Global Security: Comparative Views of Maritime Strategy as We Approach the 21st Century*, edited by Ann L. Griffiths and Peter Haydon. Halifax, NS: Dalhousie University Centre for Foreign Policy Studies, 1995.

Cromwell, William C. "Europe, the United States, and the pre-war Gulf crisis." *International Journal* 48 no. 1 (Winter 1992-1993): 124-50.

Cutter Information Corporation. *Oil Spill Intelligence Report*. International Newsletter 15 (26 March 1992).

Bibliography

Dannreuther, Roland. "The Gulf Conflict: A Political and Strategic Analysis." *Adelphi Papers* no. 264 (Winter 1991-1992).

Daponte, B.O. "A Case Study in Estimating casualties from War and its Aftermath: the 1991 Persian Gulf War." *Medecine and War: International Concerns on War and other Social Violence* 9, no. 4 (October - December 1993): 367 [summary].

David, Charles-Philippe (avec la collaboration de Martin Girard et Charles Van Der Donckt). *La Guerre du Golfe : L'Illusion de la Victoire*. Montréal: Art Global, 1992.

Deere, Captain David, ed. *Desert Cats: The Canadian Fighter Squadron in the Gulf War*. Stoney Creek, Ont: Fortress Publications, 1991.

de la Billière, General Sir Peter. *Storm Command: A Personal Account of the Gulf War*. London: Harper Collins, 1992.

France. Le Service d'information et de relations publiques de la Marine. *Marine et guerre du Golfe : août 1990 - août 1991. Une année d'opérations navales au Moyen-Orient*. [Paris:] Addim, 1992.

Freedman, Lawrence and Efraim Karsh. *The Gulf Conflict 1990-1991: Diplomacy and War in the New World Order*. Princeton, NJ: Princeton University Press, 1993.

Friedman, Norman. *Desert Victory: The War for Kuwait*. Annapolis, Md.: Naval Institute Press, 1991.

Gaffen, Fred. *In the Eye of the Storm: A History of Canadian Peacekeeping*. Toronto: Deneau & Wayne, 1987.

Gagnon, Réginald. *Faits d'armes à Oka*. Québec: Arion, 1994.

Gilchrist, Peter. *Sea Power. Desert Storm Special 3: The Coalition and Iraqi Navies*. London: Osprey, 1991.

Gimblett, Lieutenant-Commander Richard H. "MIF or MNF? The Dilemma of the 'Lesser' Navies in the Gulf War Coalition." In *A Nation's Navy: In Quest of Canadian Naval Identity*, ed. Michael L. Hadley, Rob Huebert and Fred Crickard. Montreal: McGill-Queen's Press, 1996.

Gimblett, Lieutenant (N) Richard H. "Multinational Naval Operations: The Canadian Navy In the Persian Gulf, 1990-91." *Canadian Defence Quarterly* 22, no. 1 (Special no 2/1992): 25-31.

Granatstein, J.L. and David J. Bercuson. *War and Peacekeeping: from South Africa to the Gulf - Canada's Limited Wars*. Toronto: Key Porter, 1991.

Gray, Charlotte. "War Games." *Saturday Night* 106, no. 2 (March 1991): 10-14.

Grove, Eric. *Battle for the Fiords: NATO's Forward Maritime Strategy in Action*. London: Ian Allen, 1991.

Grove, Eric, ed. *Britain's Gulf War: Operation Granby*. London: Harrington Kilbride, 1991.

Hales, Grant M. "Air Power in DESERT SHIELD / DESERT STORM: Part II - Tactical Aircraft Employment." *Air Power History* 38, no. 4 (Winter 1991): 43-47.

Hallion, Richard P. *Storm Over Iraq: Air Power and the Gulf War*. Washington, DC: Smithsonian Institution, 1992.

Bibliography

Hewitt, Lieutenant-Commander James Terrence. *Desert Sailor: A War of Mine*. Draft manuscript, 1992.

Hine, Air Chief Marshal Sir Patrick (RAF). "Despatch by [the] Joint Commander of Operation Granby, August 1990-April 1991." Supplement to *The London Gazette*, 28 June 1991.

Hiro, Dilip. *Desert Shield to Desert Storm: The Second Gulf War*. New York: Routledge, 1992.

Horner, Lieutenant-General Charles A. (USAF). "Air Power in DESERT SHIELD / DESERT STORM: Part I - An Overview." *Air Power History* 38, no. 3 (Fall 1991): 5-9.

Irving, Group Captain Niall (RAF). "The Gulf Air Campaign - An Overview." *The RUSI Journal* 137, no. 1 (February 1992): 1-5.

Jane's Weapons Systems. Coulsdon, Surrey: Jane's Information Group, [var.].

Karsh, Efraim, and Inari Rautsi. *Saddam Hussein: A Political Biography*. New York: The Free Press, 1991.

Keaney, Thomas A., and Eliot A. Cohen. *Gulf War Air Power Survey – Summary Report* [short title: *GWAPS*]. Washington, DC: US Government Printing Office, 1993.

Korwin-Szymanowski, Capt M.M. "AETE Support of Operations in the Persian Gulf." *Flight Comment* (1992, no 1), pp. 22-24.

Landry, André. «Le golfe de l'après-guerre». Dans *La crise du golfe : Implications et perspectives, Sécurité et Stratégies Asie*, Bruno P. Munier (dir.). Centre de recherche sur l'Asie, Hull (avril 1991), pp. 55-61.

Lauterpacht, E., C.J. Greenwood, Marc Weller and Daniel Bethlehem, eds. *The Kuwait Crisis: Basic Documents*. Cambridge International Documents Series, vol. 1. Cambridge: Grotius, 1991.

Mahmoudi, Said. "Passage of warships through the Strait of Hormuz." *Marine Policy* 15, no. 5 (September 1991): 338-48.

Maloney, Sean M. "'Missed Opportunity': Operation Broadsword, 4 Brigade and the Gulf War, 1990-1991." *Canadian Military History* 4, no. 1 (Spring 1995): 36-46.

Marolda, Edward J. (USNHC). "A Host of Nations: Coalition Naval Operations in the Persian Gulf." Paper presented to the Conference of the Society for Military History, Fredericksbrug, Va., 12 April 1992.

Masson, Philippe. «L'opération Prométhée». *Sommaire: 150 ans d'actions extérieures* n° 186 (mars 1992):124-29.

Matthews, Lieutenant-Colonel Donald C. "Squadron Commander." *Canadian Defence Quarterly* 21, no. 6 (June 1992): 37-41.

McCluskey, Captain Steve. "View From the Turret." *Legion* 67, no. 7 (February 1993): 6-10.

McKinnon, Michael, and Peter Vive. *Tides of War : Ecodisaster in the Gulf*. London: Boxtree, 1991.

McLaren, Captain P. (RN). "The Gulf Revisited - Why?" *The Naval Review* 78, no. 3 (July 1990): 196-204.

Bibliography

Meinhart, Lieutenant-Colonel Richard M. (USAF). "Joint Task Force Proven Force: An Outstanding Success." In *Joint Military Operations Department*. Naval War College, Newport, 1994.

Menarchik, Douglas. *Powerlift - Getting to Desert Storm: Strategic Transportation and Strategy in the New World Order*. Westport, Conn: Praeger, 1993.

Morin, le major Jean. «Les tribulations d'un historien officiel». *La revue légion* 67, n° 5 (novembre 1992): 14-15.

Pagonis, Lieutenant-General William G. (US Army), with Jeffrey L. Cruikshank. *Moving Mountains: Lessons in Leadership and Logistics from the Gulf War*. Boston: Harvard Business School Press, 1992.

Palmer, Michael A. *On Course to Desert Storm: The United States Navy and the Persian Gulf* [Contributions to Naval History, no. 5]. Washington, DC: USNHC, 1992.

Palmer, Michael A. *Guardians of the Gulf: A History of America's Expanding Role in the Persian Gulf, 1833-1992*. New York: Free Press, 1992.

Puddington, Lieutenant (N) [David S.]. "The New and Improved Canadian AOR, Part One: Equipment Changes and Increased Capabilities." *Maritime Warfare Bulletin* no. 1 (1992): 149-52.

Ranger, Robin. *The Military Balance 1990-1991*. London: Brassey's/IISS, 1990.

Ranger, Robin. "Special Report: Military Affairs: The Gulf War." In *Encyclopaedia Britannica Book of the Year, 1992 [Events of 1991]*. Chicago: Britannica, 1992.

Rosenthal, Capitán Eduardo Alfredo (ArA). "La Armada Argentina en el Golfo Pérsico." *Boletin del Centro Naval [Argentina]* 109, no. 763 [Winter 1991]: 255-68. [Translation held by DHist.]

Ross, Major-General Robin. "Some Early Lessons from Operation Haven." *RUSI Journal* 136, no. 4 (Winter 1991): 19-25.

Rost, Ronald F., John F. Addams, and John J. Nelson. *Sealift in Operation Desert Shield/ Desert Storm: 7 August 1990 to 17 February 1991*. Alexandria, Va.: Center for Naval Analyses, 1991.

Salinger, Pierre, and Eric Laurent. *Guerre du Golfe : Le dossier secret*. [Paris:] Olivier Orban, 1991.

Salinger, Pierre, and Eric Laurent. *Secret Dossier: The Hidden Agenda Behind the Gulf War*. Translated by Howard Curtis. New York: Penguin, 1991.

Schneller, Robert J. (USNHC). "Persian Gulf Turkey Shoot: The Destruction of Iraqi Naval Forces During Operation Desert Storm." Paper presented to the Conference of the Society for Military History, Kingston, Ont., May 1993.

Schwarzkopf, General H. Norman, and Peter Petre. *The Autobiography: It Doesn't Take a Hero*. New York: Bantam Books, 1992.

Sifry, Micah L., and Christopher Cerf, eds. *The Gulf War Reader: History, Documents, Opinions*. Toronto: Random House of Canada, 1991.

Silkett, Wayne A. "Alliance and Coalition Warfare." *Parameters: US Army War College Quarterly* 23, no. 2 (Summer 1993): 74-85.

Bibliography

Smith, Jean Edward. *George Bush's War*. New York: Henry Holt, 1992.

Smith, Major-General Rupert. "The Gulf War: The Land Battle." *The RUSI Journal* 137, no. 1 (February 1992): 1-5.

Summers, Commodore Kenneth J. "Operation FRICTION: A Personal Perspective." In *Canada's Navy Annual 1991/92*. Corvus, 1992.

Terasawa, Katsuaki L., and William R. Gates. "Burden-Sharing in the Persian Gulf: Lessons Learned and Implications for the Future." *Defense Analysis* 9, no. 2 (August 1993): 171-95.

Thyrard, Jean. *Golfe*. [Paris:] Addim, 1992.

United Nations. Department of Public Information. *The Blue Helmets: A Review of United Nations Peace-keeping*. August 1990.

United States. Department of Defense. *Conduct of the Persian Gulf War: Final Report to Congress*. 3 vols. Washington, DC: April 1992. [Short title: *Title V Report* or *CPGW*]

United States. Department of the Air Force. *Reaching Globally, Reaching Powerfully: The USAF in the Gulf War*. Washington, DC: September 1991.

Wiener, Robert. *Live from Baghdad - Gathering News at Ground Zero*. Toronto: Doubleday, 1992.

Winnefeld, James A., Preston Niblack, and Dana J. Johnson. *A League of Airmen: U.S. Air Power in the Gulf War*. Santa Monica, Calif: Rand Project Air Force, 1994.

Winter, James. *Common Cents: Media Portrayal of the Gulf War and Other Events*. Montréal: Black Rose, 1992.

Woodward, Bob. *The Commanders*. New York: Simon & Schuster, 1991.

York, Geoffrey, and Loreen Pindera. *People of the Pines: The Warriors and the Legacy of Oka*. Toronto, Little, Brown, 1991.

Young, Thomas-Durell. "Preparing the Western Alliance for the Next Out-of-Area Campaign." *Naval War College Review* 45, no. 3, seq. 339 (Summer 1992): 28-44.

Video

Canada. Défense nationale. *Un Appel du clairon : Les forces canadiennes dans le golfe Persique*. Directeur général des affaires publiques (DGAP), n° de catalogue : 31-0549 (93 minutes).

Canada. Department of National Defence. *A Cry of Bugles: The Canadian Forces in the Persian Gulf*. Director General of Public Affairs (DGPA), cat.# 31-0548 (93 minutes).

New Releases

The following works appeared when this manuscript was in final preparation. Although not available in time for citation in the text, they will make useful further reading on various aspects covered in this volume:

Bland, Douglas. *Chiefs of Defence: Government and the Unified Command of the Canadian Armed Forces*. Toronto: Canadian Institute of Strategic Studies, 1995.

Bibliography

Cordesman, Anthony H., and Abraham R. Wagner. *The Lessons of Modern War*. Vol. 4, *The Gulf War*. Boulder, Col.: Westview, 1996.

Craig, Captain (RN) Chris. *Call for Fire*. London: John Murray, 1995.

Gordon, Michael R., and General (US Army, retd) Bernard E. Trainor. *The Generals' War: The Inside Story of the Conflict in the Gulf*. Boston: Little, Brown and Co., 1995.

Hutchison, Kevin Don. *Operation Desert Shield/ Desert Storm: Chronology and Fact Book*. Westport, Conn.: Greenwood Press, 1995.

Maloney, Sean M. *War Without Battle: Canada's NATO Brigade in Germany, 1951-1993*. Toronto: McGraw-Hill, 1996.

Miller, Commodore Duncan (Dusty) E., and Sharon Hobson. *The Persian Excursion: The Canadian Navy in the Gulf War*. Clementsport, NS: Canadian Peacekeeping Press, 1995.

Miller, Ronnie. *Following the Americans to the Persian Gulf: Canada, Australia, and the Development of the New World Order*. London and Toronto: Associated University Presses, 1994.

Powell, Colin. *My American Journey*. New York: Random House, 1992.

Index

285

W

Z

IQ Crisis Management Organization, 1990–1991

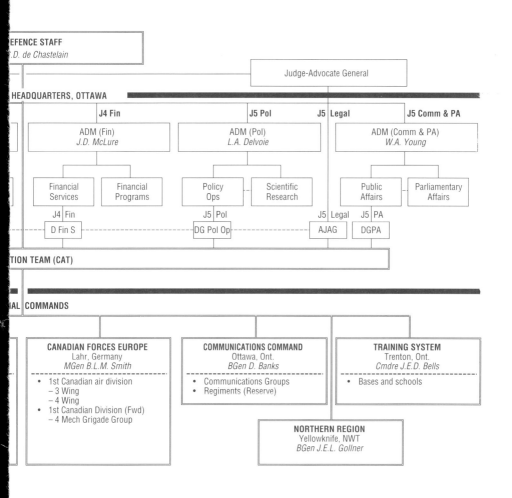

EFENCE STAFF
.D. de Chastelain

Judge-Advocate General

HEADQUARTERS, OTTAWA

J4 Fin	J5 Pol	J5 Legal	J5 Comm & PA
ADM (Fin) J.D. McLure	ADM (Pol) L.A. Delvoie		ADM (Comm & PA) W.A. Young

Financial Services — Financial Programs

Policy Ops — Scientific Research

Public Affairs — Parliamentary Affairs

J4 Fin	J5 Pol	J5 Legal	J5 PA
D Fin S	DG Pol Op	AJAG	DGPA

TION TEAM (CAT)

IAL COMMANDS

CANADIAN FORCES EUROPE
Lahr, Germany
MGen B.L.M. Smith
- 1st Canadian air division
  - 3 Wing
  - 4 Wing
- 1st Canadian Division (Fwd)
  - 4 Mech Grigade Group

COMMUNICATIONS COMMAND
Ottawa, Ont.
BGen D. Banks
- Communications Groups
- Regiments (Reserve)

TRAINING SYSTEM
Trenton, Ont.
Cmdre J.E.D. Bells
- Bases and schools

NORTHERN REGION
Yellowknife, NWT
BGen J.E.L. Gollner

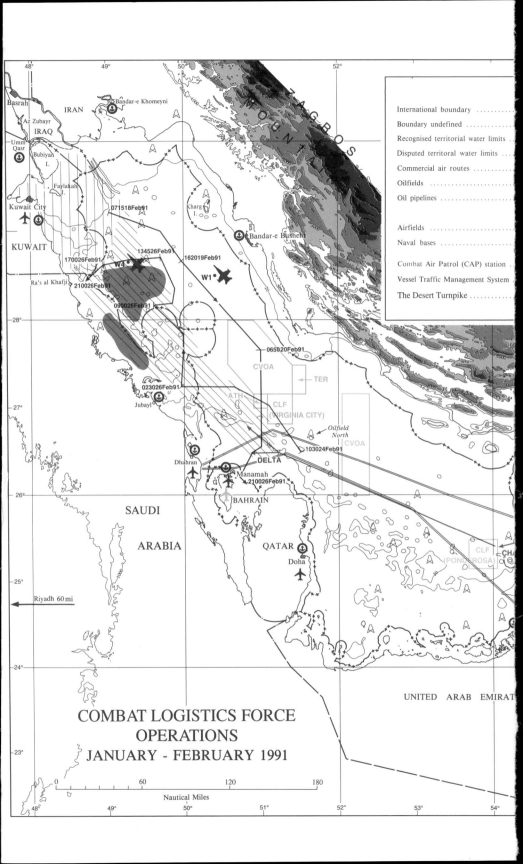

COMBAT LOGISTICS FORCE
OPERATIONS
JANUARY - FEBRUARY 1991

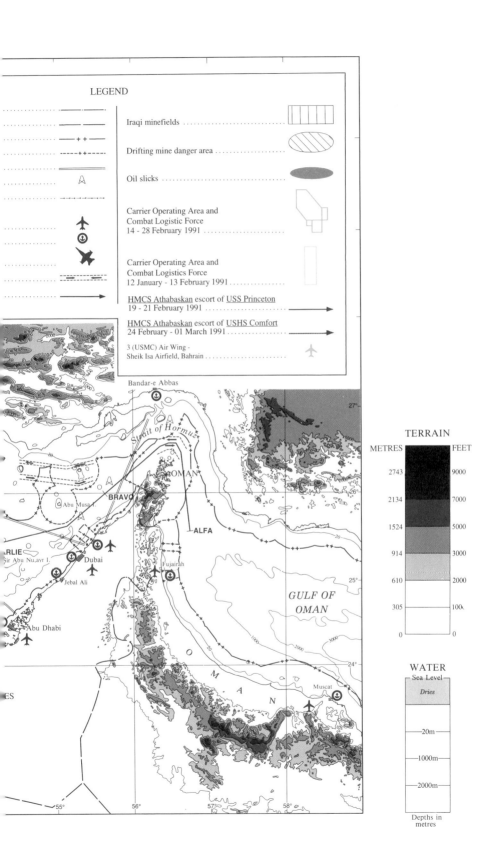

LEGEND

Iraqi minefields ....

Drifting mine danger area ....

Oil slicks ....

Carrier Operating Area and
Combat Logistic Force
14 - 28 February 1991 ....

Carrier Operating Area and
Combat Logistics Force
12 January - 13 February 1991 ....

HMCS Athabaskan escort of USS Princeton
19 - 21 February 1991 ....

HMCS Athabaskan escort of USHS Comfort
24 February - 01 March 1991 ....

3 (USMC) Air Wing -
Sheik Isa Airfield, Bahrain ....

Bandar-e Abbas

Strait of Hormuz

OMAN

BRAVO

Abu Musa I.

ALFA

RLIE

ir Abu Nu,ayr I.   Dubai

Jebal Ali

Fujairah

Abu Dhabi

GULF OF
OMAN

ES

O

M

A

N

Muscat

TERRAIN

METRES		FEET
2743		9000
2134		7000
1524		5000
914		3000
610		2000
305		100
0		0

WATER

Sea Level

Dries

20m

1000m

2000m

Depths in
metres

NDI

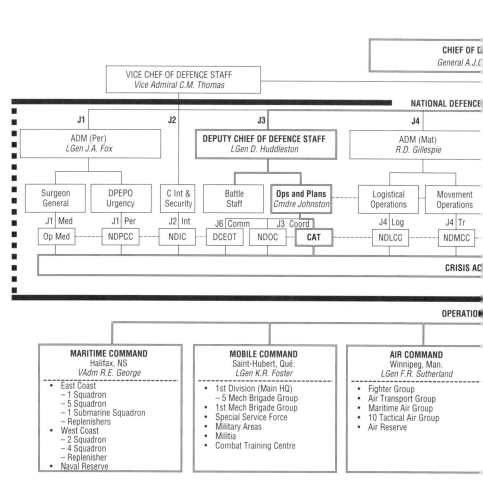

CHIEF OF D
General A.J.(

VICE CHEF OF DEFENCE STAFF
Vice Admiral C.M. Thomas

NATIONAL DEFENCE

J1	J2	J3	J4
ADM (Per) *LGen J.A. Fox*		DEPUTY CHIEF OF DEFENCE STAFF *LGen D. Huddleston*	ADM (Mat) *R.D. Gillespie*

Surgeon General	DPEPO Urgency	C Int & Security	Battle Staff	**Ops and Plans** *Cmdre Johnston*	Logistical Operations	Movement Operations

J1	Med	J1	Per	J2	Int	J6	Comm	J3	Coord	J4	Log	J4	Tr
Op Med		NDPCC		NDIC		DCEOT		NDOC		**CAT**		NDLCC		NDMCC

CRISIS AC

OPERATIO

MARITIME COMMAND Halifax, NS *VAdm R.E. George*	MOBILE COMMAND Saint-Hubert, Qué. *LGen K.R. Foster*	AIR COMMAND Winnipeg, Man. *LGen F.R. Sutherland*

• East Coast
  – 1 Squadron
  – 5 Squadron
  – 1 Submarine Squadron
  – Replenishers
• West Coast
  – 2 Squadron
  – 4 Squadron
  – Replenisher
• Naval Reserve
	• 1st Division (Main HQ)
	  – 5 Mech Brigade Group
	• 1st Mech Brigade Group
	• Special Service Force
	• Military Areas
	• Militia
	• Combat Training Centre
		• Fighter Group
		• Air Transport Group
		• Maritime Air Group
		• 10 Tactical Air Group
		• Air Reserve

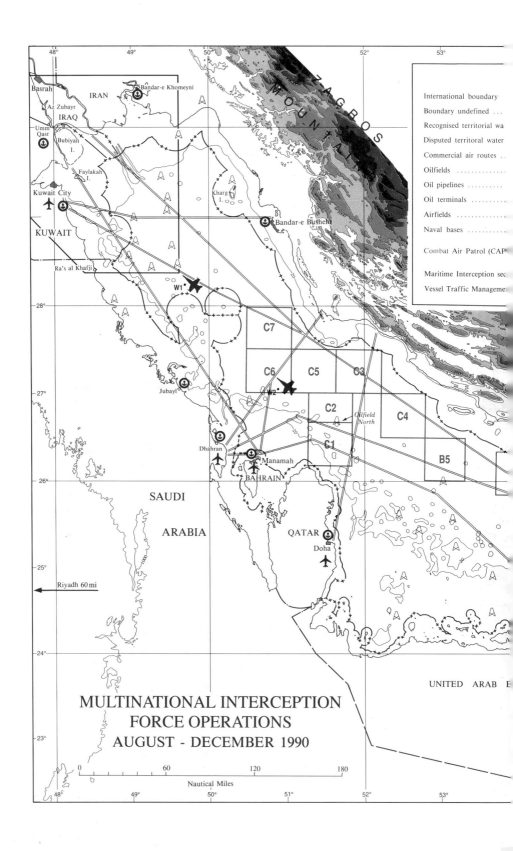

MULTINATIONAL INTERCEPTION
FORCE OPERATIONS
AUGUST - DECEMBER 1990